LEXICAL ACCULTURATION
IN NATIVE AMERICAN LANGUAGES

Lexical Acculturation in
Native American Languages

CECIL H. BROWN

New York   Oxford
Oxford University Press
1999

Oxford University Press

Oxford   New York
Athens   Auckland   Bangkok   Bogotá   Buenos Aires   Calcutta
Cape Town   Chennai   Dar es Salaam   Delhi   Florence   Hong Kong   Istanbul
Karachi   Kuala Lumpur   Madrid   Melbourne   Mexico City   Mumbai
Nairobi   Paris   São Paulo   Singapore   Taipei   Tokyo   Toronto   Warsaw

and associated companies in
Berlin   Ibadan

Published by Oxford University Press, Inc.
198 Madison Avenue, New York, New York 10016

Oxford is a registered trademark of Oxford University Press

Library of Congress Cataloging-in-Publication Data
Brown, Cecil H., 1944–
   Lexical acculturation in Native American languages / Cecil H.
Brown.
     p. cm. (Oxford studies in anthropological linguistics : 20)
   Includes bibliographical references and index.
   ISBN 0-19-512161-9
   1. Indians—Languages—Lexicology, Historical.   2. Languages in
contact—North America—History.   3. Languages, Mixed—North
America—History.   4. Indians—Cultural assimilation.   I. Title.   II. Series.
PM220.B76   1999
497—dc21   98-13835

9 8 7 6 5 4 3 2 1

Printed in the United States of America
on acid-free paper

Dedicated to the memory of

Stanley R. Witkowski

PREFACE

Research on which this book is based began in 1991. Preliminary results were reported in five articles published in *Current Anthropology* (Brown 1994), *Journal of Linguistic Anthropology* (Brown 1995a), *Language in Society* (Brown 1996a), *Anthropological Linguistics* (Brown 1996b), and *International Journal of American Linguistics* (Brown 1998). The present work builds on these publications and offers further information and observations.

The first draft of this manuscript contained three appendices that reported in substantial detail the considerable cross-language data on which this work is based. Because of considerations about length, only one in its original form is presented here (Appendix B). Appendix A is in a much truncated form that, unfortunately, omits 231 tables on individual items of acculturation. The third appendix, detailing distribution of similar native terms for acculturated items across the 292 language cases, has been entirely eliminated. Readers who wish to examine the original appendices are invited to contact me and make arrangements for doing so.

I am grateful for the support provided for this project by the Center for Latino and Latin American Studies, the Department of Anthropology, the College of Liberal Arts and Sciences, and the Graduate School of Northern Illinois University (NIU), and by the National Science Foundation (through grants BNS-9020699 and SBR-9222311). A number of individuals contributed to this study by reading and commenting on the manuscripts, by supplying data, or by assisting in other important ways. For this help I would like to thank Rani Alexander, Gene Anderson, Peter Bakker, William L. Ballard, MaryBeth Branigan, William Bright, George Aaron Broadwell, Carolyn R. Brown, Pamela Brown, Lyle Campbell, Michael Carr, Wallace Chafe, Emanuel J. Drechsel, David Dwyer, Richard Ford, Kay Fowler, Gayle J. Fritz, Dan Gebo, Michael Gonzales, Anthony P. Grant, John H. Hann, Don Hardy, Heather Hardy, Eugene Hunn, George Huttar, Dell Hymes, Frances Karttunen, Geoffrey Kimball, Fred Kitterle, Clark S. Larsen, Kent Lightfoot, Michael H. Logan, Gary Martin, Jack Martin, Carl Masthay, Mark Mehrer, Pamela Munro, James Norris, Peter Ohlin, Amadeo M. Rea, Willem J. de Reuse, Blair A. Rudes, Susan Russell, Janine Scancarelli, Linda Schwarz, Fred H. Smith, Julie Spangler, Ronald Spores, Brian Stross, William C. Sturtevant, Robert Suchner, John Swenson, Nancy J. Turner, Jack Weiner, the late Stanley R. Witkowski, Jerrold Zar, and Robert Zerwekh. I am also indebted to the interlibrary loan team at Founders Memorial Library (NIU), headed by Tobie Miller, for their tireless effort in tracking down often elusive lexical sources. Finally, many thanks to my golf buddies, Mike Gabriel, Jim Nelson, Dan Piazza, and especially, Bob "Bubba" Suchner, who helped keep me sane while working on this project.

CONTENTS

LEXICAL ACCULTURATION
IN NATIVE AMERICAN LANGUAGES

INTRODUCTION

In 1493, as head of an armada of 17 ships, Columbus made his second voyage to America. In addition to 1,200 men, on board these vessels were animals and plants never before seen by Native Americans: horses, pigs, cattle, chickens, sheep, and goats; and barley, wheat, chick-peas, melons, radishes, salad greens, sugarcane, and fruit trees in the forms of seeds, stones, and cuttings (Crosby 1991:77–79; Viola 1991:12). Thus began the first major episode in the great Columbian exchange in which objects and concepts were transferred from the Old World to the New and vice versa (cf. Crosby 1972). Columbus and subsequent travelers to the Americas would return to Europe with various items of New World origin, including many food plants that would become common fare in Western diets, for example, cacao (chocolate), chili pepper, corn (maize), peanut, potato, pumpkin, raspberry, strawberry, sunflower, sweet potato, tomato, and vanilla (Foster and Cordell 1992:163–167).

Both Native Americans and Europeans adjusted in various ways to novel items encountered in the great exchange. This adjustment often initially entailed the linguistic problem of deciding what names to give new things. Various solutions were found by Europeans. For example, the tomato is a close relative of the eggplant, and Europeans seized on this fact in naming the new fruit (Davidson 1992:7). In France, the eggplant was called *pomme des Maures*, "fruit of the Moors," because of its popularity among Arabs. This name was applied to the introduced tomato but mispronounced as *pomme d'amour* ("love fruit"), thus yielding an early French label for the item. (A similar process produced *pomodoro* in Italy which is the current Italian term for tomato.) Another approach was to create descriptive labels for things of New World origin, for example, French *pomme de terre* for the potato, literally, "apple of the earth." Frequently, Native American words for introduced entities were borrowed. For example, the English word "tomato" (cf. Spanish *tomate*) is a loanword modeled on *tomatl*, the Nahuatl (Aztec) term for the fruit.

These European naming strategies are examples of *lexical acculturation*, which refers to the accommodation of languages to new objects and concepts encountered as a result of culture contact. Although the systematic study of how European languages named items introduced from the New World to the Old has yet to be undertaken (and, clearly, this would be richly informative), the focus of this book is on linguistic aspects of the Columbian exchange that involve Old to New World transfers. This entails a survey of Amerindian names for 77 objects and concepts (including both living things and artifacts) introduced by Europeans to the Americas. These words are garnered from approximately 196 Native American languages spoken from the Arctic Circle to Tierra del Fuego. The 77 items of acculturation are listed alphabetically in table 1.1.

The present study has been stimulated in part by an observation made some time ago by Salzmann:

> It would be of some importance for the study of culture change in general,
> if one could efficiently compare the lexical responses of different languages
> to the more or less consistent impact of Occidental culture; what is needed,
> however, is a uniform measuring rod. (1954:137)

The "measuring rod" proposed by Salzmann (p. 139) is a test list of occidental objects and concepts that have been diffused widely. Languages can be compared for lexical acculturation by observing how these items have been named. Salzmann's program has not been realized since he proposed it over four decades ago. The present investigation of American Indian languages is a modest attempt to implement it.

Background

Numerous references to preceding studies of lexical acculturation in Native American languages are cited in this section. I make no claim for the thoroughness of this bibliographic treatment other than that I am sure it encompasses all major works in the field, and most minor published studies as well. I did not undertake a systematic search

Table 1.1. Alphabetical listing of the 77 occidental objects and concepts used to investigate lexical acculturation in Native American languages.

APPLE	COLT	MILE	SCHOOL
APRICOT	CORIANDER	MONEY	SCISSORS
BARLEY	COW	MULE	SHEEP
BEET	CUP	NAIL	SHOVEL
BOARD	DONKEY	NEEDLE	SOAP
BOOK	FLOUR	OATS	SOLDIER
BOTTLE	FORK	ONION	SPOON
BOX	GARLIC	ORANGE	STORE/SHOP
BREAD	GOAT	OX	SUGAR
BULL	GRAPES	PAPER	TABLE
BUTTER	HEN	PEACH	TEA
BUTTON	HORSE	PEAS	THREAD
CABBAGE	HOUR	PIG	TOWN
CALF	HUNDRED	PISTOL	TURNIP
CANDLE	KEY	RIBBON	WAGON
CAT	LEMON	RICE	WATERMELON
CHEESE	LETTUCE	RICH	WEDNESDAY
CHICKEN	MARE	ROOSTER	WHEAT
CLOCK/WATCH	MATCH	SATURDAY	WINDOW
COFFEE			

for references, and those included here were opportunistically encountered in my general preparatory reading on the topic.

The earliest published study that I have seen is A. F. Chamberlain's "New Words in the Kootenay Language," which appeared in the *American Anthropologist* in 1894. Kutenai is a language isolate, which in Chamberlain's time was spoken by about 1,000 people residing in British Columbia and in Idaho and Montana (of which there are now some 200 speakers remaining). Chamberlain provides a list of "new things" encountered by Kutenai speakers, followed by their Kutenai labels. Some of the listed items in fact were known to Kutenai speakers before contact, for example, DOG, MOUSE, and RAT (referents are given in uppercase letters). Others were certainly new to the Kutenai but nonetheless of New World origin, such as CORN (MAIZE), POTATO, and TOMATO. Only one item on Chamberlain's list, CAT, is a European-language loanword, that is, *pūs* (from English). All the other terms are fashioned from native Kutenai vocabulary. A total of 23 items of acculturation on my list of 77, in addition to CAT, are also found on Chamberlain's list. These are as follows (in the original orthography), with literal translations and other information provided by Chamberlain:

APPLE	gō′tlwā (also: ROSE-HIP)
APRICOT	gō′tlwā (also: ROSE-HIP)
BEET	ki′tEnūs kō′ktcik'nāhā′tkā ("to paint red sweet" ?)
CABBAGE	kē′kō'ktla′kpē′kā′tl ("edible leaf-plant")
CALF	ā′qkinkō′mātl
CHICKEN	gūtskā′kōminū′k'mā′Enām (name refers to a prominent tail)
COW	tlū′k'pū ("female buffalo")
BULL	ni′tltsik ("male buffalo")
GOAT	gī′ānū′kqō (also: MOUNTAIN-GOAT)
HEN	stō′kwātl gūtskā′kōminū′k'mā′Enām ("female chicken")
HORSE	k'k'ā′tlāQā′Etltsin ("elk-dog")
LETTUCE	kē′kō'ktla′kpē′kā′tl ("edible leaf-plant")
MULE	gū′witlk·ū′āt ("big ear")
OATS	k'k'ā′tlāqā′Etltsin kī′ēk ("horse's food")
ONION	āqk·ō′ātl (also: WILD ONION)
ORANGE	gūwī′tk·ā gō′tlwā ("big rose-hip")
PEACH	gō′tlwā (also: ROSE-HIP)
PEAS	āqk nā′nā (also: [GUN]SHOT)
PIG	gy′inūk·tsā′tlā ("? + nose")
ROOSTER	kE′skō gūtskā′kōminū′k'mā′Enām ("male chicken")
SHEEP	sūyä′pī ni′tlyäp
TURNIP	āqktlE′mātlu′kEnām (of doubtful etymology)
WHEAT	ā′qkinkū′tlātl (of doubtful etymology)

These acculturated items are all living things. The only introduced artifacts listed by Chamberlain are religious in nature and include such items as CHURCH, CRUCIFIX, and ROSARY. (No religious items are on my list, for reasons explained in chapter 2.)

Studies of Individual Languages

Like Chamberlain's (1894) early effort, the vast majority of studies deal with lexical acculturation in individual Native American languages (as opposed to comparative treatments; see following sections). For the most part, these studies focus on European-language loanwords for items of acculturation rather than on native terms constructed from indigenous vocabulary, such as the Kutenai words listed above. Also, in most instances, European loans are Spanish in origin.

The following works emphasize Spanish loanwords in individual Amerindian languages, typically by merely listing them. Studies are identified here by the languages treated and are grouped according to geographic location. Within geographic groupings, references are listed by year of publication, from earliest to latest: (1) South America: Araucanian (Lenz 1893), Guaraní (Morínigo 1931), Inca (Rowe 1950), Waunana (Loewen 1960), Mataco (Tovar 1962), Aymara (Briggs 1981; Sharpe 1981), Arawak (van Baarle 1995); (2) Central America: Central American Carib (D. Taylor 1948), Kekchi (Campbell 1976); (3) Caribbean region: Island Carib (D. Taylor 1946); (4) Mexico: Nahuatl (Sanchez 1885), Nahuatl (Boas 1930), Nahuatl (González Casanova 1934), Yaqui (Johnson 1943), Yaqui (Spicer 1943), Zoque (Wonderly 1946), Otomi (Bartholomew 1955), Isthmus Nahuat (Law 1961), Pame (Olson 1963), Tlaxcalan Nahuatl (Thiel 1963), Zapotec (Fernández de Miranda 1964), Tlaxcalan Nahuatl (Bright and Thiel 1965), Nahuatl (Dávila Garibi 1967), Nahuatl (Karttunen and Lockhart 1976), Tarahumara (Ornstein 1976), Sayula Popoluca (L. E. Clark 1977), Ocuiltec (Muntzel 1985), Tlaxcalan Nahuatl (Hill and Hill 1986), Cora (Casad 1988), Nahuatl (K. C. Hill 1990), Kanjobalan languages (Peñalosa 1990), Mixe and Chinantec (G. J. Martin 1992); (5) Southwestern United States: Chiricahua Apache (Hoijer 1939), Tiwa of Taos (Trager 1944), Keres (Spencer 1947), Tiwa of Taos (Hall 1947), Hopi (Dockstader 1955), Keres of Acoma (Miller 1959, 1960), Western Apache (Greenfeld 1971), Arizona Tewa (Kroskrity 1978, 1982, 1993), Cocopa (Crawford 1979), Walapai (Barto 1979), Western Apache (de Reuse 1995); (6) California: Patwin (Bright and Bright 1959), Wappo (Sawyer 1964a, 1964b), Eastern Pomo (McLendon 1969), Cahuilla (Bright 1979a), Wintu (Schlichter 1980), Western Mono (Kroskrity and Reinhardt 1985), Wikchamni (Gamble 1989); Alaska: Eskimo (A. R. Taylor 1962).

Other studies of European loans in individual Native American languages are as follows (organized by loanword origin): (1) English loanwords: Island Carib (D. Taylor 1946), Central American Carib (D. Taylor 1948), Hopi (Kennard 1963), Akwesasne Mohawk (Bonvillain 1978), Wintu (Schlichter 1980), Cree (Pentland 1982), Eskimo (de Reuse 1994), Massachusett, Narragansett, Pequot, Montauk, and Unquachog (Rees-Miller 1996); (2) French loanwords: Island Carib (D. Taylor 1946), Tunica (Haas 1947), Central American Carib (D. Taylor 1948), Kalispel (Mullen 1976), Akwesasne Mohawk (Bonvillain 1978), Cree (Pentland 1982), Carrier (Prunet 1990); (3) Russian loanwords: Eskimo (Hammerich 1954), Pomo (Oswalt 1958, 1994), Alaskan Eskimo (Worth 1963); (4) Dutch loanwords: Delaware (Goddard 1974), Munsee (Swiggers 1985, 1988), Arawak (van Baarle 1995); (5) German loanwords: Labrador Eskimo (Heinrich 1971); (6) Basque loanwords: Micmac (Bakker 1989b).

Special note should be made of Bakker (1992, 1997) and Douaud (1985), which are treatments of Michif (or Métis), a language that developed around 1800 in the central

Canadian provinces. This language is a mixture of Cree (Algonquian) verbs, postpositions, question words, and demonstratives plus French nouns, articles, adjectives, and numerals. The language retains morphological complexities from both sources including verb morphology, article usage, and gender distinctions (cf. Callaghan 1994:108).

Some treatments of individual Amerindian languages focus on lexical acculturation in general, including native terms for acculturated items, as well as European loans. These are as follows (organized by date of reference): Kutenai (Chamberlain 1894; also above discussion), Pima (Herzog 1941), Wintu (Lee 1943), Kutenai (Garvin 1948), Mohawk (Huot 1948), Arapaho (Salzmann 1951), Karok (Bright 1952), Comanche (Casagrande 1954a, 1954b, 1955), Trique (Hollenbach 1973), Dakota (Froke 1975), Cherokee (King and King 1976), Kiliwa (Mixco 1977), Kiowa (Hickerson 1985; treatment limited to terms for currency and financial transactions), Blackfoot (Baldwin 1994), Yucatec Mayan (Anderson 1997; treatment limited to terms for plants and animals). Basso (1967) lists native Western Apache terms for automobile parts.

The preponderance of individual language studies that focus on European loans deals with languages that show loanwords from Spanish. For the most part, Amerindian languages that were influenced mainly by Spanish speakers have freely borrowed Spanish words for items of acculturation. On the other hand, native languages that were influenced by speakers of other European languages (with the major exceptions of Russian and Portuguese) have only rarely borrowed European loans for introduced items (see following sections and chapter 6). Consequently, Spanish-influenced languages have been attractive subjects for loanword studies, whereas other Native American languages have not.

Dates of references show that the study of lexical acculturation in the languages of Amerindians is a relatively young endeavor in linguistic anthropology, most works having appeared since World War II. In addition, the 1940s, 1950s, and 1960s witnessed the most productive period for such studies, although there has been a renewal of interest in recent years.

Comparative Studies

Comparative studies of lexical acculturation in Native American languages are more akin to the present work. In all instances, these studies list labels for certain items of acculturation found in two or more Amerindian languages (usually spoken in the same geographic area). Some authors take us no farther than mere comparative lists, but most use cross-language data to generalize the nature of lexical acculturation and/or to show how labels (both native terms and European loans) have been diffused (i.e., have been borrowed) across languages.

The earliest comparative study known to me is that of Nordenskiöld (1922), *Deductions Suggested by the Geographical Distribution of Some Post-Columbian Words Used by the Indians of South America.* It is a Herculean effort to chart the distribution of terms (both European loans and native labels) for several items of acculturation across the languages of all of South America. Acculturated items include CHICKEN, HEN, ROOSTER, HORSE, COW, BANANA, IRON, FIREARMS, and SCISSORS, described as "indisputably post-Columbian cultural elements," and

KNIFE, NEEDLE, and FISHHOOK, described as "partly post-Columbian cultural elements." I estimate that words for introduced items were extracted by Nordenskiöld from as many as 150 languages and dialects. Little in the way of analysis is offered beyond a few comments that note postcontact interactions suggested by distributions, for example, extensive post-Columbian migrations of the Guaraní, possibly accounting for the widespread distribution of a term for SCISSORS (p. 106).

In several papers, Kiddle (1952a, 1952b, 1964, 1978) discusses the distribution of terms in Amerindian languages for acculturated items that have been borrowed from Spanish. In the most comprehensive of these, Kiddle (1952a) charts the distribution of Spanish loans across 19 languages spoken in South America, Mexico, southwestern United States, and Texas. Loanwords include terms that refer to religious items, material culture, domestic animals, and money. Another work published in the same year (Kiddle 1952b) surveys Spanish loans for HORSE and for each of the seven days of the week, found in 49 languages and dialects spoken in the areas just mentioned and in some additional areas, including Central America, southeastern United States, the Plains, the North American plateau, and California. In a later paper, Kiddle (1978) considers again Spanish loans for HORSE by surveying an even larger sample of languages and, in addition, offers some observations concerning the etymologies of native terms for HORSE in the languages that show such labels. Another contribution along the same lines is Kiddle's (1964) presentation of the distribution of Amerindian reflexes of two archaic Spanish words for CAT, *miz* and *mozo* (see also Bright 1960b; C. J. Crowley 1962; and Landar 1959, 1961).

Some other works propose that loanword distributions are explained, at least in part, by indirect diffusion, whereby European loans have been borrowed into some Amerindian languages without the direct involvement of European-language speakers (see chapter 9). Sturtevant (1962) and J. B. Martin (1994) assemble evidence that the diffusion of some Spanish loans in languages of the southeastern United States results from the movement of these words from one native language to another (see chapter 9 for additional evidence). Shipley (1962) proposes the existence of chains of diffusion followed by Spanish loans across native languages of central California. Barto (1979) discusses Spanish loans that entered Walapai (Yuman of Arizona) via other Indian languages. More recently, A. R. Taylor (1990) reconstructs diffusional paths of related French and Dutch terms for PIG across many languages of northern North America (see chapter 9). Other studies that attest to indirect diffusion of European loans include Grimes (1960), A. R. Taylor (1962), McLendon (1969), Bright (1979b, 1993), and Nordell (1984). Also of note are Karttunen's (1985) analysis of Spanish loans into Mayan and Nahuatl, Bakker's (1995) treatment of Dutch loanwords in North American Indian languages, and Bright's (1997) list of Spanish loans in languages of California.

Very little attention has been paid to the comparative study of native terms for items of acculturation. One such treatment is Shimkin's (1980) compilation of labels for acculturated items in dialects of the Shoshone-Comanche linguistic group during 1786–1848. In this study, early native terms that show considerable similarity across these languages attest to a uniform linguistic response to European-based culture in the Great Basin and adjacent regions of the western United States. In a follow-up study of Shoshone-Comanche neologisms, Shaul (1981) shows the deterioration of this similarity in later periods with the breakdown of communication networks that link dialects. Witkowski and Brown (1983) have used comparative data, mostly from

Amerindian languages, to illustrate how native terms tend to change in nomenclatural structure with shifts in the cultural importance of the introduced things they denote. This study is discussed at length in chapter 3.

Comparative investigations of lexical acculturation in general are not numerous. In two articles (Brown 1987b, 1989b), I discuss how languages, including many spoken by Amerindians, have accommodated concepts of time—that is, WEEK and its seven days—introduced to the world at large by Europeans. An earlier study by Voegelin and Hymes (1953) surveys terms (both European loans and native labels) for items of acculturation as found in dictionaries for nine Amerindian languages, of which seven (Tonkawa, Shawnee, Ojibwa, Chipewyan, Southern Paiute, Dakota, and Klamath) are spoken in North America north of Mexico and two (Lokono and Aymara) in South America. These authors were the first to observe that Spanish-influenced languages have been considerably more inclined to adopt Spanish loans for introduced items than English-influenced languages have been inclined to incorporate English loans.

Seven years later, Voegelin and Hymes's (1953) observation found support in a study by Bright (1960a) who surveys words for European-introduced animals in native languages of California. He reports that Indian languages primarily influenced by Spanish culture (southern and central California) have heavily borrowed Spanish terms for domesticated creatures, while those of groups influenced primarily by Anglo-American culture (northern California) have coined native terms for most of the same animals. (I make the same observation for Amerindian languages in general; see Brown 1994 and chapter 6.) Bright relates this difference to "a lower incidence of bilingualism" (p. 233) among northern California Indians, connecting it in turn to the fact that the Spanish were considerably more disposed than Anglo-Americans to integrate Indian peoples into colonial culture.

Comparative studies have shown that attitudinal factors can influence the extent to which European loans are incorporated into languages. Dozier (1956) examines borrowing in two Amerindian languages of the American Southwest, Yaqui and Tewa, both influenced by contact with Spanish speakers. Yaqui has been exceptionally affected by the Spanish language (as measured, in part, by the number of Spanish loans), whereas Tewa has not. Dozier relates this difference to the nature of the contact. The early Spaniards used little coercion in introducing European and Catholic cultural patterns to Yaqui speakers; in contrast, contact with Tewa speakers involved the imposition of European cultural elements, and as a result Tewa speakers consciously resisted the adoption of both the introduced cultural patterns and the language of Europeans who brought them.

The findings of these studies and of others (e.g., Diebold 1962; Spencer 1947; Scotton and Okeju 1973; Mixco 1977) challenge the long-held assumption of linguists that structural features of some languages make them more inclined than others to adopt loanwords for introduced items (e.g., Sapir 1921:205-210; Herzog 1941:74; Haugen 1956:66; Bonvillain 1978:32). For example, Haugen writes that "loanwords are easily accepted by languages with unified, unanalyzed words, but not by languages with active methods of word compounding" (p. 66). Thomason and Kaufman (1988) assemble considerable evidence that indicates—reminiscent of Bright (1960a)—that sociolinguistic factors, such as the degree of bilingualism, rather than language structure, significantly affect the extent of borrowing, especially when grammatical features are involved.

Overview Studies

Several works offer summary discussions addressed to the general topic of language contact, either involving languages in general or limited to native languages of the New World. Most notable among the former are Bloomfield (1933), Haugen (1950), Weinreich (1953), Emeneau (1962), and Thomason and Kaufman (1988) (also consult Muysken 1984, Appel and Muysken 1987, and Lehiste 1988). Haugen (1956) presents a bibliography and research guide to bilingualism in the Americas, with a chapter devoted to language contact. Dozier (1967) surveys linguistic acculturation studies in the Southwest. Bakker (1993) reviews European-Amerindian language interaction in North America. A useful bibliographic compilation of languages of Canada, Alaska, and adjacent areas has been prepared by Bakker and Grant (1994). Bright's (1973) overview of language contact in North America is a classic work that has influenced this book in many ways. Callaghan and Gamble (1996) and Silverstein (1996) are the most recent surveys of the same topic.

METHODOLOGY

The basic research approach for this study entails (1) a list of objects and concepts introduced to the New World by Europeans (i.e., items of acculturation) and (2) a set of Native American languages whose vocabularies are searched for words that denote items on the list. The following considerations pertain to the derivation and investigative use of (1) and (2).

Items of Acculturation

Salzmann (1954) describes two strategies for developing a test list of imported items for studying lexical acculturation, one "inductive" and the other "deductive." The inductive approach, which proceeds from the particular to the general, is linguistic in nature since it arrives at a composite set of acculturated objects by surveying vocabularies of individual languages for such items. Salzmann (1954:138) sees a problem with this method because "lexical materials [such as bilingual dictionaries] are of uneven value and size and...represent the native languages rather haphazardly." The deductive method is anthropological in nature since it entails constructing a list through reference to ethnographic knowledge of what items have actually been introduced to different groups (without reference to lexical materials).

Despite Salzmann's (1954) misgivings about the inductive strategy, I chose this method to construct a test list. I first consulted published studies of lexical acculturation, which for the most part focus on words of European-language origin (European loans) in Amerindian languages. The languages involved, 20 in all, and their sources are Cherokee (King and King 1976), Chiricahua Apache (Hoijer 1939), Comanche (Casagrande 1954a, 1954b, 1955), Eastern Pomo (McLendon 1969), Hopi (Dockstader 1955), Isthmus Nahuat (Law 1961), Keres (Miller 1959; Spencer 1947), Mocho (Kaufman 1967), Navajo (Young and Morgan 1980), Pame (Olson 1963), Sayula Popoluca (L. E. Clark 1977), Tarahumara (Ornstein 1976), Tewa (Dozier 1956), Tiwa (Trager 1944), Tlaxcalan Nahuatl (Bright and Thiel 1965), Western Mono (Shipley 1962; Kroskrity and Reinhardt 1985), Wappo (Sawyer 1964a, 1964b), Wikchamni (Gamble 1989), Yaqui (Johnson 1943; Spicer 1943), and Zoque

(Wonderly 1946). With only a very few exceptions, all European loanwords in these languages are Spanish in origin. From these studies, I developed a master list of all referents, 930 items, denoted by European loans in the 20 languages.

Seventy-seven referents from the master list were included in my investigative set of items of acculturation. These are presented in table 2.1, where they are listed by rank order according to the number of languages (of the 20) in which they are designated by European loanwords; for example, first-listed HORSE is denoted by a loanword in 15 of the 20 languages, and last-listed TURNIP is so designated in 2. The selection process involved identifying from among the 930 items all referents labeled by loans in *3 or more languages*. This group was then culled to a list of 69 items that have been introduced to the Americas by Europeans. (The additional 8 items are explained in the following discussion.)

I used this approach because these items, through their repetitive designation by European loanwords across languages, demonstrate high salience (for both speakers of Amerindian languages and language investigators) that is predictive of their productive use in my cross-language investigation. By "productive use" I mean that words for these referents, either European loans or native terms, will tend to be found in lexical sources for Native American languages (mostly bilingual dictionaries). Another advantage is that European loanwords for these referents should typically be well-established loans in the languages surveyed rather than merely nonce borrowings (cf. Sankoff, Poplack, and Vanniarajan 1990; van Hout and Muysken 1994).

Table 2.1. Seventy-seven items of acculturation rank-listed by the number of languages in which these are designated by a European-language loanword as attested in literature dedicated to the description of lexical acculturation in individual Amerindian languages. (See table 1.1 for an alphabetical listing of the 77 items.)

HORSE (15)	RICE (7)	WINDOW (5)
COW (14)	BUTTON (7)	BOARD (4)
COFFEE (13)	NAIL (7)	BOOK (4)
MULE (13)	THREAD (7)	CORIANDER (4)
PIG (13)	WAGON (6)	FORK (TABLE) (4)
SOLDIER (13)	CALF (6)	HOUR (4)
DONKEY (12)	FLOUR (6)	KEY (4)
GOAT (11)	GRAPES (6)	MILE (4)
SATURDAY (11)	MONEY (6)	OATS (4)
SUGAR (11)	PAPER (6)	ONION (4)
TABLE (11)	TOWN (6)	RIBBON (4)
BOTTLE (10)	WHEAT (6)	SCHOOL (4)
NEEDLE (10)	CABBAGE (5)	SCISSORS (4)
BULL (9)	CANDLE (5)	TEA (4)
CAT (DOMESTIC) (9)	CHICKEN (5)	WEDNESDAY (4)
CHEESE (9)	CUP (5)	BUTTER (3)
CLOCK (9)	HEN (5)	OX (3)
HUNDRED (9)	LEMON (5)	APRICOT (2)
SOAP (9)	MATCH (5)	BARLEY (2)
SPOON (9)	ORANGE (5)	BEET (2)
STORE (9)	PEACH (5)	COLT (2)
WATERMELON (9)	PISTOL (5)	GARLIC (2)
APPLE (8)	RICH (5)	LETTUCE (2)
BOX (8)	ROOSTER (5)	PEAS (2)
BREAD (8)	SHOVEL (5)	TURNIP (2)
MARE (8)	SHEEP (5)	

The final adjustment of the list involved some ad hoc additions. To the original 69 items I added 8 others, each of which is designated by a loanword in only 2 of the 20 languages. All of these are natural kinds (i.e., living things) imported to the Americas, all but one of which are botanical. These were included to augment the number of natural kinds on the list so that they more closely approached in quantity the number of artifacts included (discussed further below).

Among the 930 items on the master list, 95 are designated by European loanwords in 3 or more of the 20 languages but were not selected for the final list of 77. These are rank-ordered in table 2.2. Many were not included in the final set simply because they are not Old World items, for example, CORN, CHOCOLATE, POTATO, SWEET POTATO, TOBACCO, TOMATO, and TURKEY, which originated in the Americas, and AXE, BASKET, GLUE, HAT, KNIFE, MELON, and SHIRT, which are native to both the Old and New Worlds. There are various reasons for other exclusions. Items associated with religion—for example, CROSS, FATHER, GODFATHER, MASS, and SAINT—were avoided because some of them may not have been common to all areas of the Americas. The same may be true of government and military referents, such as CAPTAIN, KING, LIEUTENANT, and MAJORDOMO.

Table 2.2. Ninety-five items rank-listed by number of languages in which they are designated by a European-language loanword as shown in the literature treating lexical acculturation in Amerindian languages, which are not included among the 77 items of acculturation on the test list in table 2.1.

GODFATHER (11)	CAPTAIN (4)	CRIPPLED (3)
CHAIR (10)	CORN (MAIZE) (4)	DEBT, TO OWE (3)
PESO (10)	COWBOY (4)	DOCTOR (3)
GODMOTHER (9)	DRUM (4)	FESTIVAL (3)
GOD (9)	FATHER (PRIEST) (4)	GLUE (3)
GOLD (9)	FILE (TOOL) (4)	HANDKERCHIEF (3)
SUNDAY (8)	FOUR BITS (4)	JESUS (3)
TOMATO (8)	FRIDAY (4)	LAMP (3)
CROSS (7)	FRYING PAN (4)	LIEUTENANT (3)
HOT PEPPER (7)	HAT (4)	MANGO (3)
JUG/PITCHER (7)	JACKET (4)	MIRROR (3)
SACK (7)	KITCHEN (4)	PIE (3)
THOUSAND (7)	MAJORDOMO (4)	PLANTATION (3)
WEEK (7)	MILK (4)	PLATE/DISH (3)
CORRAL (6)	PIN/BROOCH (4)	POOR (3)
KING (6)	PLAYING CARDS (4)	RING (3)
KNIFE (6)	POTATO (4)	SEA (3)
MASS (RELIGIOUS) (6)	POWDER (4)	SHOES (3)
PEAR (6)	SHIRT (4)	SILVER (3)
POCKET (6)	SILK (4)	SOCKS/STOCKINGS (3)
POCKETKNIFE (6)	TROUSERS (4)	SOUP/STEW (3)
AUTHORITY (5)	THURSDAY (4)	SPANISH (3)
BEANS (5)	TUESDAY (4)	SWEET POTATO (3)
DRINKING GLASS (5)	AIRPLANE (3)	TAME (3)
DRUNK (5)	AMERICAN (3)	TEACHER (3)
MELON (5)	BASKET (3)	TOBACCO (3)
MONDAY (5)	BENCH (3)	TOWEL (3)
RANCH (5)	CANDY (3)	TO WORK (3)
SAINT (5)	CHOCOLATE (3)	TURKEY (3)
VEST (5)	CIGAR (3)	WINE (3)
AXE (4)	COMB (3)	YEAR (3)
BUCKET (4)	CRAZY (3)	

Some items were discarded so that referents related to the same narrow semantic domain would not be overrepresented on the final list (see table 2.3). For example, SUNDAY, MONDAY, TUESDAY, THURSDAY, and FRIDAY were excluded, whereas SATURDAY and WEDNESDAY were included; and the referent THOUSAND did not make the final list, whereas HUNDRED did. Other items presented problems of an analytical nature. For instance, CHAIR (the second referent on the 95-item list) was not included because of the semantic ambiguity of its Spanish label, *silla*. *Silla* commonly denotes SADDLE as an alternate referent; therefore, it is difficult to ascertain whether or not the term designates CHAIR in Spanish-Amerindian bilingual dictionaries. Very recent referents, such as AIRPLANE, were eliminated mainly to avoid inclusion of items that are more likely to be nonce borrowings.

Several other referents of the 95-item set—for example, BUCKET, CANDY, COWBOY, FILE (TOOL), MANGO, PIE, PLAYING CARDS, SILK, SPANISH, and WINE—would have made appropriate constituents of the final list; they were not included, however, because of practical considerations about the list's length.

Salzmann (1954:139) suggests that "750 words (plus or minus one hundred words or so)" would constitute an adequate test list of acculturated items. My final list is only about one-tenth the size of that recommended by Salzmann. Nonetheless, the list is of such a magnitude that searching for, recording, and analyzing words in the large set of lexical sources for Amerindian languages (see discussion below) proved an exceptionally prolonged undertaking, consuming approximately 18 months of research time. I estimate that investigation of each acculturated item alone involved, on the average, roughly one week of work. Each item added beyond the set of 77 would have resulted in considerable additional research time. The final number of referents constitutes what I consider to be the best balance of investigative effort vis-à-vis scholarly payoff. Clearly, a list the size suggested by Salzmann would have been impractical for the task I envisioned.

Table 2.3 organizes the 77 acculturated items by semantic domain. There are two basic classes of referents, 35 natural kinds (living things) and 42 artifacts (human-made things). For analytical reasons, it is desirable to have a close balance in number between natural kinds and artifacts. Indeed, to approach parity in these categories, 8 natural kinds were added to the list, despite the fact that none of them were labeled by European loanwords in 3 or more of the 20 languages.

With one exception, RICH, all of the items are substantives, and words for them in the languages surveyed are typically nouns. While the attribute RICH is often lexically realized in Amerindian languages as an adjective, more than occasionally it turns up only in nominal expressions comparable to "rich man" or "rich person" (in which case, I nonetheless judge RICH to be present in a language). Of the 76 substantives, all but 5 or 6 are concrete things. The few conceptual (nonconcrete) items include HOUR, HUNDRED, MILE, SATURDAY, WEDNESDAY, and, possibly, SCHOOL. The last is ambiguous because although words for SCHOOL in Amerindian languages sometimes refer to the educational concept, mostly they seem to denote the edifice in which learning occurs, that is, the schoolhouse.

Table 2.3. Seventy-seven items of acculturation sorted by semantic domain.

Natural kinds

Fruits	APPLE, APRICOT, GRAPES, LEMON, ORANGE, PEACH, WATERMELON
Vegetables	BEET, CABBAGE, CORIANDER, GARLIC, LETTUCE, ONION, PEAS, TURNIP
Grains	BARLEY, OATS, RICE, WHEAT
Livestock	BULL, CALF, COLT, COW, DONKEY, GOAT, HORSE, MARE, MULE, OX, PIG, SHEEP
Other domestic creatures	CAT, CHICKEN, HEN, ROOSTER

Artifacts

Prepared Foods	BREAD, BUTTER, CHEESE, COFFEE, FLOUR, SUGAR, TEA
Tools for eating and drinking	CUP, FORK, SPOON, TABLE
Storage	BOTTLE, BOX
Clothing	BUTTON, NEEDLE, RIBBON, THREAD
Hygiene	SOAP
Fire	CANDLE, MATCH
Educational and intellectual	BOOK, PAPER, SCHOOL
Time	CLOCK (WATCH), HOUR, SATURDAY, WEDNESDAY
Numbers	HUNDRED
Measurement	MILE
Commerce	MONEY, STORE
Construction	BOARD, NAIL, WINDOW
Miscellaneous tools	KEY, SCISSORS, SHOVEL
Warfare	PISTOL, SOLDIER
Society	RICH, TOWN
Transport	WAGON

Some items on the test list are related to other items as subtypes. These include (1) COLT and MARE, subtypes of HORSE; (2) CALF, BULL, and OX, subtypes of COW (in its generic sense); and (3) HEN and ROOSTER, subtypes of CHICKEN. A strong human tendency to recognize such inclusive relationships, as we shall see, has important consequences for how subtypes are typically treated nomenclaturally by Amerindian languages (see especially chapter 4).

All items on the list are presumed to have been unknown to Native Americans before contact with Europeans. However, some introduced referents, such as NEEDLE, ONION, PAPER, RICH, and TOWN, probably had closer native analogs—sometimes very close indeed—in some parts of the Americas than did other items, such as APPLE, CHEESE, CLOCK, HORSE, and SCISSORS. Recognition of native analogs by Amerindians clearly influenced their naming of many introduced items (see especially chapter 4).

Language Cases

Two hundred and ninety-two language cases, involving languages distributed from the Arctic Circle to Tierra del Fuego, emerged as the definitive set of Amerindian languages investigated for lexical acculturation (see appendix B for language cases; their genetic affiliations, locations, lexical sources; and other pertinent information). Derivation of this set involved an exhaustive search for the 77 items of acculturation in as many lexical sources for Native American languages as I could possibly assemble, given the resources available to me at the time of the investigation (during 1991–1993). Lexical sources were primarily bilingual dictionaries, vocabularies, word lists, glossaries, and grammars, including published and unpublished works for all time periods since sustained contact between the Old and New Worlds began. I also used studies, mostly journal articles, focusing on lexical acculturation in individual Amerindian languages, such as Casagrande's (1954a, 1954b, 1955) "Comanche Linguistic Acculturation" (see chapter 1). In a few instances, scholars directly supplied data to me from individual languages they had studied firsthand.

Approximately 2,000 lexical sources were consulted. Many of these were from my personal library, possibly the most extensive aggregation of readily available, reasonably thorough to near-complete lexical sources for Native American languages assembled anywhere by an individual. Most items by far were gathered through interlibrary loans (at Northern Illinois University). I also visited large institutional collections, such as those at the Library of Congress, the Newberry Library, Tulane University, the University of Chicago, the University of Illinois at Champaign-Urbana, and the University of Texas at Austin. A number of bibliographies were helpful in my search, most notably, Pilling's (1887a, 1887b, 1888, 1889, 1891, 1892, 1893a, 1893b, 1894) multivolume treatment of languages of North America (north of Mexico), Bright's (1967) inventory of descriptive materials on languages of Middle America, and bibliographies in Loukotka's (1968) and Tovar's (1961) books on the classification of South American Indian languages. Source coverage of languages of North America (including Mexico) and northern Central America is reasonably comprehensive and thorough, especially for extant languages. In contrast, there are few dictionaries for languages of South America and southern Central America, and not many of these are extensive lexical treatments.

Of the approximately 2,000 sources consulted, roughly 1,300 yielded information pertinent to this project. This included words for items on the list in approximately 600 Amerindian languages and dialects. Not all of the data collected relate to the 292 language cases that form the comparative core of this study. A language or dialect was excluded from the sample if only 30 or fewer of the 77 items were found to have names in any source or combination of sources for that language or dialect. Some lexical sources systematically omit European loanwords (e.g., Bright 1968), and it was assumed that sources showing 30 or fewer items may have done so. Labels for at least 31 of the 77 items are in evidence for each of the 292 language cases (see appendix B).

While most of the 292 cases represent only one language, for example, Aguaruna, Mazahua, and Tunica, in some instances two or more cases represent two or more dialects of a single language, for example, Tzeltal (Bachajón) and Tzeltal (Oxchuc), or two or more time states of a single language, for example, Klamath (1890) and Klamath (1963). I estimate that altogether the 292 language cases are affiliated with roughly 196 distinct languages. Dialectal and chronological discriminations made by language cases were largely dictated by the nature of lexical sources. For example, if 31 or more of the 77 items were found in sources for two or more distinct dialects of a single language, two or more language cases were recognized. Similarly, if 31 or more items were found in sources for two or more time states of a single language, more than one language case represented that language. As a convention, I considered a single time state of a language to range over a chronological period of no greater than 50 years, with gaps between time states usually in the neighborhood of at least 20 years. Thus, for example, four language cases that reflect different time states of Tupí are Tupí (1621), Tupí (1795), Tupí (1854–1894), and Tupí (1950–1979). The chronological ranges of the latter two cases reflect the earliest and latest dates of combined lexical sources for these cases (of course, with ranges contained within a period of 50 years).

Analysis of Words for Acculturated Items

Each of the 77 items of acculturation was searched for in all my lexical sources. When found and recorded, lexical items were then judged to be either loanwords from European languages or native terms. Identifying European loans was rarely a problem since these are usually obvious. In addition, many bilingual dictionaries specify words that are derived from European languages and also, frequently, terms from those languages on which these words are modeled.

I investigated words recognized as native labels for details of referential application and semantic content. In some instances, sources provided complete and "ready-to-use" analyses of words. This is especially true of those sources dedicated to the description of lexical acculturation in individual languages such as Casagrande's (1954a, 1954b, 1955) study of Comanche. Thus, for example, Casagrande (1954b:219) directly informs us that the Comanche word for CLOCK also denotes SUN and that the language's term for PEACH is literally "hairy plum" (p. 223). Similar information is offered by some of the more thorough bilingual dictionaries, such as Morice's (1932) lexicon of Carrier, which, for example, supplies "hair of the foreigners" as the literal translation of the language's term for BARLEY.

When literal translations of native labels were not supplied by lexical sources, as was commonly the case when dictionaries were involved, I attempted to determine the semantic content of constituents of each label, insofar as this was possible, given the limitations of individual sources. For example, the word for WINDOW in Romano and Cattunar's (1916) two-way bilingual dictionary of Chiriguano (and Spanish) is *honquerái* (I use original orthography throughout). Reference to constituent elements of the label, *honque* and *rái*, in the Chiriguano-Spanish section of the dictionary yielded the glosses "door" and "little," and thus "little door" as the literal meaning of the term.

When the dictionaries consulted were not two-way, analysis was more difficult. For example, the word for SHEEP in Córdova's (1942) sixteenth-century Spanish-Zapotec dictionary is *màni pècoxilla*. The meanings of the constituents of this label could not be easily determined from the dictionary since it lacks a Zapotec-Spanish section. I reached the final nomenclatural analysis of the term, that is, "cotton dog animal," after using an educated-guess approach in searching Spanish-Zapotec listings for Spanish words that were possibly glossed by constituent elements of the Zapotec term. Since I am acquainted with many languages of Mesoamerica, I had little difficulty with this example from Zapotec. However, there are many native labels for acculturated items whose literal meanings I could either not retrieve or only partially establish through dictionaries. As discussed in the next chapter, this failure is due in part to the fact that many native terms are loans from other Amerindian languages and, hence, often cannot be etymologized in recipient languages.

All labels for items of acculturation, including both European loanwords and native terms, are presented in this work in the orthography of the original sources from which they were extracted. While it would have been desirable to employ a standard orthography throughout, to do so would have required a major research undertaking for which resources and time were lacking.

NOMENCLATURE

This chapter describes strategies used by speakers of Native American languages for naming objects and concepts introduced to the New World by Europeans. Four major processes are widely recognized (see, e.g., Herzog 1941; Haugen 1950; Casagrande 1954a, 1954b, 1955; Salzmann 1954; Basso 1967; Bright 1976): (1) adoption of loan-words, (2) use of loan shifts (loan translations and semantic loans), (3) extension of terms, and (4) coining of descriptive expressions. Onomatopoeia, or sound-mimicking, can be added to this list as a minor process. (The expression "native term" is used here to refer to labels created through the last three major processes and onomatopoeia.)

Loanwords

Loanwords for items of acculturation in Native American languages are of two types: those borrowed from European languages and those borrowed from other Amerindian languages.

To characterize words as being "borrowed" into one language from another or as being "loans" is to use a traditional metaphor of linguistics. A literal and descriptively more accurate approach is to describe words of one language as being "copied" from another and thus so-called loanwords as being "copies" of words in another language (cf. T. Crowley 1992). With this clarification in mind, I proceed in a traditional manner by using the standard metaphor. I also follow Poplack, Sankoff, and Miller (1988:52) by conferring the status of loanword only on words that "recur relatively frequently [in language use], are widely used in the speech community, and have achieved a certain level of recognition or acceptance, if not normative approval." Since this study is based primarily on dictionary sources, I assume that most "copied" forms found there have loanword status, while I recognize that some nonce forms may have sometimes fooled even the best lexicographers.

Loanwords from European languages

American Indian languages have adopted words for acculturated items from several European languages, including Basque, Danish, Dutch, English, French, German,

Norwegian, Portuguese, Russian, and Spanish (cf. A. R. Taylor 1981:176). Appendix A identifies the number of language cases that label each of the 77 referents by using one or more European loanwords. Appendix B, among other things, specifies for each language case that has European loans for one or more items the European language or languages from which labels have been acquired.

Table 3.1 lists each of the 77 items of acculturation by rank order (from highest to lowest) of the European loan percentage, or in other words, the percentage of language cases that show a European-language loanword for the item among all the language cases for which a term for the item has been recorded (see appendix A). (This does not include referentially extended European loans and most loan blends; see the following discussion.) Of course, words for items that are not European loans are native terms.

Analysis of the information in table 3.1 shows a fairly strong and statistically significant association between the type of acculturated item (either a living thing or an artifact) and the use of European loanwords (gamma = .66; chi square = 10.82336; p < .01). (Gamma ranges in value from -1.00, a perfect negative correlation, to 1.00, a perfect positive correlation, with zero indicating no correlation.) Amerindian languages tend to use European loans for imported natural kinds more strongly than they do for introduced artifacts. This correlation would be even stronger if terms for subtypes of imported creatures (e.g., MARE, OX, CALF, ROOSTER, and COLT) were removed from consideration (see table 5.1). These items, unlike introduced living things in general, tend to be named by native terms rather than by European loans. Further discussion of this observation is found in subsequent chapters.

European loans have often undergone phonological modification in Amerindian languages. For example, the Spanish word for HORSE, *caballo*, has acquired these different manifestations in the following language cases: Osage *ká-wa*, Southern Ute *kavá*, Tewa *kaváźuʰ*, Pima *kavio*, Washo *gawá.yuʔ*, Seri *cáay*, Chatino *cuayu*, Tzotzil (San Andrés) *ca'*, Chaque *kabayi*, Uarao *cavari*, Ashluslá y (1915) *kyuaiyu*, Ranquelche *cauell*, and Colorado *calu* (cf. Kiddle 1978). Phonological alteration usually results from assimilation of adopted words to sound patterns of individual languages. The degree of assimilation is thought to depend on the length of time a loan has been part of a language's lexicon. Thus, as Spicer (1943:421–422), Trager (1944:145), Spencer (1947:132–133), Haugen (1950:216), Casagrande (1954b:229), L. E. Clark (1977), Brown (1989a:546–547), and others have observed, older loanwords tend to be more adapted to patterns of borrowing languages than younger ones.

Loans from European languages are sometimes semantically modified as well. For example, the Pima word for introduced PEAS is *wihol*, a loan based on the Spanish term for BEAN, *frijol*. The loan in question has acquired a referent it did not have in Spanish. Similarly, the Heiltsuk word for MONEY, *dála*, is based on English "dollar" (which, of course, does not denote MONEY in general), and the Miskito term for COW, *bip*, is based on English "beef." In these examples, European loans have been extended in reference to items of acculturation. (For analytical purposes in this work, these are considered to be native terms rather than European loanwords.)

In table 3.2, each of the 77 acculturated items is rank-listed by the percentage of language cases in which it is named by a referentially extended European loan among language cases that show analyzable native terms. An analyzable native term is either a polysemous word whose alternative referents are given in a lexical source or a

Table 3.1. Seventy-seven items of acculturation ranked by percentage of language cases showing (nonextended) European-language loans.

Item	Percentage	Item	Percentage
COFFEE	81 (156/192)	SCISSORS	35 (86/245)
*CORIANDER	72 (28/39)	WEDNESDAY	35 (54/155)
*CAT	70 (194/279)	MATCH	34 (64/186)
*GARLIC	69 (70/101)	NAIL	33 (74/224)
*ORANGE	67 (122/182)	CANDLE	32 (68/216)
CHEESE	66 (88/134)	* MARE	31 (42/135)
*DONKEY	64 (116/182)	SPOON	31 (79/256)
*LEMON	60 (80/133)	SHOVEL	30 (51/172)
*APPLE	59 (91/155)	STORE	30 (51/172)
*COW	58 (153/266)	BREAD	29 (78/269)
SATURDAY	56 (95/170)	FLOUR	29 (68/232)
*PIG	55 (151/277)	* OX	29 (45/153)
SOLDIER	55 (110/202)	BOARD	28 (60/215)
*PEACH	54 (66/122)	BUTTER	28 (34/122)
*MULE	54 (87/161)	WAGON	28 (42/151)
*GOAT	53 (103/196)	* PEAS	28 (29/105)
SUGAR	53 (121/227)	CUP	27 (52/196)
TEA	53 (63/119)	MILE	27 (16/60)
*HORSE	52 (143/273)	PISTOL	27 (29/108)
*RICE	52 (96/184)	WINDOW	27 (59/218)
TABLE	52 (127/244)	CLOCK	25 (47/191)
SOAP	51 (124/244)	* GRAPES	25 (34/136)
BOTTLE	51 (107/208)	* OATS	23 (17/74)
*WATERMELON	49 (71/144)	BOOK	22 (53/247)
RIBBON	48 (72/149)	NEEDLE	21 (57/272)
*CABBAGE	47 (66/140)	PAPER	20 (53/263)
*LETTUCE	47 (42/89)	HUNDRED	19 (40/215)
HOUR	45 (69/153)	* BEETS	18 (9/51)
*SHEEP	44 (105/241)	THREAD	17 (43/255)
*ONION	41 (82/202)	* CALF	16 (28/176)
KEY	41 (91/221)	* CHICKEN	16 (28/180)
*BULL	40 (76/191)	TOWN	15 (38/258)
*BARLEY	39 (23/59)	RICH	13 (29/225)
*TURNIP	39 (37/95)	* ROOSTER	12 (27/222)
BUTTON	38 (69/180)	* COLT	11 (12/109)
*WHEAT	38 (66/172)	MONEY	11 (30/263)
*APRICOT	37 (10/27)	FORK	10 (17/165)
BOX	36 (79/221)	* HEN	10 (23/229)
SCHOOL	35 (65/185)		

*Identifies living things.

complex label for which the meanings or referents of its constituent elements can be determined or retrieved, at least in part, from a lexical source; see the introduction to appendix A. The original referents of loans and their languages of origin are also presented. Thus, for example, the sixth-ranked item in table 3.2, BULL, is labeled by a semantically extended European loan in 18.2% of the language cases in which an analyzable native term for this item is found (20/110). Table 3.2 also indicates that words for HORSE and BEEF from English (E) and words for COW and OX from

Table 3.2. Seventy-seven items of acculturation ranked by percentage of language cases with extended European-language loans, the languages of origin, and their original referents.

MONEY: 50.8 (93/183) (dollar[E], silver coin?[S], hard cash[F], peso[S], real[S], silver[E,S], le piastre[F], tomin[S], medio[S], centavo[S], Dutch sixpenny-piece[F], cinq sous[F], virutas[S: "wood shaving?"])

*CHICKEN: 32.7 (18/55) (rooster[F,P,S], hen[S], Spanish[S])

*OX: 27.1 (26/96) [cow[E,S], cattle[S], bull[S], beef[E], tame[S], young bull, steer [S], yoke of draft animals[S])

BOOK: 25.4 (33/130) (paper[E,P,S], letter[P,S])

PAPER: 22.3 (25/112) (book[R], Spanish[S], letter[P,S])

*BULL: 18.2 (20/110) (horse[E], cow[S], ox[S], beef[E])

*CORIANDER: 16.7 (1/6) (onion[S])

*LEMON: 15.2 (7/46) (orange[E,S], lime[E,S])

CUP: 14.4 (13/90) (bottle[F], half pint[F], pitcher[S], glass[S], beater[S], basin[E], chocolate cup[S])

*WHEAT: 13.6 (9/66) (tortilla[S], flour[S], grass[Mexican S], bread[S], oats[S], Spanish[S])

RIBBON: 13.5 (5/37) (silk[E,S], kerchief for head[S])

*DONKEY: 13.1 (8/61) (mule[E,F,S], Mexican[S], horse[S])

*GRAPES: 11.6 (5/43) (grapevine[S], wine[E,S], grape arbor[S])

HOUR: 11.4 (8/70) (clock[R], one[G], time[E,S], watch[E])

*MULE: 11.1 (7/63) (donkey[P,S], horse[S])

*HEN: 10.7 (12/112) (rooster[F,S], Spanish[S] {8 languages show this one})

*TURNIP: 9.1 (3/33) (radish[S], sweet potato[S])

*PIG: 8.5 (8/94) (cow[R], bacon[E], back cut of meat[R], shoat[E])

FORK: 8.2 (8/98) (small pitchfork[S], carving knife[S], piquette?[F])

*PEAS: 8.0 (4/50) (bean[S], garbanso[S])

BOTTLE: 7.8 (4/51) (glass[S], liter bottle[S], pint bottle[S])

CANDLE: 7.3 (9/123) (wax[S,P], tallow [S], lamp[E], light[E])

*APRICOT: 6.7 (1/15) (peach[S])

*OATS: 6.5 (3/46) (seed[S], oatmeal[E])

*COW: 6.3 (6/95) (horse[E], ox [Dan.], cattle[S], bull[S], beef[E])

*ROOSTER: 6.3 (9/142) (chicken[S], Spanish[S], hen[S])

BOX: 6.2 (4/65) (chest[S], cardboard box[S], trunk[S])

*SHEEP: 6.1 (6/98) (goat[S], male[S])

*WATERMELON: 6.0 (3/50) (melon[S], squash[S])

*HORSE: 4.8 (5/105) (dog[R], mule[S], beast[S])

BREAD: 4.7 (5/106) (broad thin cake[F], tortilla[F], semite[S])

*PEACH: 4.4 (2/45) (apple[E], melon[S])

*RICE: 4.1 (3/74) (groats[R])

THREAD: 4.1 (4/98) (cotton[E,P], rope, cord[S])

*CABBAGE: 3.9 (2/51) (collard[E], lettuce[S])

CLOCK: 3.8 (5/131) (bell[E], hour[S])

NAIL: 3.8 (3/80) (tack[S], needle[S])

SOLDIER: 3.6 (2/55) (guard (body of armed men)[S], troops[S])

BUTTON: 3.5 (2/58) (key[S], clasp[S])

*BARLEY: 3.3 (1/30) (straw[S])

WAGON: 3.3 (2/61) (cart[S])

TOWN: 3.0 (3/99) (store[S], the street[S])

Table 3.2. (*continued*)

STORE: 2.8 (3/106) (company[R], commissary[E], a gambling game[S])
FLOUR: 2.3 (2/89) (wheat[S])
RICH: 2.2 (2/90) (to have[S], Christian[S])
*GOAT: 1.9 (1/54) (sheep[S])
SCHOOL: 1.8 (2/112) (college[S], primary school?[S])
PISTOL: 1.6 (1/61) (carbine[S])
*ORANGE: 1.5 (1/66) (Portugal[S])
*COLT: 1.1 (1/92) (horse[P])
*MARE: 1.1 (1/91) (horse[S])
WINDOW: 1.03 (1/97) (mirror[S])
MATCH: 1.01 (1/99) (cigarette[S])
KEY: 1.0 (1/100) (button[P])
TABLE: 0.97 (1/103) (board[S])
*CALF: 0.8 (1/130) (cow[S])

E = English, F = French, P = Portuguese, R = Russian, S = Spanish.
*Identifies living things.

Items showing percentages of zero include *APPLE, *BEETS, BOARD,
BUTTER, *CAT, CHEESE, COFFEE, *GARLIC, HUNDRED,
*LETTUCE, MILE, NEEDLE, *ONION, SATURDAY, SCISSORS,
SHOVEL, SOAP, SPOON, SUGAR, TEA, WEDNESDAY.

Spanish (S) are loans into Amerindian languages that have been referentially extended to BULL.

A notable result in table 3.2 is that first-ranked MONEY far surpasses other referents in designation through semantically expanded European loans. MONEY has a percentage of 50.8, whereas the second-highest percentage, for CHICKEN, is only 32.7. Typically, European loanwords for some particular denomination of money have been referentially expanded to MONEY (in general). The inclination to make such a semantic adjustment has been robust among speakers of Amerindian languages—so strong, in fact, that it may constitute a universal naming tendency (see chapter 4).

Analysis of data in table 3.2 shows a reasonably strong and statistically significant correlation between the type of acculturated item (either a living thing or an artifact) and the use of extended European loans (gamma = .66; chi square = 10.62286; p < .01). Imported natural kinds tend more strongly than introduced artifacts to acquire labels in Amerindian languages through referential extension of European loans.

European loanwords are sometimes constituents of *loan blends*, hybrid constructions in which European loans are combined with native terms. Most loan blends encountered in the current sample designate some category of introduced animal inclusively related to some other class of imported creature. For example, Cayuvava's label for ROOSTER, *torota'korako*, is literally "bull chicken," combining Spanish *toro* "bull" with the native word for CHICKEN, *ta'korako*. Another example is Lake Miwok's term for MARE, *póccikawaj*, literally "female horse," in which a loan for HORSE, *kawaj*, modeled on Spanish *caballo*, is compounded with a native term for FEMALE. Other loan blends occasionally involve introduced referents other than animals or even other than living things. For example, Cuna (1980–1913) *nas-nalas* "lemon" combines the language's native term for SOUR with its loan for ORANGE from Spanish (*naranja*); Yuki shows *papel han* for SCHOOL, which compounds a loan based on Spanish *papel* "paper" with a native term for HOUSE.

For analytical purposes in this work, loan blends, such as the preceding examples, are considered to be native terms rather than European loanwords. An exception is the fairly rare case in which a loan blend for an item of acculturation combines a European loan for that same acculturated item with another element, for example, the combination of a loan that denotes COW in a European language (e.g., Spanish *vaca*) with a native term for FEMALE, which forms a compound term for COW (e.g., "female *vaca*"). Such loan blends are formally considered to be European loanwords rather than native terms. In this, as in other, similar examples, the referent of the borrowed European term has been altered, Spanish *vaca* having developed as a term for bovine in general.

Loanwords from other Amerindian languages

Native words for items of acculturation have very frequently been diffused from one Amerindian language to another (chapter 8). Indeed, because of its ubiquity, inter-Amerindian language borrowing constitutes a major focus of this study (see chapters 8–11). Diffusion across Native American languages has entailed not only native terms for imported items but also European loanwords for these referents. European loans have been introduced into some languages directly by speakers of European languages and, subsequently, have been diffused therefrom to other languages (chapter 9).

Like European loans, some borrowed native terms have been semantically modified through referential extension to new (imported) referents. For example, terms for WHEAT in at least two languages of the Gran Chaco region of South America, Toba (1943–1980) and Mataco—respectively, *tanta* and *tantán*—are modeled on a widely diffused term for BREAD, *tanta*, which probably originated in and was diffused from Peruvian Quechua (chapter 11). Thus, in the two Gran Chaco languages, a borrowed native term for BREAD has become referentially extended to WHEAT. Borrowed native words are also found as constituents of loan blends in Amerindian languages. For example, the Mataco word for WHEAT (borrowed from Quechua) is a constituent of the language's label for FLOUR, *múc-tanta-muc*, literally, "dust wheat dust."

Many native terms for introduced items borrowed from other Amerindian languages are not analyzed in this work (see appendix A) because they cannot be semantically etymologized in the adopting languages. For example, in the southeastern United States, Creek has donated its word for MONEY, *cvto-kunáwv*, to neighboring Koasati. While the Creek label translates literally as "stone beads," the borrowed Koasati MONEY term, *Tokná:wa*, is opaque. Indeed, Koasati shows entirely different words for both STONE and BEADS from those of Creek, respectively, *talí* and *copí*. Nevertheless, when native words for imported items are loaned by one Amerindian language to another language that belongs to the same genetic grouping, borrowed terms are often analyzable because related languages frequently show the same or closely similar words for constituent elements of such labels.

Loan Shifts

Loan shifts are "loans" that do not necessarily employ the phonemic shapes of donor languages. Two basic types are observed: loan translations (or calques) and semantic loans (Weinreich 1953:47–53; Haugen 1956:60–61; Hoenigswald 1960:22). Loan translations occur when labels in one language are translated, morpheme by morpheme, into words of another language, for example, Spanish *rascacielos* from English "skyscraper" and *perro caliente* from "hot dog." Semantic loans are like loan translations except that they entail single words rather than compounds (Haugen 1956:61); for example, Portuguese *correr* "run" became extended to mean "run for office," copying the English usage (Hoenigswald 1960:22).

Loan shifts from European languages

Loan translations in Amerindian languages based on European labels for the 77 items of acculturation are extremely rare. Indeed, only one plausible example emerges in the large language sample consulted here. The Crow word for WATERMELON, *kukúmbirè*, is literally "squash water," which, of course, may be modeled on English "watermelon." A couple of other language cases, Plains Cree ("Y" dialect) and Dieugueño, have labels for WATERMELON that combine words for WATER with unknown elements (UE). These, too, may be calques based on the English. This is somewhat less likely for Dieugueño since it has been primarily influenced by Spanish rather than English. In addition, Big Smokey Valley Shoshoni's WATERMELON term is literally "water to eat that which is," which may be partially modeled on the English term. Possibly, all of these examples may instead represent instances of independent invention (see chapter 4).

Among English labels for the 77 acculturated items, only "watermelon" has constituent elements that are completely semantically analyzable. No other English labels for these referents manifest constituent parts with distinct meanings in terms of which loan translations might be derived. (English "window" is partially analyzable as WIND plus a now opaque element that originally designated EYE.) This is also true of virtually all words for acculturated items found in other European languages that have contributed loans to languages of the New World. As Casagrande (1954b:233) notes, models for loan translations themselves must be descriptive. Thus, it is not particularly surprising to learn that calques from European languages for imported items are rare in Amerindian tongues.

Semantic loans from European languages are also rare. Bright (1973) mentions an interesting example involving PEAR, an item of acculturation not on my list. In Karok (an isolate) of northern California, the word for BEAR, *vírusur*, is used to designate PEAR. This is the result of the speakers' tendency to equate the English words "bear" and "pear" since their language lacks voiceless stops. Parallel developments pertain to both Tuscarora (Iroquoian) and Comanche (Uto-Aztecan). The Tuscarora term for BEAR also denotes PEAR (Rudes 1987:127). Tuscarora's phonetic inventory lacks bilabial stops (*b*'s and *p*'s). The Comanche word for PEAR, *wasápeʔa tɨhkapɨ*, is literally "bear food." Casagrande (1954b:234) explains this usage as the result of no *p-b* distinction in the language and the addition of FOOD to "rationalize the word."

The only possible example of a semantic loan from a European language in my sample involves words for TOWN in several languages influenced by Spanish. The common Spanish word for TOWN in Hispanic America is *pueblo*. In addition to TOWN, the term denotes, among several other referents, PEOPLE. In three languages of Latin America—Zoque (Copainalá), Tucano, and Cayuvava—words for PEOPLE also designate TOWN, perhaps the result of semantic extensions of native terms for the former referent to the latter in analogy with use of Spanish *pueblo*.

The dearth of semantic loans in the sample, like the scarcity of loan translations, probably reflects the general nature of European words for items of acculturation. As far as I can determine, they rarely show salient referents in addition to acculturated items. European terms, then, infrequently involve conspicuous semantic equations, such as TOWN = PEOPLE, in terms of which Native American languages are motivated to fabricate compelling semantic loans.

Loan shifts from other Amerindian languages

The transfer of names for acculturated items from one Amerindian language to another through loan shifts is probably a fairly common phenomenon (chapters 10 and 11). Casagrande (1954b:234–235) calls attention to possible examples in two languages of the current sample, Kiowa and Comanche, noting the close historical association of their speakers. Among several possible loan translations, he mentions similar descriptive terms for the introduced PEACH in the two languages, which are, respectively, "fuzz plum" and "hairy plum." Other similar descriptive labels from Kiowa and Comanche for items on my list that are possible calques include, respectively, "liquid black" and "black water" for COFFEE; "there to look" and "through see" for WINDOW; and for both languages, "writing house" for SCHOOL and "little Sunday" for SATURDAY. However, these may not be true calques since the labels in question could have been independently invented by the two languages. Many other languages show similar labels for these items, no doubt in many instances the result of universal naming tendencies rather than loan translations (see chapter 4).

Languages of the southeastern United States provide a more certain example of loan shift. Most of these languages designate SHEEP by a term for RABBIT, for example, Biloxi (a Siouan language) *tcĕtkohí* "sheep" and Tunica (a language isolate) *rúštatɛ* "sheep," both of which are literally "rabbit big." Two factors strongly suggest that this usage is a loan translation, at least in some languages: (1) the feature does not occur in Amerindian languages outside the southeastern United States, and (2) its distribution in the southeastern United States cuts across language genetic boundaries. Factor 1 indicates lack of a universal tendency to coin the feature (see chapter 4) and, consequently, strongly suggests that innovation has not occurred more than *once* in southeastern U.S. languages. The feature must have been diffused as a loan translation from a single innovating language to some other area languages since, because of factor 2, its distribution across languages of the region cannot be entirely explained by inheritance from a common ancestral language (Brown 1996a). Diffusion of the calque was probably facilitated by a lingua franca, Mobilian Jargon, a pidgin trade language of the region (see chapters 8–11).

Another North American example involving SHEEP comes from neighboring, but genetically unrelated, languages of the western subarctic—Chipewyan (Athapascan-

Eyak) and Cree (Algonquian). In these languages, terms for SHEEP are respectively *edshenn slini* and *mayattik*. The former is literally "caribou bad" and the latter "bad caribou" (preserving respective syntactic orders). Since no other languages in the sample show this semantic construction for SHEEP, one of these languages almost certainly calqued its label from the other. Cree was probably the donor since this language is known to have contributed several lexical loans to other Athapascan-Eyak languages of the region (see chapter 9 and Silverstein 1996:118).

In Mesoamerica (southern Mexico and northern Central America), labels for imported BREAD have spread as loan translations. In several genetically unrelated languages of the area, BREAD terms are compound labels consisting of a loanword from Nahuatl that originated in Spanish—that is, *caxtillan* (Karttunen and Lockhart 1976:128; Bright 1979b:270; see chapter 11), variously meaning SPANISH or FOREIGN—and a language-particular word for TORTILLA—for example, Huave (San Mateo) *peats castil* "bread" and Zapotec (1578) *quetaxoopa castilla* "bread" (these labels roughly translate as "Spanish tortilla"). Since Nahuatl was an important lingua franca of the area, it almost certainly was the source of this calque, as well as the source of the diffused modifier *caxtillan* (see chapter 11). Compound labels for both HEN and WHEAT, which respectively combine words for TURKEY and MAIZE with Nahuatl *caxtillan*, also were diffused widely across Mesoamerican languages, such as Zoque (1672) *castellan-tunuc* "hen" and Tzotzil (Zinacantán, late sixteenth century) *castillan ʔixim* "wheat." Spread of these loan translations was almost certainly facilitated by lingua franca Nahuatl (chapter 11).

Mesoamerican languages also provide a possible example of a semantic loan. Several genetically unrelated languages of the region refer to both COTTON and SHEEP by a single term, for example, Nahuatl (1571) *ichcatl* "cotton or sheep"; Yucatec (1850–1883) *taman* "sheep, cotton"; Tequistlatec *glomoɬ* "sheep, cotton"; Huave (San Mateo) *sap* "sheep, cotton." When sheep were introduced, some area language possibly extended its term for native COTTON to the imported creature. This usage could have served as a model for the development of semantic loans for SHEEP in other Mesoamerican languages. (However, an alternative explanation of the genesis of COTTON/SHEEP polysemy is proposed presently.)

A somewhat complex example of a semantic loan is observed in languages of the southeastern United States. Virtually all languages of the area have terms for the introduced PEACH that serve as constituents of compound labels for the native WILD PLUM, for example, Choctaw *takkon* "peach" and *takkono-ši* "plum" (literally, "peach little"); Tunica *kiru* "peach" and *kirumili* "plum" (literally, "peach red"). (These are examples of marking reversal, development of which is discussed in this chapter.) While this usage was possibly independently invented by two or more southeastern languages, in most instances it probably was diffused across area languages as a semantic loan—no doubt facilitated by Mobilian Jargon, which shows the feature. (Details of this development are discussed at length in chapter 10.) A similar widespread feature of southeastern languages is use of a term for the introduced PIG as a constituent element of a compound label for the native OPOSSUM, for example, Atakapa *híyen* "pig" and *kákip híyen* "opossum" (literally, "forest pig"), and Alabama *sokha* "pig" and *sokhàatka* "opossum" (literally, "pig white"). This usage, too, was diffused as a semantic loan (chapter 10).

Referential Extension

Newly encountered items are commonly named by extending referential use of a word for some familiar object or concept to a somewhat similar introduced object or concept. The referentially extended word may, in some instances, be a European loan, for example, a borrowed term for some particular currency denomination (say, English "dollar") extended to MONEY in general (see table 3.2). More commonly, however, the referentially expanded word is a term that originated in an Amerindian language.

Nomenclatural manifestations of referential extension

Referential extension can result in different types of nomenclature for introduced items, including *polysemy, overt marking, double overt marking,* and *marking reversal.* In polysemy a single term is used to denote two similar referents, one of which is typically a native item and the other an introduced thing—for example, Beaver *klin*, which denotes both DOG (native) and HORSE (introduced), and Creek *tvláko*, which designates both BEANS (native) and PEAS (introduced). In these examples, polysemy developed when native terms for indigenous items were referentially expanded to introduced items.

In overt marking, a word for one referent (typically native) also serves as a constituent element in a compound label for a similar introduced referent—for example, Dakota (Teton, c. 1970) *omnica*, which denotes BEANS, and *omnicagmigmi*, literally, "beans round," designating PEAS. In this example, *gmigmi* "round" constitutes a modifying overt mark and *omnica* a base element. Double overt marking is apparent when two compound labels, which denote respectively two similar referents, share a constituent element—for example, Tzeltal (1888) *tetiquil chig*, literally, "wild X," which denotes native DEER, and *stunimal chig*, literally, "cotton X," which refers to introduced SHEEP (X stands for the shared constituent). Here, both *tetiquil* "wild" and *stunimal* "cotton" are overt marks, whereas *chig* is a common base.

Overt marking constructions sometimes entail base elements that designate introduced referents rather than native ones. For example, it is common for language cases of the sample to denote PEACH by compound labels in which a term for introduced APPLE is a constituent—Tewa *bè fóʔñ* "peach," literally, "apple hairy," and Cheyenne (1915) *meovemaxemeu* "peach," literally, "fuzzy apple." In some instances, the base may be a loan from a European language—Southern Ute *pųų̃masáana* "peach," literally, "fur apple," where *-masáana* is a loan based on Spanish *manzana* "apple"; and Arikara *apostaánux* "peach," literally, "apple hairy," where *apos* is a loan based on English "apple." These, of course, are further examples of loan blends.

Marking reversals show the same basic pattern as overt marking constructions—Montagnais (Chipewyan dialect) *djie ͨgayé*, which refers to PEAS, and *djie ͨgayé ͨ kalè*, literally, "peas flat," denoting BEANS. Marking reversals are distinguished from overt marking constructions through reference to ethnographic and historical considerations: typically the compound term denotes a native item (e.g., BEANS), whereas its unitary counterpart refers to an introduced item (e.g., PEAS).

It is not uncommon for more than one of these nomenclatural patterns to pertain to a single referent in a single language. For example, as noted, Beaver *klin* demonstrates polysemy since it denotes both DOG and HORSE. The term *klin* is also used as a base in an overt marking construction, *klin chok* (literally, "dog/horse large"), which designates only HORSE. Similarly, in Comanche a single word, *pihúra* (from Spanish *frijol* "bean"), denotes both PEAS and BEANS. To refer unambiguously to PEAS, one uses the overt marking construction *toponibihuuraʔ* (literally, "round bean/peas"). Choctaw demonstrates a marking reversal in which a compound label for native RABBIT, *chukfi luma*, consists of a polysemous word, *chukfi*, denoting both RABBIT and introduced SHEEP, and a modifier (*luma* "hidden"). Presumably, in situations such as these, optional compound constructions are there to be used when context does not render the intended referent absolutely clear.

Salience, marking value, and nomenclature

Witkowski and Brown (1983) outline circumstances under which referential extension results in nomenclatural patterns discussed above. The primary determining factor is change in the relative cultural salience (importance) of nomenclaturally linked referents. Change in salience affects the frequency of use of terms for referents, which in turn influences their "marking values."

The framework of marking as described by Greenberg (1966, 1969, 1975) and others draws on the earlier work of Zipf (1935, 1949) and of Prague school linguists such as Jakobson (1941) and Trubetzkoy (1939). A major aspect of this approach is a distinction between unmarked and marked linguistic items that extends to all components of language: phonology, grammar, and lexicon. Some of the criteria that tend to co-occur in typical marking relationships are as follows (for a more detailed consideration of these features and how they are interrelated, see Brown and Witkowski 1980):

Unmarked	Marked
1. The implied in an implicational relationship	1. The implier in an implicational relationship
2. Greater frequency of use within language	2. Less frequency of use
3. In neutralized context	3. Not in neutralized context
4. Less complex phonologically or morphologically	4. More complex
5. Not overtly marked	5. May be overtly marked
6. Early childhood acquisition	6. Late acquisition

Application of this framework to nomenclature for acculturated items can be illustrated through reference to overt marking (feature 5). Referents related through overt marking form a "marking pair" (unmarked vs. marked). For example, in Slave (dialect of Chipewyan), an Athapaskan language of northern Canada, *klin* (unmarked) denotes DOG, while *klintcho* (marked), literally, "dog big," labels HORSE. In the expression *klintcho*, the first element is a base, the second an overt mark. Because of co-occurrence relationships between features of marking, other associations tend to hold for this pair; for example, we expect *klin* to be more frequent in use and acquired earlier by children than *klintcho*. The deeper circumstance that underlies these relationships is that dogs are common in northern Canada and culturally important among the Slave and other area groups, whereas horses are rare and have virtually no cultural significance.

In the model presented by Witkowski and Brown (1983), overall salience of referents determines the marking values of referents by affecting label frequency. Terms for highly salient referents are used more frequently, and this in turn affects other features of marking, such as brevity and acquisition. Thus, frequent terms (e.g., *klin*) tend to be less complex and more readily acquired by children than less frequent lexical items (e.g., *klintcho*).

Shifts in cultural importance can drastically alter marking value and, by influencing frequency of use, can lead to brevity of form through abbreviation or substitution (cf. Zipf 1935). Thus alteration in marking-value assignment, resulting from a change in cultural salience, can lead to nomenclatural change.

Marking reversals are dramatic examples of nomenclatural change that results from shifts in cultural importance. In Tenejapa Tzeltal, a Mayan language spoken in the Mexican state of Chiapas, one reversal has involved the relative cultural significance of native deer and introduced sheep (Berlin 1972). At the time of the Spanish conquest, DEER were designated *čih*. When sheep were introduced, they were equated with deer. This almost certainly was first realized nomenclaturally through the referential extension of *čih* to SHEEP, thus creating a polysemous label that designates both referents. As sheep increased in cultural salience, an overt marking construction, *tunim čih*, literally, "cotton deer," developed as a means for lexically distinguishing SHEEP from DEER (in this expression, *čih* is a base and *tunim* "cotton" is an overt mark). Today, however, the Tenejapa term for SHEEP is simply *čih*, while DEER is labeled by the overtly marked expression *teʔtikil čih*, literally, "wild sheep." This development may have been immediately preceded by a stage of double overt marking in which both DEER and SHEEP were labeled by overt marking constructions (as attested for Tzeltal [1888]; see preceding discussion). Clearly, this marking flip-flop developed in response to the greatly increased cultural importance of sheep in highland Chiapas in comparison to deer (Laughlin 1969; Vogt 1969; Hunn 1977).

Referential extension that entails introduced items does not always result in marking reversals. For example, in another dialect of Tzeltal, Bachajón, SHEEP are designated by the overt marking construction, *tumin čix*, literally, "cotton deer." Bachajón Tzeltal is spoken in the Chiapas lowlands where sheep are uncommon (Blom and La Farge 1927; Villa Rojas 1969). Sheep prefer higher elevations with cooler climates. In contrast, the Tenejapa Tzeltal live in the Chiapas highlands, where sheep are common and the manufacture of woolen products is customary. Apparently, for speakers of Bachajón Tzeltal sheep never acquired a degree of high cultural salience relative to that of deer to motivate a marking reversal.

Referential extension and accompanying nomenclatural developments have not been limited to introduced natural kinds (living things). For example, in Karok of northern California (Bright 1952), two marking reversals have occurred that involve paraphernalia of hunting. In the past, *sá·k* was ARROWHEAD and *xuská·mhar* designated BOW, but today these terms mean BULLET and GUN. Not surprisingly, the optionally marked form *('arara)xúska·mhar*, literally, "Indian gun," currently denotes BOW, and a similarly marked form labels ARROWHEAD. For the contemporary Karok, the introduced gun and its bullets presumably have become more important than the aboriginal bow and arrow. Another example involves Bodega Miwok's word for imported BREAD, *cíppa*, which originally denoted a native bread-like concoction made from acorns. In contemporary times the native concoction is designated by *ʔúmpan cíppa*, which is literally "acorn bread," almost certainly a nomenclatural response to the enhanced significance of the imported food item.

Witkowski and Brown's basic model can be summarized as follows. When an introduced item is first encountered, a term for a similar native item may be appropriated to name it. This typically entails referential extension and the development of polysemy. Subsequently, the introduced item may become designated through overt marking. Even later, the native referent itself may become demoted to secondary, overtly marked status, while the introduced item is named by the original unmarked term. These nomenclatural shifts are caused by concomitant changes in the relative importance of the cultural items in question. Witkowski and Brown (1983:575–577) offer a generous number of examples to document such changes. In addition, they describe in considerable detail specific mechanisms that pertain to these dynamic processes. For further details, readers are directed to their work.

Primary and secondary polysemy

Polysemy frequently results when an object or concept is newly experienced and a term for a similar native item is referentially extended to it. This development involves a procession from unmarked to marked (Witkowski, Brown, and Chase 1981; Brown and Witkowski 1983; Witkowski and Brown 1985), whereby a term for a salient (usually native) referent expands to include a less salient (recently encountered) referent. Witkowski and Brown (1985:204) refer to this as *primary polysemy*, in contrast to *secondary polysemy*, which results from an entirely different process.

Secondary polysemy develops when an overt marking construction is truncated, leaving the overt mark on its own to refer both to its original referent and to the acculturated item. For example, there is a strong tendency among speakers of Amerindian languages to name the introduced PEACH through the use of overt marking expressions in which the base element designates some fruit (other than peach) and the overt mark translates as HAIRY or FUZZY—Arikara *apostaánux* "peach," literally, "apple hairy," and Comanche *pihisîhkiĺ* "peach," literally, "fuzzy plum." In at least one language case, Miami, a word for PEACH (*päweoča*) also means FUZZY, a polysemous situation that probably developed when a fruit term was dropped from the language's overt marking construction for PEACH.

COTTON/SHEEP polysemy in several languages of Mesoamerica may have also developed secondarily. As observed above, one area language, Tzeltal, uses the expression "cotton deer" to denote SHEEP. Similar overt marking constructions for SHEEP are found in other Mesoamerican languages—Zapotec (1578) *pèhuexílla* "sheep," literally, "wild pig cotton," and Zoque (1672) *tzoa-muca* "sheep," literally, "cotton deer." Languages that show COTTON/SHEEP polysemy may do so as a result of deleting from overt marking labels words for native creatures (e.g., WILD PIG and DEER) nomenclaturally equated with sheep.

Summary statistics

Tables 3.3, 3.4, and 3.5 provide summary statistics relating to names for acculturated items that involve polysemy, overt marking, and marking reversals. These data are extracted from information in appendix A.

Table 3.3 lists each of the 77 introduced items by rank order (from highest to lowest), according to the percentage of language cases that show extended constructions for the item among those language cases of the sample of 292 for which an analyzable native term for the item is recognized. *Extended constructions are inferred from polysemy.* Thus, by convention, an extended construction is judged to be apparent if a word denotes two or more similar referents, one of which is an item of acculturation. This is taken to suggest that the word in question originally denoted one of these referents and, subsequently, was referentially extended to its introduced counterpart (for more details, consult the introduction to appendix A). Of course, polysemy does not necessarily result from referential extension since processes such as secondary polysemy are clearly operative in languages. Extended constructions in table 3.3 include both referentially extended native terms and extended European loanwords (cf. table 3.2).

As in table 3.2, MONEY is the referent most often involved in referential extension largely because of the strong tendency for Amerindian languages to extend European loans, originally denoting a specific currency denomination, to the item. Native terms are also so expanded. Some of these are labels that originally denoted some type of aboriginal MONEY or CURRENCY, for example, BEAVER (referring to beaver pelts used in trade) in Okanagan, Kalispel, and Shuswap, and DENTALIUM SHELLS used by speakers of Karok in commercial exchange. The most common expansions of native words to MONEY involve terms for METAL (IN GENERAL) or types of metal such as SILVER and GOLD. Other common referential extensions among the top ten items in table 3.3 include (terms for) FIRE and LIGHT extended to CANDLE; SINEW, SINEW THREAD, ROPE, STRING, and CORD to THREAD; BIRD, TURKEY, and HEN to CHICKEN; DUST, POWDER, CORNMEAL, and ACORN MEAL to FLOUR; CONTAINER, TYPE OF CONTAINER, and GLASS (SUBSTANCE) to BOTTLE; SUN and CLOCK to HOUR; RECEPTACLE, BAG, and SACK to BOX; WARRIOR to SOLDIER; and GOURD, GOURD SPOON, SHELL, and SHELL SPOON to SPOON.

Analysis of table 3.3 shows a reasonably strong and statistically significant association between the type of introduced item (either living thing or artifact) and the use of extended constructions involving both European loans and native labels (gamma = .61; chi square = 8.07978; p < .01). Terms for imported artifacts tend more strongly than introduced natural kinds to show extended constructions. This correlation would be even stronger if referentially extended European loans were removed from consideration.

While terms for introduced living things typically are not extended constructions, one of the acculturated biological items, CHICKEN, is among the top four referents in table 3.3. This is in large part explained by a very strong inclination for Amerindian languages to denote CHICKEN through referential extension of borrowed European terms for HEN and ROOSTER (see table 3.2).

Table 3.3. Seventy-seven items of acculturation ranked by percentage of language cases with extended constructions, involving both referentially extended native terms and extended European-language loans.

Item	Percentage	Item	Percentage
MONEY	85 (155/183)	*LEMON	26 (12/46)
CANDLE	59 (72/123)	*ONION	23 (12/53)
THREAD	57 (56/98)	*WHEAT	23 (15/66)
*CHICKEN	53 (29/55)	*APPLE	22 (10/45)
FLOUR	52 (46/89)	*OATS	22 (10/46)
BOTTLE	51 (26/51)	WINDOW	22 (21/97)
HOUR	51 (36/70)	*HEN	21 (24/112)
BOX	46 (30/65)	*LETTUCE	21 (8/38)
SOLDIER	46 (25/55)	*ROOSTER	20 (29/142)
SPOON	46 (25/55)	*APRICOT	20 (3/15)
TEA	44 (23/52)	FORK	18 (18/98)
TOWN	42 (42/99)	*MULE	18 (11/63)
CUP	41 (37/90)	*WATERMELON	18 (9/50)
PAPER	41 (46/112)	*BEETS	17 (7/41)
*OX	40 (38/96)	BUTTER	17 (14/84)
SUGAR	40 (33/83)	*GOAT	17 (9/54)
MILE	39 (13/33)	*PEACH	16 (7/45)
*COW	36 (34/95)	*DONKEY	15 (9/61)
BREAD	35 (37/106)	WAGON	15 (9/61)
BOOK	34 (44/130)	TABLE	14 (14/103)
*SHEEP	34 (33/98)	*COLT	13 (12/92)
*CORIANDER	33 (2/6)	*MARE	12 (11/91)
*TURNIP	33 (11/33)	*ORANGE	12 (5/42)
MATCH	32 (32/99)	SHOVEL	11 (7/65)
RIBBON	32 (12/37)	*BARLEY	10 (3/30)
BUTTON	31 (18/58)	SOAP	10 (10/96)
NEEDLE	31 ((33/108)	*CALF	9 (11/130)
*RICE	31 (23/74)	COFFEE	8 (3/38)
NAIL	30 (24/80)	*GARLIC	8 (2/26)
BOARD	29 (32/110)	STORE	7 (7/106)
*CABBAGE	29 (15/51)	CHEESE	6 (3/52)
*BULL	28 (31/110)	SCISSORS	5 (5/93)
*CAT	28 (11/40)	SATURDAY	4 (3/76)
CLOCK	28 (36/131)	SCHOOL	4 (4/112)
*GRAPES	28 12/43)	HUNDRED	3 (3/100)
*PEAS	28 (14/50)	KEY	3 (3/100)
*PIG	27 (25/94)	PISTOL	3 (2/61)
RICH	26 (23/90)	WEDNESDAY	0 (0/96)
*HORSE	26 (27/105)		

*Identifies living things.

Table 3.4 rank-orders each of the 77 items according to the percentage of language cases that show an overt marking construction for it among languages for which an analyzable label for the item has been determined. Analysis of table 3.4 shows a strong and statistically significant correlation between the type of acculturated item (living thing or artifact) and overt marking (gamma = .78; chi square = 17.46032; p < .001). Imported living things tend much more strongly to be labeled by overt marking constructions than do introduced artifacts.

For the top ten items in table 3.4, the following overt-marking expressions are most commonly found. For BARLEY: a term for some grain (e.g., CORN, RICE, WHEAT) plus (+) a modifier (e.g., BIG, HORSE, HAIRY); for LEMON: ORANGE + SOUR, BITTER, or ACIDIC; for DONKEY: HORSE + LONG EARED; for GOAT: DEER

Table 3.4. Seventy-seven items of acculturation ranked by percentage of language cases with overt marking constructions.

Item	Percentage	Item	Percentage
*BARLEY	70 (21/30)	FORK	20 (20/98)
*LEMON	65 (30/46)	PISTOL	20 (12/61)
*GOAT	59 (32/54)	*ONION	19 (10/53)
*DONKEY	56 (34/61)	NEEDLE	18 (19/108)
*APRICOT	53 (8/15)	*OX	18 (17/96)
CLOCK	50 (65/131)	SUGAR	18 (15/83)
*GARLIC	50 (13/26)	CUP	17 (15/90)
*PEAS	48 (24/50)	TEA	17 (9/52)
*SHEEP	43 (42/98)	*BULL	16 (18/110)
*HORSE	41 (43/105)	SCISSORS	16 (15/93)
*ORANGE	41 (17/42)	FLOUR	15 (13/89)
*PEACH	40 (18/45)	*CHICKEN	13 (7/55)
*APPLE	38 (17/45)	BOX	12 (8/65)
*MULE	38 (24/63)	*CALF	12 (15/130)
*WATERMELON	36 (18/50)	SOLDIER	11 (6/55)
*CAT	35 (14/40)	NAIL	10 (8/80)
*RICE	34 (24/74)	*COLT	9 (8/92)
*WHEAT	33 (22/66)	*HEN	8 (9/112)
*COW	30 (28/95)	*LETTUCE	8 (3/38)
*BEETS	29 (12/41)	RIBBON	8 (3/37)
*PIG	28 (26/94)	SHOVEL	8 (5/65)
THREAD	28 (27/98)	WAGON	7 (4/61)
BREAD	27 (29/106)	*MARE	6 (5/91)
SPOON	26 (14/55)	SOAP	5 (5/96)
WINDOW	26 (25/97)	TABLE	4 (4/103)
*OATS	24 (11/46)	*CABBAGE	2 (1/51)
*TURNIP	24 (8/33)	TOWN	2 (2/99)
*GRAPES	23 (10/43)	MATCH	1 (1/99)
BOTTLE	20 (10/51)	*ROOSTER	1 (2/142)

*Identifies living things.

Items showing percentages of zero include BOARD, BOOK, BUTTER, BUTTON, CANDLE, CHEESE, COFFEE, *CORIANDER, HOUR, HUNDRED, KEY, MILE, MONEY, PAPER, RICH, SATURDAY, SCHOOL, STORE, WEDNESDAY.

or SHEEP + STINK, ODOR, or BAD SMELLING; for APRICOT: APPLE or PEACH + a modifier (e.g., LITTLE, SMOOTH, HAIRY); for CLOCK: SUN + MEASURE or COUNT; for GARLIC: ONION + STINKING; for PEAS: BEAN + ROUND; for SHEEP: DEER + FUR, WOOLLY, HAIRY, or COTTON; and for PEACH: a term for some fruit (e.g., APPLE, BERRY, PLUM) + FUZZY or HAIRY.

Table 3.5 lists each of the 77 items ranked by percentage of language cases that show marking reversals involving the item among those cases of the sample of 292 for which an analyzable native term for the item is recognized. Analysis shows a strong and statistically significant association between the type of acculturated item and marking reversal (gamma = .75; chi square = 15.41604; p < .001). Introduced natural kinds tend much more strongly than acculturated artifacts to be involved in marking reversals.

Table 3.5. Seventy-seven items of acculturation ranked by percentage of language cases with marking reversals.

Item	Percentage	Item	Percentage
*PIG	47.0 (44/94)	FLOUR	2.0 (2/89)
*HORSE	25.0 (26/105)	*MULE	2.0 (1/63)
*CAT	18.0 (7/40)	NEEDLE	2.0 (2/108)
*PEACH	18.0 (8/45)	*ORANGE	2.0 (1/42)
*COW	15.0 (14/95)	PAPER	2.0 (2/112)
BREAD	9.0 (9/106)	SUGAR	2.0 (2/83)
*CHICKEN	9.0 (5/55)	THREAD	2.0 (2/98)
*SHEEP	8.0 (8/98)	*WATERMELON	2.0 (1/50)
*APPLE	7.0 (3/45)	*BULL	1.0 (1/110)
*GRAPES	7.0 (3/43)	*CALF	1.0 (1/130)
SPOON	7.0 (4/55)	*MARE	1.0 (1/91)
*HEN	6.0 (7/112)	MONEY	1.0 (2/183)
*PEAS	6.0 (3/50)	*RICE	1.0 (1/74)
*OX	5.0 (5/96)	*ROOSTER	1.0 (2/142)
*GOAT	4.0 (2/54)	TOWN	1.0 (1/99)
*ONION	4.0 (2/53)	BOOK	0.8 (1/130)
*CABBAGE	2.0 (1/51)		

*Identifies living things.

Items showing percentages of zero include *APRICOT, *BARLEY, *BEETS, BOARD, BOTTLE, BOX, BUTTER, BUTTON, CANDLE, CHEESE, CLOCK, COFFEE, *COLT, *CORIANDER, CUP, *DONKEY, FORK, *GARLIC, HOUR, HUNDRED, KEY, *LEMON, *LETTUCE, MATCH, MILE, NAIL, *OATS, PISTOL, RIBBON, RICH, SATURDAY, SCHOOL, SCISSORS, SHOVEL, SOAP, SOLDIER, STORE, TABLE, TEA, *TURNIP, WAGON, WEDNESDAY, *WHEAT, WINDOW.

The referent PIG is by far more frequently involved in marking reversals than any other of the 77 acculturated items. PIG shows a percentage of 47, while the second highest percentage, for HORSE, is 25. The marked counterpart to PIG in most marking reversals is WILD PIG (or PECCARY), especially in languages spoken south of the U.S.-Mexico border. In languages of the southeastern United States, the native OPOSSUM is typically marked vis-à-vis PIG (see chapters 10 and 11, and table 11.1). Marked indigenous counterparts of introduced HORSE tend to differ across major areas of the Americas. Languages of northern North America (United States and Canada) mark DOG vis-à-vis HORSE. Those of Mexico and northern Central America tend to mark DEER relative to HORSE, and those of southern Central America and South America mark TAPIR vis-à-vis HORSE (cf. Kiddle 1978; see also chapter 4).

Also among the top five items involved in marking reversals are CAT, PEACH, and COW. CAT is typically unmarked vis-à-vis some native wild cat (e.g., LYNX, JAGUAR, PUMA, BOBCAT). PLUM is frequently the marked counterpart of PEACH, especially in languages of the southeastern United States (see the detailed discussion in chapter 10). Some large native mammal (e.g., MUSK OX, MOOSE, BISON, DEER, TAPIR) is typically marked relative to COW (see chapter 4).

BREAD and SPOON are most frequently involved in marking reversals among artifacts on the list, with respective percentages of 9 and 7. Typically, BREAD is unmarked vis-à-vis some indigenous bread-like concoction such as the TORTILLA. Native spoons or materials out of which native spoons are fabricated (e.g., GOURD and SHELL) are frequently marked counterparts of the imported SPOON.

Descriptive Labels

Complex labels typically name items of acculturation through reference to their more salient features. A few examples are Cheyenne *sòkomen-vohokass* "candle," literally, "slender light"; Carrier *etna-tši-ra* "barley," literally, "hair of the foreigners"; Siberian Yupik Eskimo *igaghyaghqaq* "paper," literally, "to write it down, something that will"; and Cherokee *so'-qui-li'* "horse," literally, "he carries heavy things." Descriptive labels tend to range from very literal (as in Seneca's "people spread with it" for BUTTER) to very figurative (as in Pima's "Chinaman's brain" for BUTTER).

One of the nomenclatural forms discussed earlier, overt marking, might be viewed as a type of descriptive construction. Clearly, such labels as "stink deer" for GOAT and "sour orange" for LEMON are highly descriptive, while nonetheless entailing overt marking. However, in this work *descriptive label* or *term* is used to refer only to descriptive constructions that are not also overt marking expressions. Thus, to know what labels are formally viewed here as descriptive, it is necessary to understand what labels are formally considered overt marking constructions. The introduction to appendix A gives the criteria for formally recognizing overt marking.

Table 3.6 rank-orders each of the 77 items of acculturation according to the percentage of language cases that show a descriptive label (as narrowly defined) for the item among languages for which an analyzable label for the item is determined. Analysis reveals a reasonably strong and statistically significant association between the type of introduced item and the use of descriptive terms (gamma = .63; chi square = 9.483851; p < .01). Imported artifacts tend more strongly than acculturated biological items to be denoted by descriptive labels.

Among those introduced living things that are typically labeled by descriptive terms (i.e., items with percentages greater than 60), 6 (out of 11) designate subtypes of imported creatures, such as ROOSTER, CALF, MARE, COLT, HEN, and BULL. Examples of such labels include Chiriguano *uru cuimbae* "rooster," literally, "hen male"; Tojolabal *tan yal wakax* "calf," literally, "that son of cattle"; Lengua *yatnatzling apkilana* "mare," literally, "horse female"; Cree *mistutimosis* "colt," literally, "horse son"; Cherokee *tsataga-agisi* "hen," literally, "chicken female"; and Piro *waka jeji* "bull," literally, "cow male." The exceptional nomenclatural treatment of these items among introduced biological items is discussed further in following chapters.

Some descriptive constructions, and other native terms as well, may not have been devised by Native Americans but rather developed or created for them by Europeans. For example, Lyle Campbell (personal communication) cites Nahuatl *teopan* "church," literally, "god place," as a creation of Spanish missionary priests to avoid Nahuatl *teocalli*, literally, "god house," with its pagan connotations.

Table 3.6. Seventy-seven items of acculturation ranked by percentage of language cases with descriptive labels.

Item	Percentage	Item	Percentage
WEDNESDAY	100 (96/96)	*ONION	59 (31/53)
HUNDRED	99 (99/100)	TEA	58 (30/52)
SCHOOL	98 (110/112)	HOUR	57 (40/70)
KEY	97 (97/100)	CANDLE	55 (67/123)
SATURDAY	97 (74/76)	SOLDIER	55 (30/55)
CHEESE	96 (50/52)	*WHEAT	55 (36/66)
STORE	95 (101/106)	*GARLIC	54 (14/26)
COFFEE	92 (35/38)	*OX	53 (51/96)
*ROOSTER	89 (126/142)	BOX	52 (34/65)
BUTTER	88 (74/84)	CUP	52 (47/90)
TABLE	87 (90/103)	*ORANGE	52 (22/42)
SHOVEL	86 (56/65)	*WATERMELON	52 (26/50)
*CALF	85 (111/130)	*GRAPES	51 (22/43)
*MARE	85 (77/91)	*MULE	51 (32/63)
SOAP	85 (82/96)	*TURNIP	49 (16/33)
RICH	84 (76/90)	FLOUR	46 (41/89)
WAGON	84 (51/61)	SUGAR	45 (37/83)
SCISSORS	83 (77/93)	*RICE	43 (32/74)
*COLT	82 (75/92)	*DONKEY	41 (25/61)
*LETTUCE	82 (31/38)	*APPLE	40 (18/45)
*CABBAGE	80 (41/51)	*COW	40 (37/95)
BUTTON	79 (46/58)	BREAD	37 (39/106)
BOARD	76 (84/110)	SPOON	38 (21/55)
BOOK	75 (97/130)	*SHEEP	34 (33/98)
*HEN	75 (84/112)	*APRICOT	33 (5/15)
PISTOL	74 (45/61)	BOTTLE	33 (17/51)
FORK	73 (71/98)	*GOAT	33 (18/54)
MATCH	70 (69/99)	CLOCK	32 (42/131)
NAIL	69 (55/80)	*BARLEY	30 (9/30)
RIBBON	69 (25/37)	*LEMON	30 (14/46)
*BULL	67 (74/110)	*CHICKEN	29 (16/55)
*CORIANDER	67 (4/6)	*PEACH	29 (13/45)
*BEETS	66 (27/41)	THREAD	26 (25/98)
TOWN	66 (65/99)	*CAT	25 (10/40)
WINDOW	65 (63/97)	*HORSE	23 (24/105)
MILE	64 (21/33)	*PEAS	20 (10/50)
*OATS	63 (29/46)	MONEY	19 (34/183)
PAPER	63 (70/112)	*PIG	11 (10/94)
NEEDLE	61 (66/108)		

*Identifies living things.

Onomatopoeia

Onomatopoeia refers to naming things with labels that mimic sounds associated in some way with those things. Onomatopoeic words for acculturated items imitate either sounds produced by these items or sounds, such as animal calls, made by humans, usually in the presence of the items.

I have identified onomatopoeic terms for two introduced artifacts, CLOCK and WAGON. Eskimo (North Slope Iñupiaq) and Makká (South America) have words for CLOCK, respectively *tuktuktak* and *tik-tik*, that seem to reflect its characteristic sound.

Onomatopoeic labels for WAGON mimic the clicking and clacking sounds typically produced by this object, such as Zapotec (1578) (Mexico) *quili quili quili*, and a number of similar terms are found in languages of the Pacific Northwest Coast that probably were diffused from Chinook Jargon, the regional trade language (see chapter 11), for example, Gitksan *ts'ixts'ik*, Haida *ts'akts'ak*, and Quileute *t'síkt'sik*.

Imported animals are more common referents of onomatopoeic names. Mixtec (San Juan Colorado, Mexico) and Kaingang (Brazil) have terms for GOAT that reproduce the creature's bleat—respectively, *mbèè* and *be*. Terms for ROOSTER in three South American languages appear to copy the cock's cry: Quechua (Ayacucho, 1905) *toccorocco*, Chaque *kikiriki*, and Aymara (1940–1989) *kokorichii*. The Chaque term is probably derived from Spanish *quiqueriquí* "cock-a-doodle doo" rather than directly from the rooster's cry (William Bright, personal communication). A word for COW, widely diffused through languages of the Northwest Coast and adjacent areas by Chinook Jargon (see chapter 11), may imitate this animal's familiar moan: Quileute *bósbos*, Wintu *mu.smus*, Karok *músmus*, and Songish *mósmʌs*. Conceivably, the term may be a borrowing from Cree with *mustus* "ox, bison" (Bright, personal communication). The Makká term for HORSE, *tip-tip*, probably mimics the acoustics of trotting.

A number of languages show words for introduced animals based on sounds commonly used by humans to call them. A Spanish call for domestic fowl (*pio-pio*) has been converted into terms for CHICKEN and its subtypes in dialects of Nahuatl (Mexico)—for example, Nahuatl (Xalita) *pio* "hen" and Nahuatl (Huazalinguillo) *piyoh* "chicken"—and probably were diffused to neighboring languages—for example, Popoluca (Sayula) *píyu* "hen, chicken" and Popoluca (Oluta) *piyu* "chicken." The same development took place in languages of southern South America, for example, Tehuelche *peyo* "hen, rooster" and Mapuche (1944–1990) *pió* "hen." Widespread European loans for CAT in languages of northern North America—for example, Squamish *puš*, Blackfoot *púsa*, and Inuit Eskimo *puusi*—are derived from English "pus-pus" or "pussy," which probably were originally calls. Similarly, related terms for CAT found in most languages of Latin America—for example, Mazahua *miši*, Chol *mis*, Cuna *misi*, Cofan *mishi*, and Chayahuita *misho*—were probably originally calls for felines used by Spanish intruders (Kiddle 1964). French and Dutch words for PIG, which were probably originally calls, account for terms for the creature distributed across languages of northern North America (A. R. Taylor 1990), for example, Plains Cree *kookos*, Algonquin (1984) *kòkòsh*, Inuit Eskimo *kuukkusi*, Oneida *koskos*, and Mohawk *kweskwes* (see chapter 9). Finally, three genetically unrelated languages of northern California have similar terms for COW—Wintu *wuh*, Yuki *woho* or *wohe*, and Maidu *wóha*—which are probably from a yell, *Whoa! Haw!*, used by early Anglo-American immigrants when driving ox teams (Shipley 1963:193).

Utilitarian Versus Morphological Terms

Native terms for items of acculturation in general may be either utilitarian or morphological (Brown 1995b). When a label literally refers to the use or function of a thing it designates, it is utilitarian: for example, Cherokee "he carries heavy things" for HORSE, and Siberian Yupik Eskimo "to write it down, something that will" for

PAPER. When not utilitarian, such names are morphological (metaphorically speaking), referring (either directly or indirectly) to some perceptual aspect(s) of a thing—its size, shape, color, texture, smell, or behavior: for example, Carrier "hair of the foreigners" for BARLEY, and Cheyenne "slender light" for CANDLE.

Table 3.7 lists each of the 77 items of acculturation ranked (this time from lowest to highest) by the percentage of language cases that show an analyzable native term of a utilitarian nature for the item among all analyzable native words for the item. I have taken a common sense approach to identifying labels as either utilitarian or morphological in preparing table 3.7. If a term for an introduced entity refers to some aspect of *its use by humans*, I have judged it to be utilitarian; some reasonably obvious examples include "to write it down, something that will" for PAPER (Siberian Yupik Eskimo), "which we buy with" for MONEY (Blackfoot), "raw-eating thing" for WATERMELON (Cheyenne), and "the one that makes milk" for COW (Inuit Eskimo). Perhaps less obvious examples are such labels as "pig food" for BARLEY (Montagnais [dialect of Cree]), "mouse food" for CHEESE (Plains Cree), and "worm food" for RICE (Comanche). Names for these items could be taken to refer primarily to their consumption by pigs, mice, and worms, respectively. However, in at least two of these cases, interpretations more in line with common sense suggest otherwise: labels for BARLEY and CHEESE almost certainly primarily mirror the common human use of the former to feed pigs and of the latter to trap mice. "Worm food" is a somewhat different matter, referring to the fact that humans are accustomed to consuming a grain that resembles little worms or maggots; RICE = MAGGOTS is a common nomenclatural equation among northern North American Indian languages.

I have also followed the convention of judging a label as utilitarian when a constituent refers to some other (usually native) item whose significance resides *entirely*, from a commonsense perspective, in its usefulness. For example, "wood sack" for BOX (Illinois), "Spanish tortilla" for BREAD (Zapotec [Mitla]), and "black medicine" for COFFEE (Dakota), are considered utilitarian labels since sacks, tortillas, and medicines are obviously important only in terms of their use. Similarly, native words for such items that are directly extended referentially to introduced objects are considered utilitarian labels: for example, terms for DOLLAR, WARRIOR, SINEW THREAD, CORNMEAL, and MEASURE extended, respectively, to MONEY, SOLDIER, THREAD, FLOUR, and HOUR.

If an analyzable label for an item of acculturation is not identified as utilitarian by these criteria, it is considered morphological. There are no specific criteria, other than not being utilitarian, for identifying a label as morphological. However, for the most part, the semantic content of morphological terms tends to relate to some perceptual aspect(s) of an introduced entity. Thus, for example, using a term for TAPIR in reference to HORSE (Yucatec) is a morphological naming approach since tapirs are obviously not *solely* important in terms of their use. There is, of course, a perceptual basis for equating these two creatures: both are four-legged mammals (which happen to belong to the same scientific order, Perissodactyla). Across the board in this treatment, naming strategies that equate a particular plant or animal (usually native to the New World) with an introduced plant or animal are considered nonutilitarian.

Some analyzable labels are ambiguous and thus difficult to assign definitively to either category. For example, while "little sun" for CLOCK (Karok) is judged here to be morphological, that is, nonutilitarian, a reasonable case can be made for its utilitarian nature. Such an argument would involve the proposition that the sun is

Table 3.7. Seventy-seven items of acculturation ranked by percentage of language cases with utilitarian native terms.

Item	Percentage	Item	Percentage
*APPLE	0.0 (0/45)	*LETTUCE	34.2 (13/38)
*APRICOT	0.0 (0/15)	TEA	38.5 (20/52)
*CALF	0.0 (0/130)	*WHEAT	42.4 (28/66)
*CAT	0.0 (0/40)	*WATERMELON	44.0 (22/50)
*COLT	0.0 (0/92)	*OATS	45.7 (21/46)
*GOAT	0.0 (0/54)	CLOCK	46.6 (61/131)
*MARE	0.0 (0/91)	HOUR	47.1 (33/70)
*PIG	0.0 (0/94)	FLOUR	47.2 (42/89)
*ROOSTER	0.0 (0/142)	MATCH	50.5 (50/99)
*BULL	0.9 (1/110)	MONEY	53.6 (98/183)
WEDNESDAY	1.0 (1/96)	CANDLE	54.5 (67/123)
*RICE	1.4 (1/74)	SPOON	56.4 (31/55)
*CHICKEN	1.8 (1/55)	MILE	57.6 (19/33)
*HEN	1.8 (2/112)	BOX	66.2 (43/65)
*LEMON	2.2 (1/46)	NAIL	67.5 (54/80)
*PEACH	2.2 (1/45)	NEEDLE	70.4 (76/108)
HUNDRED	3.0 (3/100)	BUTTON	70.7 (41/58)
*GARLIC	3.9 (1/26)	BOTTLE	72.6 (37/51)
*PEAS	4.0 (2/50)	SOAP	75.0 (72/96)
*SHEEP	4.1 (4/98)	THREAD	76.5 (75/98)
*ORANGE	4.8 (2/42)	TOWN	76.8 (76/99)
*BEETS	4.9 (2/41)	RIBBON	78.4 (29/37)
*DONKEY	4.9 (3/61)	PAPER	78.6 (88/112)
*COW	5.3 (5/95)	SHOVEL	83.1 (54/65)
*ONION	5.7 (3/53)	WINDOW	83.5 (81/97)
BOARD	6.4 (7/110)	FORK	84.7 (83/98)
*MULE	6.4 (4/63)	BREAD	84.9 (90/106)
BUTTER	7.1 (6/84)	SCISSORS	85.0 (79/93)
SUGAR	9.6 (8/83)	WAGON	85.3 (52/61)
*HORSE	10.5 (11/105)	SOLDIER	85.5 (47/55)
CHEESE	11.5 (6/52)	RICH	86.7 (78/90)
*OX	15.6 (15/96)	TABLE	87.4 (90/103)
*CORIANDER	16.7 (1/6)	BOOK	93.1(121/130)
*CABBAGE	17.7 (9/51)	KEY	94.0 (94/100)
*BARLEY	20.0 (6/30)	PISTOL	95.1 (58/61)
*GRAPES	20.9 (9/43)	CUP	97.8 (88/90)
SATURDAY	23.7 (18/76)	STORE	98.1(104/106)
*TURNIP	27.3 (9/33)	SCHOOL	99.1(111/112)
COFFEE	34.2 (13/38)		

*Identifies living things.

Source: Adapted from Cecil H. Brown, Lexical acculturation and ethnobiology: Utilitarianism versus intellectualism, *Journal of Linguistic Anthropology* (1995), 5:51–64, with the permission of the American Anthropological Association.

important to people everywhere only insofar as it relates to time-reckoning activities. Indeed, terms for CLOCK in many languages of the sample are, literally, "sun count" or "to measure sun" and similar constructions (which are judged to be utilitarian in this study). Nevertheless, common sense suggests that the sun is typically significant simply as an ever-present, highly conspicuous object in the daytime sky. If so, the use of "little sun" for CLOCK—and also direct referential extension of terms for SUN to

CLOCK—should not be considered utilitarian naming strategies, at least by the strict criteria I have outlined. In any event, such ambiguous cases are relatively few in the current sample, and consequently, interpretations of them (whatever they might be) would not significantly affect the conclusions reached (see especially the conclusions reached in chapter 12).

Analysis of table 3.7 shows an extraordinarily robust correlation between the nature of the introduced items (either living thing or artifact) and the extent to which they are named by utilitarian constructions (gamma = .95; chi square = 39.48891; p < .001): artifacts are vastly more likely to be given utilitarian names than are natural kinds. In addition, only 10% of introduced living things have utilitarian names, whereas 63% of imported artifacts do. This finding is perhaps not surprising since most artifacts are manufactured by humans for some specific function or purpose. Indeed, when an artifact is first encountered, a natural human response is to ascertain the nature of its intended use. Similar observations, of course, would not seem to apply to living things. These matters are considered further in chapter 12, where they are related to a current debate concerning the essential nature of folk biological classification and naming.

Conclusion: Living Things Versus Artifacts

Approaches adopted by Native American languages for naming items of acculturation have been illustrated in this chapter. In addition, information has been compiled in seven tables (3.1–3.7), displaying various ways in which terms for acculturated items compare across languages with respect to different nomenclatural variables. These tables, in all instances, reveal profound differences in how speakers of Amerindian languages have typically assigned names to imported living things as opposed to names for introduced artifacts.

In summary, these differences are as follows: (1) Amerindian languages tend to use European loans for natural kinds more strongly than they do for artifacts (table 3.1). (2) Natural kinds tend more strongly than artifacts to acquire labels through referential extension of European loans (table 3.2). (3) Artifacts tend more strongly than natural kinds to have labels that are extended constructions based on native terms (table 3.3). (4) Natural kinds tend much more strongly to be labeled by overt marking constructions than do artifacts (table 3.4). (5) Natural kinds tend much more strongly than artifacts to be involved in marking reversals (table 3.5). (6) Artifacts tend more strongly than natural kinds to be denoted by descriptive labels (table 3.6). (7) Artifacts are vastly more likely to be given utilitarian names than are natural kinds (table 3.7). In the following chapters, some of these findings are discussed further and some provisional explanations for them are proposed.

4

Lexical Universals

Contemporary linguistics has focused on language universals with the idea that they reflect the fundamental nature of the human language faculty (Witkowski and Brown 1978; Brown and Witkowski 1980). Since the midcentury development of generative grammar and related linguistic theories, it has been convincingly argued that design principles of human language are innate. The investigation of cross-language regularities is one approach to fleshing out cognitive structures innately shared by humankind on which individual languages are constructed.

Studies of language universals have dealt with uniformities in all components of language: phonology, grammar, and the lexicon. Historically, however, phonological and grammatical regularities have received the most attention. This chapter contributes to a small but expanding literature on lexical universals, produced mainly by linguistic anthropologists over the past quarter century or so. Geographically and genetically unrelated Amerindian languages have tended to develop semantically similar native labels for introduced objects and concepts, for example, Central Yupik Eskimo "maggot imitation" and Cheyenne (c. 1980) "little maggots" for imported RICE.

Previously Identified Lexical Universals

As noted in the preceding chapter, the framework of marking helps to explain the development of nomenclatural structures such as polysemy, overt marking, and marking reversals. Chapter 3 shows that principles of marking hold across independent language cases of the current sample. This and findings of other cross-language studies of the lexicon suggest that marking is a kind of lexical universal, albeit of a very general nature (see Brown and Witkowski 1980 for a summary discussion).

In addition to general uniformities such as marking, the inventory of lexical universals thus far assembled includes many which are quite specific in nature (e.g., Tagliavini 1949; Bierwisch 1967; Nerlove and Romney 1967; Berlin and Kay 1969; Witkowski 1972; Berlin, Breedlove, and Raven 1973; Kronenfeld 1974, 1996; Brown 1976, 1977a, 1977b, 1979, 1983, 1984, 1985b, 1987b, 1989a, 1989b, 1989c, 1990; Brown et al. 1976; Williams 1976; Andersen 1978; Burris 1978; Greenberg 1978;

Canart 1979; Brown and Witkowski 1981, 1983; Witkowski, Brown, and Chase 1981; Witkowski and Brown 1985; Brunel 1987; Berlin 1992; Hays 1994; Hunn 1994, 1996; Parker 1996; Wierzbicka 1996).

These lexical regularities are often manifested as frequently occurring nomenclatural relationships between two referents. Such associations typically involve polysemy and/or overt marking. For example, with regard to polysemy, approximately two-thirds of the world's languages use a single term to designate both WOOD and TREE (Witkowski, Brown, and Chase 1981), and over one-third designate HAND and ARM by a single word (Witkowski and Brown 1985). With regard to overt marking, approximately 60% of all languages nomenclaturally associate EYE and FACE through such constructions as "background of eye" in reference to FACE and "seed of face" in reference to EYE (Brown and Witkowski 1983).

Descriptive constructions for specific referents that are identical or nearly identical in semantic content also occur over and over again in unrelated languages. Brown and Witkowski (1981) assemble cross-language data that attest to the independent invention of the same figurative expressions for various parts of the human body: for example, "baby of the eye" (and similar constructions) for PUPIL (of the eye) in 36% of the world's languages (cf. Tagliavini 1949), "child of hand/foot" for FINGER/TOE and "mother of hand/foot" for THUMB/GREAT TOE in 36%, and "mouse of arm" (and similar constructions) for MUSCLE in 20%.

These examples are not absolute universals since they are not found in all languages of the world. Rather they attest to *universal naming tendencies*, or in other words, inclinations shared by all peoples for devising certain names for certain referents. I have encountered no type of naming behavior with cross-language tendencies more robust than that for items of acculturation. With two exceptions (Brown 1987b, 1989b), the rich array of cross-language regularities for acculturated items has not been systematically described before this study.

Naming Tendencies

In the preceding chapter, use of a European term for a specific currency denomination (e.g., English "dollar" and Spanish *peso*) as a label for MONEY (in general) is reported to be widespread among Amerindian languages. Of 183 language cases with analyzable native terms for MONEY, 81, or 44%, have referentially extended European currency words. In contrast, only 30 of the 263 language cases for which some term for MONEY is recorded have simply borrowed European words for MONEY, for example, English "money" or Spanish *dinero*. Languages so extending European words are spoken in North, Central, and South America. While diffusion almost certainly accounts for part of this feature's distribution (see chapters 8 and 11), it seems unlikely that borrowing could explain it all. Clearly, there is a reasonably strong inclination for Amerindian languages to independently develop terms for MONEY through referential extension of borrowed European terms. This is probably a universal naming tendency. (I hesitate to assert definitively that any naming inclination is universal until it is attested in a sample of globally distributed languages.)

At least 200 native names for acculturated items, like terms for MONEY, show similar derivational histories across languages of the sample or, like descriptive terms for RICE already cited, show similar semantic analyses. In many instances, these similarities are explained by loan shift (see chapters 3 and 10). However, languages to which similarities pertain are often geographically removed from one another so that loan shift (and the language contact it implies) is highly unlikely as an explanation of resemblances.

Songish, Quileute, and Tupí (1950–1979), for example, have semantically similar words for BOTTLE, "rum container," "whiskey inside," and "alcohol container," respectively. No other languages of the sample have terms similar in semantic content to these. Songish and Quileute are spoken in the same general part of the Americas, the Pacific Northwest, so that language contact may account for the resemblance of their BOTTLE labels. On the other hand, Tupí is spoken thousands of miles away in South America and thus independently developed its term for the introduced item. There is, then, a tendency for languages to autonomously coin BOTTLE terms through reference to the intoxicating liquid frequently contained in such receptacles. However, this naming inclination appears to be weak since it occurs in only 6% (3/51) of language cases showing analyzable terms for BOTTLE. Many of the naming tendencies for items of acculturation are similarly weak, although a substantial number can be characterized as strong.

Table 4.1 lists acculturated items whose labeling has involved one or more strong naming tendency. Here, a naming tendency is considered strong when an acculturated item is labeled by semantically similar native terms in at least 50% of the language cases for which analyzable native words for the item have been identified. Thus, for example, the fourth item, CLOCK, shows similar native terms in 109 of the 131 language cases manifesting analyzable native labels for the item, yielding a naming tendency percentage of 83. In table 4.1, acculturated items are ranked from the highest (89) to the lowest (50) percentage.

All of the 109 similar labels for CLOCK use a constituent element that denotes SUN or the closely semantically allied referent DAY, for example, Chaque "sun to measure" and Tunica "day counter." In table 4.1, SUN is presented as the semantic focus of similar constituents of similar labels for CLOCK. A *semantic focus* is usually the most frequently occurring referent of similar constituent elements (e.g., SUN, associated with CLOCK) but sometimes is a cover term for a set of similar referents (e.g., NATIVE "BREAD," associated with BREAD). Affiliated with each semantic focus is a semantic range, which is a listing of all semantically similar referents of constituents of similar labels for items of acculturation (see table 4.2). The semantic range associated with the SUN focus of similar terms for CLOCK includes both SUN and DAY.

Thirty-seven of the 77 items of acculturation are associated with strong naming tendencies, 23 of which are artifacts and 14, living things (see table 4.1). In a few instances, a single acculturated item is listed more than once. For example, BUTTER is associated with two different percentages, 82 and 66, and with two semantic foci, FAT and MILK(2). BUTTER is also listed a third time, where it is associated with a percentage of 56 and with two conjoined semantic foci, FAT and MILK(2). These indicate (1) that BUTTER shows semantically similar terms that have constituents whose referents are focused on FAT (with an associated range that includes FAT, OIL, GREASE, and LARD) in 82% of the language cases showing analyzable terms for BUTTER; (2) that BUTTER shows semantically similar terms with constituent referents focused on MILK(2) (range: MILK, BREAST, COW, BEEF) in 66% of the languages; and (3) that BUTTER shows similar terms, each entailing a combination

Table 4.1. Items of acculturation ranked by percentage (of 50 or greater) of language cases with content-similar native terms.

Item	Percentage	Semantic Focus
CHEESE	89 (46/52)	"MILK(1)"
*MARE	89 (81/91)	"FEMALE(1)"
*BEETS	88 (36/41)	"RED"
CLOCK	83 (109/131)	"SUN"
BUTTER	82 (69/84)	"FAT"
*CALF	82 (107/130)	"COW(1)"
*MARE	81 (74/91)	"HORSE(1)"
*COLT	80 (74/92)	"HORSE(2)"
MATCH	80 (79/99)	"FIRE(1)"
CANDLE	79 (97/123)	"FIRE(2)"
TABLE	77 (79/103)	"EAT"
STORE	77 (82/106)	"TRADE"
*PEAS	76 (38/50)	"BEAN"
WEDNESDAY	76 (73/96)	"THREE"
BOARD	76 (83/110)	"WOOD"
*CALF	75 (97/130)	"SMALL"
SCHOOL	75 (84/112)	"LEARN"
PISTOL	74 (45/61)	"FIREARM"
*BULL	72 (79/110)	"COW(2)"
*COLT	72 (66/92)	"LITTLE"
*MARE	71 (65/91)	"FEMALE(1)" and "HORSE(1)"
*BARLEY	70 (21/30)	"WHEAT"
TEA	69 (36/52)	"LEAF"
SUGAR	68 (56/83)	"SWEET"
SOAP	67 (64/96)	"WASH"
BUTTER	66 (55/84)	"MILK(2)"
*BULL	66 (69/110)	"MALE(1)"
*OX	65 (62/96)	"COW(3)"
*ROOSTER	65 (92/142)	"MALE(2)"
*CALF	61 (79/130)	"SMALL" AND "COW(1)"
COFFEE	61 (23/38)	"BLACK"
SHOVEL	60 (37/65)	"DIG"
*PIG	59 (55/94)	"PECCARY"
SCISSORS	58 (54/93)	"CUT"
STORE	57 (60/106)	"PLACE(1)"
BUTTER	56 (47/84)	"FAT" and "MILK(2)"
SCHOOL	56 (63/112)	"PLACE(2)"
WAGON	56 (34/61)	"ROLL"
*CAT	55 (22/40)	"WILDCAT"
*HEN	55 (61/112)	"FEMALE(2)"
*ROOSTER	55 (78/142)	"HEN"
*COLT	54 (50/92)	"LITTLE" and "HORSE(2)"
*GARLIC	54 (14/26)	"ONION"
*LEMON	54 (25/46)	"SOUR"
KEY	53 (53/100)	"OPEN"
BOOK	52 (67/130)	"MARK"
NEEDLE	52 (56/108)	"SEW"
BREAD	51 (55/107)	"NATIVE 'BREAD'"
BUTTON	50 (29/58)	"FASTEN"
*GARLIC	50 (13/26)	"SMELL"

*Identifies living things.

Table 4.2. Semantic range for each focus in table 4.1.

Semantic Focus	Semantic Range
"BEAN"	BEAN
"BLACK"	BLACK
"COW(1)"	COW, CATTLE, OX, BULL, BEEF
"COW(2)"	COW, CATTLE, BOVINE, OX
"COW(3)"	COW, CATTLE, BULL, BOVINE
"CUT"	CUT, CUTTER, CUTTING, CLIP, TRIM, PINCH, SHEAR, SHEARING, SEVER, SHAVE
"DIG"	DIG, DUG, DIGGING, DIGGER, SCOOP, SHOVEL, SHOVELED, SPOON OUT, UPROOT, CLOD-RAISER, EXTRACT, TAKE UP, THROW AWAY, MAKE HOLE, CULTIVATE, BREAK, POUR, RAISER
"EAT"	EAT, EATING, FEED, FOOD, DINE
"FASTEN"	FASTEN, LATCH, TUCK IN, TUCKING, CLASP, TIE, TIED, TYING, ADHERE TO, STUCK ON, LACING, BUTTON, UNITE, SEW, JOINING, CLOSE
"FAT"	FAT, OIL, GREASE, LARD
"FEMALE(1)"	FEMALE, FEMALE OF ANIMALS, FEMALE BREAST, WOMAN, MOTHER
"FEMALE(2)"	FEMALE, FEMALE ANIMAL, WOMAN, WIFE, MOTHER, FEMININE
"FIRE(1)"	FIRE, BURN, CAMPFIRE, BLAZE, LIGHT, TORCH
"FIRE(2)"	FIRE, START A FIRE, FIREBRAND, BURN, TORCH, SHINE, LIGHT, LIGHTING, LIT, BRIGHT, FLAME, BLAZE
"FIREARM"	FIREARM, GUN, RIFLE, BOW, ARMS, CARBINE, SHOTGUN
"HORSE(1)"	HORSE
"HORSE(2)"	HORSE, MARE
"LEAF"	LEAF, LEAVES, WEEDS, PLANT, GRASS, HERB
"LEARN"	LEARN, LEARNING, READ, READING, PAPER-TALK, TALK, WRITE, WRITING, MARK, MARKED, DRAW, STUDY, STUDIED, TEACH, TAUGHT, TEACHER, INSTRUCT, INSTRUCTION, COUNT, COUNTING, KNOW, UNDERSTAND, KNOWLEDGE, LESSON
"MALE(1)"	MALE, MAN, BOY, TESTICLES, HUSBAND, FATHER, MALE ANIMAL, BULL MOOSE, MALE MOOSE, BUFFALO BULL, COCK

Table 4.2 *(continued)*

Semantic Focus	Semantic Range
"MALE(2)"	MALE, MALE BIRD, MALE TURKEY, MAN, HUSBAND, BOY, FATHER, GRANDFATHER, MASCULINE
"MARK"	MARK, MARKS, MARKED, WRITE, WRITING, WRITTEN, DRAW, PICTURE, DOTTED, PAINT, PAINTED, STRIPED
"MILK(1)"	MILK, TEAT
"MILK(2)"	MILK, COW, BREAST, BEEF
"NATIVE 'BREAD'"	NATIVE BREAD, TORTILLA, BROAD THIN CAKE, CORNBREAD, PIKI BREAD, TAMALE, ACORN BREAD, TUBER BREAD, INDIGENOUS BISCUIT, MANIOC CAKE, TORTILLA OF GOOSEFOOT
"ONION"	ONION
"OPEN"	OPEN, OPENED, OPENER, OPEN UP, OPENING, UNLOCK, UNLOCKER
"PECCARY"	PECCARY, WILD PIG
"PLACE(1)"	PLACE, WHERE, HOUSE, HOME, LODGE, HOGAN, BUILDING, ENCLOSURE
"PLACE(2)"	PLACE, WHERE, HOUSE, BUILDING, WIGWAM, PULPIT
"RED"	RED, BLOOD
"ROLL"	ROLL, ROLLER, ROLLING, ROLLED, TURN, TURN OVER, TURN END OVER END, REVOLVE, CIRCLE, FLY AROUND IN CIRCLES, CIRCULAR THING, ROUND, WHEEL
"SEW"	SEW, SEWER, SEWN, PRICK, PIERCE THROUGH, DRAG THROUGH, GO THROUGH, PULL OUT, POKE, BORE, DRAW OUT, CARRY (STRING), PENETRATE
"SMALL"	SMALL, LITTLE, DIMINUTIVE, YOUNG, YOUNG ANIMAL, FAWN, YOUNG DEER, REINCALF, SUCKLING TAPIR, NEW, TO BE TWO YEARS OLD, OF LITTLE AGE, BABY, CHILD, OFFSPRING, SON
"SMELL"	SMELL, SMELLY, BAD SMELLER, BAD SMELL, FETID, STINKY, STINKING, DREADFUL
"SOUR"	SOUR, BITTER, ACIDIC

(continued)

Table 4.2 *(continued)*

Semantic Focus	Semantic Range
"SUN"	SUN, DAY
"SWEET"	SWEET, SWEETEN, SWEETNESS
"THREE"	THREE, THIRD
"TRADE"	TRADE, TRADING, TRADER, BUY, BUYING, BOUGHT, BUYER, SELL, SELLING, SELLER, SHOP, MERCHANDISE, GOODS, CHANGE, BUSINESS
"WASH"	WASH, WASHING, WASHER, CLEAN, SCRUB, BLEACH, WIPE, SOAP HIM
"WHEAT"	WHEAT
"WILDCAT"	WILDCAT, LYNX, LION, MOUNTAIN LION, JAGUAR, PUMA, TIGER, BOBCAT

of two constituent referents focused on FAT and MILK(2) (with respective attendant ranges) in 56% of the languages.

The naming tendencies reported in table 4.1 in addition to compound terms (i.e., descriptive labels and overt marking expressions) entail extended constructions. For example, the semantic focus associated with BREAD (at 51%) is NATIVE "BREAD" with a range encompassing various kinds of indigenous breadlike concoctions such as ACORN BREAD, TUBER BREAD, and TORTILLA. Many BREAD terms in this naming tendency are such labels as Ixil "Spanish tortilla," which are compound expressions. In other instances, pertinent BREAD terms are extended constructions in which a word for a type of NATIVE "BREAD" has been referentially extended to the introduced item. This is deduced from polysemous terms, which denote both the native concoction and European BREAD, for example, Diegueño *ʔepap* "tortilla and bread."

With one exception, COW, all animal subtypes on the list of 77 items are listed in table 4.1: BULL, CALF, COLT, HEN, MARE, OX, and ROOSTER. There is, then, a strong cross-language tendency for animal subtypes to be given semantically similar native names. In the vast majority of instances, these names are descriptive labels (as formally defined in this work; see the introduction to appendix A) such as "male cow" for BULL, "female horse" for MARE, and "male hen" for ROOSTER. As noted in chapter 3, there is also an inclination for creature subtypes to be labeled by native terms rather than European loans (see table 3.1). Thus, speakers of different Amerindian languages are not only inclined to use native terms for such referents but are also strongly predisposed to devise native labels that are semantically very similar.

Terms for bovine subtypes tend to employ constituent elements whose referents are focused on COW (see table 4.1). Across Amerindian languages, words for COW generally seem to function as generic labels for BOVINE, at least in terms for bovine subtypes (cf. Kronenfeld 1996:97–98). Thus, for example, an appropriate free translation for the commonly occurring "male cow" (for BULL) would be "male bovine." Similarly, terms for ROOSTER often take the form "male hen." HEN terms, like words for COW, tend to be used generically in Amerindian languages—as if they referred to CHICKEN. This usage is further indicated by the substantial number of language cases in which a single term denotes both HEN and CHICKEN. A total of 69 language cases show HEN/CHICKEN polysemy, suggesting the frequent referential extension of a term for HEN to CHICKEN. Across Amerindian languages, as expressed in jargon of the framework of marking (see chapter 3), ROOSTER tends to be marked vis-à-vis HEN, which is unmarked, and BULL, CALF, and OX tend to be marked vis-à-vis unmarked COW.

Semantically similar labels for other introduced living things in table 4.1 are overt marking constructions. Their base elements typically denote natural kinds that display considerable perceptual resemblance to named acculturated items. In some instances, pertinent natural kinds are indigenous biological things: PEA is equated with native BEAN, PIG with indigenous PECCARY, and CAT with WILDCAT. In others, they are themselves imported: BARLEY is equated with introduced WHEAT and GARLIC with introduced ONION. In these examples, PEA, PIG, CAT, BARLEY, and GARLIC are marked relative to, respectively, BEAN, PECCARY, WILDCAT, WHEAT, and ONION, which are unmarked.

Sometimes the significant aspect of similarity resides in overt marks (modifiers) rather than in base elements. For example, LEMON is in table 4.1 because a large number of language cases (54%) designate the item through constructions in which SOUR (range: SOUR, BITTER, ACIDIC) is an overt mark. In this example, various base elements are employed in compound terms in conjunction with the frequently occurring overt mark (SOUR), including APPLE, LIME, MAYAPPLE, ORANGE, PEACH, and PLUM. However, none of these bases occurs across Amerindian languages at frequencies that, when setting SOUR apart from consideration, would have led to the inclusion of LEMON in table 4.1. The same is true of terms for BEETS, which show a frequently occurring overt mark, RED (with a range of RED and BLOOD), and less frequently occurring base elements. One botanical referent, GARLIC, is in table 4.1 because of high frequencies of both a base element (ONION) and an overt mark (SMELL) in semantically similar terms for the item.

Of the 23 artifacts in table 4.1, 12 have similar labels relating to *utility* (BOOK, BUTTON, CLOCK, KEY, MATCH, NEEDLE, SCHOOL, SCISSORS, SHOVEL, SOAP, STORE, TABLE), and 11 have similar names relating to *morphology* (BOARD, BREAD, BUTTER, CANDLE, CHEESE, COFFEE, PISTOL, SUGAR, PEACH, WAGON, WEDNESDAY). As mentioned in chapter 3, artifacts are important mainly because they are designed for some specific function or purpose. Not unexpectedly, speakers of many different languages have focused on the same primary use of an imported artifact for naming it. Thus, a CLOCK "measures the sun," a MATCH "makes fire," a TABLE is a "place for eating," a STORE is a "house for trading," and so on. Thus, it is perhaps surprising to find that names for 11 of the 23 artifacts are based on morphology rather than utility. Two of these, BUTTER and BREAD, have already been discussed. Some widely occurring morphological labels for other artifacts include "day three" for WEDNESDAY, "flat wood" for BOARD, "leaf liquid" for TEA, "black water" for COFFEE, and "rolling wood" for WAGON. In these examples artifact morphology seems to be of greater significance for speakers of many Amerindian languages than artifact utility.

The reason for this is not entirely clear; however, a partial explanation is as follows: of the 11 artifacts with names based on morphology, 6 are prepared foods (BREAD,

BUTTER, CHEESE, COFFEE, SUGAR, and TEA). These include all of the prepared foods on the list of 77 items except one, FLOUR (see table 2.2). Since these are important to people mainly because they are eaten, native terms based on utility would naturally refer to consumption, for example, "thing for eating" or "thing for drinking." However, such names would not be particularly discriminating because the range of things eaten and drunk by any human group is usually quite large. Consequently, there may be a tendency for languages to develop terms for these items based on morphology in order to circumvent referential ambiguities that might arise if the labels were semantically focused on their primary use. It is interesting that of the 7 prepared foods on the list of 77 items, only FLOUR is not "ready to consume" but must first be transformed into BREAD or other products.

Explanatory Observations

Documentation of language universals is an important first step in fleshing out the nature of the human language faculty. Significant further strides toward this goal are made when these regularities are plausibly explained (Witkowski and Brown 1978; Brown and Witkowski 1980). A few provisional explanatory observations are offered here.

Since publication of Chomsky's (1959) review of Skinner's (1957) *Verbal Behavior* and the rise of generative grammar, it has been argued that the underlying template of human language is innate. Chomsky (1975:219) proposes that humans start life with innate knowledge of "the form and character of grammars and the principles by which grammars operate." In other words, Chomsky claims that the design properties of language are "wired" or "programmed" in the neural circuitry of humans.

The question at issue is the degree of specificity of design principles. Chomsky (1975) seems to favor a "detailed wiring" point of view. His discussion of universals of syntax stresses the detailed nature of these regularities. Similarly, he rejects attempts by others to account for language universals by appealing to very general learning principles based on very general neurophysiological wiring. Cognitive psychologists and others tend to appeal to information-processing models of the human language faculty. They explain language learning by innate but very general mechanisms for processing primary linguistic data. A position that lies between detailed wiring and information processing is proposed by Witkowski and myself (Witkowski and Brown 1978; Brown and Witkowski 1980; Brown 1984). Our "rich cognition" model entails that some aspects of language design conform to the detailed wiring model; however, the remainder and much the larger part of the human language faculty is probably explained by information-processing devices, some of which are quite specific but most of which are very general.

An information-processing approach best accounts for cross-language naming tendencies for items of acculturation. For example, when different human groups are faced with the problem of giving a name to the same newly encountered object or concept, information-processing mechanisms shared by all humans are utilized to accomplish the task. This involves, at least in part, analysis of both the item to be named and of sources from which a label for the item might be retrieved. Since information-processing devices are panhuman, similar, if not the same, analyses will tend to be made, resulting in similar names for the item in question especially if sources for labels are similar.

In the case of naming introduced living things, information processing has frequently involved the association of these biological things with perceptually similar, already named living things. The introduced organism is assigned a name already assigned to a living thing it most closely resembles among all living things labeled in a language, that is, the "closest analog." When the closest analog turns out to be the same (or very similar) for speakers of different languages, similar names will emerge in those languages for the same imported biological item. In this interpretation, the more often speakers of different languages have closest analogs in common, the more frequently the introduced organism will show semantically similar labels across languages.

I have shown (Brown 1992) that English names for British birds have typically been applied by Anglo-Americans to those American birds, among all American birds, that are closest to British birds in scientific (Linnaean) classification. Thus, for example, "coot," a label for *Fulica atra* in Britain, designates in America a species of *Fulica* (*F. americana*) that does not occur natively in Britain; *F. atra* is not found in America. The British coot constitutes in scientific taxonomy the closest analog to the American coot. Similarly, "cuckoo," which designates *Cuculus canorus* in Britain, denotes in America birds belonging to the genus *Coccyzus*, none of which occur natively in Britain. Members of the genus *Cuculus* are not native to America. However, birds of the genera *Cuculus* and *Coccyzus* belong to the same family (i.e., Cuculidae). The British cuckoo constitutes scientifically the closest analog to American cuckoos.

Among the 14 natural kinds in table 4.1, 7 are animal subtypes, attesting to a strong tendency for creature subtypes in general to have semantically similar labels across languages. In terms of the closest analog model, this is not unexpected since speakers of *all* languages necessarily will share closest analogs for such creatures. For example, a typical label for MARE across Amerindian languages is "female horse," indicating that its closest analog is HORSE. Indeed, there can be no closer analog for MARE in perceptual similarity than HORSE since these two referents pertain to the same species. In addition, the presence of MARE logically implies the presence of HORSE (since a MARE is a kind of HORSE). Similarly, ROOSTER has no analog closer than HEN, and BULL has no analog closer than COW.

Such relationships are so robustly compelling that they tend to motivate universal marking hierarchies in which creature subtypes (e.g., BULL, MARE, and ROOSTER) are perceived as marked vis-à-vis corresponding superordinate animal concepts (e.g., respectively, COW, HORSE, and CHICKEN), which are unmarked. These hierarchies account not only for the strong inclination for animal subtypes to be labeled by semantically similar terms across languages but also for the finding that, unlike most other introduced natural kinds, animal subtypes are more typically labeled by native terms than by European loans (see table 3.1). The powerful tendency to use native labels such as "female horse" for MARE and "male hen" for ROOSTER apparently forestalls any proclivity for naming such creatures through European loans.

Analogs of other natural kinds in table 4.1, while typically showing a close resemblance to their introduced counterparts, are not similarly conspecific with the latter. The imported PIG is *Sus scrofa*, whereas native American species of PECCARY (or WILD PIG) are *Tayassu pecari* and *Tayassu tajacu*. Nevertheless, peccaries and introduced pigs show considerable similarity, although mostly of a superficial nature (*Tayassu* and *Sus* are genera of the same order of mammals,

Artiodactyla). The introduced CAT is *Felis catus*, while New World wildcats either belong to species of *Felis* other than *catus*, for example, *F. concolor* (MOUNTAIN LION), or to other genera like *Lynx rufus* (BOBCAT). Of course, all cats, domestic and wild, show substantial similarity since they belong to the same family, Felidae. In the botanical domain, GARLIC and ONION belong to the same genus, *Allium*, but not to the same species; PEAS and BEANS belong to the same family, Leguminosae, but not to the same genus; and WHEAT and BARLEY share the family Gramineae but belong to different genera.

In the New World, PECCARY, WILDCAT, ONION, BEANS, and WHEAT are typically the closest analogs, respectively, to the introduced PIG, CAT, GARLIC, PEAS, and BARLEY (see table 4.1). That the former items are especially widespread through the Americas helps to explain why native terms for them are used repeatedly in Amerindian languages to designate their introduced counterparts. Of these items, the PECCARY probably shows the most circumscribed distribution, occurring widely in South and Central America and Mexico but not in most parts of northern North America. ONION and WHEAT, both introduced items, achieved their broad distributions in the Americas in postcontact times; these two items were possibly introduced into various parts of the New World before and/or more widely than GARLIC and BARLEY. It is plausible that because these five closest analogs and their introduced counterparts are *not* conspecific, similarity relationships between them have not been so compelling as to forestall using European loans, as is the case with introduced animal subtypes (see the previous discussion). These imported items, with the exception of PEAS, tend to be given imported, European names (table 3.1).

Other introduced living things, like COW and HORSE, are not included in table 4.1 because their naming tendency percentages are less than 50. The highest percentage for COW is 33 (31/95), which relates to the semantic focus BISON (with a range encompassing only BISON). Taxonomically, COW and BISON are closely related, both belonging to the same family, Bovidae, in the order Artiodactyla. Thus, nomenclatural evidence suggesting BISON to be the closest analog to COW for numerous Amerindian groups is not surprising. That a relatively low percentage is associated with BISON/COW almost certainly reflects the fact that BISON do not occur widely in the Americas (at least relatively speaking): these creatures are limited to North America, excluding the Arctic and most of Mexico. If BISON were more broadly distributed, a percentage greater than 33 might be apparent.

As it is, BISON/COW is associated with the largest naming tendency percentage observed for COW. Other analogs for COW are TAPIR at 8% (8/95), DEER at 7% (7/95), CARIBOU at 5% (5/95), MOOSE at 4% (4/95), ELK at 3% (3/95), and DOG and MUSK OX at 1% (1/95). With the possible exception of MUSK OX, none of these analogs resembles COW as closely as BISON does—that is, if scientific classification can be taken as a reasonably good guide to perceptual similarity (but see Brown 1992). TAPIR and DOG belong to orders of mammals (respectively, Perissodactyla and Carnivora) that do not include COW. DEER, CARIBOU, MOOSE, and ELK, while members of the order Artiodactyla (which includes COW), belong to a family (Cervidae) different from that of COW (Bovidae). In most New World localities in which BISON and one or more of the other creatures are cohabitants, BISON is the closest analog to COW. Consequently, words for BISON have displayed a strong tendency to be used in reference to COW in languages spoken in such localities. Words for TAPIR, DEER, CARIBOU, MOOSE, ELK, and DOG appear to have been referentially extended to COW in localities in which, for whatever reasons, these animals were not competing with BISON for the title of COW's closest analog.

As a member of the family Bovidae, MUSK OX could compete with BISON as COW'S closest analog. However, the native MUSK OX and BISON do not live in the same regions of North America, so such a head-to-head competition has probably never actually taken place. That a substantially greater percentage pertains to BISON/COW (33) than to MUSK OX/COW (1) simply reflects MUSK OX's drastically smaller geographic range (i.e., Arctic regions of North America) than that of BISON.

The largest naming tendency percentage for HORSE, 45 (47/105), pertains to the inclination of languages to designate the horse by a term for DOG. Terms for other animals include labels for DEER at 18% (19/105), for ELK at 8% (8/105), for TAPIR at 8% (8/105), for CARIBOU at 4% (4/105), and for GUANACO at 1% (1/105). Among these, HORSE is most closely related to TAPIR, both belonging to the order Perissodactyla, so that this naming association is understandable in terms of the closest analog model. The tapir's geographic range encompasses South and Central America and, in the past, extended into lowland regions of southern Mexico. With a few exceptions, extended constructions for HORSE found in languages spoken in this vast area are based on TAPIR. Languages of Latin America usually show Spanish loans for HORSE rather than native terms.

Most extended constructions for HORSE based on labels for CARIBOU, DEER, DOG, and ELK occur in languages spoken in North America, including Mexico. Terms for HORSE based on CARIBOU, ELK, and DOG are restricted to North America, excluding Mexico. Labels for HORSE based on DEER occur in both Mexico and northern North America. From a taxonomic perspective, HORSE is equally dissimilar to each of these four animals: CARIBOU, DEER, and ELK are affiliated with the order Artiodactyla, and DOG with Carnivora. GUANACO, restricted to Andean South America, belongs to Artiodactyla.

From a commonsense perspective, one might expect that among CARIBOU, DEER, DOG, and ELK, Amerindians would typically have analyzed DOG as being least similar to HORSE because of its relatively small size. Nonetheless, terms for DOG are considerably more commonly extended to HORSE than are labels for the other, more-horselike-in-size creatures. DOG may have often been viewed as the closest analog to HORSE because, like HORSE, it is a domesticated creature and was so in precontact America. Thus, DOG is more like HORSE than are nondomesticated CARIBOU, DEER, and ELK since it alone shares with HORSE a special cultural affinity to humans. Indeed, in many areas of aboriginal North America, dogs, like horses, have been used as hauling animals.

The ubiquity of DOG/HORSE in northern North America may have been motivated by an additional factor. In some instances, terms for CARIBOU, DEER, or ELK may not have been applied to HORSE simply because they were not available, having already been appropriated as labels for other introduced creatures that they more closely resemble. For example, words for CARIBOU in two subarctic languages, Chipewyan (Athapascan-Eyak) and Cree (Algonquian), have been applied to SHEEP—caribou and sheep are both affiliated with Artiodactyla. The Chipewyan and Cree terms for HORSE are based on DOG. Similarly, labels for SHEEP in two languages of northern California, Karok (isolate) and Atsugewi (Palaihnihan), are based on terms for DEER—sheep and deer are both Artiodactyla—while their respective HORSE terms are based on DOG. Conceivably, terms for another member of Artiodactyla, BISON, could have been used by North American Indians in reference to HORSE. This, apparently, never occurred, possibly because of the frequent appropriation of such labels for the introduced COW (see previous discussion). In most languages in which a term for BISON designates COW, a label for DOG denotes HORSE (e.g., Beaver, Big Smokey Valley Shoshoni, Cree, Crow, Dakota, Hidatsa, Nez Perce, Mandan, and Ojibwa). However, it is difficult to reconcile this proposal with the probable historical priority of HORSE over COW, especially among native groups of the North American Plains.

In summary, the degree to which items of acculturation have similar native labels across different Amerindian languages appears to relate, at least in part, to the extent to which closest analogs to the introduced items are found in the environments of their speakers: the more often the same closest analog is found, the more often the item will have similar labels in different languages.

This conclusion is based solely on observations about the naming of introduced living things. It is not clear to what extent it applies as well to the naming of introduced artifacts. In addition, these explanatory observations do not take account of all types of cross-language regularities. For example, explicative discussion does not include the tendency of different languages to develop similar names that allude to especially salient properties of introduced things, for example, the SOUR taste of LEMON or the SMELL of GARLIC (see table 4.1). Also, no mention is made of the role of metonymy in creating similar labels, such as the fabrication of BUTTER and CHEESE from MILK or of BOARD from WOOD. Nevertheless, all naming tendencies reported here almost certainly are linked to information-processing mechanisms, which may constitute some of the design properties of the human language faculty.

5

LEXICAL BORROWABILITY

Lexical borrowability refers to the ease with which a word or a category of words can be borrowed (van Hout and Muysken 1994:39). Over a century ago William Dwight Whitney (1881) proposed a hierarchy of categories based on borrowability, in which nouns are observed to be most readily borrowed, followed by other parts of speech and then by suffixes, inflections, and sounds. While this hierarchy has been extended and variously revised over the years by scholars such as Haugen (1950), Moravcsik (1978), Muysken (1981), and Singh (1981), the privileged status of nouns has not been seriously challenged (see especially Poplack, Sankoff, and Miller 1988:62-64). Van Hout and Muysken (p. 42) explain this as follows: "one of the primary motivations for lexical borrowing . . . is . . . to extend the referential potential of a language. Since reference is established primarily through nouns, these are the elements borrowed most easily."

Within the category of nouns, and other word classes as well, some items seem more susceptible to borrowing than others. Words that occur more frequently in a donor language may be more readily appropriated by a recipient language than those that occur less frequently (van Hout and Muysken 1994:52–54). Cultural (peripheral) vocabulary may be more easily incorporated into a language as loanwords than is core vocabulary (Thomason and Kaufman 1988:77; C. J. Crowley 1992:168–169). This book highlights the general understanding that words for novel entities are readily accepted as loans (Weinreich 1953:56; Mougeon and Beniak 1989), probably more so than other words.

This chapter examines lexical borrowability within the category of words for novel things. Cross-language evidence assembled here attests to the differential borrowability of terms for items of acculturation. Why some words for acculturated items should be more borrowable than words for other introduced things is the present focus.

Borrowability and Words for Acculturated Items

Table 3.1 ranks the 77 items of acculturation by European loan percentages, or in other words, by the percentage of language cases showing a European loanword for an item among all language cases for which a term for the item has been recorded; pertinent loanwords do not include most loanblends nor referentially extended European loans, both of which are formally treated in this work as native terms. European loan percentages are in fact indices of borrowability. Table 3.1, then, shows that items of acculturation differ in the degree of borrowability: COFFEE, with the largest European loan percentage (81), is greatest in borrowability among the 77 items, and FORK and HEN, tied with the smallest percentage (10), are least in borrowability; items between show varying degrees of borrowability.

The analysis of information in table 3.1 shows a fairly strong and statistically significant association between the type of acculturated item (either living thing or artifact) and term borrowability (gamma = .66, chi square = 10.82336, p < .01). Words for introduced natural kinds tend more strongly than those for introduced artifacts to be associated with high borrowability. In addition, labels for creature subtypes (e.g., CALF, MARE, and ROOSTER) tend to show considerably lower indices of borrowability than those for other natural kinds. In other words, European terms for subtypes of animals do not tend to be borrowed into Amerindian languages as strongly as European words for other living things. In chapter 4, this is explained as the result of a robust inclination for animal subtypes to be named by descriptive terms, such as "female horse" for MARE and "little cow" for CALF, motivated by universal marking hierarchies in which subtypes are perceived as marked vis-à-vis corresponding superordinate animal concepts that are unmarked.

Table 5.1 rank-lists 70 of the 77 items of acculturation by index of borrowability (i.e., European loan percentage) from highest to lowest. Information in this table is identical to that of table 3.1, except that the 7 creature subtypes are removed. Analysis of table 5.1 data shows an exceptionally strong and highly statistically significant association between the type of acculturated item and borrowability (gamma = .82, chi square = 17.62391, p < .001). When animal subtypes are removed from consideration, introduced living things are even more strongly named by European loans than are introduced artifacts, with the pertinent correlation coefficient (gamma) increasing from .66 (table 3.1, including animal subtypes) to .82 (table 5.1, excluding animal subtypes).

Within the category of words for introduced living things, terms for animals tend to show greater borrowability scores than words for plants. Table 5.2 lists acculturated natural kinds (minus the 7 creature subtypes) ranked by indices of borrowability. Analysis shows a strong and statistically significant correlation between the type of living thing (either animal or plant) and borrowability (gamma = .71, chi square = 4.093567, p < .05). Thus, European words for animals tend to be incorporated into Amerindian languages as loans more strongly than European words for plants.

Explanatory Possibilities

An explanation of why European terms for creature subtypes are less borrowable than European words for other introduced living things is proposed in chapter 4. The following comments explore factors that may account for other aspects of lexical borrowability, especially the finding that introduced living things tend more strongly than introduced artifacts to be named through use of European loans. Several different

Table 5.1. Items of acculturation, minus 7 creature subtypes, ranked by index of borrowability (European loan percentage).

Item	Percentage	Item	Percentage
COFFEE	81 (156/192)	*APRICOT	37 (10/27)
*CORIANDER	72 (28/39)	BOX	36 (79/221)
*CAT	70 (194/279)	SCHOOL	35 (65/185)
*GARLIC	69 (70/101)	SCISSORS	35 (86/245)
*ORANGE	67 (122/182)	WEDNESDAY	35 (54/155)
CHEESE	66 (88/134)	MATCH	34 (64/186)
*DONKEY	64 (116/182)	NAIL	33 (74/224)
*LEMON	60 (80/133)	CANDLE	32 (68/216)
*APPLE	59 (91/155)	SPOON	31 (79/256)
*COW	58 (153/266)	SHOVEL	30 (51/172)
SATURDAY	56 (95/170)	STORE	30 (51/172)
*PIG	55 (151/277)	BREAD	29 (78/269)
SOLDIER	55 (110/202)	FLOUR	29 (68/232)
*PEACH	54 (66/122)	BOARD	28 (60/215)
*MULE	54 (87/161)	BUTTER	28 (34/122)
*GOAT	53 (103/196)	WAGON	28 (42/151)
SUGAR	53 (121/227)	*PEAS	28 (29/105)
TEA	53 (63/119)	CUP	27 (52/196)
*HORSE	52 (143/273)	MILE	27 (16/60)
*RICE	52 (96/184)	PISTOL	27 (29/108)
TABLE	52 (127/244)	WINDOW	27 (59/218)
SOAP	51 (124/244)	CLOCK	25 (47/191)
BOTTLE	51(107/208)	*GRAPES	25 (34/136)
*WATERMELON	49 (71/144)	*OATS	23 (17/74)
RIBBON	48 (72/149)	BOOK	22 (53/247)
*CABBAGE	47 (66/140)	NEEDLE	21 (57/272)
*LETTUCE	47 (42/89)	PAPER	20 (53/263)
HOUR	45 (69/153)	HUNDRED	19 (40/215)
*SHEEP	44 (105/241)	*BEETS	18 (9/51)
*ONION	41 (82/202)	THREAD	17 (43/255)
KEY	41 (91/221)	*CHICKEN	16 (28/180)
*BARLEY	39 (23/59)	TOWN	15 (38/258)
*TURNIP	39 (37/95)	RICH	13 (29/225)
BUTTON	38 (69/180)	MONEY	11 (30/263)
*WHEAT	38 (66/172)	FORK	10 (17/165)

*Identifies living things.

plausible influences are considered, most of which appear to have only minimal influence on borrowability, if any at all.

Frequency of use

The high borrowability of words for imported living things may relate to some factor that these words have in common other than their obvious reference to biological organisms. Such a factor may be frequency of use. One version of a word frequency model of borrowability proposes that the probability of borrowing a specific term relates to its frequency of use in a donor language. That is, a recipient language should

Table 5.2. Introduced living things, minus 7 creature subtypes, ranked by index of borrowability (European loan percentage).

Item	Percentage	Item	Percentage
CORIANDER	72 (28/39)	WATERMELON	49 (71/144)
*CAT	70 (194/279)	CABBAGE	47 (66/140)
GARLIC	69 (70/101)	LETTUCE	47 (42/89)
ORANGE	67 (122/182)	*SHEEP	44 (105/241)
*DONKEY	64 (116/182)	ONION	41 (82/202)
LEMON	60 (80/133)	BARLEY	39 (23/59)
APPLE	59 (91/155)	TURNIP	39 (37/95)
*COW	58 (153/266)	WHEAT	38 (66/172)
*PIG	55 (151/277)	APRICOT	37 (10/27)
PEACH	54 (66/122)	PEAS	28 (29/105)
*MULE	54 (87/161)	GRAPES	25 (34/136)
*GOAT	53 (103/196)	OATS	23 (17/74)
*HORSE	52 (143/273)	BEETS	18 (9/51)
RICE	52 (96/184)	*CHICKEN	16 (28/180)

*Identifies animals.

tend to adopt as loans those words that are frequently used in a donor language, more so than words infrequently used (van Hout and Muysken 1994:52–54). Words of greater frequency in a donor language will tend to be more often encountered by speakers of a recipient language than less frequently used words. Thus, greater exposure of a word to potential recipients should promote its chances for becoming a loanword.

The word frequency model predicts that terms for introduced living things should be more frequently used in donor languages than words for introduced artifacts. To test this prediction, data from 3 European languages, English, French, and Spanish, are respectively assembled in tables 5.3, 5.4, and 5.5. These 3 languages have made substantial contributions to the loanword inventories of Native American languages (see appendix B). In each of the 3 tables, words for the 77 items of acculturation are rank-listed according to their frequency of use in European languages. Frequency information is extracted from word frequency books for the languages in question: Francis and Kučera (1982) for English, Vander Beke (1929) for French, and Juilland and Chang-Rodriguez (1964) for Spanish.

Analysis of tables 5.3, 5.4, and 5.5 does not conform with predictions of the word frequency model of borrowability. In each case, there is a strong and statistically significant association between the type of acculturated item (living thing or artifact) and word frequency (table 5.3: gamma = .86, chi square = 23.21762, p < .001; table 5.4: gamma = .72, chi square = 14.0473, p < .001; table 5.5: gamma = .78, chi square = 17.46032, p < .001). However, for all 3 European languages, words for introduced artifacts tend to show greater frequency of use than those for introduced living things. This finding is *exactly the opposite* of that predicted by the word frequency model.

Data from word frequency books for contemporary European languages may not accurately reflect how often words were used in the past, when Amerindian languages were activity assigning names (both borrowed and native) to introduced items. Since in earlier time periods, European terms for living things might have been more

Table 5.3. Items of acculturation ranked by frequency of use (in written language) of English words denoting them.

SCHOOL	687	*COLT	21
HOUR	325	NEEDLE	21
BOOK	292	BUTTON	20
BOARD	285	FORK	20
MONEY	275	NAIL	20
TABLE	242	THREAD	20
TOWN	218	*ONION	19
MILE	217	*PIG	19
HUNDRED	215	*MARE	18
PAPER	208	RIBBON	18
*HORSE	203	*CALF	17
WINDOW	172	*OX	17
STORE	102	*BULL	16
SOLDIER	98	*LEMON	16
BOTTLE	90	*APPLE	15
BOX	82	*ORANGE	15
COFFEE	78	*DONKEY	11
SATURDAY	72	*ROOSTER	11
WAGON	72	*GRAPES	10
KEY	71	CHEESE	9
RICH	71	*WHEAT	9
CLOCK	59	FLOUR	8
CUP	58	*GOAT	8
*CHICKEN	49	*OATS	8
*COW	46	SHOVEL	8
*CAT	42	*MULE	7
BREAD	41	*BARLEY	6
WEDNESDAY	37	SPOON	6
SUGAR	34	*CABBAGE	4
PISTOL	31	*GARLIC	4
TEA	29	*PEACH	4
BUTTER	27	*BEET	2
*HEN	27	*APRICOT	1
SOAP	25	*CORIANDER	1
MATCH	24	SCISSORS	1
*PEAS	24	*TURNIP	1
*RICE	24	*WATERMELON	1
*SHEEP	24	*LETTUCE	0
CANDLE	23		

*Identifies living things. The total number of words counted is 1,014,000.

Source: Based on W. Nelson Francis and Henry Kučera, *Frequency Analysis of English Usage: Lexicon and Grammar* (Boston: Houghton Mifflin, 1982).

frequently used than words for artifacts, the word frequency model of borrowability cannot be totally dismissed at present. Indeed, I reconstruct presently complex word frequency patterns of the past that probably influenced the borrowability of terms for acculturated items.

Utilitarianism versus non-utilitarianism

As noted in chapter 3, there is an extraordinarily robust correlation between the nature of introduced items (living thing or artifact) and the extent to which they are named by

Table 5.4. Items of acculturation ranked by frequency of use (in written language) of French words denoting them.

HOUR	804	WEDNESDAY	22
HUNDRED	478	*DONKEY	20
TABLE	347	*MARE	19
MONEY	312	RIBBON	19
*GRAPES	283	*COW	18
TOWN	271	*ROOSTER	18
BOOK	222	BUTTON	17
WINDOW	203	*HEN	15
COFFEE	184	SUGAR	15
PAPER	165	*CHICKEN	13
*HORSE	157	PISTOL	10
SCHOOL	141	MILE	9
RICH	125	NAIL	9
SOLDIER	124	WAGON	9
BREAD	109	*PEAS	8
BOX	97	*PEACH	8
BOTTLE	90	MATCH	7
CUP	82	SHOVEL	7
NEEDLE	69	SOAP	7
*WHEAT	62	*CABBAGE	6
THREAD	61	*RICE	6
CLOCK	55	*GOAT	5
KEY	48	*APRICOT	<5
*APPLE	45	*BARLEY	<5
*OX	45	*BEET	<5
BUTTER	39	*BULL	<5
BOARD	37	*COLT	<5
*CALF	36	*CORIANDER	<5
*CAT	36	*GARLIC	<5
FORK	36	*LEMON	<5
SATURDAY	32	*LETTUCE	<5
CANDLE	31	*MULE	<5
STORE	30	*OATS	<5
*ONION	28	*ORANGE	<5
SPOON	27	SCISSORS	<5
CHEESE	24	TEA	<5
*PIG	24	*TURNIP	<5
FLOUR	23	*WATERMELON	<5
*SHEEP	23		

*Identifies living things. The total number of words counted is 1,147,748.

Source: Based on George E. Vander Beke, *French Word Book* (New York: Macmillan, 1929).

utilitarian native terms (see table 3.7). Artifacts are vastly more likely to be given utilitarian names than are natural kinds. Perhaps the lack of focus on utilitarian aspects of living things implied by this association (see chapter 12) leads to their naming through use of European loans as opposed to native terms. However, this does not appear to be the case. Only a moderate association, lacking statistical significance, is shown when living things are analyzed alone (gamma = .54, chi square = 2.333333, $p < .20$). In other words, living things that are named by utilitarian native terms less often than other living things do not more strongly tend to be labeled by European loans than the latter. Similarly, artifacts named through use of utilitarian terms less often than other artifacts also do not tend to be labeled by European loans more

Table 5.5. Items of acculturation ranked by frequency of use (in written language) of Spanish words denoting them.

HUNDRED	450	*LEMON	7
TOWN	385	NAIL	7
HOUR	331	MILE	6
BOOK	302	*APPLE	<5
MONEY	135	*APRICOT	<5
RICH	112	*BARLEY	<5
PAPER	102	*BEET	<5
SCHOOL	100	BUTTER	<5
TABLE	80	*CABBAGE	<5
WINDOW	73	*CALF	<5
*BULL	69	CHEESE	<5
*PIG	65	*COLT	<5
COFFEE	53	*CORIANDER	<5
BOARD	46	*COW	<5
*HORSE	45	*DONKEY	<5
BREAD	44	FLOUR	<5
SOLDIER	43	FORK	<5
BOX	31	*GARLIC	<5
KEY	30	*GRAPES	<5
CLOCK	27	*LETTUCE	<5
*RICE	25	*MARE	<5
*CAT	20	MATCH	<5
STORE	20	*MULE	<5
*CHICKEN	19	*OATS	<5
*WHEAT	18	*ONION	<5
THREAD	16	*ORANGE	<5
CANDLE	14	*OX	<5
PISTOL	14	*PEAS	<5
SATURDAY	14	*PEACH	<5
TEA	14	*ROOSTER	<5
*GOAT	13	SCISSORS	<5
*HEN	12	*SHEEP	<5
BOTTLE	11	SHOVEL	<5
BUTTON	11	SPOON	<5
NEEDLE	11	*TURNIP	<5
SOAP	11	WAGON	<5
CUP	10	*WATERMELON	<5
SUGAR	10	WEDNESDAY	<5
RIBBON	9		

*Identifies living things. The total number of words counted is 500,000.

Source: Based on Alphonse Juilland and E. Chang-Rodriguez, *Frequency Dictionary of Spanish Words* (The Hague: Mouton, 1964).

strongly than the latter. The conception of items of acculturation as being either utilitarian or not apparently affects borrowability only minimally, if at all.

On the other hand, a utilitarian focus is clearly robustly associated with frequency of use; that is, names of artifacts, which tend strongly to be utilitarian, are frequently used, and names of living things, which tend strongly to be nonutilitarian (morphological), are less frequently used (see table 3.7 and tables 5.3, 5.4, and 5.5). The human inclination to focus on utilitarian aspects of artifacts may serve to enhance the salience of artifacts and, hence, the frequency of use of words that denote them.

Analogs

Borrowability may be influenced by the occurrence of reasonably close New World analogs to introduced items. Acculturated items with close analogs may tend to be labeled by native terms rather than by European loanwords. Conversely, items that lack close analogs may tend to be labeled by loanwords rather than by native terms, at least in comparison to items with close analogs. For example, among introduced artifacts, TOWN shows one of the lowest indices of borrowability, while CHEESE shows one of the highest (table 5.1). Any precontact Amerindian settlement, regardless of size, might be construed as being a reasonably close analog to TOWN. In contrast, there are few, if any, Native American groups who have developed prepared foods similar to CHEESE and thus, this artifact generally lacks a close analog in the Americas. As a possible consequence, TOWN is typically labeled by native terms (which originally denoted analogs closely similar to the item), whereas European loans typically designate CHEESE.

Using original referents of extended native terms as a guide to what may or may not be analogs of introduced items, I cross-tabulated close analogs (present or absent) against indices of borrowability. For introduced living things alone, no correlation of any kind was observed. For just artifacts, a moderate association, lacking statistical significance, emerged (gamma = .53, chi square = 3.436364, p < .10). In other words, there does seem to be a tendency for introduced artifacts with close analogs to be denoted by native terms more often than artifacts without close analogs (which tend to have European loanwords as names). However, the observed correlation is weak since it lacks both statistical significance and pertinence to living things.

Specific historical circumstances

Specific historical circumstances surrounding the introduction of individual items to the Americas may have affected the magnitude of indices of borrowability. For example, COFFEE's high index is possibly related to the fact that this item was a relatively late introduction to the New World, probably arriving in the 1660s. Indeed, coffee growing did not become established in Brazil until the 1700s. For the most part, coffee probably did not spread to most other parts of the Americas until much later, by which time many Amerindian groups had developed significant bilingualism in their native language and a European language. This may well have promoted adoption of European loans. (A major proposal of this work, discussed at length in chapters 6, 7, and 8, is that bilingualism strongly facilitates lexical borrowing.)

A possible explanation of the very low index of borrowability for CHICKEN (see table 5.1) also involves date of introduction, in this case a very early one. Nordenskiöld notes that at least on his second voyage, Columbus had brought fowls: "Wherever Europeans chose to settle and found colonies, they evidently brought fowls with them, and the Indians would no doubt begin to keep fowls themselves" (1922:3). This occurred very early, especially in Brazil and on the coasts of Guiana and in the north of South America. Once having obtained chickens, Native American groups frequently passed them on to other Amerindian peoples without the involvement of colonists. In South America, chickens were taken inland by Indian traders to far-off places long before these areas were explored by Europeans. In fact, Nordenskiöld (p. 9) speculates that chickens probably reached the Andes long before the conquest of the Inca empire by Pizarro (cf. Carter 1971).

Thus, in general, the diffusion of chickens in the New World not only occurred very early but also, for the most part, involved very little direct contact with the Europeans who had introduced them. When first encountering chickens, therefore, many Amerindians were neither bilingual nor typically exposed to European names for this bird and so may have been strongly motivated to name CHICKEN with native terms. In this regard, it is interesting that Amerindian languages spoken on the coast of Guiana and in the north of South America, in contrast to native languages of other parts of Latin America, strongly tend to show European loanwords for HEN. This part of the Americas is precisely the area Nordenskiöld (1922) identifies as the region in which chickens were very early on *directly* acquired by Native Americans from Spaniards.

Since specific historical situations tend to involve specific imported objects or concepts, these situations probably will not figure prominently into explanations of the borrowability characteristics of *classes* of acculturated items—such as the finding that introduced living things tend more strongly to be labeled by European loans than imported artifacts. A model that may best accommodate the borrowability properties of classes is one taking directly into consideration interactions between Native Americans and Euro-Americans that were focused on items of acculturation.

The Sociolinguistic Model

The sociolinguistic model is constructed on the premise that some items of acculturation have more often been foci of Native American/Euro-American interaction than other items. (For ease of reference, the former are called "N-E context items" and the latter "other context items.") Native American/Euro-American encounters that involve acculturated items have typically taken place in Euro-American settings—for example, at the farm, ranch, mission, church, store, trading post, or garrison. It is plausible that Native Americans have more commonly been exposed to European words for N-E context items than to European terms for other context items. This may have resulted in a greater inclination for Amerindians to borrow European names for the former than for the latter. For example, Lockhart (1992:271) attributes early Nahuatl (Mexico) adoption of the Spanish label for HORSE in part to "the frequency with which the Spanish word must have been pronounced in Spanish-Nahua contact episodes."

Table 5.6 presents a typology of acculturated items in which objects and concepts on the list of 77, except the 7 creature subtypes, are identified as being either (A) N-E context items or (B) other context items. Within A, items are classified as farm produce, livestock, perishable material artifacts, or other artifacts; within B, as either garden produce, (smaller) domestic creatures, durable material artifacts, or nonmaterial artifacts.

The typology of table 5.6 is not intended to be universally applicable to Native American peoples. It is presented only as an attempt to capture in its categories prevailing or dominant patterns that probably existed in most parts of the Americas when acculturated items were first named in the languages of Amerindians. Its derivation is based largely on impressions I have developed over many years of studying indigenous New World groups, both past and present.

Table 5.6. Typology of acculturated items, minus 7 creature subtypes, based on presumed differences in frequencies of interactions between Native Americans and Euro-Americans.

A. *N-E context items*: Items of acculturation more often constituting the foci of Native American/Euro-American interaction (e.g., at the marketplace, trading post, town, farm, ranch, mission, church, garrison)

  1. Farm produce: APPLE, APRICOT, BARLEY, CORIANDER, GARLIC, GRAPES, LEMON, OATS, ORANGE, PEACH, RICE, WHEAT

  2. Livestock (larger creatures): COW, DONKEY, GOAT, HORSE, MULE, PIG, SHEEP

  3. Perishable material artifacts: BREAD, BUTTER, CANDLE, CHEESE, COFFEE, FLOUR, MATCHES, SOAP, SUGAR, TEA

  4. Other artifacts: SATURDAY (typically, payday), SOLDIER

B. *Other context items*: Items of acculturation less often constituting the foci of Native American/Euro-American interaction

  1. Garden produce: BEETS, CABBAGE, LETTUCE, ONION, PEAS, TURNIP, WATERMELON

  2. Domestic animals (smaller creatures): CAT, CHICKEN

  3. Durable material artifacts: BOARD, BOOK, BOTTLE, BOX, BUTTON, CLOCK, CUP, FORK, KEY, MONEY, NAIL, NEEDLE, PAPER, PISTOL, RIBBON, SCHOOL, SCISSORS, SHOVEL, SPOON, STORE, TABLE, THREAD, TOWN, WAGON, WINDOW

  4. Nonmaterial artifacts: HOUR, HUNDRED, MILE, RICH, WEDNESDAY

The typology was constructed with several general considerations in mind. Euro-Americans have typically controlled (and, of course, still do) vastly more economic resources than Native Americans, including land, raw materials, and labor. This has entailed a New World monopoly by Euro-Americans of the production and primary distribution of high demand goods (including most of the items of acculturation dealt with in this study). In contrast, postcontact Native Americans have typically had little in the way of land-holdings, have had severely restricted access to raw materials, and have been frequently engaged (often through coercion) in work forces mobilized by Euro-Americans. Compared to Euro-Americans, Native Americans have had virtually no major influence on the production and primary distribution of widely sought commodities.

Of the 28 introduced living things in table 5.6 (which do not include animal subtypes), 19 are classified as N-E context items, 12 of which pertain to the category farm produce, and 7 to livestock. These items are all primarily associated with larger-scale agricultural enterprises, that is, the farms, ranches, and missions of Euro-Americans. While some Amerindian groups have from time to time cultivated introduced fruits and grains, such as APPLES, GRAPES, and WHEAT, and have kept large animals like COWS, HORSES, and SHEEP, they have rarely done so on a scale comparable in magnitude to that typically associated with Euro-Americans. For the most part, Native Americans have simply lacked the resources (land, food, water, labor, etc.) necessary to sustain a level of production of these items equivalent to that of Euro-Americans.

Nine living things are part of category B in table 5.6, including 7 items classified as garden produce and 2 as domestic creatures. Plants such as BEETS, LETTUCE, and TURNIPS, which are typically grown in garden plots, probably have been frequently incorporated into Amerindian inventories of cultivated plants. Limited access of Native Americans to substantial expanses of arable land would not have precluded frequent cultivation of smaller gardens. The 2 domestic creatures, CAT and CHICKEN, are included among other context items by virtue of being frequently kept by Amerindian groups. Maintenance of these smaller creatures obviously would not have strained the resources of Amerindians nearly as much as the upkeep of larger domestic animals like COWS and HORSES.

Native American/Euro-American interaction has almost certainly focused on farm produce and livestock to a considerably greater extent than on garden produce and smaller domestic creatures. Amerindians who developed familiarity with the former items have probably often encountered them in Euro-American settings such as stores and trading posts (where the items could be purchased) or at farms, ranches, and missions (where Amerindians often worked or visited). In such contexts, European words for farm produce and livestock would have been frequently heard by Native Americans. In contrast, since garden produce and smaller domestic animals have been less closely associated with Euro-American contexts, European words for these items were probably less commonly heard by Amerindians.

Of the 42 introduced artifacts on the list of 77 items of acculturation, 12 are N-E context items and 30 are other context items (table 5.6). With two exceptions, the former are designated as "perishable material artifacts." These are items that are typically rapidly consumed and, consequently, require frequent replacement. Among the 30 other context items, 25 are identified as "durable material artifacts." In contrast to perishable artifacts, these are commonly slowly consumed, if consumed at all, and therefore do not require frequent replacement.

Replenishment of items by Native Americans has typically involved interaction with Euro-Americans at stores and trading posts—bearing in mind, however, that artifacts, especially durable ones, have frequently diffused from one Amerindian group to another without the direct intervention of Euro-Americans. Since perishable artifacts necessarily entail more frequent replacement than durable ones, conditions would have been conducive for more frequent exposure of Native Americans to European terms for such artifacts as CHEESE, COFFEE, SOAP, and SUGAR than to European words for such items as BOOK, FORK, SCISSORS, and SHOVEL.

Category B in table 5.6 includes five items identified as nonmaterial artifacts: HOUR, HUNDRED, MILE, RICH, and WEDNESDAY. These "conceptual" artifacts might be regarded as more similar to durable material artifacts than to perishable ones since they are not used up and, consequently, do not require regular replenishment and the special contacts with Euro-Americans this would entail. Indeed, it is unclear why words (European or otherwise) for these concepts should have been more often heard by Amerindians in Euro-American settings than words for other acculturated artifacts in category B.

One nonmaterial artifact, SATURDAY, is included in category A in table 5.6 subsumed under "other artifacts." This day of the week, unlike WEDNESDAY (which is classed as category B), may have commonly constituted a special focus of Euro-American/Amerindian interaction since in many parts of the New World SATURDAY was the traditional day on which workers, often Native Americans, were paid by their Euro-American employers. The only other item listed in category B under "other artifacts," SOLDIER, would have been mainly encountered by Amerindians in Euro-American settings like the local garrison. SOLDIER, then, may have been a fairly common focus of Native American/Euro-American encounters.

The correlation

Table 5.7 ranks the items of acculturation, minus the 7 animal subtypes, by index of borrowability, flagging by an asterisk (*) all items identified in table 5.6 as N-E context. Analysis of table 5.7 attests to an extremely robust and statistically significant correlation between the type of acculturated item (either N-E context or other context) and borrowability (gamma = .91, chi square = 25.27898, p < .001). Items of acculturation that have frequently been the focus of Native American/Euro-American interaction, that is, N-E context items, are substantially more likely to be labeled by European loans than other context items. If we consider only living things, minus creature subtypes, the pertinent correlation coefficient is .89 (chi square = 8.0233392, p < .01), and if we consider only artifacts, gamma is .68 (chi square = 5.049545, p < .05).

This correlation is stronger than any other association considered in this chapter that involves borrowability and, hence, indicates that the sociolinguistic model best accounts for lexical borrowability of acculturated items. For example, the correlation that uses living things and artifacts as variables (table 5.1), while considered robust at .82 by statistical standards, is almost ten-hundredths of a point lower than that pertaining to the sociolinguistic model (.91).

That introduced living things tend more strongly than acculturated artifacts to be labeled by European loans may simply reflect a deeper and more significant finding that living things are more inclined than artifacts to be N-E context items (gamma = .68, chi square = 10.50868, p < .01; see table 5.6 for data on which these statistics are based). The finding that animals tend more strongly to be named by European loans than plants (table 5.2) may, in a parallel manner, entail an inclination for creatures to be N-E context items more often than plants, but this relationship does not prove to be strong (gamma = .34) and lacks statistical significance (chi square = .598475, p < .30).

Table 5.7. Items of acculturation, minus 7 creature subtypes, ranked by index of borrowability (European loan percentage) and showing N-E context.

Item	Percentage	Item	Percentage
*COFFEE	81 (156/192)	*APRICOT	37 (10/27)
*CORIANDER	72 (28/39)	BOX	36 (79/221)
CAT	70 (194/279)	SCHOOL	35 (65/185)
*GARLIC	69 (70/101)	SCISSORS	35 (86/245)
*ORANGE	67 (122/182)	WEDNESDAY	35 (54/155)
*CHEESE	66 (88/134)	*MATCH	34 (64/186)
*DONKEY	64 (116/182)	NAIL	33 (74/224)
*LEMON	60 (80/133)	*CANDLE	32 (68/216)
*APPLE	59 (91/155)	SPOON	31 (79/256)
*COW	58 (153/266)	SHOVEL	30 (51/172)
*SATURDAY	56 (95/170)	STORE	30 (51/172)
*PIG	55 (151/277)	*BREAD	29 (78/269)
*SOLDIER	55 (110/202)	*FLOUR	29 (68/232)
*PEACH	54 (66/122)	BOARD	28 (60/215)
*MULE	54 (87/161)	*BUTTER	28 (34/122)
*GOAT	53 (103/196)	WAGON	28 (42/151)
*SUGAR	53 (121/227)	PEAS	28 (29/105)
*TEA	53 (63/119)	CUP	27 (52/196)
*HORSE	52 (143/273)	MILE	27 (16/60)
*RICE	52 (96/184)	PISTOL	27 (29/108)
TABLE	52 (127/244)	WINDOW	27 (59/218)
*SOAP	51 (124/244)	CLOCK	25 (47/191)
BOTTLE	51 (107/208)	*GRAPES	25 (34/136)
WATERMELON	49 (71/144)	*OATS	23 (17/74)
RIBBON	48 (72/149)	BOOK	22 (53/247)
CABBAGE	47 (66/140)	NEEDLE	21 (57/272)
LETTUCE	47 (42/89)	PAPER	20 (53/263)
HOUR	45 (69/153)	HUNDRED	19 (40/215)
*SHEEP	44 (105/241)	BEETS	18 (9/51)
ONION	41 (82/202)	THREAD	17 (43/255)
KEY	41 (91/221)	CHICKEN	16 (28/180)
*BARLEY	39 (23/59)	TOWN	15 (38/258)
TURNIP	39 (37/95)	RICH	13 (29/225)
BUTTON	38 (69/180)	MONEY	11 (30/263)
*WHEAT	38 (66/172)	FORK	10 (17/165)

*Identifies N-E context items.

While exceptionally robust, the sociolinguistic model/borrowability correlation is not perfect. Not in conformance with the correlation, for example, are 3 other context items: 2 durable, nonmaterial artifacts, BOTTLE and TABLE, and a smaller domestic creature, CAT. These 3 are unexpectedly found among the first 23 items that show the highest indices of borrowability—of which 20 are expected N-E context items (table 5.7). The following are tentative explanations of these anomalies within the framework of the sociolinguistic model.

BOTTLE may be the least durable of the 25 acculturated items identified as durable artifacts (table 5.6). Bottles, of course, are easily broken and perhaps more like perishable objects than durable ones, tending to require frequent replacement. As a result, BOTTLE, more often than most other durable artifacts, may have been the focus of Native American interaction with Euro-Americans. Another possibility relates to the common synecdochic use of words for BOTTLE in reference to distilled alcoholic beverages like whiskey and rum. Liquor is typically consumed rapidly, necessitating frequent replenishment. BOTTLE's high borrowability index may reflect frequently occurring situations that involve both Native Americans and Euro-Americans in which European words for BOTTLE denote alcoholic drink.

The unusually high index of borrowability associated with TABLE may relate to the extent to which Amerindians typically have culturally adopted this introduced item. Most of the acculturated artifacts considered in this work are smallish items (BUTTON, CUP, KEY, SPOON, THREAD, etc.) that could have been easily transported from a Euro-American setting to a Native American one. This, of course, is not generally true of tables, which tend to be large and heavy objects requiring considerable energy and effort to move them. Such physical constraints may have substantially limited the extent to which most American Indian groups incorporated tables into their material culture. If so, tables may have been primarily experienced by Amerindians in Euro-American settings rather than in native ones. Another possibility relates to the use in Latin America of the Spanish word for TABLE (*mesa*) in reference to the communion table or altar. The latter item, of course, is canonically encountered in religious edifices and primarily found in Euro-American settings.

CAT is an imported domestic creature traditionally kept by Native Americans (Kiddle 1964). Its high index of borrowability is surprising since it probably would not have been encountered in Euro-American settings any more often than the other smaller domestic creature commonly kept by Amerindians, CHICKEN, which shows an especially low borrowability index. The CAT anomaly is perhaps explained by the peculiarity of European loans for the item, the vast majority of which are based on traditional ways of calling felines, for example, "pus-pus" in English. Plausibly, cat calls, considerably more so than actual European words for felines such as English "cat" and Spanish *gato*, were especially striking or fetching to Native Americans, motivating their frequent incorporation into their languages as formal labels for the creature.

Several N-E context items, for example, GRAPES and OATS, are unexpectedly included among items that show especially low indices of borrowability (table 5.7). Plausible explanations of these anomalies are unknown at the present time. Perhaps other variables mentioned earlier, such as close native analogs and/or specific historical circumstances, will figure prominently in forthcoming explanations.

The sociolinguistic model is another version of a word frequency explanation of borrowability since it is based on the assumption that Native Americans have tended to adopt as loans those European terms to which they have been most frequently exposed. Since, in the model, degree of exposure is viewed as primarily influenced by factors other than gross frequency of use in a donor language, the sociolinguistic model is substantially different from the word frequency proposal considered earlier in this chapter. Investigation of word frequency, at least as implied in the sociolinguistic model, appears to be a productive approach to understanding lexical borrowability involving words for items of acculturation.

Conclusion

Cross-language investigation indicates that words for objects and concepts introduced by Europeans to native peoples of the New World vary considerably with respect to their borrowability as measured by percentage of Amerindian languages showing loanwords for an acculturated item. Some findings related to classes of introduced items are: (1) terms for living things are more borrowable than words for artifacts; (2) terms for animals are more borrowable than words for plants; and (3) terms for creature subtypes are less borrowable than words for other living things.

While the sociolinguistic model appears to be most productive among those considered, it alone does not explain all findings related to word borrowability. Marking hierarchies entailing introduced creature subtypes also figure significantly into an explanatory account. Some evidence, albeit weak, indicates that lack of close New World analogs to introduced things may have influenced adoption of European loans by speakers of Amerindian languages. Although not investigated at length here, specific historical circumstances surrounding the introduction of individual items to the Americas should not be discounted as contributing factors. Finally, other influences, not envisioned in this work, may emerge as components of a comprehensive explanatory framework in future research.

6

REGIONAL PATTERNS AND BILINGUALISM

This chapter describes regional patterns of lexical acculturation. As discussed in chapter 1, Voegelin and Hymes's (1953) comparative study of nine Amerindian languages suggests that languages of Latin America have tended to borrow European terms for introduced items, whereas languages of non-Hispanic North America have tended to coin terms and only very occasionally have borrowed European labels. Similarly, Bright (1960a) reports that Indian languages of Hispanic California have heavily borrowed (Spanish) terms for introduced domesticated animals, whereas languages of non-Hispanic (northern) California have typically produced native terms for these creatures.

Bright (1960a:233) relates this finding to "a lower incidence of bilingualism" among California groups influenced by Anglo-Americans, linking this in turn to the fact that the Spanish were considerably more inclined to integrate Indian groups into colonial culture. This interpretation contrasts with the position long held by linguists that structural features of some languages make them more disposed than others to adopt loanwords (e.g., Sapir 1921:205–10; Herzog 1941:74; Haugen 1956:66; Bonvillain 1978:32). For example, Haugen writes, "[L]oanwords are easily accepted by languages with unified, unanalyzed words, but not by languages with active methods of word compounding" (p. 66). In addition to Bright's contribution, evidence presented by Spencer (1947:133), Dozier (1956), Mixco (1977), Thomason and Kaufman (1988), and others suggests that the degree of borrowing is largely dependent on sociolinguistic factors such as bilingualism rather than on language structure.

The extensive cross-language data that follows confirm Voegelin and Hymes's (1953) interpretation, based on a small sample, that Spanish-influenced Amerindian groups have been heavier borrowers of European words than Anglo-influenced groups. Comparative data also indicate that language structure factors, while sometimes influencing lexical borrowing, do so much less than sociolinguistic factors.

Regional Patterns

Table 6.1 sorts the 292 language cases of the sample by culture area and ranks them by European loanword percentage from highest to lowest. Also given for each language case is the genetic group affiliation and the type of European influence(s) to which its speakers were subjected. (Much of this information is also presented in appendix B, in which language cases are listed alphabetically.) North American culture areas correspond to those outlined in the *Handbook of North American Indians* published over the years by the Smithsonian Institution (e.g., Trigger 1978), and South American culture areas are more or less isomorphic with those identified by Loukotka (1968). The European loanword percentage is calculated by dividing the total number of items of acculturation labeled by European loans (excluding extended European loans and most loan blends) by the total number of items for which terms are found in a lexical source (or in a combination of sources) for a case (see also table 3.1).

Genetic groupings referred to in table 6.1 are, with one notable exception, well established or at least noncontroversial (cf. Kaufman 1994a, 1994b, 1994c; Tait 1994). Controversial genetic groupings such as Hokan, Penutian, and Equatorial (cf. Greenberg 1987), which at best unite very distantly related languages, are avoided. The exception is Quechumaran, a proposed genetic linkage of Aymara and Quechua in the Andean region of South America. Andean linguists do not question that Aymara and Quechua, especially southern Peruvian Quechua, share much of the same vocabulary and also show numerous phonological and grammatical similarities. In debate is whether these similarities result from borrowing between these languages or from a close genetic relationship (Mannheim 1991).

For each language case, sources of European influence were identified by consulting readily available works on Amerindian groups such as the *Handbook of South American Indians* (Steward 1946). For reasons that will become clear presently, I have characterized the intensity of the influence of Spanish speakers on speakers of Amerindian languages as either direct (dS) or indirect (iS). Where Native American groups have been more or less strongly incorporated into Hispanic society in the New World, displaying significant bilingualism, intermarriage, and active participation in Hispanic cultural institutions such as the church and regional economies, I have judged Spanish influence to be direct. Where Spanish influence has taken the form of periodic but minimal direct contact with explorers, priests, traders and so on in areas that were essentially outposts of the Spanish empire; of military encounters in which Spanish speakers were generally unsuccessful in subduing native peoples; and of diffusion through contact with other Native American groups who interacted with Spanish speakers, I have judged Spanish influence to be indirect.

Table 6.2 presents average European loanword percentages for culture areas based on percentages associated with languages of those regions (table 6.1). Culture areas that had no substantial direct Spanish influence (Arctic, North America Plateau, Subarctic, North America Northwest Coast, North America Northeast, North America Southeast, and North America Plains) show average European loanword percentages of 31 or less. In contrast, percentages that are greater than 31 are found for culture areas in which Spanish and/or Portuguese influence has been considerable. Low average loanword percentages (less than 31) also occur for the Central South America Tropical Forest, the Extreme South of South America, and the South America Gran Chaco, all remote and/or interior regions of the continent, which for the most part have been heavily penetrated by Europeans only relatively recently.

Table 6.1. European loanword percentages for 292 Amerindian language cases.

Language Case	Genetic Group	ei	%	t	l
ARCTIC					
Pacific Gulf Yupik	Eskimo-Aleut	R/E	73	45	33
Eskimo (Kuskoquim district)	Eskimo-Aleut	R/E	58	33	19
Central Yupik Eskimo	Eskimo-Aleut	R/E	55	53	29
Siberian Yupik Eskimo	Eskimo-Aleut	R/E	41	37	15
Inuit Eskimo	Eskimo-Aleut	E/F/G/N	30	64	19
West Greenlandic Eskimo	Eskimo-Aleut	Da/N	19	59	11
Eskimo (North Slope Iñupiaq)	Eskimo-Aleut	R/E	17	42	7
East Greenlandic Eskimo	Eskimo-Aleut	Da/N	14	44	6
Eskimo (Siglit)	Eskimo-Aleut	E	13	38	5
Eskimo (Uummarmiut)	Eskimo-Aleut	E	13	32	4
Eskimo (Kangiryuarmiut)	Eskimo-Aleut	E	11	38	4
SUBARCTIC					
Tanaina	Athapascan-Eyak	R/E	72	50	36
Central Koyukon	Athapascan-Eyak	R/E	52	31	16
Ingalik	Athapascan-Eyak	R/E	47	38	18
Minto (= Lower Tanana)	Athapascan-Eyak	R/E	47	34	16
Ahtna	Athapascan-Eyak	R/E	43	44	19
Carrier	Athapascan-Eyak	E/F	29	63	18
Eyak	Athapascan-Eyak	R/E	25	52	13
Northern Tutchone	Athapascan-Eyak	E/F	22	32	7
Gwichin (1976)	Athapascan-Eyak	E/F	17	36	6
Cree	Algonquian	E/F	14	72	10
Chipewyan	Athapascan-Eyak	E/F	13	61	8
Montagnais (Cree dialect, c. 1980)	Algonquian	E/F	9	55	5
Montagnais (Cree dialect, 1901)	Algonquian	E/F	8	73	6
Beaver	Athapascan-Eyak	E/F	8	51	4
Slave	Athapascan-Eyak	E/F	7	55	4
Montagnais (Chipewyan)	Athapascan-Eyak	E/F	6	70	4
Plains Cree ("Y" dialect)	Algonquian	E/F	5	75	4
Gwichin (1876)	Athapascan-Eyak	E/F	2	56	1
Peaux-de-Lièvres (= Hare)	Athapascan-Eyak	E/F	2	56	1
NORTH AMERICA NORTHEAST					
Mahican (c. 1755)	Algonquian	E/Du	48	31	15
Passamaquoddy	Algonquian	E/F	33	43	14
Delaware (eighteenth century)	Algonquian	E/Du	29	52	15
Maliseet (Passamaquoddy dialect)	Algonquian	E/F	24	33	8
Abenaki (Penobscot dialect, 1691)	Algonquian	E/F	23	40	9
Micmac (1984)	Algonquian	E/F/G	22	58	13
Micmac (1888)	Algonquian	E/F/G	19	69	13
Mississaga	Algonquian	E/F	17	35	6
Mohawk	Iroquoian	E/F/Du	14	59	8

Table 6.1. *(continued)*

Language Case	Genetic Group	ei	%	t	l
Kickapoo	Algonquian	iS/E/F	14	42	6
Algonquin (1886)	Algonquian	E/F	13	46	6
Delaware (1839)	Algonquian	E/Du	13	32	4
Iroquois	Iroquoian	E/F	13	40	5
Eastern Ojibwa	Algonquian	E/F	10	63	6
Onondaga (eighteenth century)	Iroquoian	E/F/Du	9	56	5
Algonquin (1984)	Algonquian	E/F	9	43	4
Oneida	Iroquoian	E/F/Du	8	38	3
Menominee	Algonquian	E/F	7	70	5
Onondaga (seventeenth century)	Iroquoian	E/F/Du	6	48	3
Ojibwa (Mille Lacs)	Algonquian	E/F	5	59	3
Ojibwa (Odawa dialect)	Algonquian	E/F	5	42	2
Seneca	Iroquoian	E/F	4	57	2
Chippewa (Red Lake and Pillager)	Algonquian	E/F	2	41	1
Miami	Algonquian	E/F	2	54	1
Southern Ojibwa	Algonquian	E/F	2	53	1
Illinois (c. 1700)	Algonquian	E/F	0	48	0

NORTH AMERICA NORTHWEST COAST

Language Case	Genetic Group	ei	%	t	l
Squamish	Salishan	E/F	36	31	11
Heiltsuk (Kwakiutl dialect)	Wakashan	E/F?	27	33	9
Songish (North Straits Salish)	Salishan	E/F	26	38	10
Quileute	Chimakuan	E/F	26	41	11
Gitksan	Tsimshianic	E/F?	13	31	4
Haisla	Wakashan	E/F	9	33	3
Haida (Kaigani dialect)	Isolate	E/F	8	36	3
Klamath (1963)	Isolate	E/F	56	46	26
Klamath (1890)	Isolate	E/F	37	57	21
Okanagan (Colville)	Salishan	E/F	34	50	17
Shuswap	Salishan	E/F	32	41	13
Thompson (Nitklakapamuk)	Salishan	E/F	21	43	9
Kalispel	Salishan	E/F	16	67	11

NORTH AMERICA PLATEAU

Language Case	Genetic Group	ei	%	t	l
Yakima (Sahaptin dialect)	Sahaptin-Nez Perce	E/F	13	38	5
Nez Perce	Sahaptin-Nez Perce	E/F	3	59	2

NORTH AMERICA PLAINS

Language Case	Genetic Group	ei	%	t	l
Comanche	Uto-Aztecan	iS/E/F	17	69	12
Tonkawa	Isolate	?S/E	13	39	5
Arikara	Caddoan	E	8	62	5
Blackfoot Proper (Siksika dialect)	Algonquian	E/F?	7	59	4
Blackfoot (Peigan dialect)	Algonquian	E/F?	6	53	3
Kiowa	Tanoan	E	5	42	2
Dakota (Santee dialect)	Siouan	E	4	75	3

(continued)

Table 6.1. *(continued)*

Language Case	Genetic Group	*ei*	%	*t*	*l*
Dakota (Teton dialect, 1866)	Siouan	E	4	49	2
Osage	Siouan	iS/E	3	61	2
Cheyenne (1976–1984)	Algonquian	E	2	69	1
Crow	Siouan	E/F?	2	42	1
Hidatsa	Siouan	E	2	43	1
Mandan	Siouan	E	2	44	1
Cheyenne (1862)	Algonquian	E	0	32	0
Cheyenne (1915)	Algonquian	E	0	71	0
Dakota (Teton dialect, 1970–1974)	Siouan	E	0	68	0

NORTH AMERICA SOUTHEAST

Language Case	Genetic Group	*ei*	%	*t*	*l*
Choctaw	Muskogean	iS/E/F	17	71	12
Creek (= Muskokee)	Muskogean	iS/E	16	76	12
Alabama	Muskogean	iS/E/F	13	71	9
Koasati	Muskogean	iS/E/F	12	74	9
Chickasaw	Muskogean	iS/E/F	11	70	8
Biloxi	Siouan	iS/E/F	7	59	4
Cherokee	Iroquoian	iS/E	7	72	5
Tunica	Isolate	E/F	5	56	3
Atakapa	Isolate	E/F	5	60	3
Natchez	Isolate	E/F	2	47	1
Ofo	Siouan	E/F	0	38	0

NORTH AMERICA GREAT BASIN

Language Case	Genetic Group	*ei*	%	*t*	*l*
Panamint Shoshone	Uto-Aztecan	?S/E	71	58	41
Kawaiisu	Uto-Aztecan	?S/E	70	37	26
Washo	Isolate	iS/E	65	40	26
Big Smokey Valley Shoshoni	Uto-Aztecan	?S/E	35	34	12
Ute (1849–1880)	Uto-Aztecan	?S/E	18	40	7

NORTH AMERICA SOUTHWEST

Language Case	Genetic Group	*ei*	%	*t*	*l*
Yaqui	Uto-Aztecan	dS	83	40	33
Cahita	Uto-Aztecan	dS	78	37	29
Pima	Uto-Aztecan	dS/E	76	67	51
Keresan (Santa Ana Pueblo)	Isolate	dS/E	68	38	26
Tewa	Tanoan	dS/E	65	34	22
Tarahumara (1915–1920)	Uto-Aztecan	dS	57	44	25
Cocopa	Yuman	dS/E	56	71	40
Tarahumara (1952–1972)	Uto-Aztecan	dS	49	51	25
Jicarilla Apache	Athapascan-Eyak	dS/E	40	57	23
Southern Ute	Uto-Aztecan	iS/E	38	61	23
Pame	Otomanguean	dS	34	47	16
Mojave	Yuman	iS/E	34	47	16
Mescalero Apache	Athapascan-Eyak	?S/E	30	46	14
Hopi	Uto-Aztecan	iS/E	28	68	19

Table 6.1. *(continued)*

Language Case	Genetic Group	*ei*	%	*t*	*l*
Zuni	Isolate	iS/E	27	52	14
Yavapai (Tolkapaya dialect)	Yuman	iS/E	24	62	15
Western Apache	Athapascan-Eyak	iS/E	20	64	13
Navajo (1910)	Athapascan-Eyak	iS/E	18	56	10
Navajo (1950–1980)	Athapascan-Eyak	iS/E	18	72	13
Seri	Isolate	iS	17	41	7
Comecrudo (1886)	Isolate	?S/E	14	36	5
Apache (1870s and 1880s)	Athapascan-Eyak	?S/E	11	47	5
Yavapai (Tonto dialect)	Yuman	iS/E	0	35	0

CALIFORNIA

Language Case	Genetic Group	*ei*	%	*t*	*l*
Cupeño	Uto-Aztecan	dS/E	97	62	60
Cahuilla	Uto-Aztecan	dS/E	94	70	66
Plains Miwok	Miwok-Costanoan	dS/E	91	58	53
Northern Sierra Miwok	Miwok-Costanoan	?S/E	88	60	53
Wappo	Yukian	dS/E	87	67	58
Bodega Miwok	Miwok-Costanoan	dS/E	87	47	41
Lake Miwok	Miwok-Costanoan	?S/E	82	65	53
Southern Sierra Miwok	Miwok-Costanoan	?S/E	81	63	51
Diegueño	Yuman	dS/E	80	39	31
Maidu	Maiduan	iS/E	54	39	21
Wintu	Wintun	iS/E	38	42	16
Yuki	Yukian	iS/E	33	42	14
Karok	Isolate	E	24	50	12
Atsugewi	Palaihnihan	iS/E	12	34	4
Kiliwa	Yuman	iS	0	56	0

MIDDLE AMERICA

Language Case	Genetic Group	*ei*	%	*t*	*l*
Mocho	Mayan	dS	91	58	53
Totonac (Xicotepec de Juárez)	Totonacan	dS	83	52	43
Cora	Uto-Aztecan	dS	80	46	37
Pipil	Uto-Aztecan	dS	79	53	42
Nahuatl (Tetelcingo)	Uto-Aztecan	dS	78	50	39
Ixil	Mayan	dS	78	59	46
Pocomam	Mayan	dS	78	32	25
Tzotzil (Zinacantán,1950–1975)	Mayan	dS	77	64	49
Zapotec (Mitla)	Otomanguean	dS	77	62	48
Nahuatl (Xalitla)	Uto-Aztecan	dS	75	47	35
Tojolabal	Mayan	dS	75	71	53
Tzotzil (San Bartolome)	Mayan	dS	74	43	32
Tequistlatec	Isolate	dS	72	58	42
Jacaltec	Mayan	dS	71	41	29
Huave (San Mateo)	Isolate	dS	70	47	33
Popoluca (Sayula)	Mixe-Zoque	dS	70	40	28
Kekchi	Mayan	dS	69	64	44
North Mam	Mayan	dS	68	56	38

(continued)

Table 6.1. *(continued)*

Language Case	Genetic Group	*ei*	%	*t*	*l*
Aguacatec	Mayan	dS	68	38	26
Mopan	Mayan	dS	68	38	26
Tzeltal (Bachajón)	Mayan	dS	67	51	34
Popoloca (San Vicente Coyoctepec)	Otomanguean	dS	66	50	33
Cuicatec	Otomanguean	dS	62	74	46
Tzotzil (San Andrés)	Mayan	dS	61	51	31
Trique (Copala)	Otomanguean	dS	61	54	33
Zapotec (Juárez)	Otomanguean	dS	61	49	30
Cakchiquel (1956–1981)	Mayan	dS	60	67	40
Totonac (La Sierra dialect)	Totonacan	dS	58	36	21
Popoluca (Oluta)	Mixe-Zoque	dS	58	45	26
Tzeltal (Tenejapa)	Mayan	dS	58	50	29
Chol (Tila)	Mayan	dS	57	60	34
Otomi (Santiago Mexquititlán)	Otomanguean	dS	55	73	40
Nahuatl (1611)	Uto-Aztecan	dS	53	34	18
Huichol	Uto-Aztecan	dS	52	33	17
Mazahua	Otomanguean	dS	49	45	22
Mixe (Totontepec)	Mixe-Zoque	dS	48	52	25
Tzeltal (Oxchuc)	Mayan	dS	47	36	17
Otomi (1826–1841)	Otomanguean	dS	47	68	32
Nahuatl (Sierra de Zacapoaxtla)	Uto-Aztecan	dS	46	33	15
Ixcatec	Otomanguean	dS	46	37	17
Zoque (Copainalá)	Mixe-Zoque	dS	44	32	14
Cakchiquel (c. 1650)	Mayan	dS	44	45	20
Cakchiquel (Central)	Mayan	dS	43	40	17
Nahuatl (Huazalinguillo dialect)	Uto-Aztecan	dS	42	38	16
Trique (Chicahuaxtla)	Otomanguean	dS	41	51	21
Tzotzil (Zinacantán, sixteenth century)	Mayan	dS	39	51	20
Huastec	Mayan	dS	38	32	12
Quiche	Mayan	dS	37	46	17
Nahuatl (1571)	Uto-Aztecan	dS	36	61	22
Tarascan (1559)	Isolate	dS	35	54	19
Chatino (Tataltepec)	Otomanguean	dS	35	34	12
Mixtec (Chayuco)	Otomanguean	dS	30	37	11
Mixtec (San Juan Colorado)	Otomanguean	dS	29	42	12
Otomi (Mezquital dialect)	Otomanguean	dS	26	51	13
Otomi (c. 1770)	Otomanguean	dS	26	47	12
Tzeltal (1888)	Mayan	dS	22	45	10
Zapotec (1578)	Otomanguean	dS	21	57	12
Zoque (1672)	Mixe-Zoque	dS	16	32	4
Zapotec (sixteenth century)	Otomanguean	dS	12	42	5
Amuzgo	Otomanguean	dS	9	35	3
Yucatec (1850–1883)	Mayan	dS	9	45	4
Chinantec (Ojitlán)	Otomanguean	dS	5	38	2
Mixtec (1593)	Otomanguean	dS	4	50	2

Table 6.1. *(continued)*

Language Case	Genetic Group	*ei*	%	*t*	*l*
NORTH ANDEAN REGION					
Central American Carib	Maipuran	dS/E/F	78	58	45
Cayápa	Barbacoan	dS	71	41	29
Sumo	Misumalpan	dS/E	71	62	44
Miskito (1948–1986)	Misumalpan	dS/E	68	66	45
Guaymi	Chibchan	dS/E	61	33	20
Páez	Panaquitan	dS	58	43	25
Miskito (1848–1894)	Misumalpan	dS/E	55	49	27
Cágaba	Chibchan	?S	54	37	20
Colorado	Barbacoan	dS	42	31	13
Cuna (1890–1913)	Chibchan	dS	40	38	15
Cuna (1944–1985)	Chibchan	dS	39	69	27
NORTH-CENTRAL ANDEAN REGION					
Cofan	Isolate	?S	61	36	22
SOUTH-CENTRAL ANDEAN REGION					
Aymara (1940–1989)	Quechumaran	dS	82	61	50
Quechua (Cajamarca)	Quechumaran	dS	81	43	35
Quechua (Ayacucho, 1969)	Quechumaran	dS	81	58	47
Quechua (Cochabamba)	Quechumaran	dS	75	36	27
Quechua (Cuzco, 1976)	Quechumaran	dS	74	42	31
Quechua (Ancash, 1905)	Quechumaran	dS	73	37	27
Quechua (Junin, 1976)	Quechumaran	dS	73	44	32
Quechua (Junin, 1905)	Quechumaran	dS	68	37	25
Quechua (Ayacucho, 1905)	Quechumaran	dS	62	37	23
Aymara (1612)	Quechumaran	dS	59	34	20
Quechua (Ancash, 1972)	Quechumaran	dS	58	31	18
Quechua (Cuzco, 1905)	Quechumaran	dS	57	37	21
Aymara (1870–1907)	Quechumaran	dS	49	41	20
Peruvian Quechua (1864–1908)	Quechumaran	dS	40	40	16
Ecuadorean Quechua (1892–1924)	Quechumaran	?S	22	36	8
Ecuadorean Quechua (1942–1955)	Quechumaran	?S	20	40	8
Peruvian Quechua (1560–1619)	Quechumaran	dS	16	31	5
SOUTH ANDEAN REGION					
Mapuche (1898–1916)	Araucanian	dS	66	50	33
Ranquelche	Araucanian	?S	64	53	34
Mapuche (1944–1990)	Araucanian	dS	62	52	32
Mapuche (1777)	Araucanian	dS	32	38	12
EXTREME SOUTH OF SOUTH AMERICA					
Tehuelche	Chon	?S	33	34	11
Ona	Chon	?S	14	44	6

(continued)

Table 6.1. *(continued)*

Language Case	Genetic Group	*ei*	%	*t*	*l*
NORTHEASTERN SOUTH AMERICA TROPICAL FOREST					
Chaque	Carib	?S	48	40	19
Taurepän	Carib	dS/P	43	40	17
Uarao	Uarao	dS/E/Du	42	53	22
Insular Carib (1665–1666)	Maipuran	?S/E?/F	31	35	11
NORTH-CENTRAL SOUTH AMERICA TROPICAL FOREST					
Arawak	Maipuran	dS/E/Du	69	32	22
Chayahuita	Cahuapanan	?S	68	59	40
Campa (1979–1980)	Maipuran	?S	67	33	22
Huambisa	Jivaroan	?S	66	38	25
Guahibo	Guahiban	?S	66	38	25
Guajira (1963–1977)	Maipuran	dS	65	57	37
Aguaruna	Jivaroan	?S	62	42	26
Piro	Maipuran	?S	62	61	38
Guajira (1878–1913)	Maipuran	dS	60	45	27
Ticuna	Isolate	?S/P	59	41	24
Cayuvava	Isolate	?S	52	31	16
Guarayo	Tupí-Guaraní	dS	52	33	17
Jíbaro	Jivaroan	?S	50	36	18
Oyampi	Tupí-Guaraní	F/P/Du	50	32	16
Guaraní (1903–1928)	Tupí-Guaraní	dS	49	41	20
Campa (1878–1908)	Maipuran	?S	45	42	19
Guaraní (1947–1987)	Tupí-Guaraní	dS	39	70	27
Piaroa	Salivan	dS	39	51	20
Tupí (Nheengatu dialect)	Tupí-Guaraní	P	35	46	16
Amoishe	Maipuran	?S	32	34	11
Tupí (1854–1894)	Tupí-Guaraní	P	29	42	12
Chiriguano	Tupí-Guaraní	dS	28	46	13
Kaapor	Tupí-Guaraní	P	23	39	9
Guajajara	Tupí-Guaraní	?S/P	21	39	8
Guaraní (c. 1639)	Tupí-Guaraní	dS	21	42	9
Tupí (1950–1979)	Tupí-Guaraní	P	20	49	10
Tupí (1795)	Tupí-Guaraní	P	9	33	3
Tupí (1621)	Tupí-Guaraní	P	0	31	0
CENTRAL SOUTH AMERICA TROPICAL FOREST					
Tucano	Tucanoan	?S/P	38	42	16
Makú	Kalianan	?S/P	34	35	12
Huitoto	Huitotoan	?S	18	39	7
Ocaina	Huitotoan	?S	14	35	5
SOUTH-CENTRAL SOUTH AMERICA TROPICAL FOREST					
Cavineña	Pano-Takanan	?S	63	38	24

Table 6.1. *(continued)*

Language Case	Genetic Group	*ei*	*%*	*t*	*l*
Cashinahua	Pano-Takanan	iS	18	40	7
Cháma	Pano-Takanan	?S	15	33	5
CENTRAL BRAZIL					
Kaingang (1986)	Ge	P	65	65	42
Guaraní (Mbüa dialect)	Tupí-Guaraní	?S/P	37	41	15
Kaingang (1888–1920)	Ge	P	22	36	8
SOUTH AMERICA GRAN CHACO					
Toba (1943–1980)	Guaycuruan	?S	35	51	18
Toba (1884–1925)	Guaycuruan	?S	29	41	12
Mocovi	Guaycuruan	?S	27	33	9
Abipon (c. 1760)	Guaycuruan	?S	22	46	10
Mataco	Matacoan	?S	20	49	10
Vejoz	Matacoan	?S	15	39	6
Ashluslály (1940–1979)	Matacoan	?S	12	42	5
Ashluslály (1915)	Matacoan	?S	9	32	3
Lengua	Maskoian	?S	8	40	3
Choróti	Matacoan	?S	8	39	3
Makká	Matacoan	?S	7	42	3

ei = European influence
% = European loanword percentage
t = total number of items of acculturation labeled in sources for a language
l = total number of items labeled by European loanwords
dS = direct influence of Spanish-speaking people
iS = indirect influence of Spanish-speaking people
?S = influence of Spanish-speaking people, intensity unknown
Da = influence of Danish-speaking people
Du = influence of Dutch-speaking people
E = influence of English-speaking people
F = influence of French-speaking people
G = influence of German-speaking people
N = influence of Norwegian-speaking people
P = influence of Portuguese-speaking people
R = influence of Russian-speaking people

Source: Cecil H. Brown, Lexical acculturation in Native American languages, *Current Anthropology* (1994), 35:95–117, with permission of the University of Chicago Press.

Examination of language cases broken down by type of European influence (excluding the infrequent instances of Danish, German, and Norwegian) reveals a significant pattern (table 6.3): Spanish-, Russian-, and Portuguese-influenced

Table 6.2. Average loanword percentages by culture area.

Average (%)	N	Culture Area
63	15	California
61	1	North Central Andean Region
58	11	North Andean Region
58	17	South Central Andean Region
56	4	South Andean Region
52	63	Middle America
52	5	North America Great Basin
44	28	North-Central South America Tropical Forest
41	3	Central Brazil
41	4	Northeastern South America Tropical Forest
39	23	North America Southwest
32	3	South-Central South America Tropical Forest
31	11	Arctic
27	8	North America Plateau
26	4	Central South America Tropical Forest
24	2	Extreme South of South America
23	19	Subarctic
21	7	North America Northwest Coast
18	11	South America Gran Chaco
14	26	North America Northeast
9	11	North America Southeast
5	16	North America Plains

Source: Adapted from Cecil H. Brown, Lexical acculturation in Native American languages, *Current Anthropology* (1994), 35:95–117, with permission of the University of Chicago Press.

Table 6.3. Number and percentage of Amerindian languages with European loanwords at 35% or above and below 20%, arranged by type of European influence.

European influence	Loanword percentage	
	35% or Above	Below 20%
Dutch	4 (44%)	5 (56%)
English	41 (35%)	75 (65%)
French	5 (10%)	46 (90%)
Portuguese	5 (71%)	2 (29%)
Russian	9 (90%)	1 (10%)
Spanish	129 (77%)	38 (23%)

Source: Cecil H. Brown, Lexical acculturation in Native American languages, *Current Anthropology* (1994), 35:95–117, with permission of the University of Chicago Press.

languages tend to show percentages of 35 or more, whereas English- and French-influenced languages tend to show percentages below 20. When language cases only indirectly influenced by Spanish are removed from consideration, the number of Spanish-influenced cases that show percentages at or above 35 is 125 (86%), and a mere 21 (14%) show percentages below 20. Direct Spanish influence appears to have strongly motivated adoption of Spanish loans. In contrast, where direct Spanish influence has not been a factor, Amerindian languages have been disinclined to borrow European terms for items of acculturation. These findings, paralleling the results of Voegelin and Hymes's (1953) pilot study, indicate that the type of European influence has played a strongly determinant role in lexical acculturation in Native American languages.

Bilingualism

As noted, Bright (1960a:233) relates the degree of lexical borrowing from European languages by California Indian languages to the degree of bilingualism (in a native and a European language). In brief, he proposes that speakers of California languages primarily influenced by Spanish-American culture have experienced more bilingualism in the past than have speakers of California languages primarily influenced by Anglo-American culture. As a consequence, according to Bright, speakers of Spanish-influenced languages have been significantly more disposed to borrow Spanish terms for items of acculturation than those of English-influenced languages have been inclined to borrow English terms.

Bright (1960a) provides no data to support his proposal that bilingualism is the determining factor. This omission is hardly surprising. Compiling such information would be difficult, if not impossible, given that detailed data on levels of bilingualism have been systematically recorded for only a few contemporary Amerindian groups and probably not at all for Native American peoples in the past. Despite such shortcomings, it seems reasonable to assume that the regional patterns observed here are explained by regional differences in bilingualism. Indeed, enough is known about the postconquest experiences of Native American peoples to indicate that in general speakers of English-influenced languages were significantly less bilingual than speakers of Spanish-influenced languages.

The histories of native peoples of North America not influenced by Spanish are characterized by exploitation, forced migrations, removal to reservations, and lack of any long-term government and/or religious programs to integrate them culturally, socially, and linguistically into the dominant culture (see Berkhofer 1978). As a result, very few North American Indians are strongly bicultural today. Instead, they have either retained traditional cultural patterns or totally replaced them with those of the dominant culture. This has almost certainly resulted in a general failure to develop extensive and sustained bilingualism. While it is true that many contemporary Amerindians in Anglo-influenced areas of North America speak English, many now lack knowledge of their native tongue. In most instances they have probably learned English without bilingualism as a significant intervening developmental stage. Such developments in part explain why many North American Indian languages are now extinct or close to extinction. Diamond succinctly summarizes the situation for Native Americans of the United States:

[W]e [have] insisted that Indians could be "civilized" and taught English only by removing children from the "barbarous" atmosphere of their parents' homes to English-language-only boarding schools, where use of Indian languages was absolutely forbidden and punished with physical abuse and humiliation . . . . The usual result is that minority young adults tend to become bilingual, then their children become monolingual in the majority language. Eventually the minority language is spoken only by older people, until the last of them dies. (1993:82)

In contrast, while Spanish conquerors certainly exploited Native Americans, Indian groups that were under the direct influence of Spanish-American culture were systematically brought into colonial society by both religious and secular authorities. The manner in which this was done had the effect of creating "creolized" cultures (Gillin 1947; Voegelin and Hymes 1953). "Creolization" entailed the retention of native languages by those Indians who came to learn the language of their conquerors and, consequently, promoted sustained bilingualism for many Latin American Indian groups.

Russian influence (in Alaska) also seems to have promoted lexical borrowing (see table 6.3). There are certain parallels between Russian and Spanish contact activities in the New World. Russian and Spanish administrators directly incorporated native peoples into the work forces of their colonial communities. The multiethnic character of these communities promoted bilingualism and, consequently, lexical borrowing. In contrast, Anglo-Americans typically did not integrate native peoples into work forces but, rather, imported laborers from Africa or used inexpensive European workers (Kent Lightfoot, personal communication). In addition, both Spanish Catholic and Russian Orthodox churches, in contrast to Anglo-American Protestants, were historically persistent (and successful) in their attempts to convert Native Americans.

Direct documentation of the influence of bilingualism on lexical borrowing has yet to be assembled—an observation first made some years ago by Martinet (1952:7). Probably as a consequence, few if any textbooks dealing with language contact discuss a possible causal connection between bilingualism and borrowing. For example, a contemporary text entitled *Language Contact and Bilingualism* (Appel and Muysken 1987) fails to mention this possibility either in its chapter devoted to lexical borrowing or anywhere else. To my knowledge, the only serious attempt to link these phenomena is a study by Poplack, Sankoff, and Miller (1988), but this treatment does not focus so much on the degree of bilingualism as on individual bilingual proficiency in English and French.

Perhaps this study will stimulate scholars to undertake investigations of the relationship between bilingualism and lexical borrowing, including not only quantification of bilingualism for individual borrowing groups (especially those of the past) but also examination of what kinds of bilingualism are relevant to lexical borrowing. As Kroskrity (1982:68) points out, we are ignorant of the kinds and degrees of bilingualism that may facilitate lexical diffusion. Does it matter whether bilingualism is societal or individual in nature (Gumperz 1962:34; Miller 1978:614)? For example, Lehman proposes "that often all that is needed for the borrowing of foreign terms may be the existence of a small number of persons who *are* bilingual and who are socially well-placed in the recipient population" (1994:110). Similarly, Casson (1994:109) notes that in thirteenth- and fourteenth-century England, only a small number of educated people spoke Latin, but nonetheless hundreds of Latin words entered English through translations of scholarly works. Does it matter whether code switching or diglossia is involved? Whether the donor language is used mainly as a trade language or is in general usage? What role might "incipient bilingualism" (Diebold 1961) play in lexical borrowing?

Proulx in response to an earlier presentation of this subject (Brown 1994), suggests that observed areal patterns in borrowing may be due to "Spaniards' and Russians' having colonized for the most part more sedentary people and the French and the English more nomadic ones" (Proulx 1994:112). This suggests that the degree of lexical borrowing is associated with the mode of subsistence, sedentary people being agricultural, and nomadic people largely nonagricultural (cf. Brown 1985a). While I was initially inclined to entertain this suggestion (Brown 1994:113), close examination of cross-language materials assembled here indicates that it has little if any merit.

It is highly likely that the experiences of speakers of languages of North America not influenced by Spanish have been uniformly different from those of speakers of Spanish-influenced languages of Latin America (Gillin 1947). Clearly, the fact that speakers of the former languages have strongly resisted lexical borrowing while speakers of the latter have freely adopted European loans is linked to these different historical conditions.

Structural Features of Languages

The findings discussed here do not necessarily rule out the possible influence of language structure features on lexical borrowing. If such features are influential, languages with similar structural features should show similar degrees of lexical borrowing. This hypothesis can be tested by observing lexical borrowing in languages that are closely related genetically, the assumption being that they have retained many, if not most, of the structural features of their common parent language and consequently are structurally similar.

Mixco (1977), for example, has observed that Kiliwa, a language of the Yuman family spoken in Baja California, has been remarkably resistant to the importation of Spanish terms. Kiliwa constitutes a case in the current sample and shows the lowest possible European loan percentage—zero. In contrast, other Yuman languages, such as Diegueño, spoken in southern California, have freely incorporated Spanish loans. Diegueño is also a case in the current sample, with an exceptionally high European loanword percentage—80. Mixco writes, "[S]ince Kiliwa is in no relevant way structurally unique *vis-à-vis* its sister [Yuman] languages, the reason for the small number of loanwords cannot be sought in structural difference" (p. 20). Instead he argues that Kiliwa's resistance to borrowing is based on the fact that speakers of the language have successfully resisted proselytizing by Spanish-speaking clerics.

When language cases are classified by their genetic group, it is apparent that there is considerable variation in the degree of lexical borrowing among those that are closely related. European loan percentages for Uto-Aztecan languages (table 6.4) range from a high of 97 to a low of 17 and percentages for Athapascan-Eyak languages (table 6.5) from 72 to 2. Assuming the structural similarity of languages of each grouping (because of common inheritance) and the considerable diversity of

Table 6.4. European loanword percentages and European influence in Uto-Aztecan languages.

Language	Loanword Percentage	European Influence
Cupeño	97	dS/E
Cahuilla	94	dS/E
Yaqui	83	dS
Cora	80	dS
Pipil	79	dS
Cahita	78	dS
Nahuatl (Tetelcingo)	78	dS
Pima	76	dS/E
Nahuatl (Xalitla)	75	dS
Panamint Shoshone	71	?S/E
Kawaiisu	70	?S/E
Tarahumara (1915–1920)	57	dS
Nahuatl (1611)	53	dS
Huichol	52	dS
Tarahumara (1952–1972)	49	dS
Nahuatl (Sierra de Zacapoaxtla)	46	dS
Nahuatl (Huazalinguillo dialect)	42	dS
Southern Ute	38	iS/E
Nahuatl (1571)	36	dS
Big Smokey Valley Shoshoni	35	?S/E
Hopi	28	iS/E
Ute (1849–1880)	18	?S/E
Comanche	17	iS/E/F
Average	59	

Source: Cecil H. Brown, Lexical acculturation in Native American languages, *Current Anthropology* (1994), 35:95–117, with permission of the University of Chicago Press.

lexical borrowing observed, we can conclude that language structure in these instances has had little if any influence on lexical acculturation.

Mayan and Otomanguean language cases from Middle America also show considerable internal variation in the extent of lexical borrowing. European loanword percentages for Mayan languages (table 6.6) range from 91 to 9 and percentages for Otomanguean (table 6.7) from 77 to 4. These further instances of diversity in lexical borrowing among structurally similar languages again suggest that language structure plays at most a small role in lexical acculturation.

Since all of the Mayan and Otomanguean languages have been directly influenced by Spanish speakers, the observed variation among them in lexical borrowing cannot be explained by differences in the type of European influence. Some diversity may be due to the fact that sources for some Mayan and Otomanguean language cases were compiled early in the colonial period, when the languages were not subject to Spanish influence to the same degree as contemporary ones. Language purism may explain

Table 6.5. European loanword percentages and European influence in Athapascan-Eyak languages.

Language	Loanword Percentage	European Influence
Tanaina	72	R/E
Central Koyukon	52	R/E
Ingalik	47	R/E
Minto (Lower Tanana)	47	R/E
Ahtna	43	R/E
Jicarilla Apache	40	dS/E
Mescalero Apache	30	?S/E
Carrier	29	E/F
Eyak	25	R/E
Northern Tutchone	22	E/F
Western Apache	20	iS/E
Navajo (1910)	18	iS/E
Navajo (1950–1980)	18	iS/E
Gwichin (1976)	17	E/F
Chipewyan	13	E/F
Apache (1870s and 1880s)	11	?S/E
Beaver	8	E/F
Slave	7	E/F
Montagnais (Chipewyan)	6	E/F
Gwichin (1876)	2	E/F
Peaux-de-Lièvres (Hare)	2	E/F
Average	25	

Source: Cecil H. Brown, Lexical acculturation in Native American languages, *Current Anthropology* (1994), 35:95–117, with permission of the University of Chicago Press.

some instances of variation. For example, Jane Hill (1994:110) notes that the late nineteenth century was a period of extreme purism for speakers of Yucatec (Mayan). This is roughly the period of lexical sources for Yucatec (1850–1883), a Middle America language case that shows an exceptionally low European loan percentage (9) among languages of the region. William Bright (personal communication) notes that the concept of "language purism" needs to be used with care, there being a tendency to say that loanwords are lacking because of purist attitudes and the only evidence offered is the dearth of loans (for further discussion of this topic, see chapter 7). Other diversity is probably linked to historical differences in the extent of interaction with speakers of Spanish. A few differences may simply be due to more faithful reporting of loanwords by some lexical sources.

In some instances, for example, Salishan, Siouan, Iroquoian, and Muskogean (tables 6.8–6.11), language cases in the same genetic grouping show very little variation in the degree of lexical borrowing. This might be construed as evidence that structural features of languages do significantly affect lexical acculturation, but a more likely explanation involves, once again, the type of European influence. All of these languages have historically been influenced primarily by English and/or French, and the vast majority of languages so influenced show very low European loanword

Table 6.6. European loanword percentages and European influence in Mayan languages.

Language	Loanword Percentage	European Influence
Mocho	91	dS
Ixil	78	dS
Pocomam	78	dS
Tzotzil (Zinacantán, 1950–1975)	77	dS
Tojolabal	75	dS
Tzotzil (San Bartolome)	74	dS
Jacaltec	71	dS
Kekchi	69	dS
Aguacatec	68	dS
Mopan	68	dS
North Mam	68	dS
Tzeltal (Bachajón)	67	dS
Tzotzil (San Andrés)	61	dS
Cakchiquel (1956–1981)	60	dS
Tzeltal (Tenejapa)	58	dS
Chol (Tila)	57	dS
Cakchiquel (c. 1650)	44	dS
Cakchiquel (Central)	43	dS
Tzotzil (Zinacantán, late sixteenth century)	39	dS
Huastec	38	dS
Quiche	37	dS
Tzeltal (1888)	22	dS
Yucatec (1850–1883)	9	dS
Average	59	

Source: Cecil H. Brown, Lexical acculturation in Native American languages, *Current Anthropology* (1994), 35:95–117, with permission of the University of Chicago Press.

percentages, almost certainly because English and French have not for the most part promoted incorporation of European words.

While all this evidence indicates little structural influence on lexical borrowing, there is nonetheless some evidence to the contrary. Four of five language cases of Middle America that have exceptionally low European loanword percentages (below 13) are affiliated with Otomanguean: Zapotec (sixteenth century), Amuzgo, Chinantec (Ojitlán), and Mixtec (1593). The fifth case is Yucatec (1850–1880) which, as previously explained, possibly shows a low percentage because of language purism. These four languages and other Otomanguean languages differ from all other Amerindian languages of Middle America in being tonal in structure. Zapotec's and Mixtec's low percentages perhaps can be attributed to the early dates of compilation of their sources. Statistics assembled in a Mexican census in 1970 show that among all Mexican Indian groups surveyed, Amuzgo has the lowest level of bilingualism, possibly contributing to the language's strong tendency to avoid Spanish loanwords.

Table 6.7. European loanword percentages and European influence in Otomanguean languages.

Language	Loanword Percentage	European Influence
Zapotec (Mitla)	77	dS
Popoloca (San Vicente Coyoctepec)	66	dS
Cuicatec	62	dS
Trique (Copala)	61	dS
Zapotec (Juárez)	61	dS
Otomi (Santiago Mexquititlán)	55	dS
Mazahua	49	dS
Otomi (1826–1841)	47	dS
Ixcatec	46	dS
Trique (Chicahuaxtla)	41	dS
Chatino (Tataltepec)	35	dS
Pame	34	dS
Mixtec (Chayuco)	30	dS
Mixtec (San Juan Colorado)	29	dS
Otomi (Mezquital dialect)	26	dS
Otomi (c. 1770)	26	dS
Zapotec (1578)	21	dS
Zapotec (sixteenth century)	12	dS
Amuzgo	9	dS
Chinantec (Ojitlán)	5	dS
Mixtec (1593)	4	dS
Average	38	

Source: Cecil H. Brown, Lexical acculturation in Native American languages, *Current Anthropology* (1994), 35:95–117, with permission of the University of Chicago Press.

Table 6.8. European loanword percentages and European influence in Salishan languages.

Language	Loanword Percentage	European Influence
Squamish	36	E/F
Okanagan (Colville)	34	E/F
Shuswap	32	E/F
Songish (North Straits Salish)	26	E/F
Thompson (Nitklakapamuk)	21	E/F
Kalispel	16	E/F
Average	28	

Source: Cecil H. Brown, Lexical acculturation in Native American languages, *Current Anthropology* (1994), 35:95–117, with permission of the University of Chicago Press.

Table 6.9. European loanword percentages and European influence in Siouan languages.

Language	Loanword Percentage	European Influence
Biloxi	7	iS/E/F
Dakota (Santee dialect)	4	E
Dakota (Teton dialect, 1866)	4	E
Osage	3	iS/E
Crow	2	E/F?
Hidatsa	2	E
Mandan	2	E
Dakota (Teton dialect, 1970–1974)	0	E
Ofo	0	E/F
Average	3	

Source: Cecil H. Brown, Lexical acculturation in Native American languages, *Current Anthropology* (1994), 35:95–117, with permission of the University of Chicago Press.

Table 6.10. European loanword percentages and European influence in Iroquoian languages.

Language	Loanword Percentage	European Influence
Mohawk	14	E/F/Du
Iroquois	13	E/F
Onondaga (eighteenth century)	9	E/F/Du
Oneida	8	E/F/Du
Cherokee	7	iS/E
Onondaga (seventeenth century)	6	E/F/Du
Seneca	4	E/F
Average	9	

Source: Cecil H. Brown, Lexical acculturation in Native American languages, *Current Anthropology* (1994), 35:95–117, with permission of the University of Chicago Press.

Table 6.11. European loanword percentages and European influence in Muskogean languages.

Language	Loanword Percentage	European Influence
Choctaw	17	iS/E/F
Creek	16	iS/E/
Alabama	13	iS/E/F
Koasati	12	iS/E/F
Chickasaw	11	iS/E/F
Average	14	

Source: Cecil H. Brown, Lexical acculturation in Native American languages, *Current Anthropology* (1994), 35:95–117, with permission of the University of Chicago Press.

At the same time, census figures show a level of bilingualism for speakers of Chinantec that is well within the range of that for speakers of Mexican Indian languages that have high European loanword percentages.

Table 6.12 gives the mean European loanword percentages of all genetic groupings of languages spoken in Middle America. The mean for Otomanguean languages (38) is substantially lower than that for other Middle American genetic groupings. Otomanguean languages of the current sample are all spoken in Mexico. The mean for Otomanguean is also significantly lower than that for all Mexican language cases from Middle America minus Otomanguean cases—56%. In addition, the mean, 62, for non-Otomanguean languages spoken in the same Mexican states as Otomanguean languages is significantly greater than the Otomanguean mean. If the degree of Spanish influence on speakers of Otomanguean languages in the past is in no substantial way different from that of speakers of other Amerindian languages of Mexico,

Table 6.12. Mean European loanword percentages for genetic groupings of languages spoken in Middle America.

Mean Loanword Percentage	Language Grouping
38	Otomanguean
47	Mixe-Zoque
59	Mayan
60	Uto-Aztecan
64	Others[*]

[*]These include Huave (San Mateo), Tarascan (1559), Tequistlatec, Totonac (Xicotepec de Juárez), and Totonac (La Sierra dialect).

Source: Cecil H. Brown, Lexical acculturation in Native American languages, *Current Anthropology* (1994), 35:95–117, with permission of the University of Chicago Press.

Otomanguean resistance to lexical borrowing is better explained by language structure factors than by sociolinguistic ones.

Evidence from the 1970 Mexican census strongly suggests the uniformity of Spanish-language influence on Otomanguean and other Mexican Indian languages. The census reports the degree of bilingualism (in a native language and Spanish) for speakers of 30 Amerindian languages, 10 of which are in the Otomanguean grouping. The average percentage of bilingualism for Otomanguean languages is 68, compared with a mean percentage of 71 for all others. The difference is obviously not significant, and this can be taken to suggest that the low mean European loanword percentage for Otomanguean languages is due to structural resistance to lexical borrowing rather than to sociolinguistic factors like the degree of bilingualism.

This finding for Otomanguean languages is curious given Haugen's (1956:66) claim that languages with unified, unanalyzed words easily accept loanwords. Tonal languages typically show this structural feature. Thus, it is surprising that Otomanguean languages are found to be more resistant to lexical borrowing than are nontonal languages of Middle America.

Additional evidence suggests that language structure occasionally influences lexical acculturation. Table 6.13 gives mean loanword percentages for genetic groupings of languages of North America that have been primarily influenced by English and/or French. That the average loanword percentage for Salishan languages is substantially greater than those for the other North American groupings may possibly be explained by language structure factors peculiar to Salishan languages. However, this may be explained more plausibly by the fact that speakers of Salishan languages were heavily

Table 6.13. Mean European loanword percentages for genetic groupings of languages primarily influenced by English and/or French.

Mean Loanword Percentage	Language Grouping
28	Salishan
17	Eskimo*
15	Others+
14	Muskogean
12	Athapascan*
12	Algonquian
9	Iroquoian
3	Siouan

*Mean percentages are based on loanword percentages for all languages of Eskimo and Athapascan-Eyak except those influenced by Russian.

+These include Arikara, Atakapa, Comanche, Gitksan, Haida, Haisla, Heiltsuk (Kwakiutl dialect), Kiowa, Klamath (1963), Klamath (1890), Natchez, Nez Perce, Quileute, Tonkawa, Tunica, and Yakima (Sahaptin dialect).

Source: Cecil H. Brown, Lexical acculturation in Native American languages, *Current Anthropology* (1994), 35:95–117, with permission of the University of Chicago Press.

influenced by a regional lingua franca, Chinook Jargon, which could have promoted the indirect borrowing of both English and French words (see chapter 11). Indirect borrowing refers to the diffusion of European loanwords from some Amerindian groups to others without the direct involvement of European-language speakers (see especially chapter 9). The role of lingua francas in the diffusion of terms for acculturated items is discussed in detail in chapters 8–11.

Finally, there may be evidence of language structure influence on lexical acculturation for languages spoken in South America's Gran Chaco region. Gran Chaco language cases having European loanword percentages of 22 or greater are all in the Guaycuruan genetic grouping, whereas those language cases with loanword percentages below 21 are all in the Matacoan grouping—with the exception of Lengua, which is Maskoian (see table 6.1). If Spanish influence on indigenous groups has been roughly uniform in the region since contact, the greater tendency of Guaycuruan languages to incorporate Spanish loans and/or the lesser tendency of Matacoan languages to do so is probably explained by language structure factors. However, this difference may be due to regional differences in Spanish influence; all Guaycuruan languages are spoken in the Argentine Chaco, while most Matacoan languages are in the Paraguayan Chaco.

Conclusion

The preceding analysis suggests that if language structure factors affect lexical borrowing, they do so only minimally. On the other hand, sociolinguistic factors, especially bilingualism, seem to have substantially influenced the degree to which European loans are adopted by Amerindian languages. This accords with Thomason and Kaufman's (1988) observation that language structure is subordinated to bilingualism in affecting the borrowing of grammatical features (but see Silva-Corvalán 1994 for a contrary view). Other factors, in addition to bilingualism, such as language purism (chapter 7) and indirect borrowing (chapter 9), may have also figured into processes of lexical acculturation in Native American languages. The relative importance of these factors could perhaps be ascertained through detailed investigation of individual language cases, but they clearly have not been important enough to mask the substantial effect on lexical borrowing of the type of European influence and consequent extent of bilingualism.

7

LEXICAL REPLACEMENT

In accord with the proposal that the extent of lexical borrowing is positively influenced by the degree of bilingualism is Casagrande's distinction between "primary accommodation" and "secondary accommodation" in contact situations. He relates this contrast to the four principal means by which languages enlarge their vocabularies to deal with new objects and ideas (see chapter 3):

> No knowledge of the language of an impinging culture is required for meaning extensions or new coinages and only native linguistic materials are used. This is designated PRIMARY ACCOMMODATION. A minimum knowledge of a donor language is necessary for linguistic borrowing in the form of either loanwords or loan-translations. Such linguistic borrowing is termed SECONDARY ACCOMMODATION. (1955:22)

Casagrande's (1955) proposal can be fleshed out as follows: when an Amerindian group first encounters a European language, few if any members will speak it in addition to their native tongue. Thus, in the initial stages of contact, loanwords for items introduced by Europeans tend not to be adopted because of the group's general lack of familiarity with the lexicon of the donor language; rather, introduced items are named with familiar native vocabulary. As familiarity with the European language increases—for example, as more and more members of the group become bilingual—the possibility is enhanced that words for introduced items from the donor language will gain currency in the recipient language and become established loans. This would entail both the acquisition of loanwords for previously unknown items and the *lexical replacement* of native terms by loanwords for items acquired and named earlier (during primary accommodation).

Lexical replacement here refers to the substitution in a Native American language of one term for an acculturated item by another term (cf. Brown 1989a:548–549). The type of replacement just described, in which a native word is displaced by a European loan, is formally called *European loan replacement*. There are other types of lexical replacement, including substitution of a European loan for an acculturated item by a native term, called *native term replacement*; displacement of a native term by another native word; and replacement of a European loan by another European loan. Among these different types, European loan replacement appears to have been most common in Amerindian languages.

Many of the 292 language cases comprise two or more time states of the same language, for example, Klamath (1890) and Klamath (1963); Tzotzil (Zinacantán, late sixteenth century) and Tzotzil (Zinacantán, 1950–1975); and Cheyenne (1862), Cheyenne (1915), and Cheyenne (1976–1984). In the vast majority of instances (82%), later time states show higher European loanword percentages than earlier time states (see table 6.1). This indicates that over time native terms have tended to be replaced by European loans for items of acculturation and, thus, that European loan replacement has frequently taken place in Native American languages.

A central hypothesis of this chapter is that European loan replacement has regularly developed with a shift from primary to secondary accommodation. Earlier time states of Amerindian languages generally would have entailed primary accommodation, and later states secondary accommodation. European loan percentages of later time states generally are larger than those of earlier time states, suggesting frequent European loan replacement when languages have proceeded from primary to secondary accommodation. In addition, there is direct evidence in the form of diachronic linguistic data assembled by Lockhart (1992) in his book, *The Nahuas After the Conquest.*

Nahuatl and European Loan Replacement

Nahuatl is a Uto-Aztecan language widely spoken today in Mexico. This language is represented in the current sample by six language cases, comprising different time states and dialects. The language is probably best known as the speech of the Aztec (Nahuas) who ruled a substantial portion of Middle America at the time of the Spanish invasion. Nahuatl, an areal lingua franca before the conquest, continued as such afterward. The Spanish promoted the language as a primary vehicle of administration, evangelization, and commercial interaction in many parts of New Spain (Heath 1972:15–27; Gerhard 1979:166; Suárez 1983:163–168; Edmonson 1984:345; Cotton and Sharp 1988:96–97). For this and other reasons, textual materials written in Nahuatl (using Spanish orthography) were produced in considerable abundance from the time shortly following the conquest through most of the colonial period. As a result among Amerindian languages the postcontact history of Nahuatl is especially well documented. In recent years, scholars have produced several important works, focusing on historical changes in the language through the analysis of Nahuatl textual materials (e.g., Karttunen and Lockhart 1976; Karttunen 1985; Lockhart 1992:261–325).

Lockhart recognizes three stages in the history of postcontact Nahuatl:

Stage 1, from the arrival of the Spaniards in 1519 to a time that can be set at between 1540 and 1550, was characterized by virtually no change in Nahuatl, Stage 2, extending from then until close to the mid-seventeeth century, saw massive borrowing of Spanish nouns, but the language remained little altered in other respects. Stage 3, with some advance signs coming earlier in the seventeenth century, stretches from about 1640–50 until today, wherever Nahuatl is spoken, and involves a deeper and broader Spanish influence betraying widespread bilingualism.

Of special interest here is Lockhart's characterization of the whole process: "[I]t is evident that the stages correspond to the increasing frequency and intensity of contact between Nahuas and Spaniards, eventually leading to the formation and expansion of a group of bilinguals who served as an open channel between the two speech communities." It is also apparent that Lockhart's stages for Nahuatl are isomorphic with the bipartite distinction drawn by Casagrande, wherein stage 1 represents primary accommodation and stages 2 and 3, respectively, lesser and more advanced levels of secondary accommodation.

Lockhart (1992:263), in discussing stage 1 in more detail, describes early situations that were not conducive to the acquisition of the Spanish language by significant portions of the Nahuatl-speaking populace (or, for that matter, of Nahuatl by Spanish-speaking people). For a couple of decades after conquest hostilities ceased, very few Spaniards actually resided in New Spain, and those that did were concentrated for the most part only in a very small number of broadly scattered cities and were reluctant to leave them for reasons other than dire necessity. This was the period before the development of a colonial economy, in which many indigenous peoples would be part of work forces mobilized by the Spaniards (e.g., in the silver industry, which developed in the 1540s). For the most part, the only groups of Nahuatl speakers who communicated with Spaniards on a regular basis were a small number of people, such as aides and students of Spanish clerics and servants of laity.

> Thus contact between the two populations as such can hardly be said to have existed [in stage 1], and linguistic adaptation was consequently almost nil, even though the Nahuas were experiencing new things and finding ways to express them. The new came to them in the form of direct experience of objects and actions rather than in words. They were seeing things rather than hearing about them ... Little or nothing was being borrowed ... the Nahuas were mainly not reacting to Spanish linguistically at all, but denominating in their own language out of its own means certain phenomena that they had directly observed. Lockhart (1992:263, 269)

This is unambiguously a description of primary accommodation among early postcontact speakers of Nahuatl.

Lockhart (1992:263–284) gives numerous examples of native terms coined for imported objects and concepts in stage 1 Nahuatl, including neologisms for many items on my list of 77. Nahuatl words for Spanish musical instruments are particularly notable, with labels such as "rope drum" for GUITAR, "hide something-blown drum" for ORGAN, and "metal conch horn" for TRUMPET. Lockhart's list of stage 1 native terms for European domesticated animals is extensive, encompassing all those on the list of 77 plus YEARLING and DOMESTIC DUCK. Many of these are based on Nahuatl words for New World analogs such as *maçatl* "deer" for HORSE, *totolin* "turkey" for CHICKEN, *coyametl* "peccary" for PIG, and *canauhtli* "wild duck" for DOMESTIC DUCK. Others are descriptive, for example, *quaquauhe* "one with horns" for COW, *tentzone* "bearded one" for GOAT, and *quanaca* "head flesh" for ROOSTER (referring to the bird's comb). One other—*ichcatl*, referring to both COTTON and SHEEP—is either an extended construction or derived through secondary polysemy (see chapters 3 and 11).

Stage 1 was supplanted by stage 2 after only 20 or 30 years following the initial Spanish intrusion. This second period, lasting approximately 100 years, is described by Lockhart as one in which "Nahuas were hearing and reacting to the spoken Spanish words, not just watching what happened" (1992:285). Clearly, as Lockhart suggests, stage 2 speakers of Nahuatl were becoming more and more bilingual. As a result, Nahuatl tended to incorporate any Spanish loan into its lexicon as long as it was grammatically a noun. Stage 3, characterized by ever greater levels of bilingualism, saw the relaxation of the latter restriction so that Spanish verbs and other parts of speech found their way into the language (p. 304).

One important effect of a shift from stage 1 to later stages was the replacement of native terms for many acculturated items by Spanish loanwords. Lockhart writes, for example, "With Stage 2, the Nahuas would quickly begin to borrow the Spanish words for nearly all the current introduced [musical] instruments" (1992:283). Even so, as Lockhart adds, some Stage 1 terms for musical instruments were still heard in later periods in various parts of New Spain where Nahuatl was spoken.

Perhaps no other lexical domain underwent more extensive replacement than that of domesticated animals. Table 7.1 is an adaptation of a table in Lockhart's (1992) book in which he compares stage 2 and 3 terms for introduced creatures with those of stage 1. For example, *maçatl* "deer" is identified as the stage 1 label for HORSE, which was replaced in later stages by the Spanish "horse" term, *caballo* (also written in sources for Nahuatl as *cahuallo*). Stage 1 terms in parentheses—for example, that for MARE—are not actually found in textual materials for Nahuatl but have been reconstructed by Lockhart based on strongly suggestive internal evidence. In some instances, loan blends with Spanish terms have replaced native labels: for example, the stage 2 and 3 word for MARE is *cihuacahuallo*, which is made up of the Nahuatl word for FEMALE (*cihua*) and the Spanish loan for HORSE. Native terms for animals replaced by Spanish loans or loan blends include words for HORSE, MARE, COLT, MULE, DONKEY, SHEEP, COW, OX, CALF, YEARLING, and DOMESTIC DUCK. Stage 1 native words for GOAT, PIG, ROOSTER, CHICKEN, and CAT were not similarly replaced in later stages.

Native Term Replacement

While no summary statistics are presented by Lockhart (1992), European loan replacement appears to have been the predominant form of lexical replacement after the shift from stage 1 Nahuatl. Lockhart does not discuss other replacement possibilities for Nahuatl, such as later stage displacement by native terms of earlier European (Spanish) loans for introduced items (i.e., native term replacement). This may be a simple omission, but for reasons mentioned by Lockhart—and discussed presently—it more likely reflects a true nonevent in the colonial history of Nahuatl.

Herzog cites examples of native term replacement in the postcontact history of Pima (Uto-Aztecan, Arizona), which he divides into three distinct periods: (1) an era of contact with Spanish culture, entailing colonization from Mexico, roughly between 1700 and 1850, during which words for new cultural acquisitions were mostly adopted from Spanish; (2) the "early reservation" period, which began with the American occupation and lasted until around 1920, during which the "overwhelming majority of terms to be allocated [were] Pima descriptive formations"; and (3) the "modern

Table 7.1. Nahuatl terms for main European domesticated animals in a chronological perspective.

Stage 1 (before c. 1540)		Stages 2 and 3 (after c. 1540)
HORSE	maçatl, "deer"	caballo(S) (cahuallo[S]), "horse"
MARE	(probably cihuamaçatl "female deer")	first cihuacahuallo(lb), "female horse," then yegua(S), "mare"
COLT	(probably maçaconetl, "young of the deer")	first cahualloconetl(lb), "young of the horse," then potro(S), "colt"
MULE	(probably subsumed under maçatl)	mula(S), macho(S), "female and male mule"
DONKEY	(probably subsumed under maçatl)	asno(S), "donkey"
SHEEP	ichcatl, "cotton"	still ichcatl; carnero(S), "sheep, mutton," especially for the meat
COW	quaquauhe, "one with horns"	vaca(S) or vacas(S) "cow"
BULL	quaquauhe	first quaquauhe, then toro(S), "bull"
OX	quaquauhe	first quaquauhe, then buey(S), "ox"
CALF	quaquaheconetl, "young of those with horns"	(probably ternero[S], becerro[S], "calf")
YEARLING	telpochtli quaquahe, "adolescent one with horns"	novillo(S), "yearling"
GOAT	(quaquauhe) tentzone, "bearded one (with horns)"	tentzone
PIG	pitzotl, probably "peccary"; coyametl, "peccary"	pitzotl becomes predominant
ROOSTER	Caxtillan huexolotl (lb), "Castile turkey cock"; quanaca, "(one with) head flesh"	quanaca continues to some extent
CHICKEN	Caxtillan totolin (lb), "Castile turkey hen"; caxtil(S), back-formation from Caxtillan, "Castille; also quanaca as for rooster	mainly totolin or pollo(S), "(young) chicken"; quanaca continues to some extent
CAT	mizton, "little cougar"	still mizton
DUCK*	Caxtillan canauhtli(lb), "Castile wild duck"	pato(S) or patos(S) "duck"

*European domesticated duck.

S = Spanish loanword.

lb = Loan blend of a native term and a Spanish loan (formally treated as a native term).

Source: Adapted from James Lockhart, *The Nahuas after the Conquest* (Stanford, Cal.: Stanford University Press, 1992), with the permission of the publishers. © 1992 by the Board of Trustees of the Leland Stanford Junior University.

reservation" period, in which Pima began more and more to incorporate words from English (1941:69–70).

Herzog describes the transition from the earliest era to the modern reservation period as follows:

> The earlier vocabulary is being gradually displaced. This had already begun to affect the Spanish vocabulary; "wiping thing" was substituted for the Spanish of "towel," "rolled around itself" for "cigar," and "yellow one" or "it sits" (i.e. piled up) for Spanish "centavo." Similarly, in recent years a new English vocabulary has begun to displace some of the Spanish words and more of the descriptive terms of the second period (1941:71).

Thus, not only does Herzog refer to examples of native term replacement in Pima (without, by the way, listing in his work any of the Pima or Spanish terms involved), but he also mentions lexical replacement that entails substitution of earlier European terms (Spanish) by other European terms (English) in subsequent times.

Herzog (1941) offers no explanation for why some Spanish loanwords in Pima should be subsequently replaced by descriptive terms. Similar expunging of European loans from Amerindian languages has been attributed to language purism. Jane Hill (1994:109) calls attention to Bright and Thiel's (1965) study of Tlaxcalan Nahuatl. These authors found that a consultant for the language in a field methods class at UCLA used very few loanwords, preferring Nahuatl terms. However, in their field study of the language, Hill and Hill (1986) discovered that the dialect was riddled with Spanish loans. Jane Hill explains this apparent discrepancy as follows: "The UCLA consultant had assumed an extremely purist stance (also available in Tlaxcala for certain occasions, especially by relatively cosmopolitan middle-aged men, precisely his status) which he felt was appropriate for the classroom study of Nahuatl" (1994:109).

Language purism may have been at work in two dialects of Tewa (Tanoan) spoken in Arizona and New Mexico. Both dialects, like other languages of the southwestern United States, incorporated Spanish loanwords into their lexicons at least as early as the seventeeth century. Arizona Tewa shows substantially fewer Spanish loans than New Mexico Tewa, a possible result of its speakers' relocation from New Mexico to Arizona after the Pueblo Revolt of 1680 and consequent removal from direct Spanish influence. Kroskrity proposes that the migration of Arizona Tewa may not be the entire explanation for so few Spanish words in its vocabulary:

> [T]he scarcity of Spanish loanwords in Arizona Tewa need not be interpreted as evidence of their relative absence at the times of the . . . exodus from the Rio Grande Valley [New Mexico] . . . Spanish loanwords may have been consciously purged from usage because of their symbolic association with Spanish repression. (1993:70–71)

Spicer similarly discusses a later tendency for speakers of New Mexico Tewa to look unfavorably on Spanish loanwords in their language: "[B]y the middle of the 1900 s . . . [s]peakers of Tewa were reported to be aware that many words were borrowed from Spanish and were not part of the Indian language, and so were finding ways to avoid using them." This attitude was apparently realized, leading to the incipient replacement of some Spanish loans by native terms: "[t]he tendency was to coin a new expression in Tewa . . . . There were such alternates for burro, goat, horse, and watermelon, words which had originally been borrowed from Spanish" (1962:450).

As noted, Lockhart's study of the postcontact history of Nahuatl, based primarily on colonial textual materials, does not mention instances in which Spanish loans have been replaced by native terms. He provides a good reason for believing this was not merely an omission. During much of the colonial period, speakers of Nahuatl seemed in no way concerned about Spanish influences on their language:

> Nor is there any indication that the Nahuas resisted or resented loans as in any way suspect, unpatriotic, or damaging to the integrity of their language. The conscious purism that figures in an ongoing dialectic of linguistic evolution in Nahuatl today [see the above discussion of Tlaxcalan Nahuatl and also Hill and Hill (1986)] seems to be the product of a later time. (1992:298)

In the absence of language purism, Spanish loans in colonial Nahuatl were apparently safe from displacement by native terms until very recently.

Language Cases and Lexical Replacement

Tables 7.2 and 7.3 provide detailed information on lexical replacement in two languages, Klamath (isolate, Oregon) and Zinacantán Tzotzil (Mayan, Chiapas, Mexico), based on language cases that include different time states—Klamath (1890) and Klamath (1963) and Tzotzil (Zinacantán, late sixteenth century) and Tzotzil (Zinacantán, 1950–1975). Each table lists words for items of acculturation, including synonyms (separated by a slash), that are found in sources for *both* time states of the two languages. Thirty-nine items have terms from both time states of Klamath, and 46 items from both time states of Zinacantán Tzotzil.

Although the periods between the time states of the two languages are significantly different in length—roughly 70 years between the two states of Klamath versus roughly 400 years between those of Zinacantán Tzotzil—both languages have nonetheless undergone considerable lexical replacement. In both cases, the dominant form of replacement has been the type in which native terms have been displaced by European loans (i.e., European loan replacement), but other types of replacement are also in evidence.

One notable finding is the common occurrence of synonyms for acculturated items; for example, two words, a native term and an English loan, denote ONION in the earlier time state of Klamath (table 7.2), and two words, a native term and a Spanish loan, designate CANDLE in Tzotzil's earlier time state (table 7.3). It is plausible that synonymity constitutes a kind of linguistic variability that arises from ongoing linguistic change, in this case lexical replacement. For example, in the later time state of Klamath, only the English loanword denotes ONION, and in the later version of Tzotzil, only the Spanish loanword designates CANDLE. These results may be endproducts of replacement sequences in which only native terms first denoted ONION and CANDLE (in unattested earlier time states, involving primary accommodation), later to compete with subsequently acquired European loanwords (in attested earlier time states, involving incipient secondary accommodation), and finally to be totally replaced by European loans (in attested later time states, involving full secondary accommodation). In this manner, the synonyms in question may reflect European loan replacement in progress.

Table 7.2. Klamath terms for items of acculturation at different time states.

	Late Nineteenth Century	Mid-Twentieth Century
APPLE	äplĕsh(E)	ʔeˑpal(E)
BOARD	pápkash	papg̱
BOOK	pípa(Ee)	bok(E)
BOTTLE	bunuōˑtkish/wákogsh	baˑdal(E)
BOX	iwX̌ótkish	baˑg(E)/baˑgs(E)
BREAD	shápĕle/pála-ash(Ee)	baˑlʼaˑʼ(Ee)
BULL	shluûlksháltko	lidol(F)
CALF	múshmusham lelédshi	keˑp(E)
CAT	púshish(E)	pʼoˑs(E)/pʼisʔ(E)
CHICKEN	tchíkin(E)/tchîʼkʼn(E)	ǰigin(E)
COFFEE	kōʼpe(E)/kópi(E)	koˑbi(E)
COLT	tX̌á-ush/watcham wéash	tgaˑẅkʼa
COW	múshmush/ktchîʼshlkish	mos
CUP	hashpōˑtkish/pokuága/tutísh/kapa(E)	kap(E)
FLOUR	shápĕle	baˑlʼaˑʼ(E)
FORK	sákta/shkiuX̌iūtch	sek̓ᵛiwdg̱noˑts
HORSE	wátch	wač
HUNDRED	té-unepni té-unep	tewṛipṛi tewnʼip
MATCH	match(E)	maǰ(E)
MULE	limîʼlam(F)	limiˑl(F)
NAIL	tchíkĕmen/sákta	ǰigmin
NEEDLE	spekanótkish	spiqṉoˑts
ONION	ḵó-i piluyéash/ónion(E)	ʔalyan(E)
PAPER	pípa(E)	beyba(E)
PIG	gushu(F)	goso(F)
PISTOL	shikĕnítgish	sikʼnitg
RICH	talaltko(lb)	lag̱i
SATURDAY	she-étish	seʔetʼs
SCISSORS	ktushkótkish	sisoˑ(E)
SHOVEL	köknótkish/sháwel(E)	keˑčṅoˑts
SOLDIER	shûʼldshash(E)	soˑlja(E)
SPOON	mídsho	mičʼoˑ
TABLE	pákʼlgish	teybal(E)
THREAD	skenshnútkish/knúks	gnog̱
TOWN	tchîʼsh/tá-uni(E)	tawn(E)
TURNIP	tánapsh(E)	taˑnab(E)
WAGON	tchíktchik/wäʼgĕn(E)	čʼiˑk/weˑgan(E)
WATERMELON	shánkish=pakísh	sang s pʼaṉkʼys
WEDNESDAY	ndáni tínshna súndē=giulank waíta(lb)	ndaṅniˑks
WHEAT	lólomak/húit(E)	loˑlomaq

E = English loanword.
F = French loanword.
Ee = English loanword whose meaning has been extended to the item of
       acculturation (formally treated as a native term).
lb = Loan blend of a native term and an English loan (formally treated as
       a native term).

Table 7.3. Zinacantán Tzotzil terms for items of acculturation at different time states.

	Late Sixteenth Century	Modern
APPLE	castillan potov(lb)	manȼana(S)
BOARD	jayal te?/tenal te?	tenel te?
BOOK	tzisbil Hun	vun/libro(S)
BOX	pun-te?	kahon(S)/karton(Se)
BREAD	vaj/?ot	kašlan vah(lb)/kašlan ?ot(lb)/pan(S)
BULL	xinch'ok vacas(lb)	toro(S)
CABBAGE	coles(S)	?itah/?o?on vakaš ?itah(lb)
CANDLE	tajleyabil/candela(S)	kantela(S)
CAT	gato(S)/misto(S)	čon/manu?/mašu/mošit/ šalu?/katu?(S)
CHEESE	queso(S)	kešu(S)
CHICKEN	castillan tuluk'(lb)/?alak	kašlan(Se)
CLOCK	?atob ?osil/na?ob ?osil/reloj(S)	reloho(S)
COW	vacas(S)	baka(S)/vakaš(S)
CUP	?uch ?obil/taza(S)	tasa(S)
DONKEY	asna(S)/borrico(S)/pollino(S)	buro(S)
FLOUR	castillan ch'ilim(lb)	harina(S)
GARLIC	ajos(S)	?ašuš(S)
HEN	?antzil tuluk'/tuluk'	me? ?alak/me? kašlan(lb)
HORSE	chij/caballo(S)	ka?(S)
HOUR	j-tij	?ora(S)
HUNDRED	Ho?-vinik	vo?-vinik/syen(S)
KEY	jamob na	yave(S)
LETTUCE	lechuga(S)	lečuka(S)
MARE	?antzil caballo(lb)	yevaš(S)
MONEY	manob/manojeb/tak'in/tomin(Se)	tak'in/sentavo(Se)
MULE	mula(S)	ka?(Se)
NAIL	clavo(S)	lavuš(S)
NEEDLE	aguja(S)	?akuša(S)
ORANGE	naranjas(S)	naranha(S)
OX	chij	wey(S)
PAPER	sakil Hun	vun
PEACH	durasnos(S)	turasnu(S)
PIG	chitom	čitom
RICH	?ayik'aletik	riko(S)
ROOSTER	jkotz/xinch'ok tuluk'	kelem
SATURDAY	?ok'ob xa ?oy Domingo(lb)/ sábado(S)	savaro(S)
SCHOOL	chanob na/chanantasvanab na	čanob vun
SCISSORS	tijeras(S)	tešereš(S)
SHEEP	tuxnok chij	čih
SHOVEL	pech'pech'te?	pala(S)
SOAP	ch'upak'	šavon(S)
SOLDIER	ch'ilom xanav ta?ok	h?ak'-k'ok'/soltaro(S)
TABLE	mesa(S)	meša(S)

Table 7.3. *(continued)*

	Late Sixteenth Century	Modern
THREAD	no/naul	no/naval/ʔilera(Se)
TOWN	j-tek lum/j-tek k'ulej	tek-lumal
WHEAT	castilla ʔixim(lb)	triko(S)

S = Spanish loanword.
Se = Spanish loanword whose meaning has been extended to the item of acculturation (formally treated as a native term).
lb = Loan blend of a native term and a Spanish loan (formally treated as a native term).

Synonyms from later time states may also reflect lexical replacement in progress. For example, later Tzotzil shows both a native term and a Spanish loan for BOOK, whereas its earlier state shows only the native term (in its original, more complex realization). The Spanish loan is a subsequent acquisition, which has partially replaced the native label for BOOK and, very likely, may be in the process of totally replacing it. Other synonyms in tables 7.2 and 7.3 appear to reflect types of lexical replacement in progress in addition to European loan replacement. For example, in the earlier state of Klamath a native term and an English loan both denote SHOVEL, whereas in later Klamath only the native term is in evidence. Similarly, earlier Klamath shows both a native label and an English loan for WHEAT, whereas later Klamath shows only the native term. These examples are interpreted as possibly reflecting native term replacement in progress.

Types of lexical replacement found for Klamath (table 7.2) and Zinacantán Tzotzil (table 7.3), including "in progress" replacement suggested by synonyms, are associated with individual items of acculturation as follows: (1) for European loan replacement, see BOOK, BOTTLE, BOX, BULL, CALF, CUP, FLOUR, ONION, SCISSORS, TABLE, and TOWN (table 7.2), and APPLE, BOOK, BOX, BREAD, BULL, CANDLE, CLOCK, CUP, FLOUR, HORSE, HOUR, HUNDRED, KEY, MARE, MONEY, OX, RICH, SATURDAY, SHOVEL, SOAP, SOLDIER, and WHEAT (table 7.3). Note that here, as elsewhere in this work, European loans that are extended to introduced items and most loan blends are formally treated as if they were native terms. (2) For native term replacement, see SHOVEL and WHEAT (table 7.2) and CABBAGE and MULE (table 7.3). (3) For a native term replaced by another native term, see BREAD, COLT, COW, FORK, NAIL, RICH, and THREAD (table 7.2), and BOARD, CHICKEN, HEN, ROOSTER, SCHOOL, and THREAD (table 7.3). (4) For a European loan replaced by another European loan, see CAT and DONKEY (table 7.3).

Table 7.4 presents statistics relating to lexical replacement in earlier and later time states of selected languages of Latin America. For example, Mapuche(1) compares time states represented by Mapuche (1771) and Mapuche (1944–1990). In several cases, an earlier time state of a language is compared with two or more later time states, for example, Nahuatl(1), Nahuatl(2), and Nahuatl(3), which compare Nahuatl (1571) with, respectively, Nahuatl (Xalita), Nahuatl (Huazalinguillo), and Nahuatl (Sierra de Zacapoaxtla), all modern dialects of the language. In all instances, earlier

Table 7.4. Selected languages of Latin America ranked by European loan replacement percentage (from largest to smallest), with statistics for different time states.

	A	B	C	D	E	F	G
Zapotec(2)	62.0	60.0	2.0	2.0	2.0	0.0	50
Nahuatl(4)	51.2	48.8	2.4	0.0	0.0	0.0	41
Nahuatl(1)	50.0	50.0	0.0	0.0	0.0	0.0	40
Quechua(1)	44.0	32.0	12.0	0.0	0.0	0.0	25
Zapotec(1)	40.0	40.0	0.0	2.5	2.5	0.0	40
Tzotzil(1)	39.1	26.1	13.0	6.6	4.4	2.2	46
Aymara(1)	33.3	12.1	21.2	15.1	3.0	12.1	33
Nahuatl(5)	27.6	6.9	20.7	3.5	3.5	0.0	29
Mixtec(2)	24.1	24.1	0.0	3.5	3.5	0.0	29
Nahuatl(2)	21.9	18.8	3.1	3.1	3.1	0.0	32
Tupí(1)	21.7	13.0	8.7	0.0	0.0	0.0	23
Cakchiquel(2)	21.4	4.8	16.6	14.3	4.8	9.5	42
Cakchiquel(1)	20.0	16.7	3.3	13.3	10.0	3.3	30
Mapuche(1)	20.0	6.7	13.3	3.3	0.0	3.3	30
Mixtec(1)	18.8	18.8	0.0	6.3	6.3	0.0	32
Nahuatl(3)	18.5	18.5	0.0	14.8	11.1	3.7	27
Zoque(1)	17.7	17.7	0.0	5.9	5.9	0.0	17
Otomi(1)	17.4	10.9	6.5	4.4	0.0	4.4	46
Guaraní(1)	16.7	0.0	16.7	7.2	2.4	4.8	42

A = Overall European loan replacement percentage (B + C).

B = Number of acculturated items designated by native terms in an earlier time state, which are named solely by European loans in a later time state, presented as a percentage of the total number of items for which terms are recorded in sources for both time states (G).

C = Number of acculturated items designated solely by native terms in an earlier time state, which are named by both native terms and by European loans in a later time state, presented as a percentage of the total number of items for which terms are recorded in sources for both time states (G).

D = Overall native term replacement percentage (E + F).

E = Number of acculturated items denoted by European loans in an earlier time state, which are named solely by native terms in a later time state, presented as a percentage of the total number of items for which terms are recorded in sources for both time states (G).

F = Number of acculturated items denoted solely by European loans in an earlier time state, which are named by both native terms and by European loans in a later time state, presented as a percentage of the total number of items for which terms are recorded in sources for both time states (G).

G = Total number of items of acculturation for which terms are recorded in sources for two different time states of a single language.

Table 7.4. *(continued)*

Language cases comprising time states compared:

Aymara(1)	=	Aymara (1612)/Aymara (1940–89)
Cakchiquel(1)	=	Cakchiquel (c. 1650)/Cakchiquel Central)
Cakchiquel(2)	=	Cakchiquel (c. 1650)/Cakchiquel (1956–1981)
Guaraní(1)	=	Guaraní (1639)/Guaraní (1947–87)
Mapuche(1)	=	Mapuche (1771)/Mapuche (1944–90)
Mixtec(1)	=	Mixtec (1593)/Mixtec (San Juan Colorado)
Mixtec(2)	=	Mixtec (1593)/Mixtec (Chayuco)
Nahuatl(1)	=	Nahuatl (1571)/Nahuatl (Xalitla)
Nahuatl(2)	=	Nahuatl (1571)/Nahuatl (Huazalinguillo dialect)
Nahuatl(3)	=	Nahuatl (1571)/Nahuatl (Sierra de Zacapoaxtla)
Nahuatl(4)	=	Nahuatl (1571)/Nahuatl (Tetelcingo)
Nahuatl(5)	=	Nahuatl (1571)/Nahuatl (1611)
Otomi(1)	=	Otomi (c. 1770)/Otomi (Santiago Mexquititlán)
Quechua(1)	=	Peruvian Quechua (1560–1619)/Quechua (Ayacucho, 1969)
Tupí(1)	=	Tupí (1621)/Tupí (1854–94)
Tzotzil(1)	=	Tzotzil (Zinacantán, late sixteenth century)/Tzotzil (Zinacantán, 1950–75)
Zapotec(1)	=	Zapotec (1578)/Zapotec (Juárez)
Zapotec(2)	=	Zapotec (1578)/Zapotec (Mitla)
Zoque(1)	=	Zoque (1672)/Zoque (Copainalá)

time states are eighteenth century or earlier, and in all but two instances, Nahuatl(5) and Tupí(1), later time states are twentieth century.

Languages are rank-listed in table 7.4 according to overall European loan replacement percentages (see column A), from largest [Zapotec(2)] to smallest [Guaraní(1)]. This percentage is an aggregate value yielded by the addition of percentage figures in columns B and C. Essentially, the overall European loan replacement percentage is the number of acculturated items designated by native terms in an earlier time state of a language that have been either partially or totally replaced by European loans in a later time state, divided by the total number of acculturated items for which terms are recorded in sources for both of the compared time states (column G). (See table 7.4 for a detailed explanation of how the statistics have been calculated.) Column D presents the overall native term replacement percentage, which is an aggregate value yielded by the addition of percentage figures in columns E and F. Essentially, this is the number of acculturated items designated by European loans in an earlier time state of a language that have been either partially or totally replaced by native terms in a later time state, divided by the total number of acculturated items for which terms are recorded in sources for both of the compared time states (column G).

In all instances, overall European loan replacement percentages (column A) are larger, typically considerably so, than overall native term replacement percentages (column D): the average difference between columns A and D is 24.2. Indeed, while all languages in table 7.4 have undergone European loan replacement, some—Nahuatl(1), Quechua(1), and Tupí(1)—show no evidence whatsoever of native term replacement. In addition, the average overall European loan replacement percentage is 29.8, which is more than five times greater than the average overall native term replacement percentage, which is 5.6. Thus, the languages in question have replaced native terms with European loans at a far greater rate than they have replaced European loans with native terms.

Extensive European loan replacement in Latin American Indian languages almost certainly reflects a common feature of *all* of their postcontact histories—progression from primary to secondary accommodation. In this development, some languages, such as Quechua(1) and Zapotec(2), have achieved higher levels of secondary accommodation (and of bilingualism?) than other languages, such as Guaraní(1) and Otomí(1) (see column A). The generally less extensive occurrence of native term replacement probably reflects, at least in part, the occasional tendency for speakers of some Amerindian languages to develop purist attitudes toward native ways of speaking. The data in table 7.4 suggest that such languages as Aymara(1) and Cakchiquel(1) have been affected by language purism to a considerably greater extent than such languages as Mapuche(1) and Tupí(1) (see column D).

Amerindian languages of North America north of Mexico, for which both earlier and later time states are found among sampled language cases, all (with the major exception of Klamath, see table 7.2) manifest very low European loan replacement percentages, a not unexpected finding since these languages typically show very low European loan percentages (see table 6.1). Languages influenced primarily by English and French not only have not been inclined to borrow European words for items of acculturation but also have strongly tended to avoid replacement of native terms by European loans. In terms of Casagrande's (1954a, 1954b, 1955) interpretative framework, these languages seem to have failed to proceed from primary to secondary accommodation, a probable result of a general disinclination to develop extensive bilingualism (see chapter 6).

8

NATIVE TERM DIFFUSION

In addition to adopting European loans, Amerindian languages have borrowed native terms for items of acculturation from other Amerindian languages. In fact, native labels for imported things have commonly been diffused through languages of the New World. Analysis of native terms for the 77 acculturated items reveals strong diffusional patterns.

1. In the vast majority of cases, the diffusion of native terms for acculturated items has involved languages in the same genetic grouping (e.g., those belonging to the Algonquian family, to the Mayan family, or to the Matacoan family).

2. When native labels have been diffused across languages of different genetic groupings, usually one of the languages is a lingua franca, such as a pidgin trade language (e.g., Chinook Jargon of the Pacific Northwest, and Mobilian Jargon of the southeastern United States) or a dominant indigenous language widely used in commercial interaction (e.g., Nahuatl of Middle America, and Peruvian Quechua).

3. Native terms for imported items have rarely been diffused through Amerindian languages when the languages involved do not include a lingua franca and do not belong to the same genetic grouping.

It may not be surprising to learn that lingua francas frequently influence vocabularies of other languages (cf. Pinnow 1969:98; Campbell and Kaufman 1976:82; Moravcsik 1978:109; Thomason and Kaufman 1988:43–44); however, to my knowledge, before this study (as first described in Brown 1996a) no one has assembled extensive cross-language data that thoroughly document the phenomenon. Findings reported in this chapter are related to the explanatory framework constructed in chapter 6 which proposes that the degree of bilingualism positively influences the extent of lexical borrowing. However, here the type of bilingualism involved entails proficiency in two or more non-European languages rather than in a native language and a European one.

Methodology

For each of the 292 cases, I have ascertained the number of similar native terms for introduced items a language case shares with all other language cases of the sample.

Thus Squamish, a Salishan language of the Pacific Northwest, shares 9 terms with Songish, 1 with Shuswap, and 1 with Thompson (all Salishan languages); 2 with Quileute (Chimakuan); 2 with Haisla and 1 with Heiltsuk (both Wakashan); 2 with Yakima (Sahaptin-Nez Perce); 1 with Eyak (Athapascan-Eyak); 1 with Wintu (Wintun); 3 with Haida (isolate); 3 with Klamath (1890) and 1 with Klamath (1963) (two time states of the same genetic isolate); 1 with Gitksan (Tsmishianic), and 1 with Karok (isolate). In all, Squamish shares 29 native terms for introduced items with other language cases of the sample.

Frequently, a language case shares the same native term with more than one other case. For example, the Squamish word for NEEDLE, *p'a'c'-tn*, is also found in both Shuswap (*pékweten*) and Thompson (*pat quotten*). While only one diffused label is actually involved in this example, the convention followed here requires *two* terms to be considered shared by Squamish with other cases (a label for NEEDLE that is shared with Shuswap and one with Thompson). Similarly, the Squamish word for BREAD (*səpli'n*) also occurs in another Salishan language, Songish (*sʌplíí*), and in Haida (*sablíí*), Yakima (*sa-plil*), and Klamath (1890) (*shápĕ le*). By convention, this label, which was diffused from the pidgin trade language Chinook Jargon (*sapolil*), counts as four terms shared by Squamish with other language cases. Since Chinook Jargon is not a Native American language as such, it is not included among the 292 language cases of the sample, as is also true of the pidgins Delaware Jargon, Eskimo Jargon, and Mobilian Jargon, whose vocabularies have been consulted in this study. Another Chinook Jargon term, a label for MONEY (*dolla* or *tala*), is found in Squamish (*ta'la*) and Songish (*télʌ*), as well as in Haida (*dàalaa*), Haisla (*dàla*), Heiltsuk (*dála*), Quileute (*tála*), Klamath (*tála*), Gitksan (*daala*), and Eyak (*da·na·*). This is the English term "dollar" which entered Chinook Jargon and became extended in reference to MONEY. Such referentially expanded European loanwords are formally considered to be native terms in this study. This widely spread MONEY term counts as eight native words that Squamish has in common with other languages.

For each set of language cases in the same genetic grouping, the total number of shared native labels is presented in table 8.1. Thus, among the 6 Salishan cases of the sample, Squamish, as reported, has 29 native terms in common with other cases, Songish 27, Kalispel 26, Okanagan 26, Shuswap 15, and Thompson 31. Salishan language cases, then, have a total of 154 shared native labels. For each genetic set of languages, three percentage figures are presented in table 8.1:

1. Within group—the percentage of the total number of shared terms that are held in common among languages of the same genetic grouping
2. Outside group: lingua franca—the percentage of the total number of shared terms that are held in common by languages of a single genetic grouping with languages outside the grouping and where at least one manifestation of each shared term occurs in a lingua franca
3. Outside group: no lingua franca—the percentage of the total number of shared terms that are held in common by languages of a single genetic grouping with languages outside the grouping and where no manifestation of a shared term is found in a lingua franca.

Genetic sets are rank-ordered (from highest to lowest) according to the value of their within-group percentage. Thus the Salishan set, listed eighteenth, shows a within-

Table 8.1. Number of native terms for items of acculturation shared by 292 Amerindian language cases organized by genetic affiliation.

	Total Shared Native Labels	Within Group		Outside Group: Lingua Franca		Outside Group: No Lingua Franca	
		N	%	N	%	N	%
Genetic sets of two or more cases							
Ge (2)	4	4	100.0	0	0.0	0	0.0
Misumalpan (3)	59	58	98.3	0	0.0	1	1.7
Iroquoian (7)	604	592	98.0	0	0.0	12	2.0
Algonquian (29)	5,110	5,003	97.9	0	0.0	107	2.1
Yuman (6)	96	94	97.9	0	0.0	2	2.1
Muskogean (5)	321	310	96.6	10	3.1	1	0.3
Eskimo-Aleut (11)	593	568	95.8	0	0.0	25	4.2
Southern Athapascan-Eyak (6)	472	445	94.3	24	5.1	3	0.6
Mayan (24)	2,716	2,469	90.9	199	7.3	48	1.8
Northern Athapascan-Eyak (15)	758	677	89.3	8	1.1	73	9.6
Siouan (9)	238	212	89.1	10	4.2	16	6.7
Northern Uto-Aztecan (9)	146	128	87.7	0	0.0	18	12.3
Tupí-Guaraní (14)	1,559	1,325	85.0	228	14.6	6	0.4
Otomanguean (21)	776	634	81.7	116	15.0	26	3.4
Quechumaran (17)	2,726	2,001	73.4	713	26.2	12	0.4
Uto-Aztecan (Sonoran) (7)	193	123	63.7	63	32.6	7	3.6
Matacoan (6)	181	111	61.3	48	26.5	22	12.2
Salishan (6)	154	86	55.8	38	24.7	30	19.5
Uto-Aztecan (Aztecan) (7)	532	291	54.7	232	43.6	9	1.7
Miwokan (5)	34	17	50.0	0	0.0	9	26.5
Guaycuruan (4)	159	78	49.1	60	37.7	21	13.2
Jivaroan (3)	108	44	40.7	56	51.9	8	7.4
Klamath (2)	69	28	40.6	39	56.5	2	2.9
Wakashan (2)	54	20	37.0	29	53.7	5	9.3
Araucanian (4)	525	182	34.7	334	63.6	9	1.7
Chibchan (4)	122	38	31.2	83	68.0	1	0.8
Mixe-Zoque (5)	166	32	19.3	121	72.9	13	7.8
Maipuran (9)	464	85	18.3	371	80.0	8	1.7
Sahaptin-Nez Perce (2)	25	4	16.0	15	60.0	6	24.0
Pano-Takanan (3)	140	20	14.3	111	79.3	9	6.4
Totonacan (2)	84	8	9.5	60	71.4	16	19.1
Carib (2)	81	6	7.4	71	87.7	4	4.9
Huitotoan (2)	37	2	5.4	34	91.9	1	2.7
Barbacoan (2)	159	4	2.5	155	97.5	0	0.0
Kiowa-Tanoan (2)	17	0	0.0	13	76.5	4	23.5
Chon (2)	1	0	0.0	0	0.0	1	100.0
Yukian (2)	11	0	0.0	0	0.0	11	100.0
Subtotals	19,494	15,699	80.5	3,241	16.6	546	2.8

(continued)

Table 8.1 *(continued)*

	Total Shared Native Labels	Within Group		Outside Group: Lingua Franca		Outside Group: No Lingua Franca	
		N	%	N	%	N	%
Genetic sets of only one case							
Caddoan (Arikara)	2	0	0.0	0	0.0	2	100.0
Cahuapanan (Chayahuita)	103	0	0.0	97	94.2	6	5.8
Chimakuan (Quileute)	24	0	0.0	24	100.0	0	0.0
Guahiban (Guahibo)	27	0	0.0	27	100.0	0	0.0
Kalianan (Makú)	9	0	0.0	9	100.0	0	0.0
Maiduan (Maidu)	6	0	0.0	0	0.0	6	100.0
Maskoian (Lengua)	3	0	0.0	0	0.0	3	100.0
Palaihnihan (Atsugewi)	0	0	0.0	0	0.0	0	0.0
Panaquitan (Páez)	22	0	0.0	18	81.8	4	18.2
Salivan (Piaroa)	9	0	0.0	9	100.0	0	0.0
Tucanoan (Tucano)	21	0	0.0	21	100.0	0	0.0
Uarao (Uarao)	43	0	0.0	40	93.0	3	7.0
Wintun (Wintu)	12	0	0.0	9	75.0	3	25.0
Subtotals	281	0	0.0	254	90.4	27	9.6
Language isolates							
California (2)	12	0	0.0	9	75.0	3	25.0
Middle America (3)	91	0	0.0	87	95.6	4	4.4
North America Plains (1)	0	0	0.0	0	0.0	0	0.0
N. America Southeast (3)	4	0	0.0	0	0.0	4	100.0
N. America Southwest (4)	60	0	0.0	46	76.7	14	23.3
Northwest Coast (2)	48	0	0.0	31	64.6	17	35.4
South America (3)	62	0	0.0	54	87.1	8	12.9
Subtotals	277	0	0.0	227	82.0	50	18.1
Grand Totals	20,052	15,699	78.3	3,722	18.6	623	3.1

Source: Cecil H. Brown, Lexical acculturation, areal diffusion, lingua francas, and bilingualism, *Language in Society* (1996a), 25:261-282, with the permission of Cambridge University Press.

group percentage of 55.8, that is, the number of terms shared by Salishan cases with other Salishan cases (86), divided by the total number of shared native labels (154). The two outside-group percentages for Salishan are 24.7 (lingua franca) and 19.5 (no lingua franca). The first of these is the number of terms shared by Salishan cases with language cases of other genetic affiliations and where at least one manifestation of each shared term occurs in the local lingua franca, Chinook Jargon (38), divided by the total number of shared labels (154). The second is the number of terms shared by Salishan cases with cases of other genetic groupings, no manifestations of which are found in Chinook Jargon (30), divided by the total (154).

Genetic group affiliation and geographic location of each of the 292 language cases is given in appendix B (see also table 6.1 for genetic group affiliations). Languages affiliated with Athapascan-Eyak and Uto-Aztecan in table 8.1 are divided into geographic subgroupings. For the former these are as follows: Northern Athapascan-Eyak [including Tanaina, Central Koyukon, Ingalik, Minto, Ahtna, Carrier, Eyak, Northern Tutchone, Gwichin (1976), Chipewyan, Beaver, Slave, Montagnais (Chipewyan), Gwichin (1876), and Peaux-de-Lièvres], and Southern Athapascan-Eyak [Jicarilla Apache, Mescalero Apache, Western Apache, Navajo (1910), Navajo (1950–1980), and Apache (1870s and 1880s)]. Subgroupings for Uto-Aztecan are: Northern Uto-Aztecan [Comanche, Panamint Shoshone, Kawaiisu, Big Smokey Valley Shoshoni, Ute (1849–1880), Southern Ute, Hopi, Cupeño, and Cahuilla], Uto-Aztecan (Sonoran) [Yaqui, Cahita, Pima, Tarahumara (1915–1920), Tarahumara (1952–1972), Cora, and Huichol], and Uto-Aztecan (Aztecan) [Pipil, Nahuatl (Tetelcingo), Nahuatl (Xalita), Nahuatl (1611), Nahuatl (Sierra de Zacapoaxtla), Nahuatl (Huazalinguillo), and Nahuatl (1571)]. Statistics relating to Athapascan-Eyak and Uto-Aztecan as whole genetic groupings can be calculated by aggregating the numbers in table 8.1 pertinent to their respective geographic subgroupings.

There are three general groupings in table 8.1. The first comprises all genetic sets represented by at least two language cases of the sample (the number in parentheses following the genetic set name is the number of language cases of the sample within a set). The grouping designated by Klamath, which includes two different time states of a single language isolate, Klamath (1890) and Klamath (1963), is not a genetic grouping as such since it does not encompass two or more *distinct* languages that are genetically related. The second grouping comprises all genetic sets represented by only one language case of the sample (the name of the single language involved is in parentheses following the name of the pertinent genetic set). The third grouping comprises language cases pertaining to language isolates, that is, languages that are not known to be genetically related to any other. These are grouped according to geographic location. For example, a California set comprises two isolates of the area, Karok and Washo. The Northwest Coast isolate set has two members including Gitksan that, while in fact an affiliate of the small Tsmishianic grouping, is treated as an isolate. For sets of the last two general groupings, within-group percentages are all zero since there are no possible within-group language cases of the sample with which member cases of these sets can share native labels for acculturated items.

Lingua francas consulted in this study are generally familiar to Americanists: Eskimo Jargon, Chinook Jargon, Mobilian Jargon, Delaware Jargon, Nahuatl, Peruvian Quechua, Tupí, and Guaraní (cf. Silverstein 1996). The first four are extinct pidgin trade languages, derived primarily from Amerindian languages; they were spoken, respectively, in the American Arctic, the Pacific Northwest Coast, the southeastern United States, and the northeastern United States. Eskimo Jargon (Stefánsson 1909) developed mainly from Eskimo languages and dialects, especially Western Inuit (Mackenzie Eskimo; Drechsel 1981). Native American languages of the sample influenced by Eskimo Jargon are limited to those of the Eskimo-Aleut grouping. Chinook Jargon (Swan 1857; Gibbs 1863; Langevin 1872; Blanchet 1878; Good 1880; Gill 1884; Tate 1889; Coones 1891; Thomas 1935) developed from English, French, and certain Amerindian languages of the region, including Chinook and

Nootka (Thomason and Kaufman 1988:258–259). Native American languages of the sample influenced by Chinook Jargon include a Northwest Coast isolate; a California isolate; and all or some languages affiliated with Salishan, Northern Athapascan-Eyak, Klamath, Wakashan, Tsmishianic, Sahaptin-Nez Perce, Chimakuan, and Wintun. Mobilian Jargon (Crawford 1978; Drechsel 1979, 1996) developed primarily from Western Muskogean (Choctaw/Chickasaw). Languages of the sample that are influenced by Mobilian Jargon include those of the Muskogean grouping and two Siouan languages spoken in the southeastern United States. Delaware Jargon (Prince 1912; Thomason 1980) developed primarily from the Algonquian language Delaware. The influence of this trade language was probably fairly limited since only one term for an imported item is shared by languages of the sample, and the latter include only Delaware and Mahican (Algonquian).

Nahuatl, a Uto-Aztecan tongue primarily spoken today in Mexico, was the language of the Aztec empire that dominated much of Mesoamerica at the time of Spanish contact (see chapter 7). Languages that share native terms for introduced items with Nahuatl include three Middle America isolates; three North America Southwest isolates; and all or some languages affiliated with the groupings Mayan, Southern Athapascan-Eyak, Uto-Aztecan (Northern, Sonoran, and Aztecan branches), Otomanguean, Mixe-Zoque, Totonacan, and Kiowa-Tanoan. Peruvian Quechua was the language of the Inca empire and is still widely spoken today; languages that share native labels include one South America isolate and all or some languages associated with Quechumaran, Matacoan, Guaycuruan, Jivaroan, Barbacoan, Araucanian, Maipuran, Pano-Takanan, Huitotoan, Cahuapanan, and Panaquitan. Tupí and Guaraní are closely related members of the Tupí-Guaraní genetic grouping, the former spoken primarily in Brazil (Hartt 1872) and the latter in Paraguay; both served as lingua francas in their respective regions in postcontact times. In some areas of Brazil, Tupí was used in a pidginized version (Hancock 1971:515.) The two languages share with one another many native terms for introduced items. Languages of the sample that show native words for acculturated items in common with Tupí and/or Guaraní include two South America isolates and all or some languages respectively affiliated with Tupí-Guaraní, Guaycuruan, Chibchan, Maipuran, Carib, Guahiban, Kalianan, Salivan, Tucanoan, and Uarao.

These languages are not the only ones that have served as lingua francas in the postcontact Americas. Other pidgins derived in part from Native American languages—such as Slavey Jargon (see chapter 9), Lingua Franca Creek (chapter 9), Massachusetts Pidgin, and Basque-American Indian Pidgin (Bakker 1989b)—have been reported but do not figure in this study since little, if any, of their vocabulary has been recorded and made available to researchers. Lexicons of other American pidgins and creoles, such as Pidgin Dutch (Guyana) and Louisiana Creole French (Hancock 1971), are derived mainly from European or nonAmerindian languages; consequently, they generally have not contributed native terms for imported items to vocabularies of Native American languages. No doubt other nonpidginized Amerindian languages, like Nahuatl and Peruvian Quechua, have surfaced as areal economic languages but are nonetheless not recognized as such. Such nonsalient lingua francas are discussed presently.

Findings

The 292 language cases share 20,052 native terms for items of acculturation (table 8.1). Of these, 15,699 are labels that languages of the same genetic set share with one another, producing a within-group proportion of 78.3% for Native American languages in general. Of the 292 language cases, 31 are either genetic isolates or are the only representatives of a genetic set in the sample; thus they cannot share terms with other languages of the same genetic grouping. Removing these 31 cases from consideration and looking only at languages that can share terms with closely related languages, we see that the within-group proportion for Amerindian languages in general increases from 78.3% to 80.5% (15,699/19,494). Clearly, by far the greatest part of areal diffusion of native terms for introduced items entails sharing such words among languages of close genetic relationship.

Of the 20,052 shared labels, 4,345 are held in common by languages that do not belong to the same genetic grouping, yielding an overall outside-group proportion of 21.7%. Removing the 31 cases noted above from consideration, we find that this decreases to 19.4%. Of the 4,345 terms, 3,722 (or a striking 85.7%) have manifestations found in lingua francas (yielding 18.6%). This strongly suggests that most terms shared by genetically unrelated languages have been diffused to them from lingua francas.

In contrast, only 623 of the 4,345 terms shared by genetically unrelated languages, or a mere 14.3%, do not have manifestations found in lingua francas. In other words, only 3.1% of all shared labels are held in common by languages that are not closely related genetically and that do not include lingua francas, that is, the outside group: no lingua franca. This strongly suggests that lexical diffusion across languages of different genetic groupings rarely occurs unless there is a lingua franca in the region to promote it.

Of the 3,722 native terms shared by genetically unrelated languages with manifestations found in lingua francas, 1,129 (or 30.5%) are loanwords from European languages that have been referentially extended to items of acculturation, for example, loans in Northwest Coast languages modeled on English "dollar" and extended to MONEY. Similarly, of the 623 terms shared by genetically unrelated languages, none of which are lingua francas, 200 (or 32.1%) are referentially extended European loans. If these are not considered to be native terms, percentages for Amerindian languages in general are as follows: within group, 84.0% (15,699/18,693); outside group: lingua franca, 13.9% (2,593/18,693); outside group: no lingua franca, 2.3% (423/18,693). In short, such a revision does not alter observed patterns of lexical diffusion; indeed, it makes them even more apparent.

Examples

Some discussion of sample cases—Algonquian, Mayan, and Quechumaran —will help to flesh out the data summarized in table 8.1.

Algonquian

The 29 language cases of the Algonquian grouping share among themselves, and with languages of other North American groupings, a total of 5,110 native labels for items of acculturation—the most of any genetic set of the sample. Of these, 5,003 are held in common among Algonquian languages, yielding an exceptionally high within-group proportion of 97.9% for the genetic set. This leaves a mere 107 native terms shared by Algonquian languages with languages of other genetic groupings, none of which have a manifestation in a lingua franca; this results in a proportion of 0.0% for the outside group: lingua franca and a proportion of 2.1% for the outside group: no lingua franca.

Algonquian languages and dialects of the sample are distributed across a vast area of northern North America including the Northeast, the northern Plains, and parts of the subarctic. These are more or less geographically contiguous, except for two, Cheyenne and Blackfoot, which are spoken in Montana and southern Alberta, west of the main Algonquian area. Many Algonquian languages and dialects show massive borrowing of native words for items of acculturation from others in the genetic set. The most intense borrowing has occurred among languages of the Great Lakes region (especially Menominee, Kickapoo, Algonquin, dialects of Ojibwa, and dialects of Cree; see the following discussion). Algonquian languages east of the Great Lakes—especially Micmac and Eastern Algonquian languages like Passamaquoddy, Mahican, and Delaware—show borrowings from other Algonquian languages, but at substantially lower rates. Eastern Algonquian is the only clearly discernible major genetic subgroup within Algonquian (Goddard 1979). The geographic outliers, Cheyenne and Blackfoot, have not participated at all in postcontact inter-Algonquian lexical diffusion.

Several native terms for items of acculturation have exceptionally broad distributions, occurring in Algonquian languages of both the Great Lakes region and areas to the east. The most widespread is a word for SOLDIER found in most Great Lakes languages and in Micmac, and in several Eastern Algonquian languages as well. Examples include Cree *simaganis*, Eastern Ojibwa *zhmaagan*, Micmac *smàgnis*, Mahican *tchimaganis*, and Miami *simakanäsia*. In several languages, this term is analyzable as SPEAR,LANCE,SWORD + UE (UE = unknown element). A word for TOWN occurs in Great Lakes Algonquian languages and in Micmac, Passamaquoddy, and Delaware—for example, Chippewa *o day nung*, Cree *otenaw*, Algonquin *otenaw*, Micmac *utan*, and Delaware *uteney*. This item probably relates to a Proto-Algonquian word for a large camp or settlement (cf. Aubin 1975:118; Hewson 1993:146).

Very few native terms for acculturated items are found both in Algonquian languages and in languages of other genetic groupings. Some of these are the following:

1. A term for HEN in Inuit Eskimo (Eskimo-Aleut), *pakaakkuani* (compare Montagnais *pakakuan* and Algonquin *pakaakwan*)

2. A term for COW in Carrier (Athapascan-Eyak), *musdoos* (compare Plains Cree *mostos*)

3. A label for DONKEY in Beaver (Athapascan-Eyak), *soosoohlyeñ* (compare Cree *sosuw*)

4. A word for SOLDIER in Beaver (Athapascan-Eyak), *simakanisine* (compare Cree *simaganis* and also see above)

5. A label for CHICKEN in Comanche (Uto-Aztecan), *ko ko?*, and in Dakota (Siouan), *koh-koh'-yah-hohn-lah* (compare Cheyenne *ko-kú-yah*)

Mayan

The 24 language cases of the Mayan grouping share among themselves and with languages of other genetic groups a total of 2,716 native terms for introduced items. Of these, 2,469 (or 90.9%) are within-group sharings. In addition, Mayan shows a percentage of 7.3 for the outside group: lingua franca and a percentage of 1.8 for the outside group: no lingua franca. With one exception (Huastec in northern Mexico), Mayan languages are more or less contiguously located in Belize, Guatemala, and southern Mexico.

A number of native terms for introduced items in Mayan languages are widely distributed throughout the grouping. For example, many Mayan languages share a term for BREAD that is derived from a common Mayan word for TORTILLA. In some instances, the latter term is combined with a Spanish derived term (modified and diffused by Nahuatl), meaning FOREIGN or SPANISH, to denote European BREAD (see chapter 11). Examples of these include Tzotzil (Zinacantán dialect) *vaj*, Yucatec *castellan uah*, Chol *kaxlan waj*, and Quiche *caxlan hua*. Some Mayan terms for introduced animals are reasonably widespread. For example, reflexes of the Proto-Mayan word for DEER, **kehj* (Kaufman and Norman 1984:118) are used to designate both the SHEEP and HORSE in a number of Mayan languages (usually entailing a complementary distribution of these referents), for example, Chol *chij* "sheep," Tojolabal *chej* "sheep," Aguacatec *cen* "horse," and Quiche *quiej* "horse."

An archaic Spanish term for a certain currency denomination, *tomín*, is found in several Mayan languages in which it expansively designates MONEY, for example, Huastec *tumin*, Tzotzil (Zinacantán, late sixteenth century) *tomin*, Kekchi *tumin*. This word also occurs as a label for MONEY in Nahuatl (Aztec): Nahuatl (Xalita dialect) *tomin*. In fact, the loan, as a term for MONEY, has entered the vocabularies of a number of Middle America and Southwest languages of genetic affiliations other than Mayan and Uto-Aztecan, for example, Seri (Southwest isolate) *tom*, Pame (Otomanguean) *tumin*, Totonac (Totonacan) *tumin*, Zoque (Mixe-Zoque) *tumin*, and Tequistlatec (Middle America isolate) *el tomi*. The term and its extended application to MONEY may have been directly diffused to these languages by speakers of Spanish; but it is just as likely, if not more so, that the lexical item and its usage were spread primarily through Nahuatl, the regional lingua franca (see chapter 11).

A term for GOAT originating in Nahuatl (*tentzone*, literally, "bearded one") spread to several Mayan languages, such as Tzotzil *tentsun* and Cakchiquel *tsuntsun*, as well as to other area languages, for example, Totonac (Totonacan) *tintzun*, Huave (Middle America isolate) *teants*, and Zoque (Mixe-Zoque) *tentzun* (see chapter 11). Another Nahuatl term, *xonacatl* "onion," was diffused only to Mayan languages, such as North Mam *xhnukat* and Quiche *xonacat*.

Quechumaran

The 17 Quechumaran language cases share a total of 2,726 native terms for acculturated items among themselves and with languages of other genetic affiliations. Of these, 2,001 are within-group lexical items, yielding a within-group proportion of 73.4% for Quechumaran. There are 725 outside-group terms, of which 713, or 98.4%, show a lingua franca manifestation. The lingua franca involved is Peruvian Quechua, part of the Quechumaran grouping. Several dialects of Peruvian Quechua are represented among the Quechumaran language cases: Cajamarca, Ayacucho, Cuzco, Ancash, and Junin. The Quechumaran languages and dialects of the sample are located in three Andean countries: Ecuador, Peru, and Bolivia.

Several native terms for items of acculturation are widely spread through Quechumaran languages and dialects, most of which have been diffused to neighboring languages of other genetic affiliations (see chapter 11). Among the most widely distributed is a word for European BREAD, for example, Ecuadorean Quechua *tanda*, Peruvian Quechua *ttanta*, and Aymara *ttantta*. This term is also found in South American languages of six other genetic groupings, for example, Chayahuita (Cahuapanan) *tanta*, Cháma (Pano-Takanan) *tanta*, Aguaruna (Jivaroan) *tánta*, and Vejoz (Matacoan) *tantan*. Sixteenth- and seventeenth-century sources for both Quechua and Aymara indicate that the term originally denoted a native breadlike concoction made from a species of goosefoot, probably *Chenopodium quinoa*.

Factors that Produce Similar Native Terms

Several phenomena, in addition to straightforward lexical borrowing, can produce similar native terms for items of acculturation in two or more languages. These include loan shifts (chapters 3 and 10), universal naming tendencies (chapter 4), and chance. Genetic relatedness is not included since the importation of European objects and concepts postdates the parent languages of contemporary genetic groupings, usually by tens of hundreds of years. Terms originating in parent languages have more than occasionally acquired imported items as referents in daughter languages subsequent to contact (cf. Bloomfield 1946:106; Hockett 1948:127). While the three factors, especially the first two, are undoubtedly important contributors to cross-language lexical homogeneity, sharing of native terms can for the most part almost certainly be explained by the diffusion of words across languages. Nevertheless, no discussion of areal diffusion should fail to take note of the following.

Loan shifts

Loan shifts are "loans" that do not necessarily employ the phonetic shapes of words of the donor languages. For a detailed discussion of the two basic types—loan translations (or calques) and semantic loans—see chapter 3.

As mentioned in chapter 3, Biloxi (Siouan) and Tunica (isolate) of the southeastern United States both refer to the introduced SHEEP through loan translations that are literally "rabbit big," *tcĕ tkohí* and *rúštatɛ*, respectively. The use of words for RABBIT in reference to SHEEP occurs in most languages of the Southeast (which include languages of several different genetic affiliations) but is not found in languages outside the area. Thus, the *idea* of lexically equating RABBIT and SHEEP has regionally diffused or, in other words, is a postcontact areal phenomenon (see chapter 11). In the case of Biloxi and Tunica, this has resulted in the development of two phonologically very distinct labels for SHEEP since these genetically unrelated languages have different words for RABBIT. In contrast, languages of the area that belong to the same genetic grouping have similar terms for RABBIT and, hence, similar labels for SHEEP, for example, words for SHEEP in Muskogean languages: Chickasaw *chukulhpoba*, Choctaw *chukfi*, Koasati *cokfonapá*, and Alabama *chokfalpooba*. These lexical similarities could be due in part to straightforward lexical borrowing, but given the regionalism of the RABBIT/SHEEP equation, loan shift (involving similar words from similar languages) provides an equally plausible explanation of lexical resemblances.

Universal naming tendencies

This investigation reveals robust cross-language similarities in the naming of imported items by native terms, many of which reflect universal naming tendencies (chapter 4).

An earlier comparative investigation of a world-wide sample of languages has shown that the use of a construction for WEDNESDAY, variously "day three," "third day," and so on, qualifies as a universal naming tendency (Brown 1989b:545). From the current sample of 292 Amerindian language cases, of the 96 cases that show an analyzable native term for WEDNESDAY, 73 (or 76%) name that day of the week by using such a construction.

Languages of the Eskimo-Aleut grouping are typical. Similar terms for WEDNESDAY are distributed across the entire east-west span of the vast Arctic area of Eskimo occupation, from Greenland to the north slope of Alaska, including both Inuit-Inupiaq and Yupik Eskimo languages. Some examples are West Greenlandic Eskimo *pingasúngorpoq* (THREE + REPEATEDLY), Inuit Eskimo of Quebec *pingajuanni* (THIRD + ON THE), Kangiryuarmiut Eskimo *pingattiqtuq* (THREE + UE), and Central Yupik Eskimo *pingayirin* (THREE + UE). Only one other term, a word for WINDOW, has a distribution across Eskimo languages comparable to that of terms for WEDNESDAY. Since so few Eskimo labels for acculturated items have diffused so broadly, the observed distribution of similar "Wednesday" terms may be explained by factors other than straightforward lexical borrowing. One possibility may be a strong universal tendency for naming WEDNESDAY through the use of constructions that involve words for THREE (and related concepts such as THIRD). Since all Eskimo-Aleut languages of the sample show similar terms for THREE, realization of such a tendency would create similar labels for WEDNESDAY across these languages. Loan shift could have been another contributing factor. Indeed, the Eskimoan distribution of similar "Wednesday" terms may be explained by some complex, simultaneous involvement of a universal naming tendency, loan shift, and term borrowing.

Also among similarities produced by universal naming tendencies are those motivated by onomatopoeia (chapter 3). For example, two Mesoamerican languages, Tzeltal (Mayan) and Mixtec (Otomanguean), show similar words for the introduced GOAT: respectively, *meé tentzun* and *mvee* or *mbèè* (*tentzun* is the widely diffused Nahuatl "goat" term mentioned previously). While this similarity is probably due to lexical diffusion (facilitated by the geographic proximity of the languages involved), onomatopoeia cannot be ruled out as an explanation since a similar sound-mimicking word for GOAT, *be*, is found in distantly removed Kaingang, a Ge language of Brazil.

Chance

Simple coincidence occasionally explains the occurrence of similar terms for items of acculturation in two or more languages. Reasonably unambiguous examples of such terms are obtained only from languages considerably removed geographically from one another since chance-produced similar terms from two or more neighboring languages are difficult to distinguish from those explained by borrowing. Two examples teased out from the current sample are the following:

1. Comanche (Uto-Aztecan of western Oklahoma) *tïhka?* "fork" compared to Piaroa (Salivan of Venezuela) *tuhkua'* "fork"
2. Zoque (Mize-Zoque of Mexico) *picsi* "thread" compared to Chayahuita (Cahuapanan of Peru) *pi'shi* "thread"

Words believed to be similar by chance are not included in table 8.1.

Explanatory Framework

In chapter 6, I propose that the degree of bilingualism positively influences the extent of lexical borrowing. This proposal is made in the context of the adoption of European loans by Native American languages, but there is no reason why it should not apply equally well to the borrowing of native terms by Amerindian languages from other Amerindian languages.

Among all native terms for introduced items shared by languages of the sample, 21.7% are held in common by languages of different genetic groupings (table 8.1). Of these, an impressive 85.7% relate to sets of shared terms each of which shows at least one manifestation in a lingua franca. This is not unexpected if bilingualism significantly influences the extent of lexical borrowing. Crystal defines a lingua franca as an "auxiliary language used to enable routine communication to take place between groups of people who speak different native languages" (1980:211). By definition, then, a significant portion of people who speak any lingua franca are bilingual in the latter and in some native tongue. Thus, genetically unrelated languages spoken by groups who use the same lingua franca will tend to share vocabulary items mainly as a result of parallel acquisitions from the lingua franca.

Among all terms for items of acculturation held in common by Amerindian languages, 78.3% are shared by languages affiliated with the same genetic grouping (table 8.1). By far, then, most lexical borrowing occurs among genetically related languages. Because these languages are typically spoken in the same region, people are more apt to encounter languages closely related to their native tongue rather than otherwise. Thus, simple proximity may (at least in part) account for this finding. However, geographic propinquity does not appear to be a sufficient condition for the development of extensive lexical diffusion since the results reported here indicate that in general genetically unrelated languages, *including those spoken in the same geographic areas*, strongly tend *not* to share terms for acculturated items if a lingua franca is not involved. For example, genetically unrelated languages of the sample spoken on the North American Plains—including Algonquian, Caddoan, Siouan, and Uto-Aztecan languages, as well as a language isolate—share very few terms for items of acculturation (cf. Bright and Sherzer 1976:234–35). As far as we know, there was no widely used *spoken* lingua franca in this area. However, a sign language was employed extensively for intertribal communication (W. P. Clark 1885; A. R. Taylor 1981:187–194). A nonverbal lingua franca, of course, would have facilitated sharing of phonetically similar terms for imported items only minimally, if at all. A related argument that geographic proximity promotes bilingualism, which in turn motivates lexical borrowing, is problematic for the same reason.

Nevertheless, if bilingualism significantly influences lexical borrowing, this sociolinguistic feature may be important in explaining the fact that diffusion of terms for acculturated items is especially extensive across genetically related languages. People who speak these languages may also use the same lingua franca as an auxiliary language. If so, most terms for imported items shared by a set of genetically related languages might be expected to occur also in a lingua franca. However, this does not seem to be the case (see table 8.2).

Table 8.2 lists the same group of 37 genetic sets in table 8.1, each of which contains at least two language cases of the sample. The table shows for each set the number of within-group terms shared, the number of terms that are also found in a lingua franca, and the percentage of the latter. The genetic sets are rank-ordered according to the percentages of their within group: lingua franca, which vary from 100 [Barbacoan, Huitotoan, and Uto-Aztecan (Aztecan)] to zero (13 genetic sets). Based on aggregated numbers for all 37 genetic sets, only 26.8% of the terms for imported items shared by genetically affiliated languages are also found in lingua francas. The extensive sharing of native terms for acculturated items across genetically related languages, then, does not appear to be significantly facilitated by use of lingua francas (but see following discussions).

In a personal communication, Anthony P. Grant makes the following important observation: much postcontact-derived lexical homogeneity may be related to lexical diffusion facilitated by languages that have served as lingua francas in the past but have generally not been recognized as such. For example, in attempting to account for the massive sharing of terms for items of acculturation among Algonquian languages, Grant writes:

> Ojibwa, in one form or another, was certainly a handy language around the Great Lakes in the 17th century and afterwards. Menominees and Potawatomis learned Southwestern Ojibwa, but the converse was not true. It was a prestige language even though it wasn't the language of an empire like Quichua was.

Rhodes (1982) supports Grant's observation and further enhances our understanding of lingua francas among Algonquian peoples (cf. A. R. Taylor 1981:178; Bakker 1992:38–39). Rhodes develops several lines of (indirect) evidence to the effect that—in addition to Southwestern Ojibwa, spoken west of Lake Michigan and south of Lake Superior—two other dialects of Ojibwa (Eastern Ojibwa, east of Georgian Bay, and Ottawa, around Lake Huron and west to Lake Michigan) and Cree (north of the Great Lakes) functioned as trade languages or lingua francas in their respective regions. In addition, apparently none of these were spoken as second languages by any groups other than those having Algonquian languages as their native tongues.

All four of the lingua francas are found among the 29 Algonquian language cases in the sample. Of the 5,003 labels for items of acculturation held in common among

Table 8.2. Percentage of native terms shared within 37 genetic groupings also found in lingua francas.

	Within Group	Within Group: Lingua Franca	
		N	%
Genetic sets of two or more cases			
Barbacoan (2)	4	4	100.0
Huitotoan (2)	2	2	100.0
Uto-Aztecan (Aztecan) (7)	291	291	100.0
Tupi-Guarani (14)	1,325	1,324	99.9
Quechumaran (17)	2,001	1,989	99.4
Maipuran (9)	85	52	61.2
Muskogean (5)	310	151	48.7
Uto-Aztecan (Sonoran) (7)	123	55	44.7
Mixe-Zoque (5)	32	12	37.5
Chibchan (4)	38	14	36.8
Carib (2)	6	2	33.3
Araucanian (4)	182	60	33.0
Totonacan (2)	8	2	25.0
Pano-Takanan (3)	20	4	20.0
Eskimo-Aleut (11)	568	86	15.1
Klamath (2)	28	4	14.3
Wakashan (2)	20	2	10.0
Salishan (6)	86	6	7.0
Mayan (24)	2,469	130	5.3
Northern Uto-Aztecan (9)	128	6	4.7
Jivaroan (3)	44	2	4.5
Guaycuruan (4)	78	2	2.6
Matacoan (6)	111	2	1.8
Otomanguean (21)	634	9	1.4
Algonquian (29) (0.04)	5,003	2	0.0
Northern Athapascan-Eyak (15)	677	0	0.0
Southern Athapascan-Eyak (6)	445	0	0.0
Chon (2)	0	0	0.0
Ge (2)	4	0	0.0
Iroquoian (7)	592	0	0.0
Kiowa-Tanoan (2)	0	0	0.0
Misumalpan (3)	58	0	0.0
Miwokan (5)	17	0	0.0
Sahaptin-Nez Perce (2)	4	0	0.0
Siouan (9)	212	0	0.0
Yukian (2)	0	0	0.0
Yuman (6)	94	0	0.0
Totals	15,699	4,213	26.8

Source: Adapted from Cecil H. Brown, Lexical acculturation, areal diffusion, lingua francas, and bilingualism, *Language in Society* (1996a), 25:261–282, with the permission of Cambridge University Press.

Algonquian languages (table 8.1), 4,433 (88.6%) are found in one or more of the four proposed lingua francas. In striking contrast, in table 8.1, familiar lingua francas are found to relate to only .04% of the terms shared among Algonquian languages. It is interesting that the new percentage is almost identical to that for the number of terms shared by genetically unaffiliated languages also found in lingua francas, that is, 85.7. Thus, the extensive diffusion of labels for imported items across Algonquian languages may be due to widespread bilingualism of native Algonquian languages and "local" Algonquian lingua francas.

As noted, only 26.8% of the terms for imported items shared by genetically related languages are also found in lingua francas (table 8.2). When recognized lingua francas are extended beyond the more conspicuous ones—such as Chinook Jargon, Mobilian Jargon, Nahuatl, and Peruvian Quechua—to less conspicuous ones, such as Southeastern Ojibwa, this percentage figure almost certainly will increase significantly, perhaps in many instances approaching in magnitude that of languages of the Algonquian grouping (i.e., 88.6). Grant (personal communication) mentions several other languages, all spoken in North America north of Mexico, that may be less conspicuous lingua francas: Chinook, Nez Perce, Crow, Blackfoot, Dakota/Lakhota, Osage, Caddo, Creek, Apache, Navajo, and Shoshone (cf. Bakker 1993:19). Clearly, languages spoken in southern North America (Mexico), Central America, and South America could be added to this list.

Nonsalient lingua francas may account for much postcontact-derived lexical homogeneity in genetically related languages but this does not explain why most lexical diffusion by far entails such languages. The fact that genetically related languages are typically geographic neighbors is part of the explanation. In addition, related languages also tend to be more similar (phonologically, grammatically, and lexically) to one another than are unaffiliated languages. Perhaps similarity facilitates the development of bilingualism, while, conversely, lack of similarity hampers this development. There is at present no systematic evidence supporting such a proposal; however, it is a plausible working hypothesis. For example, commenting on certain dialectal similarities, Weinreich writes, "[T]hey diminish the interdialectal gap and simplify the problems of the bilingual" (1953:2). He also states, "[T]he greater the difference between the systems [languages or dialects], i.e. the more numerous the mutually exclusive forms and patterns in each, the greater is the learning problem" (p. 1). Thus, language similarity may not directly promote bilingualism (or bidialectalism), but it may increase the likelihood of its development when speakers of two languages come into contact (cf. Miller 1978:611; Thomason and Kaufman 1988:97).

Bidialectal skills are obviously more easily acquired than bilingual ones. Bidialectalism has probably played a significant role in the diffusion of words for imported items across dialects of the same language. Our sample of language cases includes a number of dialects, for example, the various dialects of Peruvian Quechua previously listed. These cases contribute to statistics assembled here in a way that increases the percentages of shared terms for genetic groupings of languages. These percentages are also increased by counting the same terms found in different time states of the same language as words for acculturated items shared by genetically related languages.

Loan shifts and universal naming tendencies are identified here as factors, in addition to lexical borrowing, that are involved in producing similar terms for acculturated items among Native American languages. As noted, these factors more readily facilitate the development of similar terms among languages that are related genetically than among those that are not. Loan shifts and universal naming tendencies, then, also contribute to the greater extent to which languages of the same genetic grouping show similar native terms for acculturated items than languages of different affiliations—although these factors probably constitute a fraction of that typically produced by straightforward lexical borrowing. In addition, loan shift (including loan translation), like lexical borrowing, is more likely to be realized when speakers have some familiarity with the languages in contact, like bilinguals, than when no such familiarity exists. For example, Casagrande writes, "[A] minimum knowledge of a donor language is necessary for linguistic borrowing in the form of either loanwords or loan-translations" (1955:22). Degree of loan translation, like the extent of lexical borrowing, may be primarily a function of the level of bilingualism people achieve in languages in contact (cf. Haugen 1956:101).

Finally, only 3.1% of all native terms for acculturated items shared by languages of the sample involve genetically unaffiliated languages that do not include a lingua franca (table 8.1). This is a mere 14.3% of all outside-group terms. Native words for introduced items, then, have only very rarely been diffused across two or more unrelated languages when a lingua franca is not involved. Such languages are not as frequently spoken in the same region as are genetically related ones. In addition, unaffiliated languages typically do not manifest a degree of close similarity that might facilitate or encourage bilingualism. These factors, as well as the lack of bilingualism with a lingua franca, would conspire against the extensive diffusion of native terms across unrelated languages.

Conclusion

Bilingualism, frequently involving a lingua franca as an auxiliary language, appears to constitute the single most important factor in promoting diffusion of native terms for acculturated items across languages of the Americas. In addition, reported cross-language patterns have specific implications for the study of language history. For example, detection of substantial lexical diffusion across languages of a region in which a familiar lingua franca is not known to have been employed may indicate the influence of a previously unrecognized lingua franca. Knowledge of such languages would be of significance to researchers involved in fleshing out regional sociolinguistic histories.

One finding should be of concern to comparative linguists who are pursuing language reconstruction. Reconstruction is undertaken with care to sort sets of true cognates from words whose similarity is due to lexical diffusion. The finding that lexical borrowing is often especially extensive among genetically related languages means that this task may be considerably more problematic than previously thought. Scholars should perhaps be less inclined to embrace uncritically lexical reconstructions based on widespread forms that are in fact "overreconstructions" for a genetic group's parent language (Witkowski and Brown 1981; Brown 1987a). Findings of this investigation, at the very least, constitute points of reference for the serious appraisal of such proposals (see chapter 12).

9

EUROPEAN LOAN DIFFUSION

Of the 4,345 native terms for items of acculturation shared by genetically unrelated languages (table 8.1), 1,329 (30.6%) are European loanwords that have been referentially extended (formally considered to be native terms in this study). While some Amerindian languages have occasionally independently extended the same European loan to the same acculturated item (e.g., a European word for a specific currency denomination extended to MONEY in general; see chapter 4), widespread sharing of semantically altered European loans is typically due to their diffusion across Native American languages. Distributions of referentially extended European terms are almost always regional in nature, involving languages that are more or less geographically contiguous (see chapter 11).

For example, the Russian word *zadínka*, which denotes BACK CUT OF MEAT, is used as a term for the introduced PIG in several languages spoken in the southwest corner of Alaska and the immediately adjacent areas. These include languages of two different genetic groupings, for example, Central Yupik Eskimo *sitiinkaq* and Pacific Gulf Yupik *sitiinkaaq* (both Eskimo-Aleut) and Ahtna *sidingah*, Tanaina *sidinga*, and Eyak *Sedinga'* (all Athapascan-Eyak). This usage almost certainly developed in a single language of the region (perhaps even in the local Russian) and was diffused to others.

In a few cases, geographic distributions are very broad. One of the most widely distributed extended European loans is modeled on Spanish *carta*, a label for LETTER ("epistle") also found in Portuguese. Adopted versions of *carta* denoting PAPER (and, sometimes, BOOK as well) occur in numerous Latin American Indian languages in different genetic groupings. PAPER and BOOK are commonly related nomenclaturally by languages of the sample. Languages that show semantically extended *carta* are not sporadically distributed throughout Latin America but are spoken in a more or less contiguous, but nonetheless huge, area that encompasses the circum-Caribbean region and adjacent areas (parts of Central America and Colombia, Venezuela, and the Guianas) and, to the south, Brazil and Paraguay. Examples include Insular Carib (Maipuran) *carta*; Cuna (Chibchan) *karta*; Guajira (Maipuran) *kararáuta*; Taurepän (Carib) *kareta*; and the Tupí-Guaraní languages, Oyampi *kaleta*, Chiriguano *cuatía*, Guaraní *kuatia*, and Tupí *cuatiara*. While *carta* possibly was independently expanded to PAPER in two or more languages of this vast area, its distribution as a "paper" term was probably influenced by one or both of two South American lingua francas, Tupí and Guaraní (chapter 11).

Another exceptionally widespread extended European loan is a word for MONEY that is found in northern North American Indian languages. This lexical item occurs in languages of the Northeast, Southeast, plateau, and subarctic regions, for example, Micmac (1888) *sooleawa'*, Kickapoo *sooniaah-*, Miami *šoli*, Cree *soniyaw*, Mobilian Jargon (a pidgin of the southeastern United States; Drechsel 1979, 1996) *sonak*, Thompson *snoweah*, Carrier *sooniya*, and Beaver *sooniyá*. The term was possibly originally a Spanish word for a specific currency denomination that became extended to MONEY in general in some Amerindian language and was diffused widely. This interpretation is based on observations of Frank T. Siebert, Jr., referred to in Crawford's (1978:73–74) book *The Mobilian Trade Language*. Siebert cites several Spanish words that may have been the model for the diffused form, including *sol* "silver coin" (also "sun, day"). He also mentions American Spanish *jola* "money" as a possible model, in which case the diffused form is not an extended European term but simply a diffused Spanish word for MONEY. Concerning the American history of the word, Crawford quotes Siebert:

> The term is widespread in Algonquian, and must be borrowed . . . and I think from 16th century Spanish . . . De Soto and Pardo, and other expeditions . . . into Mobilian [Jargon] . . . I suspect it may have passed from Mobilian into Illinois-Miami (who held the area about the Ohio-Mississippi confluence) . . . and thus entered Algonquian through Miami-Illinois. (p. 74)

The term probably moved subsequently from one of the Algonquian languages, almost certainly Cree, into Salishan (Thompson) and Athapascan-Eyak languages (Beaver and Carrier) of the far western part of the term's geographic range.

Since extended European loans have been diffused across Native American languages, undoubtedly semantically unchanged European words for acculturated items have been diffused as well. Often the latter instances of diffusion are difficult to distinguish from situations in which a European language has directly donated terms to several different Amerindian languages spoken in the same geographic region. However, some linguistic clues aid in detecting semantically unchanged European terms that have been diffused. These are phonological, morphological, and distributional in nature.

Phonological Clues

When two or more Amerindian languages spoken in the same region share a European loanword that is in some way significantly phonologically aberrant from the original European term, the word in question probably entered at least one of the languages indirectly (i.e., without direct involvement of a European donor language). For example, Shipley (1962:7) gives the following Spanish loanwords for WHEAT in languages of central California: Wappo *tíliku?*, Lake Miwok *tilíikuh*, Chico *tilíku*, Plains Miwok *tilíiku-*, and Southern Sierra Miwok *tilíko-*. The original Spanish word that is the model for these loans is *trigo*. Little background in phonological analysis is required to see that all of the California languages have similar aberrant versions of the Spanish term.

Shipley (1962) accounts for the observed phonological homogeneity of these loans by proposing that one of the languages, probably Wappo, borrowed the term directly from Spanish, phonologically altered it, and then loaned the changed word (either directly or indirectly) to other central Californian languages. On the basis of similar phonological evidence for many loan sets, Shipley proposes that Spanish loans have been transmitted sequentially from one Amerindian language to another along three chains of diffusion. An alternate proposal is that phonologically altered loans pertained to a pidginized version of Spanish that served as a regional lingua franca from which loans were directly diffused to individual languages of central California (cf. A. R. Taylor 1981:181–82; Bartelt 1992:26).

Another example involves a single language of California, Kashaya (Pomo), which shows loanwords from Russian (Oswalt 1958, 1994). Kashaya speakers were subjected to Russian influence at the Fort Ross colony in the early nineteenth century. Several Russian loans into Kashaya show substantial phonological deviations from Russian models. For example, the Kashaya word for CATTLE is *kuluwet*, based on the Russian word for COW, *korova* (Oswalt 1994:102). While such deviations might be explained by how Russian words were interpreted by individual Kashaya speakers, who spread them to other speakers of the language (cf. Oswalt 1958:246), we now know that other factors were at work (Oswalt 1994).

Oswalt proposes that direct lenders of Russian terms may not have been native speakers of Russian but rather Alaskan natives who were brought by Russians to the Ross colony as workers. For example, the Kashaya word for CATTLE, *kuluwet*, appears in Alutiiq (Pacific Yupik Eskimo) as *kuluwat* "cows," derived from *kuluwa-* (a loan based on Russian *korova* "cow") plus *-t*, a plural suffix that is distinctly Eskimo. Oswalt elaborates:

> Besides the expected replacement of Russian *o* with *u*, the Alaskan languages. . . will often replace the trilled *r* of Russian with *l*; *v* between vowels becomes *w*; *d* becomes *t*; and *g* becomes *k*. . . . Other [Kashaya] words also show probable influence of Alutiiq: Kashaya *tupulu* 'axe' from Russian *topor*, by way of *tupulu-q*; *'ukuluta* 'fence, garden' from Russian *ogorod'*, by way of *ukuluta-q*. (1994:102)

Allan Taylor (1990) charts the widespread distribution of certain European loans for the introduced PIG throughout languages of northern North America, citing phonological evidence for their diffusion. The words in question are found in languages of the Northeast, Great Plains, subarctic, and Arctic regions. Examples include Micmac (1984) *gulgwìs*, Seneca *kiskwi:s*, Delaware (1839) *goschgosch*, Kickapoo *koohkoos-*, Algonquin (1984) *kòkòsh*, Miami *kokoša*, Cree *kookoos*, Arikara *kúhkUx*, Dakota (Santee dialect) *koo-kOO-shay*, Peaux-de-Lièvres *kukuch*, Slave *kukuch*, Beaver *koohkoós*, and Inuit Eskimo *kuukkuusi*.

Allan Taylor (1990) persuasively argues that these labels can ultimately be traced to European terms for PIG derived from the form *koš*, words whose exact phonological shapes are now unknown. According to Taylor (p. 202), some known European reflexes of *koš* include Spanish *coche*, Galician *cocho*, French *cochon*, Rumanian *cuciu*, and Hungarian *koca*. He proposes that some loans in Amerindian languages, which I flag here by *kokosh (such as those listed above for Kickapoo,

Slave, and Beaver) are based on a partially reduplicated reflex of *koš*, which once was found in French; and others, flagged by **koshkosh* (see the Micmac, Seneca, and Delaware examples), are based on a fully reduplicated reflex that once was found in Dutch.

Allan Taylor (1990:201) postulates two separate loaning events that could have initiated diffusion of the forms. The first involved the introduction by Dutch speakers of the fully reduplicated form (**koshkosh*) probably somewhere in New Netherlands, including the Delaware valley. Later, the incompletely reduplicated form (**kokosh*) was introduced by the French, the most likely locus being the Illinois country. Taylor refers to a number of phonological peculiarities of different reflexes to demonstrate their diffusion throughout Amerindian languages. Similar to Shipley's (1962) evaluation of the central California situation, Taylor postulates "chains" of diffusion: "[T]he term was clearly passed along a chain of contiguous . . . languages, speakers of the receiving language making such substitutions as were necessary for the word to conform to the phonology of their particular language" (p. 197).

Even without the detailed phonological evidence assembled by Taylor, the terms for PIG in question clearly entered most Amerindian languages indirectly. The region in which *koš*-derived loans are found is so vast that the historically attested direct influence of French and Dutch can explain only a small part of the total distribution. The extremely broad spread of the lexical item is even more impressive when one considers the great reluctance of northern North American Indian languages to accept European loans for items of acculturation (see chapter 6). Why, then, was this particular European loan diffused so widely through languages of northern North America?

> The territory covered by *koš*-derived terms is so enormous that it is certainly the most widespread European loanword in the native languages of North America. The unprecedented success of this loan must be due to its phonetic simplicity, its recognizable onomatopoeic character [relating, according to Taylor, to hog calls], the ease with which the referent naturalized in North America, and the universal presence of pork in the colonial diet. (A. R. Taylor 1990:200)

Morphological Clues

Among the European loan sets compiled by Shipley (1962:20) for languages of central California is one encompassing loans based on the Spanish word for TABLE, *mesa*. These include forms such as Wappo *lámesaʔ*, Lake Miwok *laméesaʔ*, Patwin *lamesa*, Plains Miwok *laméesa-*, Chukchansi Yokuts *lammeesá'*, and Southern Sierra Miwok *lamesa* (and I can add Northern Sierra Miwok *lame·sa* and Bodega Miwok *laméesa*). All of these incorporate the Spanish definite (feminine) article *la* as an initial syllable. This is unusual since Spanish *mesa*, which is a frequently borrowed term among Spanish-influenced languages, is typically adopted without the definite article. Indeed, among the Latin American languages of the sample only one, Toba (1943–1980), spoken in the Argentine Chaco, shows a Spanish loan for TABLE preceded by the article—*nameesa*.

This morphologically complex loan also occurs in languages spoken in areas that abut central California, including southern California [Chumash (Whistler 1980) *lamesa*, Diegueño *lamees*, Cupeño *lamɛɛsa*, Cahuilla *laméesa*, and Kawaiisu *lameesaʔa*], Arizona (Mojave *lames* and Cocopa *lamís*), and Nevada (Panamint Shoshone *nammeesa*). Clearly both the special morphology of the item and its distribution suggest that it was diffused not only through languages of central California but through those of adjacent areas as well. There are no obvious clues to indicate which language or languages were most influential in this spread. One guess is that since southern California seems to be most central in the diffusional area in question, a language from there played the pivotal role, for example, Chumash, which may have been used as a lingua franca (Bartelt 1992:25).

Other European loans incorporate definite articles and are shared by two or more Amerindian languages spoken in the same geographic region. A particularly widespread one is a French loan for RIBBON found in languages distributed from the Great Lakes area of North America to the Pacific Northwest. Examples from the current sample are Mississaga *sénipEn*, Menominee *sɛ ˑnepaˑn*, Ojibwa (Odawa dialect) *se:nipa*, Cree *senibân*, Beaver *soónipan*, Montagnais (Chipewyan dialect) *sounibanen*, and Carrier *sunîmpal*. These ultimately can be traced to French Canadian *ses ribans* "his or her ribbons."

Distribution of this item mirrors that of two other European loans (previously mentioned)—the loan for MONEY, based on a Spanish term that possibly denoted SILVER COIN, for example, Cree *soniyaw*, and the *koš*-derived loan for PIG, for example, Cree *kookoos*. Distributions of all three lexical items encompass the region that stretches from the Great Lakes to the Pacific Northwest Coast, including languages of both the Algonquian and the Athapascan-Eyak genetic groupings. The most influential language in the diffusion of these loans was probably Cree (cf. Bakker 1993:19; Silverstein 1996:118–119), one of the four Algonquian lingua francas identified in the previous chapter (Rhodes 1982). This is strongly suggested by Cree's broad geographic distribution, which places speakers of its various dialects in close proximity to speakers of both Great Lakes Algonquian languages and Athapascan-Eyak languages of the Pacific Northwest and adjacent regions.

Languages of the Pacific Northwest and adjacent areas of the plateau and subarctic show the most examples of European loans with definite articles. Table 9.1 presents such loans for 12 introduced items in 19 Native American languages of the region. All of the loans are based on words from French. Also presented are French words from two sources for Chinook Jargon, a pidgin trade language that served as the regional lingua franca (see chapters 8 and 11).

Each loanword in table 9.1 occurs in at least 2 of the 19 listed Amerindian languages (lexical sources are listed in appendix B for language cases; additional sources are sometimes given in parentheses after the language in table 9.1). In all instances, and in Chinook Jargon as well, the initial syllable of the loan reflects a French definite article, either the masculine version (*le*) or the feminine (*la*). The most frequently occurring loan is based on the French word for SHEEP, *mouton* (13 of the 19 languages). The least frequently occurring are loans for MULE and RIBBON, based on French *mule* and *ruban*, respectively (2 languages each). While none of the 19 Amerindian languages shows French loans for all 12 introduced items, Chinook Jargon does.

Table 9.1. Loans from French in languages of the Pacific Northwest and adjacent areas that incorporate French definite articles.

	BOARD	BOTTLE	CUP	KEY	MULE	OATS	PEAS	RIBBON	ROOSTER	SHEEP	SHOVEL	TABLE
1	planche	bouteille	pot*	clef	mule	avoine	pois	ruban	coq	mouton	pelle	table
2	la plash'	la bottaile		le klee		la ween	le poof	la lupan	le coque	la mu-toń	la pell	la tamlé
3	la-plash	labooti		le-kleh	lé-mel	la-wen	le-pwau	le-ló-ba	le-cock'	lemooto	la-pellé	la-tahb
4		leputé	lepot	laklf		lewén	lipwá		likók	lmotó	lapál	latáp
5		laputáy	lpót			lawán	lipwá		likók	lemotó	lpelt	ltep
6		lpwey	l-lpot			lwen			lqʼʷuqʷoʳ		lpél	
7		(putéy)		nklf								
8					limfl	lawén	lipuá	Lálup		lamutú		latám
9	leplaš									lemǝtu		
10				lekelf				lúlupah		labatú		letem
11	leplaš		lepot	lekii						lemǝtu		letém
12	lapláš			lekelf						lemǝtú		lʌtém
13				lakʌlf						lʌmʌtól		
14			lapa't						lǝkʷa'qʷ	lmǝtu'		lata'm
15										lamatu		
16		lʌbuday	lʌbod	lʌgli					lʌgog			lʌdab
17							lé-pois		le-coq			
18										lamadú‡		
19	lebelás											
20										lamdúu		
21					limil		libwa					
22										lfbto		

* Designates POT.
' Designates CHICKEN.
‡ Designates LAMB.

EUROPEAN
1 = French

PIDGIN
2 = Chinook Jargon (Swan 1857)
3 = Chinook Jargon (Thomas 1935)

SALISHAN
4 = Kalispel (Mullen 1976)
5 = Okanagan (Colville dialect) (Doak 1983)

SALISHAN (continued)
6 = Shuswap
7 = Thompson (Thompson and Thompson 1996)
8 = Upper Chehalis (Kinkade 1991)
9 = Clallam (Fleisher 1976)
10 = Lushootseed (Bates, Hess, and Hilbert 1994)
11 = Saanich (Montler 1991)
12 = Samish (Galloway 1990)
13 = Songish
14 = Squamish
15 = Bella Coola (Nater 1990)

ATHAPASCAN-EYAK
16 = Carrier (Prunet 1990)

SAHAPTIN-NEZ PERCE
17 = Yakima (Sahaptin dialect)

WAKASHAN
18 = Heiltsuk
19 = Kwakiutl (Grubb 1977)

ISOLATES
20 = Haida (Kaigani dialect)
21 = Klamath (1963)

CHIMAKUAN
22 = Quileute

Both the special morphology of these loans and their distribution suggest their areal diffusion rather than direct adoption by individual languages from French. The occurrence of all 12 loans in Chinook Jargon, compared to their sporadic occurrence in the other languages, is a strong indication that Chinook Jargon was responsible for their areal distribution (see chapter 11). This accords with the conclusion of the preceding chapter—that extensive sharing of native terms for items of acculturation by genetically unrelated languages is typically due to bilingualism of those languages and a lingua franca. However, Prunet (1990), attending to strict phonological criteria, argues that most French loans in Carrier, including those listed for that language in table 9.1, entered Carrier directly from French rather than indirectly through Chinook Jargon. But it is almost certain that most of the 19 languages, which include languages of several different genetic affiliations (see table 9.1), acquired French loans with definite articles directly from Chinook Jargon. As a result, the Pacific Northwest and adjacent areas appear to constitute a postcontact linguistic region (see chapter 11).

Languages of the western subarctic and adjacent areas of the plateau, including some contiguous with languages of the Northwest Coast, share a French loanword for TEA in which an initial syllable incorporates a definite article:

Ahtna: *'eldiil*
Northern Tutchone: *ledyát*
Gwichin: *lidii*
Slave: *leti*
Montagnais (Chipewyan): *ledé*
Chipewyan: *lɛdí*
Beaver: *litea*
Carrier: *lʌdi*
Yakima: *le thé*
Kalispel: *lití*

Three of these, Carrier, Yakima, and Kalispel, have been influenced by Chinook Jargon (see table 9.1). All words for TEA in other languages influenced by Chinook Jargon are European loans, probably from English (but possibly from French) that do not incorporate the definite article. The Chinook Jargon word for TEA is English in origin (without a definite article), and the pidgin is the probable source of terms for TEA in most Amerindian languages whose speakers used it as an auxiliary tongue (with the exception of Carrier, Yakima, and Kalispel). The contiguous distribution of French loans for TEA that incorporate the definite article strongly suggests areal diffusion. A possible source of the item is a now extinct, probably pidginized, lingua franca known as Slavey Jargon (Bakker and Grant 1994:28–29; Silverstein 1996:120), which at one time was widely spoken in the western subarctic. Almost nothing of this language has been recorded or now survives (Bakker and Grant 1994:29).

Distributional Clues

I have frequently cited European loan distribution as suggestive of loanword diffusion across Native American languages. A highly indicative distributional clue of loan diffusion entails situations in which one native language's inventory of European loans constitutes a subset of loans in a neighboring language.

Spanish loans in Havasupai

Havasupai is a Yuman language spoken in northern Arizona. I have determined from the few published (and not particularly thorough) sources for the language (e.g., Gatschet 1892; Spier 1946) that eight Spanish loanwords have found their way into its lexicon. This low number is not especially surprising since speakers of the language have historically experienced little if any direct contact with speakers of Spanish (Schwartz 1983:15).

The eight Spanish loans in Havasupai are presented in table 9.2. Also presented are those Spanish loanwords found in Havasupai that also occur in immediately neighboring languages, including Hopi, Arizona Tewa, Southern Paiute, Western Apache, Navajo, Yavapai, and Walapai—as well as estimates of the total number of Spanish loans in each of these languages.

Only two languages, Havasupai and Hopi, share all 8 Spanish loans. Since Hopi's inventory of loanwords (45 in total) is larger than that of Havasupai, Havasupai's repertoire of Spanish loans forms a subset of Hopi's. It is highly unlikely that such a distribution would exist if Havasupai and Hopi were borrowing terms from Spanish autonomously. If, for example, these two languages were independently adopting terms from a pool of, say, 500 Spanish words (a number that is considerably smaller than the actual number of words in Spanish or, for that matter, in any natural language), Havasupai and Hopi would be expected to have by coincidence only 1 (actually, 0.72) Spanish loan in common (given the size of their respective Spanish loan lexicons). The probability of having 8 loans in common by chance is less than 1 in 100 million (Robert Suchner, personal communication). Clearly, then, Havasupai and Hopi have not adopted Spanish words independently of each other.

The obvious, and surely correct, explanation of the observed distribution is that Havasupai has borrowed all—or, at least, very nearly all—of its Spanish loans directly from Hopi. Since 82% (37/45) of Hopi's Spanish loans have come from sources other than Havasupai—most of them directly or indirectly from Pueblo languages to the east such as Keres of Acoma—it is unlikely that any of the eight shared items have moved from Havasupai to Hopi. This conclusion is in accord with other loanword evidence. Havasupai also shares with Hopi at least three native terms that are unquestionably Hopi in origin, one of which denotes an item of acculturation: Havasupai gǐdjǐ'na "a masked dancer, the name of a dance" and Hopi katsina "kachina" (Spier 1946:69); Havasupai bigá "wafer bread" and Hopi piiki "wafer-thin bread" (p. 123); Havasupai θápálá "peach" and Hopi sipala "peach" (p. 124). We know that the Havasupai obtained European fruit trees, and other introduced items as well, indirectly through the Hopi (Schwartz 1983:15). Also, the Hopi are known to have been, among

Table 9.2. Spanish loanwords in Havasupai and neighboring languages.

	BURRO "donkey"	CABALLO "horse"	CARRETA "wagon"	CASTILLA "Castile"	GUACO* "prairie chicken"	MELÓN "melon"	MOZO/A† "cat"	VACA "cow"	TOTAL NUMBER OF SPANISH LOANS
1	múlo "mule"	váwló	karˀéta	gástfla "whites"	kuágo "chicken"	mélóná "muskmelon"	muso/musóa	wagasí "cattle"	8
2	móˑro	kawaíyo	karéˑta	kástila "Spaniard"	kowáko "chicken"	melóˑni	músa	wáˑkasi	45
3	mµ:lu	wa:yu				melo:ni "mushmelon"	mu:sa	wak'a	17
4		qavaːṣ				mino'nI "cantaloupe"			9
5						bilón "cantaloupe"		magashi/bagashi	24
6							mósi	béégashii	34
7			kaaréta						16
8	mulo "mule"		kadeta		gwalyaw "chicken"			waksi	15

*See Miller (1960:44); Barto (1979:44).
†See Bright (1960b:167–168).

1 = Havasupai (Gatschet 1892; Spier 1946)
2 = Hopi (Dockstader 1955; Albert and Shaul 1985; Seaman 1985)
3 = Arizona Tewa (Kroskrity 1978)
4 = Southern Paiute (Sapir 1931)

5 = Western Apache (Perry et al. 1972)
6 = Navajo (Young and Morgan 1980)
7 = Yavapai (Shaterian 1983; Munro 1992a)
8 = Walapai (Barto 1979)

all of the Havasupai's neighbors, their most enduring friends, allies, and trading partners (p. 14). Several Spanish loans in Walapai are suggested by phonological evidence to have been acquired from Hopi (Barto 1979).

Spanish loans in languages of the southeastern United States

One or more of 20 Spanish loans are shared by two or more languages of the southeastern United States (SE). Distributional evidence involving subset relationships strongly suggests that for the most part these were not borrowed directly from Spanish but rather were diffused from one SE language to another, usually in a strikingly unidirectional manner (Brown 1998).

Crawford describes the SE as a "cultural province," geographically encompassing the area "from the Potomac and Ohio rivers to the Atlantic Ocean and Gulf of Mexico and westward beyond the Mississippi River for some two hundred miles or more" (1975:1). He lists 29 recorded languages (about which more than merely a name is known today) spoken in the region at least as late as A.D. 1700 (pp. 5–6). Twenty-two are associated with 5 different language families, 6 are language isolates, and 1 is a pidgin. These languages and their genetic affiliations are given in table 9.3 and, with the exception of the pidgin, are located on the accompanying map according to where they are believed to have been spoken between 1700 and 1800 (figure 9.1). Other languages of the area, perhaps many, have become extinct during the postcontact era, leaving little if any trace of their existence (pp. 1–2).

Lexical sources for data from SE languages used in this and subsequent chapters are included in table 9.3. Sources for some languages are especially thorough, including those for Alabama, Chickasaw, Choctaw, Creek, Koasati, Biloxi, Cherokee, and Tunica. Sources for others are often highly incomplete and fragmentary, explaining in part why Spanish loanwords of interest here are not forthcoming for them.

The 20 Spanish words, each of which has *unambiguously* yielded loans found in two or more SE languages, are listed in table 9.4. Some loans of possible Spanish origin may just as likely have been adopted from other European languages such as English or French; these ambiguous items are not included in table 9.4. Languages in which loans are found are also identified in the table. Spanish loans in addition to those derived from the 20 words in table 9.4 are relatively common only in two SE languages, Timucua, showing 50 such items, and Apalachee, with 7 (see Sturtevant 1962:66–67 for these lists). Sources for other SE languages only very occasionally attest to lexical items that are true or possible Spanish loanwords beyond the 20 in table 9.4.

Among the 19 SE languages having Spanish loanwords, Creek (CRK), with 16, shows the largest number, followed by Mikasuki (MKS), with 15; Koasati (KST) and Seminole (SML), with 10 each; Alabama (ALB) and Chickasaw (CHS), with 8 each; Choctaw (CHT) and Caddo (CDD), with 5 each; Cherokee (CHR), with 4; Mobilian Jargon (MBJ), Hitchiti (HCH), and Timucua (TMC), with 3 each; Biloxi (BLX) and Yuchi (YCH), with 2 each; and Chitimacha (CHM), Tunica (TNC), Shawnee (SHW), Quapaw (QPW), and Apalachee (APL), with 1 each. A rough correlation between the number of Spanish loans and language location is apparent: the number of loans generally decreases with a shift from southeastern languages of the region (e.g., Creek and Mikasuki) to western languages (e.g., Chickasaw, Choctaw, and Biloxi) and to northern languages (e.g., Cherokee and Shawnee).

Table 9.3. Recorded languages of the southeastern United States and lexical sources.

PIDGIN LANGUAGE: Mobilian Jargon (MBJ)

MUSKOGEAN FAMILY: Alabama (ALB), Apalachee (APL), Chickasaw (CHS), Choctaw (CHT), Creek (CRK), Hitchiti (HCH), Koasati (KST), Mikasuki (MKS), Seminole (SML)

SIOUAN FAMILY: Biloxi (BLX), Catawba (CTW), Ofo (OFO), Quapaw (QPW), Tutelo (TTL), Woccon (WCC)

IROQUOIAN FAMILY: Cherokee (CHR), Nottoway (NTT), Tuscarora (TSC)

ALGONQUIAN FAMILY: Pamlico (PML), Powhatan (PWH), Shawnee (SHW)

CADDOAN FAMILY: Caddo (CDD)

LANGUAGE ISOLATES: Atakapa (ATK), Chitimacha (CHM), Natchez (NTZ), Timucua (TMC), Tunica (TNC), Yuchi (YCH)

Adapted from Cecil H. Brown, Spanish loanwords in languages of the southeastern United States, *International Journal of American Linguistics* (1998), 64:148–167.

LEXICAL SOURCES: Sources include mainly dictionaries, vocabularies, word lists, and glossaries. Munro (1992b) served as a source for Muskogean languages in general. Sources for individual SE languages are as follows: ALB: Sylestine, Hardy, and Montler (1993); APL: Kimball (1988); ATK: Gatschet and Swanton (1932); BLX: Dorsey and Swanton (1912), Haas (1968); CDD: Wallace Chafe (personal communication), Gallatin (1836), Parsons (1941); CHM: Gatschet (1883), Swanton (1919), Haas (1947); CHR: Alexander (1971), Feeling (1975), Holmes and Smith (1976), King and King (1976); CHS: Humes and Humes (1973), Munro and Willmond (1994); CHT: Wright (1880), Watkins (1892), Byington (1915), Nicklas (1974); CRK: Pope (1792), Gallatin (1836), Gatschet (1888), Loughridge and Hodge (1890), William C. Sturtevant (1962), Hardy (1988), Haas (n.d.); CTW: Shea 1984; HCH: M. Williams (1992), Sturtevant (1962); KST: Kimball (1994); MKS: Sturtevant (1962, personal communication), Derrick-Mescua (1980), Boynton (1982), J. B. Martin (1987, personal communication); MBJ: Crawford (1978), Drechsel (1979, 1996); NTZ: Brinton (1873), Haas (1947), Van Tuyl (1979); OFO: Dorsey and Swanton (1912); QPW: Drechsel (personal communication), Rankin (1988); SHW: Voegelin (1938a, 1938b, 1939, 1940a, 1940b); SML: Nathan (1977), Sturtevant (personal communication); TMC: Granberry (1993); TNC: Haas (1953); TSC: Rudes (1987); WCC: Schoolcraft (1855); YCH: W. L. Ballard (personal communication), Rudes (personal communication), Wagner (1931, 1933–1938).

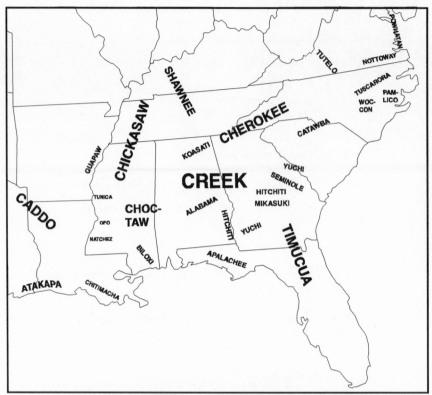

Figure 9.1. Location of recorded Native American languages in the southeastern United States from 1700 to 1800. Adapted from John R. Swanton, *The Indians of the Southeastern United States* (Washington: Government Printing Office, 1946).

Spanish loanwords (hereafter referring just to those in table 9.4 unless otherwise indicated) in ten SE languages constitute *perfect* subsets of the 16 found in Creek. For example, all 10 of Koasati's loans also occur among the 16 pertaining to Creek, all 8 of Alabama's also occur among those of Creek, as do all 3 of Mobilian Jargon. Another six languages show *near perfect* subsets of Creek loanwords wherein only one member of each respective set is not also found in Creek. Only one language, Caddo, shows a set of Spanish loans that is neither a perfect nor near-perfect subset of those in Creek.

Since it is extremely unlikely that individual SE languages would have independently borrowed the same words from Spanish, the observed distribution must be due to the diffusion of loanwords across SE languages. Thus, these languages, for the most part, have only rarely borrowed terms directly from Spanish (cf. Sturtevant 1962:51–52; J. B. Martin 1994). Indeed, Spanish loanwords in the vast majority of instances appear to have been diffused from Creek (directly or indirectly) to most other languages of the region.

There is strong distributional evidence of an impressively long diffusional chain of Spanish loans. Table 9.4 shows that all loans in Koasati are included among Creek loans, all loans in Alabama are included among Koasati loans, all but one loan in

Table 9.4. Twenty Spanish words yielding loans in at least two languages of the southeastern United States.

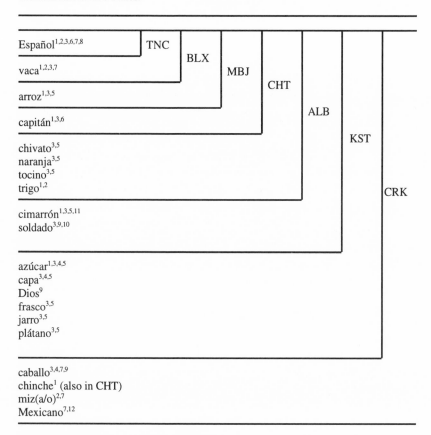

Español[1,2,3,6,7,8]

vaca[1,2,3,7]

arroz[1,3,5]

capitán[1,3,6]

chivato[3,5]
naranja[3,5]
tocino[3,5]
trigo[1,2]

cimarrón[1,3,5,11]
soldado[3,9,10]

azúcar[1,3,4,5]
capa[3,4,5]
Dios[9]
frasco[3,5]
jarro[3,5]
plátano[3,5]

caballo[3,4,7,9]
chinche[1] (also in CHT)
miz(a/o)[2,7]
Mexicano[7,12]

TNC
BLX
MBJ
CHT
ALB
KST
CRK

TRANSLATIONS OF SPANISH TERMS

Español "Spanish"
vaca "cow"
arroz "rice"
capitán "captain"
chivato "goat"
naranja "orange"
tocino "bacon"
trigo "wheat"
cimarrón "wild"
soldado "soldier"

azúcar "sugar"
capa "cloak"
Dios "God"
flasco "bottle"
jarro "jug"
plátano "banana"
caballo "horse"
chinche "bed bug"
miz(a/o) "cat"
Mexicano "Mexican"

[1]CHS, [2]CHR, [3]MKS, [4]HCH, [5]SML, [6]YCH, [7]CDD, [8]QPW, [9]TMC, [10]APL, [11]SHW, [12]CHM.

Adapted from Cecil H. Brown, Spanish loanwords in languages of the southeastern United States, *International Journal of American Linguistics* (1998), 64:148–167.

Choctaw is included among Alabama loans, all loans in Mobilian Jargon are included among Choctaw loans, all Biloxi loans are included among Mobilian Jargon loans, and the single loan in Tunica is included among Biloxi loans. Distributional data, then, robustly suggest that Creek donated Spanish loans to Koasati, Koasati to Alabama, Alabama to Choctaw, Choctaw to Mobilian Jargon, Mobilian Jargon to Biloxi, and Biloxi to Tunica (cf. J. B. Martin 1994).

In addition, data suggest other, shorter paths of diffusion not as apparent as that just described. Spanish loans in Seminole constitute a perfect subset of loans in Mikasuki, whose loans in turn constitute a near-perfect subset of loans in Creek, suggesting that Creek donated loans to Mikasuki, which in turn donated them to Seminole. Seminole is a dialect of Creek whose speakers migrated to Florida in historic times. Choctaw shows five Spanish loanwords, all of which are found among the eight loans in Chickasaw, its sister dialect, suggesting that Chickasaw contributed loans to Choctaw.

This interpretation of the diffusion of Spanish loans across languages of the SE dovetails with our somewhat limited knowledge of the Spanish presence in the area. Spanish exploration of the SE is thought to have begun with Juan Ponce de Leon's voyage along the east Florida coast in 1513. From this date until around 1565, when St. Augustine was founded, there were various Spanish expeditions into the SE interior, but none had any lasting effect on native peoples (Sturtevant 1962:46–47). In 1573, Spanish missions were established in northern Florida among the Timucua and along the Georgia coast among the Indians of Guale. Missions were extended westward to the Apalachee (in northern Florida) around 1633 (Sturtevant 1971:98). From this time onward for about 70 years, speakers of Timucua and Apalachee and the Guale Indians were more or less continuously in contact with the Spanish, thus accounting for most known Spanish loans in Timucua and Apalachee.

To the best of our knowledge, the Spanish never succeeded in establishing viable missions among other SE groups east of the Mississippi River. Perhaps with this in mind, Jack Martin (1994:17) proposes that Spanish loanwords of interest here (table 9.4) spread from languages of the missionized groups to those of hinterland peoples, specifically first to speakers of Creek and Mikasuki and later to others. John H. Hann (personal communication) cites Apalachee migrations to the Creek and Hitchiti country in the 1680s and in 1704 and 1715, which could have facilitated the diffusion of Spanish loanwords to Creek speakers. Hann also mentions Apalachee who migrated to Mobile in 1704 and who could have donated Spanish words to native groups living there; other such donations could have occurred when Apalachee moved on to the Red River in 1765. Sturtevant (1962:53) speculates, on the basis of admittedly skimpy evidence, that at the end of the mission period (c. 1700) Guale Indians moved west and joined the Creek confederacy, thus possibly explaining Spanish loanwords in Creek.

Sturtevant (1962:50) discusses another possibility with a considerably earlier date. In 1566, an exploration of the Georgia-Alabama interior was undertaken by Captain Juan Pardo and Sergeant Boyano with a force of 125 soldiers. A group led by Boyano found its way to the Creek town of Chiaha, where he and his men settled for at least a few months, building a fort and "planting wheat and barley there and spent much time visiting the Indians in the neighborhood and contracting alliances with them" (Swanton 1946:65). Many of the loanwords in question could have entered Creek at that time. (It is interesting that the Spanish word for WHEAT, *trigo*, is among the 20 items in table 9.4.) As Sturtevant (1962:53) notes, if direct borrowing by Creek speakers from

Spanish occurred in the interior, it must have taken place before 1675 since after that date Creek contact with Europeans primarily involved English speakers.

Although how and when Spanish loans entered Creek remains to be resolved, scholars tend to agree that they spread from Creek to other languages of the SE interior (e.g., Sturtevant 1962; Kimball 1994; Martin 1994). The source of Creek's influence may relate to its wide use as a lingua franca by members of the Creek confederacy, who spoke a number of different SE tongues as first languages. (Drechsel 1983 suggests the possibility that Lingua Franca Creek was pidginized.) These languages included Hitchiti, Mikasuki, Apalachee, Alabama, Koasati, Choctaw, and Chickasaw (all Muskogean); Yuchi (an isolate); and Shawnee (Algonquian) (Crawford 1975:37; Drechsel 1979:45–46, 1983:392; Derrick-Mescua 1980:13). Later, speakers of Seminole (Muskogean) in Florida probably also used Lingua Franca Creek as a second language (Drechsel 1979:47). Speakers of some of these languages are also known to have been in close proximity to Creek groups. Swanton reports that at least before 1686 part of the Koasati "had moved into the Creek country. . . and most of the tribe soon gathered there" (1946:145). Some of the Chickasaw in the eighteenth century moved eastward and settled for a while among the Creeks (p. 117). Several Shawnee settlements were located in Creek territory in the second half of the eighteenth century, and some Yuchi are known to have joined them there (pp. 184, 213).

Lingua Franca Creek was not used by speakers of some SE languages to which Spanish loanwords nonetheless were eventually diffused. These included an isolate (Tunica), a Siouan language (Biloxi), an Iroquoian language (Cherokee), and a Caddoan language (Caddo). However, speakers of all of these languages except Cherokee are known to have also spoken Mobilian Jargon, a now extinct pidgin trade language (Drechsel 1979:129–130, 1996). At its peak, in the eighteenth century, Mobilian Jargon was spoken in the lower Mississippi valley from southern or central Illinois south to the delta region, west into eastern Texas, and east to the vicinity of the Alabama-Georgia border, including the northwestern Gulf coast of Florida (p. 131).

Other users of Mobilian Jargon included speakers of five languages who also employed Lingua Franca Creek. These were groups who spoke Apalachee, Alabama, Koasati, Choctaw, and Chickasaw as first languages (Drechsel 1979:129–130). Mobilian Jargon was almost certainly a vehicle through which Spanish loanwords diffused to languages whose speakers did not also speak Lingua Franca Creek (cf. pp. 76, 169). Drechsel (1983, 1996, and personal communication) proposes that Lingua Franca Creek may have been an Eastern Muskogean-based variety of Mobilian Jargon. Spanish loans probably entered Mobilian Jargon indirectly from Creek, a transfer no doubt facilitated by people who used both Mobilian Jargon and Lingua Franca Creek, most likely speakers of Choctaw and/or Chickasaw. Western Muskogean (Choctaw/Chickasaw) constituted the predominant source of Mobilian Jargon's lexicon (Drechsel 1979, 1996; Munro 1984).

Speakers of Biloxi and Tunica, both now extinct (Crawford 1975), used Mobilian as a lingua franca, consistent with the finding that Spanish loans in these languages are subsets of those found in the pidgin (see table 9.4). Distributional evidence suggests that Biloxi contributed a loan directly to Tunica. This transfer is in accord with what is known from historical accounts of contacts among speakers of these languages. Haas (1968:81) reports that as late as the beginning of the twentieth century, speakers of Biloxi and Tunica lived together in the vicinity of Marksville, Louisiana. Speakers of Tunica settled in the Marksville area some time between 1784 and 1803 (Swanton

1946:198), and speakers of Biloxi may have arrived there around the same time (p. 97).

While Caddo, whose speakers used Mobilian Jargon, shows five loans from Spanish (see table 9.4), these do not constitute a perfect or even near-perfect subset of loans found in Mobilian Jargon, in Creek, or in any other SE language. Some or all of these items may have been borrowed directly from Spanish. The historical context dovetails with such a possibility. During the early years of the eighteenth century, Spaniards from posts in New Spain (Mexico) established missions in Caddo country in eastern Texas (Crawford 1975:16). Although these were largely unsuccessful ventures, at least one, founded among the Nacogdoches, endured until around 1772 (Swanton 1946:75, 156). Phonological evidence is also suggestive. The Spanish loan for COW in Caddo (*wa:kas*) differs from reflexes of Spanish *vaca* in other SE languages (e.g., Creek *wa:ka*, Choctaw *wa:k*, and Biloxi *wa:ka*) since it alone is modeled on the plural realization of the Spanish word (*vacas*) (Wallace Chafe, personal communication). This suggests an origin for the Caddo term independent of reflexes in other languages of the SE. In addition, the terms for CAT in Caddo (*míst'uh* and *ch'á:mis*) are based on the archaic Spanish *miz(o/a)* and thus differ from most words for CAT in other SE languages, which are derived from Spanish *gato* or English "cat" or "kitty." In fact, of the five Spanish loans in Caddo, only one, based on *Español* "Spanish," is likely to have been acquired directly from another SE language. If it were, Mobilian Jargon was the probable contributing agent.

Cherokee shares with Caddo, and only with Caddo among SE languages, a "cat" term based on Spanish *miz(o/a)*. Given the considerable geographic removal of the two languages from each other, it is unlikely that one of these donated the word to the other. Both languages probably acquired their terms independently and directly from Spanish. Sturtevant (1962:54), citing a conversation with R. D. Fogelson, writes that a Cherokee group at Chickamauga in Tennessee had trade contacts with the Spanish at New Orleans and Pensacola in the late eighteenth century, thus possibly explaining the provenience of the loan. The other three Spanish loans in Cherokee (see table 9.4) were probably directly donated to the language by Creek since the three items constitute a near-perfect subset of loans found in Creek.

Finally, an explanation of the reported correlation between number of Spanish loans and language location should now be reasonably apparent. Spanish loans generally decrease in number with a shift from more southeastern SE languages to western and northern ones because of the geographic removal of languages from the fount of Spanish influence in the southeastern part of the region, that is, in Florida and immediately adjacent areas. There was also a Spanish presence in the western part of the SE: the area known today as French Louisiana was under Spanish dominion between 1763 and 1800. However, if Spanish loanwords are any indication, the relatively brief Spanish control of Louisiana had little enduring impact on the languages of native peoples in the region.

10

LOAN SHIFT: A BRIEF CASE STUDY

In addition to diffused native terms (chapter 8) and diffused European loans (chapter 9), names for imported items have spread across Native American languages independent of phonological representation. This is typically manifested by phonologically different native labels that show the same, or virtually the same, semantic content in two or more languages. When such similarities are due to diffusion, as opposed to either universal naming tendencies (chapter 4) or to chance, they constitute loan shifts. As noted in chapter 3, loan shifts come in two varieties: (1) loan translations (or calques) in which compound labels in one language are translated, morpheme by morpheme, into words of another language, and (2) semantic loans, which are like loan translations except that they involve single words rather than compounds.

This chapter focuses on the considerable complexities of a widespread loan shift for naming the introduced PEACH in languages of the southeastern United States (SE). Formally, the loan shift in question is a semantic loan since various monolexemic labels for PEACH in SE languages are all derived from native terms for the indigenous WILD PLUM. This semantic loan has developed in conjunction with a broadly occurring loan translation in which the WILD PLUM is designated by compound labels with terms for PEACH as constituents (Brown 1996b). These nomenclatural relationships are the products of an areally pertinent marking reversal (chapter 3), which has been motivated by a radical shift in the relative cultural importance of the referents involved.

The Data

The following is a list of all words for PEACH and PLUM recorded for SE languages, which are organized by genetic grouping (see table 9.3 and figure 9.1). Also given, when possible and appropriate, are the literal translations of these. Actual terms and, occasionally, original English glosses are placed within brackets. For all Muskogean languages and for Cherokee, Shawnee, and Tunica, orthographies have been normalized after Munro (1992b). However, orthographies depart from Munro by presenting the glottal stop as ʔ and the alveopalatal or retroflex spirant as š. For other languages, original transcriptions (as found in sources) are enclosed between left (<)

and right (>) arrows. The symbol UE, found in literal translations, stands for "unknown element." For lexical sources for these data, see table 9.3.

PIDGIN LANGUAGE

Mobilian Jargon   *peach*: [tak(k)on]
                  plum: PEACH + LITTLE [tak(k)on oši]

MUSKOGEAN LANGUAGES

Choctaw   *peach*: [takkon]
            plum: PEACH + LITTLE [takkon-oši]
Chickasaw   *peach*: [takOlo]
            plum: PEACH + LITTLE ONE [takOloši?]
Alabama   *peach*: [takkola]
            plum: PEACH + TO BE SMALL [takkosawwa]
Koasati   *peach*: [takkola]
            plum: PEACH + TO BE SMALL [takkollawista], PEACH + UE
            [takkolsalba "Chickasaw plum"]
Creek   *peach*: [paka:na "a peach, sometimes apples"]
            plum: PEACH + LITTLE [paka:noci]
Seminole   *peach*: [paka:na]
            plum: —
Mikasuki   *peach*: [tohâ:ni]
            plum: [tohâ:ni]
Hitchiti   *peach*: [<tohani>]
            plum: [<osi>]

SIOUAN LANGUAGES

Biloxi   *peach*: [<tkâ'nâ>, <tokoña'>]
            plum: [<sti'iñki'>]
Ofo   *peach*: [<akô^{n}ti>]
            plum: PEACH + RED [<akó^{n}t atcû'ti>]
Catawba   *peach*: [<yēh>]
            plum: [<tchick-neh>]
Woccon   *peach*: [<yonne>]
            plum: —

IROQUOIAN LANGUAGES

Cherokee   *peach*: [kwa^{2}na]
            plum: PEACH + UE [kwa^{2}nun^{3}sḍ^2?i]
Tuscarora   *peach*: [<kwáhrak>]
            plum: —

ALGONQUIAN LANGUAGE

Shawnee   *peach*: [po?kama]
               plum: PEACH + DIMINUTIVE [po?kamaaθa]

LANGUAGE ISOLATES

Atakapa   *peach*: [<tepu′k>]
               plum: PEACH + RED [<tepû′k ku′tskuts>]
Natchez   *peach*: [<ápîshu'l>]
               plum: UE + PEACH [<antabishu'l>]
Tunica   *peach*: [kiru]
               plum: PEACH + RED [kirumili]
Yuchi   *peach*: [<?yabo>]
               plum: PEACH + LITTLE [<?yabos?i>]

In 13 of these languages a term for the European-introduced PEACH (*Prunus persica*) is used in compound labels to refer to species of WILD PLUM native to America (e.g., *Prunus angustifolia*, the Chickasaw plum). This usage constitutes a marking reversal in which native words for PLUM have shifted in reference to PEACH, with PLUM subsequently becoming overtly marked vis-à-vis PEACH; for example, "little peach" designates PLUM in Choctaw, Alabama, and Creek, and "red peach" designates PLUM in Ofo, Atakapa, and Tunica ("little" and "red" are overt marks).

Marking Reversal for Peach and Plum

As discussed at length in chapter 3, instances of marking reversal are typically observed in the context of cultural processes such as innovation and invention or interaction between markedly different cultures, for example, Old World influence on New World groups (Witkowski and Brown 1983:571). Marking reversals always entail two similar referents (e.g., PLUM and PEACH, both of which belong to same genus, *Prunus*), one overtly marked vis-à-vis the other. When foreign introductions are involved, the overtly marked referent is usually a culturally significant native item (PLUM) while its unmarked counterpart is an introduced one (PEACH). Marking reversals are motivated by radical changes in the relative cultural importance of referents, and the introduced item, which is initially low in salience, comes to surpass its counterpart (Witkowski and Brown 1983).

When the peach was first introduced to the SE (probably by the Spanish), one or more languages may have used words for an important native fruit, PLUM, in reference to PEACH creating PEACH/PLUM polysemy, such as Mikasuki (Muskogean) *tohâ:ni*, which denotes both of these referents (see preceding list). As the PEACH increased in cultural importance, it may have become overtly marked vis-à-vis PLUM in some languages, developing labels like *puhusu?kui* for PEACH in modern Comanche (Uto-Aztecan), which is literally "fuzzy plum" (Robinson and Armagost 1990). Conceivably, the importance of peaches may have increased to such an extent that it surpassed that of native plums, leading to a reversal in marking in which PLUM developed an overt marking construction based on a label for PEACH. Of course, this speculative assessment assumes changes in the relative salience of native plums and introduced peaches, but such an assumption appears to be historically justified.

Historical Context

According to Swanton (1946:279), peaches were introduced to the SE by the Spanish, probably by colonists in Florida. The English colony in the Carolinas is another possible early donor (Du Pratz 1758:II:20). The literature does not provide us with an introduction date, even an approximate one. On this point the most informative statement by Swanton is that "[p]lants and trees introduced at a comparatively early date include the passiflora, watermelon, muskmelon, peach, peanut, canna, sorghum, the cultivated sweet potato, rice, okra, apple, fig, and orange" (p. 297).

Some of the earliest writers have provided texts that cite the importance of wild plums among native peoples. Swanton (1946:265) notes that chroniclers of the De Soto expedition (1539–1543) report use by various groups of wild tree fruits, especially plums and persimmons, whose preparation often included drying. Other accounts that suggest the importance of plums, and persimmons as well, are relatively numerous, and they also occasionally mention drying. Strachey (1849) cites plums among important wild foods for Virginia groups; De Montigny (c. 1698) notes the same for the Taensa (Shea 1861:76–78); Pénicaut (c. 1699) for the Pascagoula (Margry 1883:388–391); Timberlake (c. 1761) for the Cherokee (S. C. Williams 1927:68–72); Bartram ([1792] 1909:49–50) for the Creek; Romans (1775:84–85) for the Choctaw; Swanton (1946:296) for the Caddo; Elvas (Bourne 1904:47) and Garcilaso de la Vega (1723) for the Apalachee; and MacCauley (1887:504) for the Seminole. The popularity of plums, at least among the Creeks, is illustrated by this quote from Bartram: "There is a vast collection of plums or drupes, of the size and figure of ordinary plums, which...is a delicious and nourishing food, and diligently sought after" (pp. 49–50). Gene Anderson (personal communication) writes that the Chickasaw plum, a relatively big and impressive plant with lots of fruit, was widely cultivated in the SE and may even have been domesticated by native peoples.

Some of the earliest references to peaches are following. De Montigny around 1698 observed peach and plum trees in blossom in the region of the Taensa people (Shea 1861:76–78). Pénicaut (c. 1699) in a short description of a Pascagoula village writes, "The peaches are better and larger [than in France], but the plums are not so good" (Margry 1883:388–391). The same author (c. 1706) states of the Acolapissa, "They have...peaches in the season which are even larger than in France and more sugary" (pp. 467–469). Near the beginning of the eighteenth century Beverley (1705:14) mentions peaches in Virginia. Slightly later, Catesby writes of coastal Algonquian peoples in Carolina: "In summer, they feed much on vegetables...[including] peaches, raspberries, and strawberries, which their woods abound in" (1731–1743:x). Du Pratz (1758:II: 20) refers to clingstone peaches grown by the Natchez, out of whose juice a kind of wine is prepared. Around 1761 Timberlake found that the fruits of the Cherokee country were "plums, cherries, and berries of several kinds...but their peaches and pears grow only by culture" (S. C. Williams 1927:68–72). Romans writes of Creek groups that "they dry peaches and persimmons" (1775:93–94). Swanton adds that "[w]hen Romans visited the nation, peach trees had been introduced and planted in considerable numbers about most Indian towns" (1946:286). Lawson describes for Siouan tribes of the Carolinas, "all sorts of fruits, and peaches, which they dry and make quiddonies and cakes, that are very pleasant" (1860:290–291).

Some of these quotations indicate that food preservation methods applicable to native plums and persimmons were readily transferred to the introduced peach. Indeed, Swanton notes for the SE in general that "[a]s soon as peaches were introduced they were dried and put away like plums and persimmons" (1946:73). Other remarks by Swanton strongly indicate that peaches quickly replaced plums and persimmons as fruits of first choice in the region; for example, he writes, "[B]efore peaches were introduced into the country the greatest use was made of the persimmon" (p. 363), implying that the greatest use was made of the peach subsequently. Swanton's clearest statement about the relative popularity of peaches and plums and persimmons is this: "The original 'Indian peach' was probably introduced by the Spaniards, and peach trees were soon planted about most Indian towns of any consequence. Like the native plums and persimmons, the fruit was dried and seems to have supplanted all others in the estimation of the natives" (pp. 363–364).

Insight into the considerable importance of the peach among the Natchez of the lower Mississippi is given by Du Pratz in a discussion of their system of time. The Natchez divided their year into 13 months, or moons. At the beginning of every month they celebrated a feast that took "its name from the principal fruits gathered in the preceding moon, or from the animals that are usually hunted then.... The fifth moon is that of the Peaches. It answers to our month of July" (as quoted in Swanton 1946:260). Other Natchez months and feasts with botanical names include the second moon (strawberries), the third (little corn), the fourth (watermelons), the sixth (mulberries), the seventh (great corn), the twelfth (chestnuts), and the thirteenth (nuts). Notably lacking from this list of "principal fruits" are native plums and persimmons. Thus, by the time Du Pratz visited the Natchez, peaches clearly had acquired substantial salience, probably more so than plums if botanical naming of months and feasts is a reasonably good measure of their relative significance.

While not exhaustive, this review of historical sources certainly suggests that the introduction of peaches to the SE generally resulted in a shift in the relative importance of peaches and plums which could have motivated a marking reversal.

Loan Shift and Areal Diffusion

The overt marking of PLUM vis-à-vis PEACH is in more-or-less geographically contiguous distribution only among Amerindian languages of the SE. In languages of other areas of the Americas, the marking reversal occurs hardly at all. In addition, when PEACH and PLUM are connected through overt marking elsewhere, PEACH is usually overtly marked vis-à-vis PLUM (as in the previously cited Comanche example), suggesting that the salience of the introduced peach has not exceeded that of the native plum. Only in one language of North America outside the SE have I encountered a clear example of a marking reversal that involves the native PLUM and PEACH. Ottawa (Algonquian) shows *bgesaanmin'gaawanzh* for PLUM which is its "peach" term (*bgesaan*) combined with some unknown element (Rhodes 1985). The general restriction of the nomenclatural feature to languages of the SE strongly suggests areal spread through loan shift.

Mobilian Jargon, a now extinct pidginized lingua franca of the area, shares a term for PEACH with several Muskogean languages and uses it in a compound label for PLUM (see the list of data; see also chapter 9 for Mobilian Jargon). Speakers of most of the SE languages with this nomenclatural feature are known to have spoken Mobilian Jargon as an auxiliary language. These languages include Atakapa, Alabama, Chickasaw, Choctaw, Koasati, Natchez, Ofo, and Tunica (Drechsel 1979:129–130). This suggests that the trait could have been diffused as a loan shift to these languages from Mobilian Jargon. One language, Biloxi, whose speakers used Mobilian Jargon, does not show the nomenclatural feature. Nevertheless, Biloxi has a term for PEACH, *tkâ'nâ* or *tokoⁿa'*, which is phonologically very similarly to Mobilian Jargon's "peach" word, *tak(k)on*, and could have been directly borrowed from the lingua franca.

Some SE languages whose speakers did not use Mobilian Jargon show a complex label for PLUM based on PEACH. These include Creek, Cherokee, Yuchi, and Shawnee. Speakers of three of these languages, Creek, Yuchi, and Shawnee, were members of the Creek confederacy, who along with a number of other member groups used Lingua Franca Creek as an auxiliary language (Drechsel 1983; see chapter 9). As noted in chapter 9, Mobilian Jargon and Lingua Franca Creek are known to have had users in common, including speakers of Alabama, Chickasaw, Choctaw, and Koasati (Crawford 1975:37; Drechsel 1979:45–46, 1983:392; Derrick-Mescua 1980:13). Thus, there was a natural conduit for the transfer of linguistic traits from Mobilian Jargon to Lingua Franca Creek and vice versa. One of these may have been a loan shift with overt marking of PLUM based on PEACH. While speakers of Cherokee are not known to have used either Mobilian Jargon or Lingua Franca Creek, they could have borrowed the trait from Creek, a language known to have exchanged lexical items with Cherokee (J. B. Martin 1994).

Loan shift alone may not explain the widespread distribution across SE languages of overt marking of PLUM vis-à-vis PEACH. It may be partially the result of the independent development of the feature in different SE languages. This is not so farfetched since, in addition to SE languages, the trait occurs in Ottawa (Algonquian, Ontario), an Amerindian language so distantly removed geographically from SE languages that their common possession of the feature almost certainly is due to coincidental invention rather than to historical connection. Conceivably, then, the trait's SE distribution itself could be attributable to some degree of independent development in addition to areal diffusion.

It seems unlikely that the feature in question was diffused throughout languages of the SE as a fully completed marking reversal. Before the introduction of peaches, most if not all SE languages must have had perfectly good terms for the native PLUM. Thus, after introduction, at least in the early days, there would have been little if any reason for languages to borrow a construction for PLUM from their neighbors. In at least one SE language, the acquisition of peaches led to the development of a term for the fruit through referential extension of a native word for the culturally salient and botanically similar PLUM. The lack of a word for PEACH in other area languages could have motivated borrowing of this semantically appropriate naming strategy from neighboring languages. Consequently, the lexical designation of PEACH by a term for PLUM may have been incorporated into many SE languages as a loan translation or a semantic loan. As peaches increased significantly in salience throughout the region, pressure would have been exerted over time on all area languages that nomenclaturally link the fruits to linguistically mark PLUM vis-à-vis PEACH. Presumably, this pressure would have resulted in the independent development of overt marking of PLUM vis-à-vis PEACH in some languages. Others, of course, may have acquired the feature as a result of influence from their SE neighbors.

That overt marking constructions for PLUM are not semantically identical in all languages of the SE is some support for this speculative interpretation. In Alabama, Choctaw, Creek, Koasati, Mobilian Jargon, Yuchi, and Shawnee, terms for PLUM are literally "little peach," whereas in Atakapa, Ofo, and Tunica, they are literally "red peach." If a single overt marking construction for PLUM was diffused throughout the SE, one might anticipate or project uniformity across area languages in semantic content. The lack of such semantic uniformity conforms with the proposition that some languages of the region independently developed labels for PLUM based on PEACH.

A similar situation pertains to another nomenclatural trait that is both common among and unique to SE languages. At least 16 of these languages have overt marking constructions for the native OPOSSUM based on the European introduced PIG (Alabama, Atakapa, Biloxi, Caddo, Chitimacha, Cherokee, Chickasaw, Choctaw, Creek, Koasati, Mobilian Jargon, Mikasuki, Seminole, Ofo, Quapaw, and Yuchi)—the result of marking reversal (Witkowski and Brown 1983:574). The semantic content of these labels varies across SE languages even more so than that for PLUM: "white pig" in Alabama, Caddo, Choctaw, Creek, Koasati, Mobilian Jargon, Mikasuki, and Seminole; "forest pig" in Atakapa, Chitimacha, and Ofo; "smiling pig" in Cherokee and Choctaw; "swamp pig" in Biloxi; and "small pig" and "true(?) pig" in Chickasaw (Chickasaw has several synonyms for OPOSSUM). In one language, Natchez, PIG is actually overtly marked vis-à-vis OPOSSUM (with "big opossum" designating PIG) instead of vice versa. In addition, one early writer, Adair (1775), provides a statement from which it can be inferred that the modern Cherokee word for PIG once referred polysemously to both OPOSSUM and PIG (as quoted in S. C. Williams 1930:17). This example, then, similarly suggests that some SE languages independently developed marking reversals that entailed the same two referents, probably after the idea of referentially extending a word for one of them (OPOSSUM) to the other (PIG) was diffused widely throughout the region.

11

POSTCONTACT LINGUISTIC AREAS

Data assembled in the preceding chapters attest to the diffusion of several postcontact linguistic traits across both genetically affiliated and unaffiliated languages of the southeastern United States (SE). These include Spanish loanwords for items of acculturation (see table 9.4) and loan shifts that involve the imported referents PEACH and PIG (chapter 10). Two lingua francas of the region, Mobilian Jargon and Lingua Franca Creek, are identified as probable primary agents of diffusion. This is in accord with the findings of chapter 8 that genetically unrelated languages spoken by groups who use the same lingua franca share native terms for acculturated items mainly as a result of parallel acquisitions from the lingua franca.

In addition to being a cultural province (Crawford 1975:1), the SE constitutes a postcontact linguistic area. A linguistic area is apparent when geographically contiguous languages, some of which are not genetically related to one another, share linguistic features that are largely explained by areal diffusion (i.e., borrowing) rather than by such factors as inheritance from a common ancestor, universal tendencies, or coincidence (cf. Sherzer 1973, 1976; Campbell, Kaufman, and Smith-Stark 1986; Aikhenvald 1996). In the case of native languages of the New World, when shared traits are names for objects and concepts introduced by Europeans, linguistic areas are postcontact developments. (See Campbell, Kaufman, and Smith-Stark 1986:530–536 for a detailed background discussion of linguistic areas.)

In the following pages, I compile information attesting to five major postcontact linguistic areas in the Americas, including the SE, Pacific Northwest, Andean South America, Mesoamerica, and tropical forest South America. These are not the only postcontact linguistic areas in the New World, but they are clearly among the geographically most expansive. Undoubtedly not a coincidence, historically associated with each of these five areas is a major lingua franca (see chapter 8), respectively, Mobilian Jargon, Chinook Jargon, Peruvian Quechua, Nahuatl (Aztec), and Tupí (with Guaraní).

The five postcontact linguistic areas exist because speakers of Amerindian languages there used lingua francas as auxiliary languages. The evidence for this is sometimes direct and unequivocal. For example, most of the widely shared native terms for imported items in languages of the Mesoamerican region are unambiguously identified as originating in Nahuatl. Other evidence is strongly suggestive. For example, in all five regions, lingua francas show all or nearly all of the diffused traits of the languages of the area, whereas regional non-lingua franca tongues only sporadically demonstrate them. If a lingua franca were largely responsible for the areal diffusion of traits, all or at least very nearly all the traits should pertain to its lexicon; on the other hand, this should not necessarily be true of recipient languages of the region.

Southeastern United States

Table 11.1 gives the distribution across SE languages of nine postcontact traits, features in addition to the diffused Spanish loans reported in chapter 9. All nine traits are loan shifts for acculturated items, including those for PEACH and PIG, discussed in the preceding chapter. The occurrence of a trait in a language is indicated by a plus sign. A minus sign indicates that a feature either is not present or that a lexical source fails to report the trait (these conventions are also used in tables 11.2–11.5).

All 19 languages in table 11.1 (organized by genetic grouping) are geographically confined to the SE culture province (defined in chapter 9). In addition to 18 Native American languages (including 7 Muskogean languages, 3 Siouan, 1 Iroquoian, 1 Algonquian, 1 Caddoan, and 5 isolates), table 11.1 includes information from the pidgin lingua franca Mobilian Jargon.

Only two languages, Mobilian Jargon and Choctaw, show all nine traits. The homogeneity of these two languages is not unexpected since the pidgin is largely derived from Western Muskogean, of which Choctaw is a member dialect (along with its sister dialect Chickasaw). If the traits in question were diffusing directly from the lingua franca to all other languages, it should, as it does, demonstrate all nine linguistic features. An unrecorded lingua franca of the region, Lingua Franca Creek, may have also contributed to the distribution of these features. As noted in chapter 9, Mobilian Jargon and Lingua Franca Creek are known to have had users in common; also, Drechsel (1983, 1996, and personal communication) proposes that Lingua Franca Creek may have been a variety of Mobilian Jargon.

Pacific Northwest

Table 11.2 gives the distribution of eight postcontact features across languages of the Pacific Northwest and abutting regions. These are in addition to the twelve French loanwords shared by languages of the area, all of which incorporate French definite articles as initial syllables (chapter 9). Four of the eight traits entail European loanwords: (1) the English word "apple" which is borrowed into languages in its plural version (with suffixed -s); (2) a native term for CAT, for example, Chinook Jargon *pish-pish*, which may be a corruption of an English term for calling felines, "pus-pus"; (3) a native term for MONEY, which is a referential extension of English "dollar"; and (4) a loan for PIG based on French *cochon*. The other four items are purely native terms, two of which—a word for WAGON, for example, Chinook Jargon *chik'-chik*, and a word for COW, such as Songish *mósmʌs*—are probably onomatopoeic in origin (chapter 3).

Table 11.1. Distribution of nine postcontact traits across languages of the southeastern United States.

	A	B	C	D	E	F	G	H	I
PIDGIN									
Mobilian Jargon	+	+	+	+	+	+	+	+	+
MUSKOGEAN									
Choctaw	+	+	+	+	+	+	+	+	+
Chickasaw	+	+	+	+	−	+	+	+	+
Alabama	+	+	+	+	−	+	−	−	−
Koasati	+	+	+	+	−	+	+	−	−
Creek	+	+	+	+	−	+	+	−	+
Seminole	−	+	−	+	−	−	−	−	−
Mikasuki	+	+	−	+	−	+	−	−	−
SIOUAN									
Biloxi	−	+	+	+	+	−	+	+	+
Ofo	+	+	−	−	+	−	−	−	−
Quapaw	−	+	−	−	−	−	−	−	−
IROQUOIAN									
Cherokee	+	+	−	−	−	−	−	+	−
ALGONQUIAN									
Shawnee	+	−	−	−	−	−	−	−	−
CADDOAN									
Caddo	−	+	−	−	+	−	−	−	−
ISOLATES									
Atakapa	+	+	+	−	+	−	−	−	−
Chitimacha	−	+	+	−	−	−	−	−	−
Natchez	+	+	+	−	+	−	+	−	−
Tunica	+	+	+	−	+	−	−	+	−
Yuchi	+	+	−	+	+	+	−	−	+

A = Loan shift for PEACH derived from a word for PLUM (typically realized as a marking reversal, e.g., "little peach" or "red peach" = PLUM; see chapters 3 and 10).

B = Loan shift for PIG derived from a word for OPOSSUM (typically realized as a marking reversal, e.g., "white pig" or "smiling pig" = OPOSSUM; see chapters 3 and 10).

C = Loan shift for SHEEP derived from a word for RABBIT (typically realized through overt marking, e.g., "domesticated rabbit" = SHEEP; see chapters 3 and 8).

D = Loan shift for WHISKEY derived from words for WATER and BITTER (always realized by "bitter water" = WHISKEY).

E = Loan shift for SUGAR derived from words for SALT and SWEET (always realized by "sweet salt" = SUGAR).

F = Loan shift for MONKEY derived from words for RACCOON and PERSON (always realized by "raccoon person" = MONKEY).

Table 11.1 *(continued)*

G = Loan shift for CHEESE derived from words for BREAD and
  MILK (always realized by "milk bread" = CHEESE).
H = Loan shift for GOAT derived from a word for DEER (typically
  realized through overt marking, e.g., "stinking deer" =
  GOAT).
I = Loan shift for SATURDAY derived from words for SUNDAY
  and YOUNGER BROTHER (always realized by "Sunday's
  younger brother" = SATURDAY).

Table 11.2. Distribution of eight postcontact traits across languages of the
Pacific Northwest and adjacent regions.

	A	B	C	D	E	F	G	H
PIDGIN								
Chinook Jargon	+	+	+	+	+	+	+	+
SALISHAN								
Kalispel	−	−	−	−	−	−	+	−
Okanagan	−	−	−	−	−	−	+	−
Shuswap	+	−	−	−	−	−	+	−
Thompson	+	+	−	+	−	−	+	−
Upper Chehalis	+	+	+	+	−	+	+	+
Clallam	+	+	+	+	+	−	+	−
Lushootseed	−	+	+	−	−	+	+	−
Saanich	+	+	+	+	−	+	−	+
Samish	−	+	+	+	−	−	+	−
Songish	+	+	+	+	−	+	−	−
Squamish	+	+	−	+	−	+	+	−
Bella Coola	+	+	−	+	−	+	+	+
WAKASHAN								
Haisla	−	−	−	+	−	+	+	−
Heiltsuk	−	−	−	−	+	+	−	+
Kwakiutl	−	−	−	−	−	−	+	−
SAHAPTIN-NEZ PERCE								
Nez Perce*	−	−	+	+	−	−	−	−
Yakima	−	+	+	+	−	−	−	−
ATHAPASCAN-EYAK								
Eyak	+	−	−	−	−	+	−	−
CHIMAKUAN								
Quileute	+	−	+	+	+	+	+	+
TSMISHIANIC								
Gitksan	−	−	−	−	+	+	−	+
NORTHWEST ISOLATES								
Haida	−	+	−	+	−	+	+	+

(continued)

Table 11.2 *(continued)*

	A	B	C	D	E	F	G	H
Klamath	+	+	+	+	−	+	+	+
WINTUN								
Wintu	−	−	−	+	−	−	−	−
CALIFORNIA ISOLATE								
Karok	+	−	−	+	−	−	−	−

*An additional source for this language is Aoki (1994).

A =   English loan for APPLE in its plural version [e.g., Chinook Jargon (Good 1880) *apples*; Upper Chehalis *ʔápls*].

B =   Native term for BREAD and/or FLOUR (e.g., Chinook Jargon *sapolil*; Upper Chehalis *saplíl*; see chapter 8).

C =   Native term for CAT, probably based on English "pus-pus" (e.g., Chinook Jargon *pish-pish*; Upper Chehalis *píšpiš*).

D =   Native term for COW, possibly onomatopoeic [e.g., Chinook Jargon *klootchman moos-moos* (literally, "female cattle"); Upper Chehalis *músmuski*; see chapter 3].

E =   Native term for HORSE (e.g., Chinook Jargon *kiuitan*; Quileute *kíˑyotad*).

F =   Native term for MONEY, based on English "dollar" (e.g., Chinook Jargon *dolla*; Upper Chehalis *táˑla*; see chapter 8).

G =   French loan for PIG, based on *cochon* (e.g., Chinook Jargon *kosho*; Upper Chehalis *kʷišú*).

H =   Native term for WAGON, probably onomatopoeic (e.g., Chinook Jargon *chik'-chik*; Upper Chehalis *c'íkc'ik*; see chapter 3).

Information from 24 Native American languages and 1 pidgin lingua franca, Chinook Jargon, is presented in table 11.2 (lexical sources for these languages, in addition to those listed in appendix B, are given in table 9.1). The native languages include 12 of the Salishan grouping, 3 affiliated with Wakashan, 2 with Sahaptin-Nez Perce, 1 with Athapascan-Eyak, 1 with Chimakuan, 1 with Wintun, 1 with Tsmishianic, 2 Pacific Northwest isolates, and 1 isolate from California. The languages involved are distributed along the Pacific Coast from northern California (Karok and Wintu) to southeastern Alaska (Eyak) and inland into the plateau region (e.g., Yakima and Kalispel).

Only 1 language of the 25, Chinook Jargon, shows all 8 postcontact features. This parallels the finding that only Chinook Jargon shows all 12 diffused French loanwords that incorporate definite articles (see table 9.1). The areal lingua franca, then, is strongly suggested to be the diffusional source of all 20 lexical items in question (Silverstein 1972:379).

The distribution of features presented in table 11.2 indicates a very broad area through which the influence of Chinook Jargon extended, that is, from northern California to southeastern Alaska and as far east as Montana (Kalispel) (cf. Thomason 1983:820). The greatest numbers of features are found in languages closest to the Pacific Coast in Oregon, Washington State, and British Columbia, including Klamath,

Quileute, languages affiliated with Coastal Salishan (Upper Chehalis through Bella Coola in table 11.2), and Haida. Speakers of languages in other areas which show fewer features—especially, speakers of Karok, Wintu, Eyak, and Kalispel—perhaps did not actually use Chinook Jargon as an auxiliary language but acquired pertinent traits from speakers of neighboring languages who did.

Andean Region

Table 11.3 presents the distribution of eight postcontact traits across languages of Andean South America and adjacent regions. All of these are native terms for items of acculturation.

Data from 25 languages and dialects are given (all of which are language cases of the current sample). These include 3 associated with Quechumaran (in Ecuador, Peru, and Bolivia), 2 with Barbacoan (Ecuador), 3 with Jivaroan (Ecuador and Peru), 3 with Maipuran (Peru), 1 with Cahuapanan (Peru), 2 with Pano-Takanan (Peru and Bolivia), 2 with Huitotoan (Colombia and Peru), 1 isolate (Colombia), 1 with Panaquitan (Colombia), 3 with Guaycuruan (Argentina), 2 with Matacoan (Argentina), and 2 with Araucanian (Chile and Argentina). These languages all more or less straddle the Andean chain on both of its flanks, with an extension into the Gran Chaco (Guaycuruan and Matacoan languages).

One of the 25 languages and dialects, Peruvian Quechua, is a well-known lingua franca that served as the principal language of the Inca empire and continued to be

Table 11.3. Distribution of eight postcontact traits across languages of Andean South America and adjacent regions.

	A	B	C	D	E	F	G	H
QUECHUMARAN								
Peruvian Quechua	+	+	+	+	+	+	+	+
Ecuadorean Quechua	+	+	+	+	+	+	+	+
Aymara	+	+	+	+	+	+	+	+
BARBACOAN								
Cayápa	+	−	+	+	−	−	+	−
Colorado	+	−	+	−	+	−	+	−
PANAQUITAN								
Páez	+	−	−	−	−	−	−	−
ISOLATE								
Cofan	+	−	−	−	−	−	−	−
ARAUCANIAN								
Mapuche	+	−	+	+	+	−	−	+
Ranquelche	+	−	+	+	+	−	−	−
MAIPURAN								
Amoishe	−	+	−	+	+	−	−	−
Campa	+	+	−	−	+	−	−	−

(continued)

Table 11.3 *(continued)*

	A	B	C	D	E	F	G	H
Piro	–	–	+	+	–	–	–	–
JIVAROAN								
Aguaruna	+	+	–	–	–	–	–	–
Huambisa	+	–	–	–	–	–	–	–
Jíbaro	+	+	–	–	–	–	–	–
CAHUAPANAN								
Chayahuita	+	+	+	+	–	–	–	–
HUITOTOAN								
Huitoto	+	–	–	–	–	–	–	–
Ocaina	+	–	–	–	–	–	–	–
PANO-TAKANAN								
Cavineña	–	–	–	+	–	–	–	–
Cháma	+	+	+	+	–	–	–	–
GUAYCURUAN								
Abipon	–	+	–	–	–	–	–	–
Mocovi	–	+	–	–	–	–	–	–
Toba	–	+	–	–	–	–	–	–
MATACOAN								
Mataco	–	+	–	–	–	+	–	–
Vejoz	–	+	–	–	–	+	–	–

A = Native term for HEN/ROOSTER/CHICKEN, derived from Peruvian Quechua *atahuallpa* "hen" (e.g., Páez *atall* "hen"; Chayahuita *atash* "hen"; Cháma *atapa* "hen, chicken"; Colorado *hualpa* "hen, chicken"; Campa *atyaapa* "hen, rooster").

B = Native term for BREAD/FLOUR/WHEAT (e.g., Peruvian Quechua *tanta* "bread"; Mataco *múc-tanta-muc* "flour"; Toba *tanta* "wheat"; see chapters 3 and 8).

C = Native term for HUNDRED (e.g., Peruvian Quechua *pachak*; Piro *patša*; Ranquelche *pataca*).

D = Native term for BOOK/PAPER (e.g., Peruvian Quechua *quilla* "book, paper"; Chayahuita *quirica* "book, paper").

E = Native term for SPOON (e.g., Peruvian Quechua *huislla*; Amoishe *huisllat*).

F = Native term for MONEY (e.g., Peruvian Quechua *ccollque*; Vejoz *kolki*).

G = Native term for CANDLE (e.g., Peruvian Quechua *nina*; Colorado *nin*).

H = Native term for WINDOW (e.g., Peruvian Quechua *ttco*; Mapuche *toco*).

widely used throughout the Andean region after the conquest (Mannheim 1991). Peruvian Quechua, predictably as a lingua franca, shows all eight postcontact traits—as do the other two Quechumaran examples, Ecuadorean Quechua and Aymara—while traits occur only sporadically in other languages. As noted in chapter

6, Aymara and Quechua are thought by some scholars to be genetically affiliated in a grouping called Quechumaran, but the strong similarities between these languages may in fact be due to intense borrowing rather than to a genetic relationship. Since most of the native terms involved are clearly Quechumaran in origin, there can be little doubt that their broad Andean distribution is due to the influence of the lingua franca.

Mesoamerica

Table 11.4 gives the distribution of nine postcontact features across languages of Mesoamerica and adjacent areas. Mesoamerica is a culture region of Middle America that stretches from central Mexico to northern Central America. Campbell, Kaufman, and Smith-Stark (1986) have assembled cross-language evidence that shows that Mesoamerica proper constitutes a linguistic area as well as a culture province. However, this evidence does not include traits that are clearly postcontact in nature. The features reported here are a mixture of native terms, native terms that are semantically extended European loans, and loan shifts for introduced items.

Sixty-two languages and dialects are surveyed in table 11.4. Most are language cases of the current sample or are data extracted from two or more language cases that are dialects of the same language. Some languages not included in the sample are also used, like Teco and Itza. Data for these are extracted from standard lexical sources for Middle American languages, all of which are listed in Yasugi's (1995) book on Native Middle American Languages. Most recorded languages of the region with pertinent traits are included, and these are associated with all major and minor genetic groupings of Mesoamerica and immediately adjacent areas.

Six (A, B, D, E, F, and I) of the nine traits undoubtedly diffused from Nahuatl, the regional lingua franca (see chapters 7 and 8). Nahuatl is represented in table 11.4 by Classical Nahuatl which is based on two cases of the sample, Nahuatl (1571) and Nahuatl (1611). However, five of these six traits involve terms that may have originated, at least in part, from Spanish. For example, the native term for CAT (trait A) may be related to the archaic Spanish word *miz(a/o)* "cat," but the term (e.g., Classical Nahuatl *mizton*) clearly was diffused from Nahuatl since it shows the language's diminutive suffix *-ton* (Karttunen and Lockhart 1976:136; Campbell 1977:106; Karttunen 1985:149–150). In Nahuatl, *mizton* "cat" is literally "little cougar."

Loan shifts for BREAD, CHICKEN, and WHEAT (traits D, E, and F) have involved diffusion of complex labels, literally translating as, respectively, "Spanish/foreign tortilla," "Spanish/foreign turkey" or "Spanish/foreign bird," and "Spanish/foreign maize." These are in fact "semi-loan shifts" since in all instances words translated by "Spanish/foreign" originated in Nahuatl. These are all versions of Classical Nahuatl *caxtillan* (orthographic variants: *castillan* and *castellan*). Despite the obvious similarity of this form to Spanish *castellano* "Spanish," the word is actually a Nahuatl innovation based on Spanish *Castilla* "Castile," to which the Nahuatl locative suffix, *-tlan*, has been added (Karttunen and Lockhart 1976:128; Bright 1979b:270; Lockhart 1992:276–279).

Two languages in table 11.4, Classical Nahuatl and Tzotzil, show all nine postcontact traits, while all the other languages demonstrate them only sporadically. Occurrence of all traits in Nahuatl, of course, reflects the language's status as a

Table 11.4. Distribution of nine postcontact traits across languages of Mesoamerica and adjacent areas.

	A	B	C	D	E	F	G	H	I
Mesoamerican Languages									
UTO-AZTECAN									
Classical Nahuatl	+	+	+	+	+	+	+	+	+
Pipil	+	−	−	−	+	−	+	−	+
MAYAN									
Huastec	+	−	−	−	−	−	+	+	−
Quiche	−	+	+	+	−	−	−	+	−
Cakchiquel	+	+	+	+	+	+	+	+	−
Tzutujil	−	−	−	+	+	−	−	+	−
Pocomam	−	+	−	+	+	−	−	−	−
Pocomchí	−	+	−	+	+	+	+	−	−
Kekchi	−	−	−	+	+	−	+	−	−
Mam	−	−	−	+	−	−	−	+	−
Teco	−	−	−	−	+	−	+	−	−
Ixil	−	+	−	+	+	−	−	+	−
Jacaltec	−	−	−	−	−	−	−	+	−
Chuj	+	−	−	−	+	+	+	−	−
Tojolabal	−	+	+	+	−	+	−	−	−
Chol	−	+	+	+	−	+	−	−	−
Chontal	−	+	−	+	−	−	−	−	−
Cholti	+	−	−	+	−	−	+	−	−
Chorti	−	−	−	−	−	−	+	−	−
Tzeltal	−	+	+	+	−	+	−	−	−
Tzotzil	+	+	+	+	+	+	+	+	+
Yucatec	+	−	+	+	+	−	−	−	−
Itza	−	−	−	−	+	−	−	−	−
Mopan	−	−	−	−	+	−	−	−	−
MIXE-ZOQUEAN									
Totontepec Mixe	+	+	−	−	−	−	−	−	−
Sayula Popoluca	+	+	−	−	−	−	+	−	−
Oluta Popoluca	+	−	−	+	−	−	+	−	−
Old Zoque	−	+	+	−	+	+	−	−	−
Copainalá Zoque	−	−	+	+	+	−	+	−	−
Francisco León Zoque	−	−	−	−	+	−	+	−	−
Rayón Zoque	−	−	−	−	+	−	+	−	−
Sierra Popoluca	−	−	−	+	−	−	+	−	−
TOTONACAN									
Totonac	+	+	−	+	+	−	+	−	+
OTOMANGUEAN									
Otomi	+	−	+	−	−	−	−	+	−
Mazahua	−	+	−	−	−	−	−	+	−
Matlazinca	+	+	+	−	−	−	+	+	−
Chinantec	−	−	+	−	−	−	−	+	−
Tlapanec	+	−	−	−	+	−	−	−	−
Chiapanec	+	+	+	+	−	+	+	+	−
Mixtec	+	−	+	+	−	+	−	+	−
Cuicatec	−	−	+	−	−	−	+	+	+
Amuzgo	−	−	+	−	−	−	−	+	−

Table 11.4. *(continued)*

	A	B	C	D	E	F	G	H	I
Mazatec	–	+	–	–	–	–	+	+	–
Ixcatec	–	–	+	–	–	–	–	–	–
Chocho	–	+	–	–	–	–	–	+	–
Popoloca	–	–	–	–	–	–	–	+	–
Zapotec	+	+	+	+	+	+	+	+	–
Chatino	–	–	+	–	–	–	–	–	–
XINCAN									
Xincan	+	–	–	+	+	–	+	–	–
OTHER									
Huave	+	+	+	+	–	–	+	–	–
Cuitlatec	+	–	–	+	+	–	+	–	–
Tarascan	+	+	+	+	–	–	+	–	–
Tequistlatec	+	–	+	–	–	–	+	+	–

Adjacent Area Languages

	A	B	C	D	E	F	G	H	I
UTO-AZTECAN									
Pima	+	–	–	–	–	+	+	–	+
Eudeve	+	–	–	–	–	–	–	–	–
Tarahumara	–	–	–	–	–	–	–	–	+
Cora	+	–	–	–	–	–	+	–	–
Huichol	–	–	+	–	–	–	+	–	–
MISUMALPAN									
Sumu	+	–	–	–	–	–	–	–	–
OTHER									
Seri	+	–	–	–	–	+	+	–	+
Jicaque	+	–	+	–	+	–	+	–	–
Lenca	+	–	–	–	+	–	+	–	–

A = Native term for CAT derived from Classical Nahuatl *mizton* (e.g., Totontepec Mixe *miistu*; Cora *místun*; Seri *miist*).

B = Native term for GOAT (sometimes SHEEP) derived from Classical Nahuatl *tentzone* (e.g., Ixil *tentzun*; Mazatec *tinʼo*; Huave *teants*; see chapter 8).

C = Loan shift for SHEEP derived from a word for COTTON (realized through overt marking, e.g., "cotton deer" = SHEEP, or as polysemy; see chapter 3).

D = Loan shift for BREAD derived from a combination of Classical Nahuatl *caxtillan* plus a word for TORTILLA (e.g., Classical Nahuatl *caxtillan tlaxcalli*; Yucatec *castran uah*; Huave *peats castil*; see chapters 3 and 8).

E = Loan shift for CHICKEN/HEN (occasionally ROOSTER) typically derived from a combination of Classical Nahuatl *caxtillan* plus a term for TURKEY or BIRD (e.g., Classical Nahuatl *caxtillantotolin* "chicken"; Lenca *cashlanmúni* "hen"), sometimes truncated to a derived form of *caxtillan* (e.g., Tlapanec *štiʼla*[3] "chicken, hen"; Mopan *cax* "hen"; see chapter 3).

F = Loan shift for WHEAT (or, rarely, some other imported grain) derived from Classical Nahuatl *caxtillan* plus a term for MAIZE
(continued)

Table 11.4. *(continued)*

(e.g., Classical Nahuatl *caxtillan tlaulli*; Chiapanec *nama katila*; Cakchiquel *kaxlan ixim*).

G = Native term for MONEY, based on an archaic Spanish term, *tomín*, which denoted a specific currency denomination—one-eighth of a peso (e.g., Pame *tumin*; Huave *tomian*; Seri *tom*; see chapter 8).

H = Loan shift for HORSE derived from a term for DEER, typically realized in marking reversals (e.g., Huastec "Huastec horse" = DEER) and as polysemy (see chapter 8 and also discussion of Nahuatl in chapter 7).

I = Native term for CHICKEN/HEN/ROOSTER derived from Classical Nahuatl *totolin* (e.g., San Bartolome Tzotzil *totórin* "rooster"; Pame *tolôn* "chicken"; Tarahumara *totorí* "hen").

regional lingua franca from which traits were diffused to other languages. Occurrence of all traits in Tzotzil perhaps attests to a special postcontact familiarity of speakers of the language with Nahuatl. For example, shortly before the arrival of the Spanish, an Aztec garrison is reported to have been established at the Tzotzil town of Zinacantán in Highland Chiapas, Mexico (Remesal 1932:I:378; Calnek 1962:24; Gerhard 1979:149). In addition, there were a number of postcontact Nahuatl settlements in the region, several persisting in areas surrounded by Tzotzil speakers until very recently (Lyle Campbell, personal communication).

Table 11.4 indicates that the postcontact influence of Nahuatl extended well beyond the borders of Mesoamerica proper, perhaps as far north as the Mexico-United States frontier (Pima) and as far south as Nicaragua (Sumu).

Tropical Forest South America

Table 11.5 shows the distribution of 26 postcontact traits across languages of tropical forest South America and adjacent areas. These are all entirely native terms for items of acculturation except one which is a referentially extended European word.

Nineteen languages are listed, all of which are language cases of the current sample. These include 7 affiliated with Tupí-Guaraní: Tupí (Brazil), Guaraní (Paraguay), Guarayo (Bolivia), Chiriguano (Bolivia), Kaapor (Brazil), Guajajara (Brazil), and Oyampi (French Guiana); 1 Tucanoan: Tucano (Brazil); 1 isolate: Ticuna (Colombia); 1 Carib: Taurepän (Venezuela); 4 Maipuran: Insular Carib (Caribbean islands), Central American Carib (Honduras), Guajira (Colombia), and Arawak (British Guiana); 2 Chibchan: Cuna (Panama) and Cágaba (Colombia); 1 Guahiban: Guahibo (Venezuela); 1 Uarao: Uarao (British Guiana); and 1 Kalianan: Makú (Brazil).

Two of the 19 languages, Tupí and Guaraní, are well-known lingua francas, the former spoken in Brazil and the latter in Paraguay (see chapter 8). All but 5 of the 26 postcontact traits occur in Tupí. Guaraní has the second-highest total, with 14 (tied with Kaapor), including the 5 traits not found in Tupí. At least 8 of the diffused terms found in Tupí, designating FLOUR, HEN, HUNDRED, NEEDLE, SCISSORS, THREAD, WATERMELON, and WEDNESDAY, appear to analyze only in Tupí and, therefore, probably originated in that lingua franca. The distribution plotted in table 11.5 suggests that Guarayo and Chiriguano have been directly influenced by

Table 11.5. Distribution of 26 postcontact traits across languages of tropical forest South America and adjacent regions.

	A	B	C	D	E	F	G	H	I	J	K	L	M	N	O	P	Q	R	S	T	U	V	W	X	Y	Z
TUPI-GUARANI																										
Tupí	+	+	+	+	+	+	+	+	+	+	+	+	+	+	+	+	+	+	+	+	+	−	−	−	−	−
Guaraní	+	+	−	−	+	−	−	−	−	−	+	−	+	+	+	+	+	−	−	−	−	+	+	+	+	+
Guarayo	+	+	−	+	−	−	−	−	−	−	+	−	+	−	−	−	+	−	−	−	−	+	+	+	+	+
Chiriguano	+	+	−	−	−	−	−	−	−	−	+	−	−	+	−	+	+	−	−	−	−	+	+	+	+	+
Kaapor	−	+	+	+	+	+	+	−	−	−	−	+	+	+	+	−	−	+	+	+	+	−	−	−	−	−
Guajajara	−	+	+	−	−	+	−	+	−	−	−	+	+	+	+	−	+	+	+	+	+	−	−	−	−	−
Oyampi	+	+	−	−	−	−	−	−	−	−	−	−	−	+	−	−	−	−	−	−	−	+	−	−	−	−
TUCANOAN																										
Tucano	−	−	+	−	−	+	−	−	+	+	−	−	−	−	−	−	−	−	−	−	−	−	−	−	−	−
ISOLATE																										
Ticuna	−	−	+	+	+	−	+	+	−	−	−	−	−	−	−	−	−	−	−	−	−	−	−	−	−	−
CARIB																										
Taurepän	+	+	+	−	−	−	−	−	−	−	−	−	−	−	−	−	−	−	−	−	−	−	−	−	−	−
MAIPURAN																										
Insular Carib	+	+	−	−	−	−	−	−	−	−	−	−	−	−	−	−	−	−	−	−	−	−	−	−	−	−
Central American Carib	+	−	−	−	−	−	−	−	−	−	−	−	−	−	−	−	−	−	−	−	−	−	−	−	−	−
Guajira	+	−	−	−	−	−	−	−	−	−	−	−	−	−	−	−	−	−	−	−	−	−	−	−	−	−
Arawak	+	−	−	−	−	−	−	−	−	−	−	−	−	−	−	−	−	−	−	−	−	−	−	−	−	−
CHIBCHAN																										
Cuna	+	−	−	−	−	−	−	−	−	−	−	−	−	−	−	−	−	−	−	−	−	−	−	−	−	−
Cágaba	+	−	−	−	−	−	−	−	−	−	−	−	−	−	−	−	−	−	−	−	−	−	−	−	−	−
GUAHIBAN																										
Guahibo	+	−	−	−	−	−	−	−	−	−	−	−	−	−	−	−	−	−	−	−	−	−	−	−	−	−
UARAO																										
Uarao	+	−	−	−	−	−	−	−	−	−	−	−	−	−	−	−	−	−	−	−	−	−	−	−	−	−
KALIANAN																										
Makú	−	−	+	−	−	−	−	−	−	−	−	−	−	−	−	−	−	−	−	−	−	−	−	−	−	−

A = Native term for BOOK and/or PAPER derived from Spanish or Portuguese *carta* "letter" (e.g., Tupí *cuatiara* "paper"; Guaraní *cuatía* "book, paper, letter"; see chapter 9).

B = Native term for THREAD (e.g., Tupí *inimbo*; Guaraní *inimbo*).

C = Native term for CAT (e.g., Tupí *pišana*).

D = Native term for FLOUR (e.g., Tupí *uí*).

E = Native term for RICE (e.g., Tupí *abatií*; Guaraní *abatí-i*).

F = Native term for NEEDLE (e.g., Tupí *abi* or *aui*).

G = Native term for SCISSORS (e.g., Tupí *piranha*).

H = Native term for NAIL (e.g., Tupí *itapua*).

I = Native term for HUNDRED (e.g., Tupí *jepé-papasaua*).

J = Native term for WEDNESDAY (e.g., Tupí *marapé muçapira*).

K = Native term for FLOUR (e.g., Tupí *cui*; Guaraní *cuí*).

L = Native term for HEN and/or ROOSTER (e.g., Tupí *sapucaia* "hen, rooster").

(continued)

Table 11.5 *(continued)*

M = Native term for PIG (e.g., Tupí *curé*; Guaraní *curê*).

N = Native term for MATCH (e.g., Tupí *tataiw*; Guaraní *tata'y*).

O = Native term for CAT (e.g., Tupí *maracaya*; Guaraní *mbaracaya*).

P = Native term for TABLE (e.g., Tupí *caruaba*; Guaraní *carúhaba*).

Q = Native term for BOARD (e.g., Tupí *imirá péba*; Guaraní *ibirápembí*).

R = Native term for WATERMELON (e.g., Tupí *zoromo-piw*).

S = Native term for ONION (e.g., Tupí *ma'ê-iwa nêm*).

T = Native term for GOAT (e.g., Tupí *arapuh-ran*).

U = Native term for MONEY (e.g., Tupí *témêtarêr*).

V = Native term for SCISSORS (e.g., Guaraní *yetapá*).

W = Native term for NEEDLE (e.g., Guaraní *yu*).

X = Native term for BREAD (e.g., Guaraní *mbuyapé*).

Y = Native term for TOWN (e.g., Guaraní *tetā*).

Z = Native term for MONEY (e.g., Guaraní *quarepotí*).

Guaraní, rather than by Tupí, and that Kaapor and Guajajara have been directly influenced by Tupí, rather than by Guaraní.

Discussion

Classic linguistic areas, such as the Balkans (Klagstad 1963; Georgiev 1977; Joseph 1983), South Asia (Henderson 1965; Masica 1976; Emeneau 1980), and the more recently identified Mesoamerica (Campbell, Kaufman, and Smith-Stark 1986), are predominantly recognized for regionally diffused structural features (i.e., phonological, morphological, and syntactic aspects of language). Consequently, some scholars may object to identifying linguistic areas, as I have done, solely in terms of diffused lexical traits. Of course, lexical features (i.e., words for items of acculturation) are the focus of research in this study and thus, naturally, emerge as defining features of postcontact linguistic areas. Indeed, it is difficult to imagine how one would go about sorting diffused postcontact phonological and grammatical features from those that predate contact—except in the special circumstance in which such traits were diffused from intruding European languages to Native American ones. In any case, Campbell, Kaufman, and Smith-Stark (1986) do use loan shifts as diagnostic traits in their study of Mesoamerica as a linguistic area and also allow straightforward lexical borrowing as appropriate evidence (p. 558).

Thomason and Kaufman (1988:74–76) propose a "borrowing scale" detailing the nature and type of borrowing that results from increasing degrees of interaction between languages. Casual contact allows only lexical borrowing; as interaction becomes more intense, lexical borrowing gives way to more structural borrowing. Social and linguistic intercourse that results in the development of classic linguistic areas may have typically been sustained over hundreds or tens of hundreds of years, so that areal sharing of structural features as well as of lexical items, is not unexpected. In contrast, if the extent of the contact is any indication, the nature of interaction among Native American languages that leads to development of postcontact diffusional areas may not have involved, in most instances, a degree of sustained intensity that would have promoted diffusion of structural features. It is plausible that some Native American lingua francas responsible for postcontact areal diffusion simply have not persisted long enough as regional languages to result in the areal sharing of structural traits.

Such is probably the case for the two pidgin lingua francas, Mobilian Jargon and Chinook Jargon. While some scholars have maintained that these pidgins developed before contact (e.g., Drechsel 1979, 1984; Thomason 1983), the earliest attestations for both languages are relatively late—1699 for Mobilian Jargon (Drechsel 1979:116) and the late eighteenth century for Chinook Jargon (Thomason 1983:859). The last fluent speakers of Mobilian Jargon probably died before 1980, and few if any speakers of Chinook Jargon remain today. These languages, then, have taken the path to extinction so common for Native American languages of North America (see chapter 6). The demise of Mobilian Jargon and Chinook Jargon (before possible creolization) ended any eventuality that they might contribute linguistic traits to Amerindian languages beyond simple lexical features.

Lingua francas in Mesoamerica and South America are another matter. Nahuatl and Quechua undoubtedly served as regional lingua francas both before and after contact, and both languages are still spoken today. As precontact regional languages, they may have contributed both structural and lexical features to other native languages before European arrival; they clearly facilitated lexical borrowing after contact. The precontact regional influences of Tupí and Guaraní are unclear, but like Nahuatl and Quechua, these languages are still spoken. Nahuatl, Quechua, and Tupí resemble Mobilian Jargon and Chinook Jargon since their influence on other Native American languages is much less today than in the past, especially, in the era closely following first contact. Hispanic languages have emerged as primary lingua francas in areas in which Nahuatl, Quechua, and Tupí were influential, although Guaraní still retains the status of a major lingua franca in modern Paraguay (Haugen 1956:15). Spanish and Portuguese in the past and continuing today have contributed to both the structural and lexical homogeneity of Latin American Indian languages, so much so that virtually all of Latin America can appropriately be regarded as a postcontact linguistic area (cf. Suárez 1983:161–162).

12

CONCLUSION

The preceding chapters have presented detailed information on various processes that account for lexical acculturation in Native American languages promoted by European contact. The following are summaries of major findings and conclusions.

Summaries

1. Native Americans have linguistically accommodated objects and concepts introduced by Europeans either through European-language loans or native terms. Amerindian languages of Latin America (influenced mostly by Spanish speakers) have been considerably more inclined to adopt Spanish loans for items of acculturation than native languages of Anglo-America (influenced mostly by English speakers) have been inclined to adopt English loans. This is explained by regional differences in bilingualism. Spanish-influenced Native Americans appear to have been substantially more bilingual in their native languages and Spanish than English-influenced Amerindians have been in their languages and English. Thus there is a positive association between the degree of bilingualism and the extent to which European loans for imported items have been incorporated into lexicons. Bilingualism, then, has promoted the adoption of European loans for items of acculturation, an interpretation that challenges the assumption long held by linguists that language structure is the primary factor in borrowing. However, some evidence suggests that language structure does occasionally influence borrowing, although only minimally (chapter 6).

2. Some items of acculturation tend to be designated by European loans in Amerindian languages more strongly than others, which tend to be denoted by native terms. For example, European words for introduced living things have more often been incorporated into Amerindian languages than European terms for artifacts. The "borrowability" of European labels probably relates to the extent to which the acculturated items have typically been encountered by American Indians in Euro-American settings such as trading posts, marketplaces, farms, missions, and garrisons. Some items of acculturation have typically been more frequently experienced, and

terms for these more often heard, in Euro-American contexts than other items, and therefore these terms have been adopted more often by Native Americans. Introduced living things commonly have been more frequently encountered in Euro-American settings than imported artifacts, explaining the greater borrowability of their European labels (chapter 5).

3. Some native terms for items of acculturation have been coined by Amerindians through referential extension, that is, extending the application of a native label for a usually indigenous entity to an introduced item that it resembles. This involves different types of nomenclatural structures, including polysemy, overt marking, and marking reversal. The structure that emerges depends on the relative cultural importance (salience) of the two items involved. As relative salience changes over time, so will nomenclature (Witkowski and Brown 1983). When first encountered, an introduced object is always low in salience and a native term for a similar item is directly extended to it creating polysemy. As the introduced item becomes more familiar and increases in salience, polysemy breaks down and the item develops an overt marking construction—the word for the indigenous item plus a modifier (overt mark). If the introduced referent eventually surpasses the native referent in salience, a marking reversal develops in which the original term comes to designate (without a modifier) the introduced item and the native object acquires an overt marking construction (chapters 3 and 10).

4. There are profound differences in the ways in which speakers of Native American languages have approached the naming of imported living things and of introduced artifacts. As noted in summary 2, living things tend to be labeled by European loans more strongly than artifacts. In addition, they tend more strongly to acquire labels through referential extension of European loans (see summary 7), to be labeled by overt marking constructions, and to be involved in marking reversals. Artifacts tend more strongly than living things to have labels that are extended constructions based on native terms, to be denoted by descriptive terms, and to be given utilitarian names (chapter 3).

5. Amerindian languages have strongly tended to develop independently semantically similar native labels for introduced objects and concepts, for example, compound terms for BUTTER, translating literally as "milk fat," in many languages geographically removed from one another. Such examples attest to naming tendencies that appear to be universal in scope. The naming of items of acculturation manifests cross-language tendencies more robustly than any other type of naming behavior. Fitting into the framework of lexical universals, these cross-language regularities can contribute to the investigation of the nature of the human language faculty (chapter 4).

6. Cross-language naming tendencies suggest that innate information-processing mechanisms are important components of the human language faculty. Similar names for items of acculturation probably have developed independently in languages because information-processing devices common to all humans are brought to the task of naming novel things. These mechanisms are involved in the analysis of imported items and of sources from which potential labels might be retrieved. Since information-processing devices are the same for all humans (i.e., innate and universal), similar

analyses will tend to be made, resulting in similar names for introduced items across languages, especially when sources for labels are similar across different groups of people. One mechanism involves the closest analog principle, whereby humans tend to name introduced things by native terms for items that most closely resemble introduced entities. When speakers of two languages share a closest analog, they tend to develop semantically similar names for the item (chapter 4).

7. A ubiquitous naming phenomenon among Native American languages is the use of semantically modified European loans to designate items of acculturation, in which a European term that denotes a referent other than a certain acculturated item is borrowed and referentially extended to the introduced entity. For example, more than half of all languages showing terms for MONEY have developed labels for this item through referential extension of European loans that originally denoted a specific currency denomination, such as English "dollar" or Spanish *peso*. The ubiquity of European loan extensions is due in part to both cross-language naming tendencies (see summaries 5 and 6) and diffusion across Amerindian languages (see 10 and 12) (chapter 3).

8. While introduced living things in general tend more strongly than imported artifacts to be labeled by European loans in Native American languages (see summaries 2 and 4), animal subtypes, for example, CALF, MARE, and ROOSTER, strongly tend to be labeled by native terms, respectively, "little cow," "female horse," and "male chicken." In addition, native terms across languages for creature subtypes strongly tend to show similar semantic content (see 5 and 6). These nomenclatural findings are explained by universal marking hierarchies in which animal subtypes are perceived as marked vis-à-vis corresponding superordinate creature concepts (e.g., respectively, COW, HORSE, and CHICKEN), which are unmarked (chapters 3 and 4).

9. Diachronic data indicate that native terms for introduced entities in earlier time states of languages have tended to be replaced by European loans in later time states, especially in Latin American Indian languages. This is in accord with Casagrande's (1955:22) distinction between "primary accommodation," in which speakers of recipient languages have little knowledge of donor languages and no bilingualism, and "secondary accommodation," in which recipient-language speakers have knowledge of donor languages and some bilingualism. Since earlier time states of Amerindian languages are more likely to have involved primary accommodation and later time states to have involved secondary accommodation, the diachronic data accord with the proposition that increases in bilingualism lead to increases in the adoption of European loans for items of acculturation (see summary 1). Diachronic evidence also attests to the occasional replacement of European loans for acculturated items by native terms. It is plausible that language purism promotes lexical substitution of this type (chapter 7).

10. Native terms for items of acculturation have frequently been diffused across Native American languages. Extensive or even massive diffusion of such labels through languages belonging to the same genetic grouping, like Algonquian languages, has been common. Diffusion of native terms across languages belonging to different

genetic groups is less common. In the vast majority of instances, the latter has been promoted by regional lingua francas such as Chinook Jargon, a pidgin trade language of the Northwest Coast, and Peruvian Quechua, the language of the Inca empire. Languages of different genetic affiliations that share terms for acculturated items strongly tend to do so because of parallel acquisitions directly from a common lingua franca. Bilingualism in native languages and lingua francas underlies this process, attesting to the substantial role bilingualism plays in promoting lexical borrowing (see 1 and 7); in this case, borrowing involving native rather than European labels. Languages that are not genetically related and whose speakers do not use a common lingua franca strongly tend not to share native terms for imported items, even when such languages are spoken in the same region (chapter 8).

11. Lingua francas also promote diffusion of native terms through genetically related languages, but sometimes, as in Algonquian languages, these are neither familiar American pidgins nor languages associated with influential nation states. When salient lingua francas such as Chinook Jargon and Peruvian Quechua do *not* exist in regions in which extensive diffusion of native terms across languages of the same genetic group is apparent, some less salient, "local" lingua franca may explain term dispersal. Otherwise, intragenetic group diffusion is due to the usual geographic proximity of genetically related languages and to their structural similarity. Structural similarity may facilitate the development of multilingualism in two or more languages of the same genetic group, thus promoting lexical borrowing across those languages (chapter 8).

12. European loans for items of acculturation, as well as native terms, have frequently diffused across Native American languages. These are sometimes difficult to distinguish from European loanwords which have been directly borrowed into Amerindian languages from European languages. Certain clues aid in recognizing diffused European loans, including phonological and morphological evidence and clues relating to distributional considerations. In one distributional pattern, one language shows a subset of those European loans that pertain to another, neighboring language. This pattern strongly suggests that the latter language acquired loans from the former. As in the case of diffused native terms for acculturated items (see 10 and 11), diffusion of European loanwords is often promoted by a regional lingua franca (chapter 9).

13. In addition to European loans and native terms, loan shifts (loan translations and semantic loans) for introduced items have been diffused across native languages of the Americas. Diffusion of loan shifts may have typically involved lingua francas as promoting agents (chapters 10 and 11).

14. Diffusion of labels for items of acculturation (including European loans, native terms, and loan shifts) across Native American languages has resulted in the formation of postcontact linguistic areas. A linguistic area is in evidence when geographically contiguous languages, some of which are not genetically related to one another, share linguistic features and when feature sharing is largely explained by areal diffusion. When the traits involved are names for objects and concepts introduced by Europeans, linguistic areas are postcontact developments. Five probable postcontact linguistic areas, which are among the most geographically expansive in the Americas, are recognized: the southeastern United States, Pacific Northwest, Andean South America,

Mesoamerica, and tropical forest South America. Distributional and other evidence robustly indicates that each of these linguistic regions developed as a consequence of the widespread use of lingua francas, including, respectively, Mobilian Jargon, Chinook Jargon, Peruvian Quechua, Nahuatl (Aztec), and Tupí (with Guaraní) (chapter 11).

Implications

Here and there I have alluded to implications of findings and conclusions for research beyond the primary focus of this study on lexical acculturation—for example, comments that relate cross-language tendencies in the naming of acculturated items to the study of lexical universals and the human language faculty. Another example is the observation that the detection of substantial lexical diffusion across languages of a region in which a familiar lingua franca is not known to have been employed may indicate the past influence of a previously unrecognized lingua franca (chapter 8), a proposal potentially of use to researchers in fleshing out aspects of regional sociolinguistic histories that otherwise might not be apparent. Along similar lines, the study of sociolinguistic history might also benefit from attention to European loanword percentages (table 2.1 and appendix B), which can be taken as indices of the past intensity of social and linguistic intercourse between speakers of Native American and European languages. In conclusion, I address implications of this study for two areas of scholarly concern in linguistic anthropology, which perhaps have few points of intellectual intersection other than my long-standing personal interest in them. These are ethnobiology and lexical reconstruction.

Ethnobiology

In a recent contribution to ethnobiology, Berlin (1992) outlines the positions of proponents of two contemporary schools of thought about the fundamental nature of folk classification and the naming of plants and animals. He calls these, respectively, the utilitarianists and the intellectualists. Proponents of utilitarianism (e.g., Hunn 1982; Morris 1984; Randall 1987) argue that people adjust to their environments by classifying and assigning names to those species that have important, practical consequences for human existence. In contrast, the intellectualists (e.g., Atran 1990) propose that biological organisms are categorized and named independently of the practical values and uses species may have for people. In this view, ethnobiological knowledge is motivated by intellectual curiosity—plants and animals are of interest to humans simply because they are there.

Berlin (1992:286) links these views to earlier anthropological theorizing. For example, he sees the modern utilitarianist argument as a restatement of the functionalist position of Malinowski, who emphasized pragmatic aspects of ethnobiological knowledge: "The road from the wilderness to the savage's belly and consequently to his mind is very short. For him the world is an indiscriminate background against which there stands out the useful, primarily the edible, species of plants and animals" (1974:44). On the other hand, Lévi-Strauss is seen as a precursor to contemporary intellectualists (Berlin 1992:7–8) when he writes that "animals and plants are not known as a result of their usefulness; they are deemed to be useful or interesting because they are first of all known....Classifying, as opposed to not classifying, has a value of its own" (Lévi-Strauss 1966:9).

Berlin (1990) himself is a strong advocate of the intellectualist position. He assembles evidence from two Jivaroan groups (Peru) that show that folk naming of vertebrate animals in their habitats can be predicted on the basis of how these are treated in scientific classification. Western scientific taxonomy is not based on knowledge of the cultural importance of these animals but rather solely on gross similarities and differences among species. Since Jivaroan ethnobiological classifications are in close accord with scientific taxonomy, these systems also are not informed primarily by utilitarian considerations. Rather, they are largely products of intellectualism.

The naming of organisms by folk observers of nature is not always restricted just to those plants and animals of practical significance. In this regard, Berlin again cites his work among Jivaroan groups and challenges the utilitarian view: "More than half of the mammals given linguistic recognition by the Aguaruna and Huambisa of Peru have 'no direct use either as food or for material goods'" (1992:89). He further states that the "majority of vertebrate animals known to the Jívaro cannot be shown to have any immediate utilitarian importance" (p. 90). Similarly, the majority of wild plant species named by Tzeltal speakers of southern Mexico "have little dietary importance and many have only minimal direct adaptive significance" (p. 287).

Information compiled in this work provides another approach to the issue addressed by Berlin (1992), one involving the semantic content of names for acculturated items. As noted in chapter 3, when a name literally refers to the use or function of the thing it designates, its content is utilitarian in nature. For example, the Cherokee word for HORSE (*soquili*) is, literally, "he carries heavy things," and the Miskito term for GRAPES (*wain ma*) is, literally, "wine seed." When content is not utilitarian, such names are morphological in nature, referring either directly or indirectly to some perceptual aspect(s) of a thing—its size, shape, color, texture, smell, or behavior. For example, the Mataco term for HORSE (*yelatà*) is, literally, "large tapir," and the Tucano term for GRAPES (*ʉsé dadʉca*) is, literally, "that which comes from the vine."

Artifacts are purposefully created by humans to serve specific functions, while living things are not. Given their utilitarian intent, one would expect imported artifacts to be named by labels that literally reflect their uses, for example, the Crow term for SOAP (*iwarɛckyurucígyua*), which is, literally, "with it one wipes," and the Guajajara word for CLOCK (*quarahí-mangapáu*), literally, "to measure the sun." Nonetheless, artifacts are sometimes found to be morphologically (metaphorically speaking) labeled; for example, Lengua SOAP (*aksak mopaia*), literally, "white thing," and Mescalero Apache CLOCK (*bésh nanáhaakusí*), literally, "metal that turns."

If living things are important because of their uses (as argued by utilitarianists), a reasonable prediction is that plants and animals should show utilitarian names at around the same rate demonstrated by artifacts. This prediction does not directly relate to the question of what sort of organisms (useful or nonuseful) are typically classified and named. In my view, an answer to this question would be merely one indication of whether utilitarianism or intellectualism pertains to the usual human response to living things. Here I assume that the semantic content of terms used to name introduced plants and animals is another such indication.

Data assembled in table 3.7 can be used to test directly the prediction that living things should show utilitarian names at about the same rate as do artifacts. The table lists the 77 items of acculturation, ranked (from lowest to highest) by the percentage of language cases with analyzable native terms of a utilitarian nature. These data attest to an extraordinarily strong correlation between the nature of the introduced item (as either living thing or artifact) and the extent to which it is named by utilitarian constructions; artifacts are far more likely to be given utilitarian names than are living things. Thus, the utility of living things does not seem to constitute an especially privileged aspect of their conceptual cognition, a finding that lends support to the intellectualist view of the nature of folk biological classification and naming.

While data assembled in table 3.7 largely substantiate the intellectualist view, they also show that utilitarian considerations do sometimes play a role in human cognition about living things. Several domesticated plants—LETTUCE, WHEAT, WATER-MELON, and OATS—show utilitarian naming percentages greater than 30. This suggests, as Hays (1982) anticipated some time ago, that utilitarianist factors, as well as intellectualist ones, can influence folk biological classification and naming.

Berlin (1992) provides no overt allowance whatsoever for the possibility that biological naming is sometimes informed by utilitarian concerns. However, some of his statements, when their implications are fully pursued, do contribute (if only covertly) to an understanding of how utilitarian factors might indeed be important. He observes that plants and animals of high salience strongly tend to be named, while those low in salience tend not to be named. The key here is what he means by "salience."

In one instance, Berlin (1992:31) equates salience with biological distinctiveness and, in another (p. 24), with cultural importance. I agree with him that the salience of a plant or animal can relate to either or both of these factors. Some organisms are intrinsically salient because our species is innately predisposed in some manner to perceive them as "standing out" or, in other words, as especially attention getting or fetching, for example, by having a bright color or large size or by being biologically unique in a local environment. Other organisms may be salient because they are culturally significant. Plants and animals of high utilitarian value are by definition culturally important and, hence, salient. Since utilitarian factors contribute to salience, they must contribute at times to the development of systems of folk biological classification, assuming, with Berlin, that high salience promotes the naming of living things.

The cross-language findings reported in table 3.7 bear out Berlin's (1992) emphasis on the importance of intellectualist considerations in ethnobiology. However, they also indicate that the role of utilitarian phenomena in folk biological classification and naming, while probably quite small, should not be totally discounted.

Berlin (1992) does not discuss why intellectualist considerations should be of paramount significance in folk biological classification. The work of another member of the intellectualist camp, Scott Atran (1990), may provide a clue. Atran argues that human beings are innately inclined to believe that an *essential nature* pertains to each distinct kind of organism (i.e., species). Each exemplar of a biological kind is presumed to have the same underlying essence, even if it is somehow different. Thus, a three-legged tiger is judged to be a tiger because this feline, even though truncated, is still thought to have the underlying nature of a tiger. The human predisposition to believe in underlying biological natures is due to the natural history of the human species and, hence, implies that this feature has provided some survival advantage. A possible implication of Atran's proposal is that when people encounter plants and animals, interest necessarily focuses primarily on their presumed essential natures and only secondarily, if at all, on their potential uses. Perhaps such a focus relates also to other nomenclatural differences observed in this work (see chapter 3 and summary 4) that involve acculturated living things and introduced artifacts.

Lexical reconstruction

A major goal of historical-comparative linguistics is to reconstruct languages ancestral to groups of languages that are genetically related. This entails reconstruction of all components of a protolanguage, including phonological, grammatical, and lexical elements. Lexical reconstruction—the resuscitation of words in a protolanguage—is begun by identifying cognate words in offspring languages that are descendant forms of terms in a protolanguage. Lexical reconstruction must be undertaken with considerable care to sort sets of true cognates in genetically related languages from terms whose similarity is due to lexical diffusion across those languages rather than to common ancestry. Findings of this study, especially those in chapter 8 (see summaries 9 and 10), suggest that historical linguists who pursue lexical reconstruction should do so with considerably more restraint than has sometimes been the case.

A case in point is a lexical reconstruction proposed by Bloomfield (1946:107) for Algonquian. He reconstructs a Proto-Central Algonquian word for WHISKEY, *eškoteewaapoowi (literally, "fire water"), based on similar forms found in Cree (*iskoteewaapoy*), Menomini (*eskooteεwaapoh*), and Ojibwa (*iškoteewaapoo*). This is a credible phonological reconstruction since the compared forms in these three languages all show the sound correspondences expected of words that are true cognates of one another. A major problem with Bloomfield's analysis relates to its semantics: WHISKEY was introduced to the New World by Europeans centuries after Proto-Central Algonquian ceased to be spoken.

Bloomfield (1946:106) surely recognized WHISKEY as an acculturated item, so why he offered this reconstruction is not altogether clear. Whatever the reason, this example serves to draw attention to a complication in lexical reconstruction suggested by this study. Data compiled in chapter 8 show that it is exceedingly common for words for acculturated items (such as WHISKEY) to have been diffused widely across genetically related languages. This suggests that the task of sorting true cognates from words whose similarity is due to lexical diffusion may be considerably more problematic than previously thought, especially when those words denote novel or introduced referents. In addition, the example from Bloomfield's work indicates that lexical borrowing does not necessarily preclude manifestation by diffused lexical items of sound correspondences, making them appear to be reflexes (descendant forms) of words in protolanguages (cf. Hockett 1948:127).

Bloomfield's (1946) analysis is a conspicuous example of overreconstruction in historical-comparative linguistics (cf. Witkowski and Brown 1981; Brown 1987a). Other examples of overreconstruction, while not so obvious, may nonetheless be plentiful.

Especially familiar to me are reconstructive efforts for Proto-Mayan (PM), a language, according to Campbell and Kaufman, that was spoken at the latest some 42 centuries ago. Proto-Mayan is the parent language of 31 recorded Mayan languages, for the most part contiguously located in Guatemala and southern Mexico. Campbell and Kaufman write, "Reconstructed vocabulary shows PM speakers to have been highly successful agriculturalists, with the maize complex at the core of a full range of Mesoamerican cultigens" (1985:192). The latter included, according to Kaufman in an earlier publication, "avocado, chile, chicozapote, anona, palm (two kinds), yellow squash (ayote), sweet potato, bean, achiote (*bixa*), greens, cotton, maguey, corn (= maize), corncob, ear of corn (mazorca), roasting ear (elote), tobacco, cigarette (originally cigar?), atole; to sow" (1976:105). He also lists other PM things and concepts suggested by lexical reconstruction, including items relating to commerce and social organization: "to pay, writing, paper, tribe, to lose, sale, lord." (The actual reconstructions of words for these items are found in Kaufman 1964 and in Kaufman and Norman 1984.)

There are good anthropological reasons for believing that most if not all of these items could not have pertained to PM culture. It is unlikely that any Mesoamerican group living around 2,200 B.C. could have been, at this very early date, advanced so substantially beyond a hunting and gathering way of life that it would have possessed so great an array of domesticated plants, especially one that included exotic botanicals like cotton and tobacco, which are not normally found in a subsistence enterprise. Even granting the remote possibility that *all* agricultural items of the impressive list assembled by Kaufman (1976) were known to PM speakers, it is difficult to believe that such historically progressive items as "to pay," "writing," "paper," "sale," and "lord" were relevant some 4,000 years ago anywhere in Mesoamerica, especially since these are things and concepts typically associated with civilizations—certainly not with groups who, at best, were in the process of substituting a hunter-gatherer existence for one involving horticulture.

Recent chronological revisions render these critical observations even more pertinent. Witkowski and Brown (1991) have recalculated the glottochronological date for the breakup of PM at around 6,300 years before today (4,300 B.C.). Such an early date, of course, would make it even less likely that speakers of PM had advanced significantly beyond a hunter-gatherer existence. This view is supported by recent studies of the agricultural chronology of Mesoamerica based on dates produced through accelerator mass spectrometry. A recent interpretation (Fritz 1994, 1995) is that 3,500–3,000 B.C. constitutes the period of the earliest agriculture in the region.

These considerations, then, call into question reconstructive proposals, suggesting the overreconstruction of PM's lexical inventory. Overreconstruction derives from deficiencies of traditional approaches widely employed by historical linguists. I am familiar with the cognate sets that underlie PM reconstructions. These show distributions and phonological correspondences expected of contemporary reflexes of PM words and, hence, on methodological grounds alone motivate reconstruction of respective PM forms. However, on anthropological grounds, as argued, many if not most of these words could not have pertained to PM—at least not with the referents attributed to them.

Given that native words for novel or introduced items tend to spread by borrowing through genetically related languages, many of the "cognate" sets that relate to questionably reconstructed PM forms may actually reflect extensive post-PM diffusion rather than direct inheritance from the parent language. In many instances, diffusion could have occurred so early in the language family's history that pertinent words underwent sound changes in languages into which they were borrowed, so that they now show the phonological correspondences expected of PM lexical reflexes. In other instances, cognate sets may entail forms directly inherited from PM but which have acquired in post-PM times referents relating to new cultural items that, through loan shift, were extensively diffused across Mayan languages (cf. Witkowski and Brown 1981).

It is plausible that many of the items previously listed did not become known to speakers of Mayan languages until centuries after the breakup of PM. This was probably true of the mentioned commercial and social organizational features and the two exotic cultigens, cotton and tobacco, whose innovation and development and spread were most likely associated primarily with Classic Maya civilization. Classic Maya culture began crystallizing in lowland areas of Mayaland around A.D. 250, nearly 2,500 years after the date for PM's breakup estimated by Campbell and Kaufman (1985). It is now clearly established that speakers of Cholan and Yucatecan Mayan languages were cobearers of Maya civilization (Kaufman and Norman 1984). These two languages almost certainly served as area lingua francas. Broad diffusion of terms for many items across Mayan languages frequently involved these economic tongues (cf. Kaufman and Norman 1984:145–147; Justeson et al. 1985:9–20).

In summary, two circumstances would have set the stage for substantial post-PM diffusion of native terms for new items across Mayan languages: (1) the close genetic relatedness of Mayan languages (coupled, of course, with their geographic contiguity), and (2) development of Cholan and Yucatecan as area lingua francas. There is little question that these factors did indeed facilitate considerable diffusion of native terms through languages of the Mayan grouping (for detailed examples, see Brown 1987a and 1991). In some instances, distributional and/or phonological evidence allows for sorting such diffused Mayan terms from true sets of cognates (cf. Kaufman and Norman 1984). In others, especially when great time depths have been involved, diffused items cannot be distinguished from reflexes of PM terms, which has sometimes led to overreconstruction.

This concluding discussion is intended not so much as a challenge to earlier conjecture of Mayanists as an attempt to direct the attention of historical linguists and others to the fact, thoroughly documented in this study, that lexical diffusion, especially of words for novel and introduced items, is often extensive among languages that are related genetically. So informed, scholars will be less inclined to uncritically accept lexical reconstructions yielded through traditional approaches of historical linguistics.

STATISTICAL REPORTS ON INDIVIDUAL ITEMS
OF ACCULTURATION

Statistical reports on each of the 77 items of acculturation are presented alphabetically by the English name of the item.

Cases with Terms for Item

The total number of language cases among the 292 surveyed whose sources list at least one term for a specific item of acculturation is presented. Frequently, sources for a single language case list more than one term for a single item. However, a language case, no matter how many different labels it may have for an item, has been counted only once in this statistic. The mean number of language cases for which a label for an item of acculturation is forthcoming is 180, with a standard deviation of 62. CAT has the largest number, with 279, and APRICOT the smallest, with 27.

Cases with European Language Loans

Only European loanwords for a specific acculturated item that denote the same item in European languages from which they are borrowed have been counted, and thus this statistic does not include referentially extended European loans (see chapter 3). In some instances sources may report more than one European loan for an item, either two or more different loans from the same European language and/or two or more loans from different European languages. No matter how many European loans for a single item are found for a case, the case has been counted only once for this statistic. The mean number of language cases for which a European loan for an item of acculturation is forthcoming is 67, with a standard deviation of 38. CAT shows the largest number, with 194, and BEETS the smallest, with 9.

A *European loan percentage* for an item of acculturation has been calculated by dividing the total number of language cases with European loans for an item by the total number of language cases for which terms for the item are reported. The mean European loan percentage is 38, with a standard deviation of 17. COFFEE shows the largest percentage, with 81, and FORK and HEN are tied for the smallest percentage, at 10 (see table 3.1).

Cases with Native Terms

The number of language cases for which sources list at least one native term for a specific item of acculturation is presented. In this study, native terms formally include referentially extended European loans and most loan blends, in addition to labels manufactured solely from the native vocabulary (see chapter 3). Frequently, sources for a single case list more than one native label for a single item. However, regardless of the number of different native terms a language may have for a single item, for this statistic the case has been counted only once. The mean number of cases for which a native term for an acculturated item is forthcoming is 126, with a standard deviation of 56. MONEY shows the largest number, with 244, and CORIANDER the smallest, with 13.

Given parenthetically with this statistic is the percentage of the total number of cases with terms for an item that show native terms. The mean percentage is 69 with a standard deviation of 16. HEN shows the largest percentage, with 94, and COFFEE the smallest, with 25.

Convergence Index

The convergence index ranges in value from +1.00, indicating that all language cases for which at least one term is reported for a specific item show a European loan or loans but no native terms as well, to -1.00, indicating that all language cases for which at least one term is reported for an item show a native term or terms but no European loans as well. An index of zero, for example, would indicate that among all language cases for which terms are reported for an item, just as many cases show native terms for the item as those that show European loans.

Information for WINDOW can be used to illustrate the calculation of the convergence index. Terms for WINDOW are reported in sources for 218 language cases. Among these, European loans for the item occur in 59 cases and native terms are found in 178 cases. (The apparent arithmetic discrepancy is due to the fact that both loans and native terms for WINDOW are reported for some language cases.) The convergence index is derived by subtracting the number of language cases with native terms for WINDOW divided by the total number of cases for which terms for the item are reported ($178/218 = 0.82$), from the number of cases with European loans, divided by the total number of cases with terms for the item ($59/218 = 0.27$), yielding an index for WINDOW of -0.55.

Cases with Analyzable Native Terms

The number of language cases with at least one analyzable native term for a specific item of acculturation is presented. By "analyzable" I mean either (1) that meanings or referents of constituent elements of such labels can be identified, at least in part, and thus can be expressed in English or (2) that the native term is polysemous (has two or more related meanings or referents), suggesting that its application to the acculturated item arose through referential extension.

Nomenclatural statistics for analyzable native terms are presented. Analyzable terms are *descriptive, extended, overt marking, double overt marking,* or *marking reversal* constructions. The number of language cases with descriptive constructions for an item of acculturation and/or extended constructions for the same item and/or overt marking constructions for the item and so on are presented. Given parenthetically with this information are percentage figures, for example, the percentage of analyzable native terms for an acculturated item that are descriptive constructions, the percentage that are overt marking constructions, and so on.

Chapter 3 outlines in detail what is meant by descriptive, extended, overt marking, double overt marking, and marking reversal constructions. A few further observations are in order here, involving three of these nomenclatural forms.

Descriptive and overt marking constructions are nomenclaturally very similar. In fact, these are distinguished from one another only by reference to semantic content. A convention used for making such a distinction is that overt marking is considered apparent when a base element of a construction designates an item that seems to be of the same level of semantic abstraction as the item of acculturation denoted by the construction; otherwise, description is judged in evidence. For example, the base element DEER in the compound construction COTTON + DEER (denoting SHEEP) is here considered a constituent of an overt marking construction since DEER and SHEEP are on the same level of semantic generalization; that is, both are "generic" zoological categories in folk biological taxonomy (Berlin 1992). On the other hand, the base WILD ANIMAL in COTTON + WILD ANIMAL (denoting SHEEP) is considered a constituent of a descriptive construction since WILD ANIMAL and SHEEP are on different levels of abstraction in folk biological classification; that is, the former constitutes a considerably more comprehensive zoological category than the latter.

The same convention is applied to labels for artifacts, although perhaps with somewhat less analytical ease. For example, two commonly occurring labels for the artifact WINDOW are DOOR + LITTLE and HOUSE + HOLE. By the stated convention, the former is judged to be an overt marking construction and the latter a descriptive label. The reasoning is a follows: a window is a hole, that is, a hole in a house. Similarly, a door is also a hole, that is, another kind of hole in a house. Clearly, HOLE is a considerably more comprehensive category of things than is either WINDOW or DOOR. Consequently, HOUSE + HOLE is considered a descriptive construction since HOLE and WINDOW are not on the same level of semantic abstraction. On the other hand, DOOR and WINDOW would seem at least roughly equivalent in semantic generalization, and consequently, DOOR + LITTLE is considered to be an overt marking construction.

Another convention is used in connection with terms for introduced living things. When a constituent of such a label denotes an organism of the *same* biological species as the introduced item designated by the term, the label is considered descriptive. For example, by this convention HORSE + FEMALE (denoting MARE) is descriptive since a horse and a mare are of the same species. Similarly, labels such as HEN + MALE (denoting ROOSTER) and COW + SON (denoting CALF) are judged to be descriptive.

Unless some information suggests otherwise, partial analyzes of native constructions are considered descriptive. For example, COTTON + UE (where UE signals an unknown element) may be the only analysis forthcoming given the nature of information provided by sources for a native term for SHEEP. However, if a full analysis were possible, it might yield COTTON + DEER, an overt marking construction, or even COTTON + WILD ANIMAL, a descriptive construction. In any case, COTTON + UE is, by default, considered descriptive. Readers should bear in mind, then, that such an approach tends to inflate the number of descriptive terms judged in evidence. However, some partial analyses, such as PEACH + UE (denoting ORANGE), provide enough information for accurate identification of the construction type—in this case the label is an overt marking construction.

A label judged to be an extended construction is typically a term for which sources report more than one referent, one of which is an item of acculturation. At least one other referent of the term may plausibly be considered (1) to bear some kind of similarity to the acculturated item and (2) to have been part of the cultural and/or conceptual inventory of Amerindians in precontact times (or at least before its acculturated analog was part of that inventory); these factors strongly suggest that the word in question originally designated the former referent and was subsequently semantically extended directly to the introduced referent. Readers should bear in mind, then, that for the most part extended constructions are apparent only in the form of term polysemy and that for the most part statistics for extended constructions in fact directly reflect only term polysemy.

Some examples of extended constructions unambiguously involve referential extension and not merely polysemy. In some instances, Amerindian languages have adopted a European language term that did not denote a certain item of acculturation in the European donor language and, subsequently, have referentially extended the borrowed term to that acculturated item. Such words for analytical purposes are formally considered here to be native labels for items of acculturation rather than European language loans. For example, the Pima word for the introduced PEA is *wihol*, a loanword based on the Spanish word for BEAN, *frijol*. Unambiguously, in this case, a term for BEAN, a precontact item, has been directly extended to PEA, an introduced item.

Cases with Nonanalyzable Native Terms

The number of language cases with nonanalyzable native terms for a specific acculturated item is presented. A nonanalyzable native term is a label for which the meanings of none of its constituent parts can be determined and, thus, cannot be expressed in English. In addition, a nonanalyzable term is not found to be polysemous in such a manner that suggests application to an item of acculturation through extension of reference. In most of the following reports, this statistic entails all language cases with nonanalyzable native terms. However, in a few reports, excluded from the latter are those language cases having nonanalyzable native terms that also show at least one analyzable native label. When this is the case, it is noted by an asterisk (*).

Many native terms are nonanalyzable because of deficiencies of lexical sources and/or because of the analyst's lack of familiarity with pertinent languages. Some are nonanalyzable because they are borrowed from other Amerindian languages and, consequently, have not been manufactured from the native vocabulary of the languages into which they have been borrowed (see chapters 3 and 8). Nonanalyzable native labels also include those obviously derived through onomatopoeia (see chapter 3).

1. APPLE
Cases with terms for item: 155
Cases with European language loans: 91
Loan percentage: 59%
Cases with native terms: 67 (43%)
Convergence index: +0.16
Cases with analyzable native terms: 45
Cases with descriptive constructions: 18 (40%)
Cases with overt marking constructions: 17 (38%)
Cases with extended constructions: 10 (22%)
Cases with marking reversal constructions: 3 (7%)
Cases with double overt marking constructions: 1 (2%)
Cases with nonanalyzable native terms: 27*

2. APRICOT
Cases with terms for item: 27
Cases with European language loans: 10
Loan percentage: 37%
Cases with native terms: 19 (70%)
Convergence index: -0.33
Cases with analyzable native terms: 15
Cases with overt marking constructions: 8 (53%)
Cases with descriptive constructions: 5 (33%)
Cases with extended constructions: 3 (20%)
Cases with nonanalyzable native terms: 4*

3. BARLEY
Cases with terms for item: 59
Cases with European language loans: 23
Loan percentage: 39%
Cases with native terms: 40 (68%)
Convergence index: -0.29
Cases with analyzable native terms: 30
Cases with overt marking constructions: 21 (70%)
Cases with descriptive constructions: 9 (30%)
Cases with extended constructions: 3 (10%)
Cases with nonanalyzable native terms: 10*

4. BEETS
Cases with terms for item: 51
Cases with European language loans: 9
Loan percentage: 18%
Cases with native terms: 46 (90%)
Convergence index: -0.73
Cases with analyzable native terms: 41

Cases with descriptive constructions: 27 (66%)
Cases with overt marking constructions: 12 (29%)
Cases with extended constructions: 7 (17%)
Cases with nonanalyzable native terms: 6*

5. BOARD
Cases with terms for item: 215
Cases with European language loans: 60
Loan percentage: 28%
Cases with native terms: 184 (86%)
Convergence index: -0.58
Cases with analyzable native terms: 110
Cases with descriptive constructions: 84 (76%)
Cases with extended constructions: 32 (29%)
Cases with nonanalyzable native terms: 76*

6. BOOK
Cases with terms for item: 247
Cases with European language loans: 53
Loan percentage: 22%
Cases with native terms: 214 (87%)
Convergence index: -0.65
Cases with analyzable native terms: 130
Cases with descriptive constructions: 97 (75%)
Cases with extended constructions: 44 (34%)
Cases with marking reversal constructions: 1 (0.8%)
Cases with nonanalyzable native terms: 96

7. BOTTLE
Cases with terms for item: 208
Cases with European language loans: 107
Loan percentage: 51%
Cases with native terms: 122 (59%)
Convergence index: -0.07
Cases with analyzable native terms: 51
Cases with extended constructions: 26 (51%)
Cases with descriptive constructions: 17 (33%)
Cases with overt marking constructions: 10 (20%)
Cases with nonanalyzable native terms: 72*

8. BOX
Cases with terms for item: 221
Cases with European language loans: 79
Loan percentage: 36%
Cases with native terms: 155 (70%)

Convergence index: -0.34
Cases with analyzable native terms: 65
  Cases with descriptive constructions: 34 (52%)
  Cases with extended constructions: 30 (46%)
  Cases with overt marking constructions: 8 (12%)
Cases with nonanalyzable native terms: 91*

9. BREAD
Cases with terms for item: 269
Cases with European language loans: 78
  Loan percentage: 29%
Cases with native terms: 220 (82%)
Convergence index: -0.53
Cases with analyzable native terms: 107
  Cases with descriptive constructions: 39 (37%)
  Cases with extended constructions: 37 (35%)
  Cases with overt marking constructions: 30 (28%)
  Cases with marking reversal constructions: 9 (9%)
Cases with nonanalyzable native terms: 136

10. BULL
Cases with terms for item: 191
Cases with European language loans: 76
  Loan percentage: 40%
Cases with native terms: 130 (68%)
Convergence index: -0.28
Cases with analyzable native terms: 110
  Cases with descriptive constructions: 74 (67%)
  Cases with extended constructions: 31 (28%)
  Cases with overt marking constructions: 18 (16%)
  Cases with double overt marking constructions: 3 (3%)
  Cases with marking reversal constructions: 1 (1%)
Cases with nonanalyzable native terms: 32

11. BUTTER
Cases with terms for item: 122
Cases with European language loans: 34
  Loan percentage: 28%
Cases with native terms: 93 (76%)
Convergence index: -0.48
Cases with analyzable native terms: 84
  Cases with descriptive constructions: 74 (88%)
  Cases with extended constructions: 14 (17%)
Cases with nonanalyzable native terms: 9*

12. BUTTON
Cases with terms for item: 180
Cases with European language loans: 69

Loan percentage: 38%
Cases with native terms: 121 (67%)
Convergence index: -0.29
Cases with analyzable native terms: 58
  Cases with descriptive constructions: 46 (79%)
  Cases with extended constructions: 18 (31%)
Cases with nonanalyzable native terms: 63*

13. CABBAGE
Cases with terms for item: 140
Cases with European language loans: 66
  Loan percentage: 47%
Cases with native terms: 82 (59%)
Convergence index: -0.12
Cases with analyzable native terms: 51
  Cases with descriptive constructions: 41 (80%)
  Cases with extended constructions: 15 (29%)
  Cases with overt marking constructions: 1 (2%)
  Cases with marking reversal constructions: 1 (2%)
Cases with nonanalyzable native terms: 31*

14. CALF
Cases with terms for item: 176
Cases with European language loans: 28
  Loan percentage: 16%
Cases with native terms: 152 (86%)
Convergence index: -0.71
Cases with analyzable native terms: 130
  Cases with descriptive constructions: 111 (85%)
  Cases with overt marking constructions: 15 (12%)
  Cases with extended constructions: 11 (9%)
  Cases with marking reversal constructions: 1 (1%)
Cases with nonanalyzable native terms: 22*

15. CANDLE
Cases with terms for item: 216
Cases with European language loans: 68
  Loan percentage: 32%
Cases with native terms: 175 (81%)
Convergence index: -0.50
Cases with analyzable native terms: 123
  Cases with extended constructions: 72 (59%)
  Cases with descriptive constructions: 67 (55%)
Cases with nonanalyzable native terms: 52*

16. CAT
Cases with terms for item: 279
Cases with European language loans: 194
  Loan percentage: 70%
Cases with native terms: 117 (42%)
Convergence index: +0.28

Cases with analyzable native terms: 40
  Cases with overt marking constructions: 14 (35%)
  Cases with extended constructions: 11 (28%)
  Cases with descriptive constructions: 10 (25%)
  Cases with marking reversal constructions: 7 (18%)
  Cases with double overt marking constructions: 1 (3%)
Cases with nonanalyzable native terms: 82

17. CHEESE
  Cases with terms for item: 134
  Cases with European language loans: 88
    Loan percentage: 66%
  Cases with native terms: 58 (43%)
  Convergence index: +0.22
  Cases with analyzable native terms: 52
    Cases with descriptive constructions: 50 (96%)
    Cases with extended constructions: 3 (6%)
  Cases with nonanalyzable native terms: 5*

18. CHICKEN
  Cases with terms for item: 180
  Cases with European language loans: 28
    Loan percentage: 16%
  Cases with native terms: 156 (87%)
  Convergence index: -0.71
  Cases with analyzable native terms: 55
    Cases with extended constructions: 29 (53%)
    Cases with descriptive constructions: 16 (29%)
    Cases with overt marking constructions: 7 (13%)
    Cases with marking reversal constructions: 5 (9%)
    Cases with double overt marking constructions: 1 (2%)
  Cases with nonanalyzable native terms: 108

19. CLOCK/WATCH
  Cases with terms for item: 191
  Cases with European language loans: 47
    Loan percentage: 25%
  Cases with native terms: 155 (81%)
  Convergence index: -0.57
  Cases with analyzable native terms: 131
    Cases with overt marking constructions: 65 (50%)
    Cases with descriptive constructions: 42 (32%)
    Cases with extended constructions: 36 (28%)
  Cases with nonanalyzable native terms: 24*

20. COFFEE
  Cases with terms for item: 192
  Cases with European language loans: 156

Loan percentage: 81%
Cases with native terms: 48 (25%)
Convergence index: +0.56
Cases with analyzable native terms: 38
  Cases with descriptive constructions: 35 (92%)
  Cases with extended constructions: 3 (8%)
Cases with nonanalyzable native terms: 13

21. COLT
  Cases with terms for item: 109
  Cases with European language loans: 12
    Loan percentage: 11%
  Cases with native terms: 101 (93%)
  Convergence index: -0.82
  Cases with analyzable native terms: 92
    Cases with descriptive constructions: 75 (82%)
    Cases with extended constructions: 12 (13%)
    Cases with overt marking constructions: 8 (9%)
  Cases with nonanalyzable native terms: 16

22. CORIANDER
  Cases with terms for item: 39
  Cases with European language loans: 28
    Loan percentage: 72%
  Cases with native terms: 13 (33%)
  Convergence index: +0.39
  Cases with analyzable native terms: 6
    Cases with descriptive constructions: 4 (67%)
    Cases with extended constructions: 2 (33%)
  Cases with nonanalyzable native terms: 8

23. COW
  Cases with terms for item: 266
  Cases with European language loans: 153
    Loan percentage: 58%
  Cases with native terms: 131 (49%)
  Convergence index: +0.08
  Cases with analyzable native terms: 95
    Cases with descriptive constructions: 37 (40%)
    Cases with extended constructions: 34 (36%)
    Cases with overt marking constructions: 28 (30%)
    Cases with marking reversal constructions: 14 (15%)
    Cases with double overt marking constructions: 5 (5%)
  Cases with nonanalyzable native terms: 30*

24. CUP
  Cases with terms for item: 196
  Cases with European language loans: 52
    Loan percentage: 27%
  Cases with native terms: 164 (84%)
  Convergence index: -0.57
  Cases with analyzable native terms: 90

Cases with descriptive constructions: 47
(52%)
Cases with extended constructions: 37
(41%)
Cases with overt marking constructions: 15
(17%)
Cases with nonanalyzable native terms: 72*

25. DONKEY

Cases with terms for item: 182
Cases with European language loans: 116
  Loan percentage: 64%
Cases with native terms: 83 (46%)
Convergence index: +0.18
Cases with analyzable native terms: 61
  Cases with overt marking constructions: 34
  (56%)
  Cases with descriptive constructions: 25
  (41%)
  Cases with extended constructions: 9 (15%)
Cases with nonanalyzable native terms: 31

26. FLOUR

Cases with terms for item: 232
Cases with European language loans: 68
  Loan percentage: 29%
Cases with native terms: 181 (78%)
Convergence index: -0.49
Cases with analyzable native terms: 89
  Cases with extended constructions: 46
  (52%)
  Cases with descriptive constructions: 41
  (46%)
  Cases with overt marking constructions: 13
  (15%)
  Cases with marking reversal constructions: 2
  (2%)
  Cases with double overt marking
  constructions: 1 (1%)
Cases with nonanalyzable native terms: 104

27. FORK

Cases with terms for item: 165
Cases with European language loans: 17
  Loan percentage: 10%
Cases with native terms: 151 (92%)
Convergence index: -0.81
Cases with analyzable native terms: 98
  Cases with descriptive constructions: 71
  (73%)
  Cases with overt marking constructions: 20
  (20%)
  Cases with extended constructions: 18
  (18%)
Cases with nonanalyzable native terms: 53*

28. GARLIC

Cases with terms for item: 101
Cases with European language loans: 70
  Loan percentage: 69%
Cases with native terms: 37 (37%)
Convergence index: +0.33

Cases with analyzable native terms: 26
  Cases with descriptive constructions: 14
  (54%)
  Cases with overt marking constructions: 13
  (50%)
  Cases with extended constructions: 2 (8%)
Cases with nonanalyzable native terms: 14

29. GOAT

Cases with terms for item: 196
Cases with European language loans: 103
  Loan percentage: 53%
Cases with native terms: 101 (52%)
Convergence index: +0.01
Cases with analyzable native terms: 54
  Cases with overt marking constructions: 32
  (59%)
  Cases with descriptive constructions: 18
  (33%)
  Cases with extended constructions: 9 (17%)
  Cases with marking reversal constructions:
  2 (4%)
Cases with nonanalyzable native terms: 47*

30. GRAPES

Cases with terms for item: 136
Cases with European language loans: 34
  Loan percentage: 25%
Cases with native terms: 107 (79%)
Convergence index: -0.54
Cases with analyzable native terms: 43
  Cases with descriptive constructions: 22
  (51%)
  Cases with extended constructions: 12
  (28%)
  Cases with overt marking constructions: 10
  (23%)
  Cases with marking reversal constructions:
  3 (7%)
Cases with nonanalyzable native terms: 66

31. HEN

Cases with terms for item: 229
Cases with European language loans: 23
  Loan percentage: 10%
Cases with native terms: 216 (94%)
Convergence index: -0.84
Cases with analyzable native terms: 112
  Cases with descriptive constructions: 84
  (75%)
  Cases with extended constructions: 24
  (21%)
  Cases with overt marking constructions: 9
  (8%)
  Cases with marking reversal constructions:
  7 (6%)
  Cases with double overt marking
  constructions: 1 (1%)
Cases with nonanalyzable native terms: 148

32. HORSE
   Cases with terms for item: 273
   Cases with European language loans: 143
      Loan percentage: 52%
   Cases with native terms: 161 (59%)
   Convergence index: -0.07
   Cases with analyzable native terms: 105
      Cases with overt marking constructions: 43
      (41%)
      Cases with extended constructions: 27
      (26%)
      Cases with marking reversal constructions:
      26 (25%)
      Cases with descriptive constructions: 24
      (23%)
      Cases with double overt marking
      constructions: 1 (1%)
   Cases with nonanalyzable native terms: 56*

33. HOUR
   Cases with terms for item: 153
   Cases with European language loans: 69
      Loan percentage: 45%
   Cases with native terms: 95 (62%)
   Convergence index: -0.17
   Cases with analyzable native terms: 70
      Cases with descriptive constructions: 40
      (57%)
      Cases with extended constructions: 36
      (51%)
   Cases with nonanalyzable native terms: 32

34. HUNDRED
   Cases with terms for item: 215
   Cases with European language loans: 40
      Loan percentage: 19%
   Cases with native terms: 183 (85%)
   Convergence index: -0.67
   Cases with analyzable native terms: 100
      Cases with descriptive constructions: 99
      (99%)
      Cases with extended constructions: 3 (3%)
   Cases with nonanalyzable native terms: 83*

35. KEY
   Cases with terms for item: 221
   Cases with European language loans: 91
      Loan percentage: 41%
   Cases with native terms: 150 (68%)
   Convergence index: -0.27
   Cases with analyzable native terms: 100
      Cases with descriptive constructions: 97
      (97%)
      Cases with extended constructions: 3 (3%)
   Cases with nonanalyzable native terms: 50*

36. LEMON
   Cases with terms for item: 133
   Cases with European language loans: 80
      Loan percentage: 60%
   Cases with native terms: 59 (44%)
   Convergence index: +0.16

Cases with analyzable native terms: 46
   Cases with overt marking constructions: 30
   (65%)
   Cases with descriptive constructions: 14
   (30%)
   Cases with extended constructions: 12
   (26%)
Cases with nonanalyzable native terms: 13

37. LETTUCE
   Cases with terms for item: 89
   Cases with European language loans: 42
      Loan percentage: 47%
   Cases with native terms: 52 (58%)
   Convergence index: -0.11
   Cases with analyzable native terms: 38
      Cases with descriptive constructions: 31
      (82%)
      Cases with extended constructions: 8 (21%)
      Cases with overt marking constructions: 3
      (8%)
   Cases with nonanalyzable native terms: 17

38. MARE
   Cases with terms for item: 135
   Cases with European language loans: 42
      Loan percentage: 31%
   Cases with native terms: 98 (73%)
   Convergence index: -0.42
   Cases with analyzable native terms: 91
      Cases with descriptive constructions: 77
      (85%)
      Cases with extended constructions: 11
      (12%)
      Cases with overt marking constructions: 5
      (6%)
      Cases with marking reversal constructions:
      1 (1%)
   Cases with nonanalyzable native terms: 12

39. MATCH
   Cases with terms for item: 186
   Cases with European language loans: 64
      Loan percentage: 34%
   Cases with native terms: 142 (76%)
   Convergence index: -0.42
   Cases with analyzable native terms: 99
      Cases with descriptive constructions: 69
      (70%)
      Cases with extended constructions: 32
      (32%)
      Cases with overt marking constructions: 1
      (1%)
   Cases with nonanalyzable native terms: 43*

40. MILE
   Cases with terms for item: 60
   Cases with European language loans: 16
      Loan percentage: 27%
   Cases with native terms: 48 (80%)
   Convergence index: -0.53
   Cases with analyzable native terms: 33

Cases with descriptive constructions: 21
(64%)
Cases with extended constructions: 13
(39%)
Cases with nonanalyzable native terms: 19

41. MONEY
Cases with terms for item: 263
Cases with European language loans: 30
Loan percentage: 11%
Cases with native terms: 244 (93%)
Convergence index: -0.81
Cases with analyzable native terms: 183
Cases with extended constructions: 155
(85%)
Cases with descriptive constructions: 34
('9%)
Cases with marking reversal constructions: 2
(1%)
Cases with nonanalyzable native terms: 61*

42. MULE
Cases with terms for item: 161
Cases with European language loans: 87
Loan percentage: 54%
Cases with native terms: 86 (53%)
Convergence index: +0.01
Cases with analyzable native terms: 63
Cases with descriptive constructions: 32
(51%)
Cases with overt marking constructions: 24
(38%)
Cases with extended constructions: 11
(18%)
Cases with marking reversal constructions: 1
(2%)
Cases with nonanalyzable native terms: 25

43. NAIL
Cases with terms for item: 224
Cases with European language loans: 74
Loan percentage: 33%
Cases with native terms: 166 (74%)
Convergence index: -0.41
Cases with analyzable native terms: 80
Cases with descriptive constructions: 55
(69%)
Cases with extended constructions: 24
(30%)
Cases with overt marking constructions: 8
(10%)
Cases with nonanalyzable native terms: 86*

44. NEEDLE
Cases with terms for item: 272
Cases with European language loans: 57
Loan percentage: 21%
Cases with native terms: 233 (86%)
Convergence index: -0.65
Cases with analyzable native terms: 108
Cases with descriptive constructions: 66
(61%)

Cases with extended constructions: 33
(31%)
Cases with overt marking constructions: 19
(18%)
Cases with marking reversal constructions:
2 (2%)
Cases with nonanalyzable native terms: 125*

45. OATS
Cases with terms for item: 74
Cases with European language loans: 17
Loan percentage: 23%
Cases with native terms: 59 (80%)
Convergence index: -0.57
Cases with analyzable native terms: 46
Cases with descriptive constructions: 29
(63%)
Cases with overt marking constructions: 11
(24%)
Cases with extended constructions: 10
(22%)
Cases with nonanalyzable native terms: 16

46. ONION
Cases with terms for item: 202
Cases with European language loans: 82
Loan percentage: 41%
Cases with native terms: 133 (66%)
Convergence index: -0.25
Cases with analyzable native terms: 53
Cases with descriptive constructions: 31
(59%)
Cases with extended constructions: 12
(23%)
Cases with overt marking constructions: 10
(19%)
Cases with marking reversal constructions:
2 (4%)
Cases with nonanalyzable native terms: 84

47. ORANGE
Cases with terms for item: 182
Cases with European language loans: 122
Loan percentage: 67%
Cases with native terms: 66 (36%)
Convergence index: +0.31
Cases with analyzable native terms: 42
Cases with descriptive constructions: 22
(52%)
Cases with overt marking constructions:
17 (41%)
Cases with extended constructions: 5 (12%)
Cases with marking reversal constructions:
1 (2%)
Cases with nonanalyzable native terms: 26

48. OX
Cases with terms for item: 153
Cases with European language loans: 45
Loan percentage: 29%
Cases with native terms: 122 (80%)
Convergence index: -0.50

Cases with analyzable native terms: 96
  Cases with descriptive constructions: 51 (53%)
  Cases with extended constructions: 38 (40%)
  Cases with overt marking constructions: 17 (18%)
  Cases with marking reversal constructions: 5 (5%)
  Cases with double overt marking constructions: 1 (1%)
Cases with nonanalyzable native terms: 34

49. PAPER

Cases with terms for item: 263
Cases with European language loans: 53
  Loan percentage: 20%
Cases with native terms: 220 (84%)
Convergence index: -0.64
Cases with analyzable native terms: 112
  Cases with descriptive constructions: 70 (63%)
  Cases with extended constructions: 46 (41%)
  Cases with marking reversal constructions: 2 (2%)
Cases with nonanalyzable native terms: 125

50. PEACH

Cases with terms for item: 122
Cases with European language loans: 66
  Loan percentage: 54%
Cases with native terms: 61 (50%)
Convergence index: +0.04
Cases with analyzable native terms: 45
  Cases with overt marking constructions: 18 (40%)
  Cases with descriptive constructions: 13 (29%)
  Cases with extended constructions: 7 (16%)
  Cases with marking reversal constructions: 8 (18%)
Cases with nonanalyzable native terms: 19

51. PEAS

Cases with terms for item: 105
Cases with European language loans: 29
  Loan percentage: 28%
Cases with native terms: 80 (76%)
Convergence index: -0.49
Cases with analyzable native terms: 50
  Cases with overt marking constructions: 24 (48%)
  Cases with extended constructions: 14 (28%)
  Cases with descriptive constructions: 10 (20%)
  Cases with marking reversal constructions: 3 (6%)
  Cases with double overt marking constructions: 1 (2%)
Cases with nonanalyzable native terms: 31

52. PIG

Cases with terms for item: 277
Cases with European language loans: 151
  Loan percentage: 55%
Cases with native terms: 150 (54%)
Convergence index: +0.003
Cases with analyzable native terms: 94
  Cases with marking reversal constructions: 44 (47%)
  Cases with overt marking constructions: 26 (28%)
  Cases with extended constructions: 25 (27%)
  Cases with descriptive constructions: 10 (11%)
  Cases with double overt marking constructions: 2 (2%)
Cases with nonanalyzable native terms: 76

53. PISTOL

Cases with terms for item: 108
Cases with European language loans: 29
  Loan percentage: 27%
Cases with native terms: 82 (76%)
Convergence index: -0.49
Cases with analyzable native terms: 61
  Cases with descriptive constructions: 45 (74%)
  Cases with overt marking constructions: 12 (20%)
  Cases with extended constructions: 2 (3%)
  Cases with double overt marking constructions: 2 (3%)
Cases with nonanalyzable native terms: 25

54. RIBBON

Cases with terms for item: 149
Cases with European language loans: 72
  Loan percentage: 48%
Cases with native terms: 90 (60%)
Convergence index: -0.12
Cases with analyzable native terms: 37
  Cases with descriptive constructions: 25 (68%)
  Cases with extended constructions: 12 (32%)
  Cases with overt marking constructions: 3 (8%)
Cases with nonanalyzable native terms: 59

55. RICE

Cases with terms for item: 184
Cases with European language loans: 96
  Loan percentage: 52%
Cases with native terms: 102 (55%)
Convergence index: -0.03
Cases with analyzable native terms: 74
  Cases with descriptive constructions: 32 (43%)
  Cases with overt marking constructions: 25 (34%)

Cases with extended constructions: 23
(31%)
Cases with marking reversal constructions: 1
(1%)
Cases with nonanalyzable native terms: 31

56. RICH
Cases with terms for item: 225
Cases with European language loans: 29
Loan percentage: 13%
Cases with native terms: 205 (91%)
Convergence index: -0.78
Cases with analyzable native terms: 90
Cases with descriptive constructions: 76
(84%)
Cases with extended constructions: 23
(26%)
Cases with nonanalyzable native terms: 137

57. ROOSTER
Cases with terms for item: 222
Cases with European language loans: 27
Loan percentage: 12%
Cases with native terms: 204 (92%)
Convergence index: -0.80
Cases with analyzable native terms: 142
Cases with descriptive constructions: 126
(89%)
Cases with extended constructions: 29
(20%)
Cases with overt marking constructions: 2
(1%)
Cases with marking reversal constructions: 2
(1%)
Cases with nonanalyzable native terms: 99

58. SATURDAY
Cases with terms for item: 170
Cases with European language loans: 95
Loan percentage: 56%
Cases with native terms: 90 (53%)
Convergence index: +0.03
Cases with analyzable native terms: 76
Cases with descriptive constructions: 74
(97%)
Cases with extended constructions: 3 (4%)
Cases with nonanalyzable native terms: 22

59. SCHOOL
Cases with terms for item: 185
Cases with European language loans: 65
Loan percentage: 35%
Cases with native terms: 140 (76%)
Convergence index: -0.41
Cases with analyzable native terms: 112
Cases with descriptive constructions: 110
(98%)
Cases with extended constructions: 4 (4%)
Cases with nonanalyzable native terms: 36

60. SCISSORS
Cases with terms for item: 245

Cases with European language loans: 86
Loan percentage: 35%
Cases with native terms: 176 (72%)
Convergence index: -0.37
Cases with analyzable native terms: 93
Cases with descriptive constructions: 77
(83%)
Cases with extended constructions: 5 (5%)
Cases with overt marking constructions: 15
(16%)
Cases with nonanalyzable native terms: 89

61. SHEEP
Cases with terms for item: 241
Cases with European language loans: 105
Loan percentage: 44%
Cases with native terms: 153 (64%)
Convergence index: -0.20
Cases with analyzable native terms: 98
Cases with overt marking constructions: 42
(43%)
Cases with descriptive constructions: 33
(34%)
Cases with extended constructions: 33
(34%)
Cases with marking reversal constructions:
8 (8%)
Cases with double overt marking
constructions: 1 (1%)
Cases with nonanalyzable native terms: 71

62. SHOVEL
Cases with terms for item: 172
Cases with European language loans: 51
Loan percentage: 30%
Cases with native terms: 129 (75%)
Convergence index: -0.45
Cases with analyzable native terms: 65
Cases with descriptive constructions: 56
(86%)
Cases with extended constructions: 7 (11%)
Cases with overt marking constructions: 5
(8%)
Cases with nonanalyzable native terms: 75

63. SOAP
Cases with terms for item: 244
Cases with European language loans: 124
Loan percentage: 51%
Cases with native terms: 138 (57%)
Convergence index: -0.06
Cases with analyzable native terms: 96
Cases with descriptive constructions: 82
(85%)
Cases with extended constructions: 10
(10%)
Cases with overt marking constructions: 5
(5%)
Cases with nonanalyzable native terms: 52

64. SOLDIER
Cases with terms for item: 202

Cases with European language loans: 110
  Loan percentage: 55%
Cases with native terms: 106 (53%)
Convergence index: +0.02
Cases with analyzable native terms: 55
  Cases with descriptive constructions: 30 (55%)
  Cases with extended constructions: 25 (46%)
  Cases with overt marking constructions: 6 (11%)
Cases with nonanalyzable native terms: 60

65. SPOON

Cases with terms for item: 256
Cases with European language loans: 79
  Loan percentage: 31%
Cases with native terms: 204 (80%)
Convergence index: -0.49
Cases with analyzable native terms: 55
  Cases with extended constructions: 25 (46%)
  Cases with descriptive constructions: 21 (38%)
  Cases with overt marking constructions: 14 (26%)
  Cases with marking reversal constructions: 4 (7%)
Cases with nonanalyzable native terms: 162

66. STORE/SHOP

Cases with terms for item: 172
Cases with European language loans: 51
  Loan percentage: 30%
Cases with native terms: 132 (77%)
Convergence index: -0.47
Cases with analyzable native terms: 106
  Cases with descriptive constructions: 101 (95%)
  Cases with extended constructions: 7 (7%)
Cases with nonanalyzable native terms: 39

67. SUGAR

Cases with terms for item: 227
Cases with European language loans: 121
  Loan percentage: 53%
Cases with native terms: 139 (61%)
Convergence index: -0.08
Cases with analyzable native terms: 83
  Cases with descriptive constructions: 37 (45%)
  Cases with extended constructions: 33 (40%)
  Cases with overt marking constructions: 15 (18%)
  Cases with marking reversal constructions: 2 (2%)
Cases with nonanalyzable native terms: 61

68. TABLE

Cases with terms for item: 244
Cases with European language loans: 127

Loan percentage: 52%
Cases with native terms: 143 (59%)
Convergence index: -0.07
Cases with analyzable native terms: 103
  Cases with descriptive constructions: 90 (87%)
  Cases with extended constructions: 14 (14%)
  Cases with overt marking constructions: 4 (4%)
Cases with nonanalyzable native terms: 59

69. TEA

Cases with terms for item: 119
Cases with European language loans: 63
  Loan percentage: 53%
Cases with native terms: 66 (56%)
Convergence index: -0.03
Cases with analyzable native terms: 52
  Cases with descriptive constructions: 30 (58%)
  Cases with extended constructions: 23 (44%)
  Cases with overt marking constructions: 9 (17%)
Cases with nonanalyzable native terms: 15

70. THREAD

Cases with terms for item: 255
Cases with European language loans: 43
  Loan percentage: 17%
Cases with native terms: 229 (90%)
Convergence index: -0.73
Cases with analyzable native terms: 98
  Cases with extended constructions: 56 (57%)
  Cases with overt marking constructions: 27 (28%)
  Cases with descriptive constructions: 25 (26%)
  Cases with marking reversal constructions: 2 (2%)
Cases with nonanalyzable native terms: 154

71. TOWN

Cases with terms for item: 258
Cases with European language loans: 38
  Loan percentage: 15%
Cases with native terms: 234 (91%)
Convergence index: -0.76
Cases with analyzable native terms: 99
  Cases with descriptive constructions: 65 (66%)
  Cases with extended constructions: 42 (42%)
  Cases with overt marking constructions: 2 (2%)
  Cases with marking reversal constructions: 1 (1%)
Cases with nonanalyzable native terms: 157

72. TURNIP
Cases with terms for item: 95
Cases with European language loans: 37
Loan percentage: 39%
Cases with native terms: 61 (64%)
Convergence index: -0.25
Cases with analyzable native terms: 33
Cases with descriptive constructions: 16
(49%)
Cases with extended constructions: 11
(33%)
Cases with overt marking constructions: 8
(24%)
Cases with nonanalyzable native terms: 30

73. WAGON
Cases with terms for item: 151
Cases with European language loans: 42
Loan percentage: 28%
Cases with native terms: 115 (76%)
Convergence index: -0.48
Cases with analyzable native terms: 61
Cases with descriptive constructions: 51
(84%)
Cases with extended constructions: 9 (15%)
Cases with overt marking constructions: 4
(7%)
Cases with nonanalyzable native terms: 60

74. WATERMELON
Cases with terms for item: 144
Cases with European language loans: 71
Loan percentage: 49%
Cases with native terms: 84 (58%)
Convergence index: -0.09
Cases with analyzable native terms: 50
Cases with descriptive constructions: 26
(52%)
Cases with overt marking constructions: 18
(36%)
Cases with extended constructions: 9 (18%)
Cases with double overt marking
constructions: 1 (2%)
Cases with marking reversal constructions: 1
(2%)
Cases with nonanalyzable native terms: 40

75. WEDNESDAY
Cases with terms for item: 155
Cases with European language loans: 54
Loan percentage: 35%
Cases with native terms: 108 (70%)
Convergence index: -0.35
Cases with analyzable native terms: 96
Cases with descriptive constructions: 96
(100%)
Cases with nonanalyzable native terms: 17

76. WHEAT
Cases with terms for item: 172
Cases with European language loans: 66
Loan percentage: 38%

Cases with native terms: 114 (66%)
Convergence index: -0.28
Cases with analyzable native terms: 66
Cases with descriptive constructions: 36
(55%)
Cases with overt marking constructions: 22
(33%)
Cases with extended constructions: 15
(23%)
Cases with nonanalyzable native terms: 53

77. WINDOW
Cases with terms for item: 218
Cases with European language loans: 59
Loan percentage: 27%
Cases with native terms: 178 (82%)
Convergence index: -0.55
Cases with analyzable native terms: 97
Cases with descriptive constructions: 63
(65%)
Cases with overt marking constructions: 25
(26%)
Cases with extended constructions: 21
(22%)
Cases with nonanalyzable native terms: 98

Appendix B

LEXICAL SOURCES AND OTHER INFORMATION FOR 292 LANGUAGE CASES

This appendix lists the 292 language cases in alphabetical order, giving for each (in the following order) the genetic group affiliation, geographic location, total number of items of acculturation (out of 77) for which labels are found in lexical sources (t), number of items for which European loans are found in lexical sources (l), number of items for which native terms are found in lexical sources (n), European loan percentage (%), convergence index (ci), and lexical sources.

Genetic groups identified are, with one exception, well established or at least noncontroversial (cf. Kaufman 1994a, 1994b, 1994c; Tait 1994). Controversial genetic groupings such as Hokan, Penutian, and Equatorial (cf. Greenberg 1987), which at best unite very distantly related languages, are avoided. The exception is Quechumaran, a debated proposed genetic linkage of Aymara and Quechua (see chapter 6).

Geographic location is identified by country and, when possible, by state, province, district, or town. For the most part, listed locations are the earliest known places at which a language or dialect was spoken.

For most language cases, the total number of acculturated items labeled (t) is smaller than the actual number of terms for the items found in sources because of the use of synonyms; that is, two or more labels may be found in a single case for the same item of acculturation. Also because of synonyms, the number of items designated by European loans (l) is often smaller than the actual number of European loans used by a language case to denote the items, and the number of items labeled by native terms (n) is often smaller than the actual number of native words used to denote them. The use of synonyms results as well in sums of l's and n's that exceed values of t's. For example, the aggregation of the l (26) and the n (13) given for Aguacatec (case 3) is 39, which exceeds the value of Aguacatec's t (38) by 1.

Language cases included in the sample are restricted to those whose total number of labeled items of acculturation (t) is greater than 30 (see chapter 2). The mean t across the 292 language cases is 47.6, with a standard deviation of 12.1. Creek (Muskokee, case 66) shows the largest number of labeled items (out of 77), with 76.

The number of acculturated items labeled by European loanwords (*l*) does not entail items labeled by referentially extended European loans or by loan blends (except for a certain type of loan blend that occurs only rarely; see chapter 3). Extended European loans and loan blends are formally considered here, for analytical purposes, to be native terms. European loanwords are identified by the language of origin. For example, information given for Aguaruna (case 4), *l* = S:26, indicates that 26 items of acculturation are labeled by European loans and that all the loans are from Spanish (S). A more complex example is Atakapa (case 16), where *l* = 3 (E:2, F:1) indicates that three items are labeled by European loans, two of which are designated by English (E) terms and one by a French (F) word. Since loanwords from two or more different European languages may sometimes label the same item in a single language, the aggregate of parenthesized numbers may not always equal the total number of items labeled by European loans (*l*). For example, *l* = 9 (E:9, S:3) is given for Alabama (case 6). This indicates that nine items of acculturation are denoted by European loans and that while all nine are labeled by English (E) adoptions, three are designated by Spanish (S) loans as well (9 and 3, of course, do not equal 9). Symbols used for identifying the European language of origin are as follows:

Da = Danish	N = Norwegian
Du = Dutch	P = Portuguese
E = English	R = Russian
F = French	S = Spanish
G = German	

The European loan percentage (%) is calculated by dividing the number of acculturated items labeled by a European loan (*l*) by the total number of items labeled (*t*).

The convergence index (*ci*) theoretically ranges in value from +1.00, indicating that all labeled items of acculturation for a language case are denoted by European loans but no items are labeled by native terms, to -1.00, indicating that all labeled items are designated by native terms but no items are designated by European loans. None of the 292 language cases shows a convergence index of +1.00; the largest is +0.84, shown by Cupeño (case 71). An index of 0.00, for example, would indicate that just as many items are labeled by native terms as are labeled by European loans. The *ci* is calculated by subtracting the number of items labeled by native terms (*n*), divided by the total number of labeled items (*t*), from the number of items denoted by European loans (*l*) divided by the total number of labeled items (*t*).

A standard bibliographic format is used in presenting lexical sources for language cases. In many instances, cases are based on information from two or more sources. Lexical sources for language cases are limited to those available through 1993. After this date, the set of 292 cases was considered a definitive and closed sample and no other cases (and lexical sources) were added. Since 1993, a number of other sources for Amerindian languages have been published or otherwise made accessible, many of which are cited in chapters of this book and in notes in this appendix and are appropriately listed in the general references cited section.

Readers should note that the following references are not necessarily repeated in the references section of this book, which includes only sources specifically cited in the text.

1. *Abenaki (Penobscot dialect, 1691)*
    Algonquian; Maine; $t = 40$, $l = 9$ (E:7, F:2), $n = 31$, $\% = 23$, $ci = -0.55$.

    Rasles, Sebastian (1833). *A dictionary of the Abnaki language, in North America*. In *Memoirs of the American Academy of Arts and Sciences*.

    Note: Since 1993, another Abenaki dictionary has become available (Day 1994, 1995).

2. *Abipon (c. 1760)*
    Guaycuruan; Argentine Chaco; $t = 46$, $l = $ S:10, $n = 36$, $\% = 22$, $ci = -0.57$.

    Najlis, Elena Lidia (1966). *Lengua Abipona,* Tomo II. Buenos Aires: Universidad de Buenos Aires, Centro de Estudios Lingüísticos.

3. *Aguacatec*
    Mayan; Huehuetenango, Guatemala; $t = 38$, $l = $ S:26, $n = 13$; $\% = 68$, $ci = +0.34$.

    McArthur, Harry S. (1976). *Aguacatec vocabulary with grammatical notes*. University of Chicago Library Microfilm Collection of Manuscripts on Middle American Cultural Anthropology, Chicago.

4. *Aguaruna*
    Jivaroan; Amazonas, Peru; $t = 42$, $l = $ S:26, $n = 17$, $\% = 62$, $ci = +0.21$.

    Anonymous (1979). *Palabras y frases utiles en algunos idiomas de la Selva Peruana*. Perú: Instituto Lingüístico de Verano.
    Larson, Mildred (1957). *Comparación de los vocabularios Aguaruna y Huambisa*. Cuzco, Perú: Revista Peruana de Cultura.
    Larson, Mildred (1958). *Vocabulario comparado de las lenguas Aguaruna y Castellana*. Perú: Instituto Lingüístico de Verano.
    Larson, Mildred L. (1966) *Vocabulario Aguaruna de Amazonas*. Perú: Instituto Lingüístico de Verano.
    Mori, Angel Corbera (1981. *Glosario Aguaruna-Castellano*. Lima, Perú: Universidad Nacional Mayor de San Marcos.

5. *Ahtna*
    Athapascan-Eyak; Alaska; $t = 44$, $l = 19$ (R:18, F:3, E:2), $n = 35$, $\% = 43$, $ci = -0.36$.

    Kari, James, and Buck, Mildred (1975). *Ahtna noun dictionary*. Fairbanks: Alaska Native Language Center.
    Kari, James (1990). *Ahtna Athabaskan dictionary*. Fairbanks, Alaska: Alaska Native Language Center.

6. *Alabama*
    Muskogean; Alabama, later Texas; $t = 71$, $l = 9$ (E:9, S:3), $n = 65$, $\% = 13$, $ci = -0.79$.

    Sylestine, Cora, Hardy, Heather K., and Montler, Timothy (1993). *Dictionary of the Alabama language*. Austin: University of Texas Press.

7. *Algonquin (1886)*
    Algonquian; Quebec and Ontario; $t = 46$, $l = 6$ (F:4, E:1, F:1), $n = 40$, $\% = 13$, $ci = -0.74$.

    Cuoq, Jean-André (1886). *Lexique de la langue Algonquine*. Montréal: J. Chapleau et Fils.

8. *Algonquin (1984)*
    Algonquian; Quebec and Ontario; $t = 43$, $l = $ F:4, $n = 40$, $\% = 9$, $ci = -0.84$.

    McGregor, Ernest (1984). *Algonquin lexicon*. Maniwaki, Québec: River Desert Education Authority.

9. *Amoishe*
Maipuran; Cuzco, Peru; t = 34, l = S:11, n = 23, % = 32, ci = -0.35.

Sala, Gabriel (1905–1908). Diccionario, gramática y catecismo Castellano, Inga, Amueixa y Campa. *Boletín de la Sociedad Geográfica de Lima* 17:149–227, 311–356, 469–490; 19: 102–120, 211–240.

10. *Amuzgo*
Otomanguean; Guerrero, Mexico; t = 35, l = S:3, n = 32, % = 9, ci = -0.83.

Belmar, Francisco (1901). *Idioma Amuzgo que se habla en algunas pueblos del Distrito de Jamiltepec.* Oaxaca, México: Tipografía Particular.

11. *Apache (1870s and 1880s)*
Athapascan-Eyak; Arizona and New Mexico; t = 47, l = S:5, n = 44, % = 11, ci = -0.83.

Condie, Carol J. (1980). *Vocabulary of the Apache or 'Inde" language of Arizona and New Mexico collected by John Gregory Bourke in the 1870's and 1880's.* Greeley: University of Northern Colorado.

12. *Arawak*
Maipuran; British Guiana and Surinam; t = 32, l = 22 (Du:11, S:10, E:2), n = 12, % = 69, ci = +0.31.

Goeje, Claudius Henricus de (1928). *The Arawak language of Guiana.* Amsterdam: Uitgave Van De Koninklijke Akademie. Van Wetenschappen Te Amsterdam.

13. *Arikara*
Caddoan; Nebraska, later North Dakota; t = 62, l = 5 (E:4, F:1), n = 57, % = 8, ci = -0.84.

Parks, Douglas R. (1986). *An English-Arikara student dictionary.* Roseglen, N.D.: White Shield School District 85.

14. *Ashluslây (1915)*
Matacoan; Paraguayan Chaco; t = 32, l = S:3, n = 30, % = 9, ci = -0.84.

Hunt, Richard J. (1915). *El Choratio Yófuaha.* Liverpool: Henry Young and Sons, Limited.

15. *Ashluslây (1940–1979)*
Matacoan; Paraguayan Chaco; t = 42, l = S:5, n = 37, % = 12, ci = -0.76.

Junker, Paulino, Wilkskamp, Juan, and Seelwische, José (1968). Manual de la gramática Chulupí. *Suplemento Antropológico de la Revista del Ateneo Paraguayo* 3:159–247.
Schmidt, Max (1940). Vocabulario de la lengua Churupí. *Revista de la Sociedad Científica* del *Paraguay* 5:73–97.
Seelwische, José (1979). *Diccionario Nivacle-Castellano.* Asunción, Paraguay: Centro de Estudios Antropológicos de la Universidad Católica Nuestra Señora de la Asunción.

16. *Atakapa*
Isolate; Louisiana and Texas; t = 60, l = 3 (E:2, F:1), n = 57, % = 5, ci = -0.95.

Gatschet, Albert S., and Swanton, John R. (1932). *A dictionary of the Atakapa language.* Washington, D.C.: U.S. Government Printing Office.

17. *Atsugewi*
Palaihnihan; California; t = 34, l = 4 (E:3, S:1), n = 31, % = 12, ci = -0.79.

Olmsted, David L. (1984). *A lexicon of Atsugewi.* Reports from the Survey of California and Other Indian Languages. Report 5.

18. *Aymara (1612)*
    Quechumaran; Bolivia; t = 34, l = S:20, n = 21, % =59, ci = -0.03.

    Bertonio, Ludovico (1612). *Vocabulario de la lengua Aymara*. Juli, Chucuito.

19. *Aymara (1870–1907)*
    Quechumaran; Bolivia; t = 41, l = S:20, n = 22, % = 49, ci = -0.05.

    Forbes, David (1870). On the Aymara Indians of Bolivia and Peru. *The Journal of the Ethnological Society of London* 2:193–305.
    Middendorf, Ernst W. (1891). *Die Aimara-Sprache*. Leipzig: F. A. Brockhaus.
    Religiosos Franciscanos Misioneros de los Colegios de Propaganda Fide del Perú (1905). *Vocabulario políglota Incaico*. Lima: Tipografía del Colegio de Propaganda Fide del Perú.
    Tavera-Acosta, Bartolomé (1907). *En el sur (Dialectos indígenas de Venezuela)*. Bolívar: Imprenta y Encuadernación de Benito Jimeno Castro.

20. *Aymara (1940–1989)*
    Quechumaran; Bolivia; t = 61, l = S:50, n = 31, % = 82, ci = +0.31.

    Briggs, Lucy T. (1981). Aymarization: An example of language change. In M. J. Hardman (ed.), *The Aymara language in its social and cultural context*, pp. 127–145. Gainesville, Florida: University Presses of Florida.
    Cotari, Daniel, Mejía, Jaime, and Carrasco, Víctor (1978). *Diccionario Aymara-Castellano, Castellano-Aymara*. Cochabamba, Bolivia: Instituto de Idiomas Padres de Maryknoll.
    Deza Galindo, Juan Francisco (1989). *Nuevo diccionario Aymara-Castellano, Castellano-Aymara*. Lima, Perú: Consejo Nacional de Ciencias y Tecnología Concytec.
    Deza Galindo, Juan Francisco, and Molleapasa Coello, Anselmo (1945). *Vocabulario trilingüe Castellano, Quechua i Aimara*. Puno, Perú.
    Ebbing, Juan Enrique (1965). *Gramática y diccionario Aimara*. La Paz: Editorial "Don Bosco."
    Lucca D., Manuel de (1983). *Diccionario Aymara-Castellano, Castellano-Aymara*. La Paz, Bolivia: Comisión de Alfabetización y Literatura en Aymara.
    Lucca D., Manuel de (1987). *Diccionario práctico Aymara-Castellano Castellano-Aymara*. La Paz: Editorial Los Amigos del Libro.
    Miranda S., Pedro (1970). *Diccionario breve Castellano-Aymara y Aymara-Castellano*. La Paz.
    Sebeok, Thomas A. (1951). Materials for an Aymara dictionary. *Journal de la Société des Américanistes de Paris* 40:89–151.
    Villamor, German G. (1940). *Moderno vocabulario del Kechua y del Aymara*. La Paz: Libreria "Popular."
    Yapita, Juan de Dios (1974). *Vocabulario Castellano-Inglés-Aymara*. Oruro, Bolivia: Editorial I.N.D.I.C.E.P.

21. *Beaver*
    Athapascan-Eyak; Alberta and British Columbia; t = 51, l = F:4, n = 47, % = 8, ci = -0.84.

    Garrioch, Alfred C. (1885). *A vocabulary of the Beaver Indian language*. London: Society for Promoting Christian Knowledge.

22. *Big Smokey Valley Shoshoni*
    Uto-Aztecan; Nevada; t = 34, l = 12 (E:12, S:1), n = 26, % = 35, ci = -0.41.

    Crapo, Richley H. (1976). *Big Smokey Valley Shoshoni*. Desert Research Institute Publications in the Social Sciences, No. 10, Reno, Nevada.

23. *Biloxi*
    Siouan; Mississippi; t = 59, l = 4 (E:2, S:2), n = 55, % = 7, ci = -0.86.

    Dorsey, James Owen, and Swanton, John R. (1912). *A dictionary of the Biloxi and Ofo languages*. Washington, D.C.: U.S. Government Printing Office.

24. *Blackfoot (Peigan dialect)*
    Algonquian; Alberta; t = 53, l = 3 (E:2, F:1), n = 51, % = 6, ci = -0.91.

Uhlenbeck, Christian C., and van Gulik, R. H. (1934). *A Blackfoot-English vocabulary based on material from the Southern Peigans.* Amsterdam: Uitgave Van De N.V. Noord-Hollandsche.

25. *Blackfoot Proper (Siksika dialect)*
    Algonquian; Alberta; $t = 59$, $l = 4$ (E:3, F:1), $n = 55$, % = 7, $ci = -0.86$.

    Tims, John WIlliam (1889). *Grammar and dictionary of the Blackfoot language.* London: Society for Promoting Christian Knowledge.

26. *Bodega Miwok*
    Miwok-Costanoan; California; $t = 47$, $l = 41$ (S:39, E:1, R:1), $n = 10$, % = 87, $ci = +0.66$.

    Callaghan, Catherine A. (1970). *Bodega Miwok dictionary.* Berkeley: University of California Press.

27. *Cágaba*
    Chibchan; Magdalena, Colombia; $t = 37$, $l = $ S:20, $n = 18$, % = 54, $ci = +0.05$.

    Celedón, Rafael (1886). *Gramática de la lengua Köggaba con vocabularios y catecismos.* Paris: Maisonneuve Frères and C. H. Ledero.
    Preuss, Konrad Theodor (1927). Forschungsreise zu den Kágaba-Indianern der Sierra Nevada de Santa Marta in Kolumbien. Lexicon Deutsch-Kaugian. *Anthropos* 22:357–386.

28. *Cahita*
    Uto-Aztecan; Sonora, Mexico; $t = 37$; $l = $ S:29, $n = 9$, % = 78, $ci = +0.54$.

    Lionnet, Andrés (1977). *Los elementos de la lengua Cahita (Yaqui-Mayo).* México, D.F.: Universidad Nacional Autónoma de México.

    Note: This language case may be the same dialect as Yaqui (case 281).

29. *Cahuilla*
    Uto-Aztecan; California; $t = 70$, $l = $ S:66, $n = 16$, % = 94, ci = +0.72.

    Bright, William (1960). Animals of acculturation in the California Indian languages. *University of California Publications in Linguistics* 4:215–246.
    Bright, William (1979). Hispanisms in Cahuilla. *Journal of California and Great Basin Anthropology Papers in Linguistics* 1:101–116.
    Sauvel, Katherine Siva, and Munro, Pamela (1981). *Chem'ivillu' (Let's speak Cahuilla).* Los Angeles: American Indian Studies Center.
    Seiler, Hans Jakob, and Hioki, Kojiro (1979). *Cahuilla dictionary.* Banning, Cal.: Malki Museum Press.

30. *Cakchiquel (c. 1650)*
    Mayan; Guatemala; $t = 45$, $l = $ S:20, $n = 34$, % = 44, $ci = -0.31$.

    Coto, Thomás de (1983), Vocabulario *de la lengua Cakchiquel V[el] Guatemalteca, nueuamente hecho y recopilado con summo estudio, trauajo y erudición.* México, D.F.: Universidad Nacional Autónoma de México.

31. *Cakchiquel (1956–1981)*
    Mayan; Guatemala; $t = 67$, $l = $ S:40, $n = 46$, % = 60, $ci = -0.09$.

    Blair, Robert W., Robertson, John S., Richman, Larry, Sansom, Greg, Salazar, Julio, Yool, Juan, and Choc, Alejandro (1981). *Diccionario Español-Cakchiquel-Inglés.* New York: Garland Publishing.
    Herbruger, Alfredo, Jr., and Diaz Barrios, Eduardo (1956). *Método para aprender a hablar, leer y escribir la lengua Cakchiquel.* Guatemala, C.A.: Tipografía Nacional Guatemala.

32. *Cakchiquel (Central)*
    Mayan; Chimaltenango, Guatemala; $t = 40$, $l = $ S:17, $n =25$, $\% = 43$, $ci = -0.20$.

    Munson L., Jo Ann (1991). *Diccionario Cakchiquel Central y Español.* Guatemala, C.A.: Instituto Lingüístico de Verano.

33. *Campa (1878–1908)*
    Maipuran; Cuzco, Peru; $t = 42$, $l = $ S:19, $n = 32$, $\% = 45$, $ci = -0.31$.

    Adam, Lucien (1890). *Arte de la lengua Indios Antis o Campas (Conforme al manuscrito original hallado en la Ciudad de Toledo por Charles Leclerc).* Paris: J. Maisonneuve.
    Capelo, Joaquín (1896). *La via central del Perú.* Lima: Imprenta Masias.
    Delgado, Eulogio (1896–1897). Vocabulario del idioma de las Tribus Campus. *Boletín de la Sociedad Geográfica de Lima* 5:445–457; 6:96–105, 230–240, 347–356, 393–396.
    Sala, Gabriel (1905–1908), Diccionario, gramática y catecismo Castellano, Inga, Amueixa y Campa. *Boletín de la Sociedad Geográfica de Lima* 17:149–227, 311–356, 469–490; 19:102–120, 211–240.
    Tavera-Acosta, Bartolomé (1907). *En el sur (Dialectos indígenas de Venezuela).* Bolívar: Imprenta y Encuadernación de Benito Jimeno Castro.
    Touchaux, Mauricio (1908). Apuntes sobre la gramática y el diccionario del idioma Campa, o lengua de los Antis tal como se usa en el Río Aputimas. *Revista Histórica, Organo del Instituto Histórico del Perú* 3:131–164.

34. *Campa (1979–1980)*
    Maipuran; Cuzco, Peru; $t = 33$, $l = $ S:22, $n = 13$, $\% =67$, $ci = +0.27$.

    Anonymous (1979). *Palabras y frases utiles en algunos idiomas de la Selva Peruana.* Yarinacocha, Pucallpa, Perú: Instituto Lingüístico de Verano.
    Kindberg, Lee (1980). *Diccionario Ashaninca (edición provisional).* Yarinacocha, Pucallpa, Perú: Instituto Lingüístico de Verano.
    Payne, David L. (1980). *Diccionario Asheninca-Castellano.* Yarinacocha, Pucallpa, Perú: Instituto Lingüístico de Verano.

35. *Carrier*
    Athapascan-Eyak; British Columbia; $t = 63$, $l = $ 18 (F:10, E:8), $n = 53$, $\% = 29$, $ci = -0.56$.

    Antoine, Francesca, Bird, Catherine, Isaac, Agnes, Prince, Nellie, Sam, Sally, Walker, Richard, and Wilkinson, David B. (1974). *Central Carrier bilingual dictionary.* Fort Saint James, British Columbia: Carrier Linguistics Committee.
    Morice, Adrien-Gabriel (1932). *The Carrier language,* vols. 1 and 2. St. Gabriel, Osterreich (Austria): Collection Internationale de Monographies Linguistiques, ANTHROPOS.

36. *Cashinahua*
    Pano-Takanan; Amazonas, Brazil; $t = 40$, $l = $ 7 (S:5, P:2), $n = 38$, $\% = 18$, $ci = -0.78$.

    Abreu, J. Capistrano de (1941). *Ra-txa Hu-ni-ku-i, grammatica, textos e vocabulario Caxinauás.* Brazil: Sociedade Capistrano de Abreu.
    Montag, Susan (1981). *Diccionario Cashinahua.* Yarinacocha, Pucallpa, Perú: Instituto Lingüístico de Verano.

37. *Cavineña*
    Pano-Takanan; Beni, Bolivia; $t = 38$, $l = $ S:24, $n = 15$, $\% = 63$, $ci = +0.24$.

    Camp, Elizabeth L., and Liccardi, Millicent R. (1989). *Diccionario Cavineña - Castellano, Castellano-Cavineña.* Dallas: Summer Institute of Linguistics.
    Key, Mary Ritchie de (1963). *Cavineña y Castellano.* Cochabamba, Bolivia: Instituto Lingüístico de Verano.

38. *Cayápa*
    Barbacoan; Esmeraldas, Ecuador; $t = 41$, $l = $ S:29, $n = 15$, $\% = 71$, $ci = +0.34$.

Lindskoog, John N., and Lindskoog, Carrie A. (1964). *Vocabulario Cayapa.* Quito: Instituto Lingüístico de Verano.

Seler, Eduard (1960). *Gesammelte Abhandlungen zur Amerikanischen Sprach- und Altertumskunde.* Graz: Adademische Druck-U. Verlagsanstalt.

39. *Cayuvava*
Isolate; Beni, Bolivia; $t = 31$, $l = $ S:16, $n = 16$, % $= 52$, $ci = 0.00$.

Key, Harold H. (1975). *Lexicon-dictionary Cayuvava-English.* Huntington Beach, Cal.: Summer Institute of Linguistics.

40. *Central American Carib*
Maipuran; Honduras; $t = 58$, $l = 45$ (F:23, S:16, E:7), $n = 14$, % $= 78$, $ci = +0.54$.

Stochl, John J. (1975). *A dictionary of Central American Carib.* Belize Institute of Social Research and Action.

Taylor, Douglas (1948). Loanwords in Central American Carib. *Word* 4:187–195.

41. *Central Koyukon*
Athapascan-Eyak; Alaska; $t = 31$, $l = $ R:16, $n =17$, % $= 52$, $ci = -0.03$.

Henry, David C., Hunter, Marie D., Jones, Eliza, and others (1973). *Dinaak'a: Our language.* Fairbanks, Alas.: Summer Institute of Linguistics.

42. *Central Yupik Eskimo*
Eskimo-Aleut; Alaska; $t = 53$, $l = 29$ (R:29, E:3), $n = 42$, % $= 55$, $ci = -0.25$.

Jacobson, Steven A. (1984). *Yup'ik Eskimo dictionary.* Fairbanks: Alaska Native Language Center, University of Alaska.

43. *Cháma*
Pano-Takanan; Loreto, Peru; $t = 33$, $l = $ S:5, $n = 30$, % $= 15$, ci $= -0.76$.

Alemeny, Agustín (1906). *Castellano-Shipibo.* Lima: Tip. del Colegio Apostolico de P. F. del Perú.

Armentia, Nicolás (1898). Idioma Schipibo. *Boletín de la Sociedad Geográfica de la Paz* 1:43–91.

Steinen, Karl von den (1904). *Diccionario Sipibo.* Berlin: Dietrich Reimer.

Tessmann, Günter (1929). Die Tschama-Sprache. *Anthropos* 24:241–271.

44. *Chaque*
Carib; Zulia, Venezuela; $t = 40$, $l = $ S:19, $n = 33$, % $= 48$, ci $= -0.35$.

Vegamian, Felix Mª de (1978). *Diccionario ilustrado Yupa Español, Español Yupa.* Caracas: Formateca C.A.

45. *Chatino (Tataltepec)*
Otomanguean; Oaxaca, Mexico; $t = 34$, $l = $ S:12, $n = 22$, % $= 35$, $ci = -0.29$.

Pride, Leslie, and Pride, Kitty (1970). *Vocabulario Chatino de Tataltepec.* México, D.F.: Instituto Lingüístico de Verano.

46. *Chayahuita*
Cahuapanan; Loreto, Peru; $t = 59$, $l = $ S:40, $n = 27$, % $= 68$, ci $= +0.22$.

Anonymous (1979). *Palabras y frases utiles en algunos idiomas de la Selva Peruana.* Yarinacocha, Pucallpa, Perú: Instituto Lingüístico de Verano.

Hart, Helen (1988). *Diccionario Chayahuita-Castellano.* Yarinacocha, Pucallpa, Perú: Instituto Lingüístico de Verano.

Soto Valdivia, Gloria N. (1983). *Léxico del grupo etnolingüístico Chayahuita.* Lima, Perú: Centro Amazónico de Antropología y Aplicación Práctica.

47. *Cherokee*
Iroquoian; North Carolina; $t = 72$, $l = 5$ (E:4, S:1), $n = 69$, $\% = 7$, $ci = -0.89$.

Alexander, J. T. (1971). *A dictionary of the Cherokee Indian language.* (Copy borrowed from the North Carolina State Library, Raleigh.)
Feeling, Durbin (1975). *Cherokee-English dictionary.* Tahlequah: Cherokee Nation of Oklahoma.
Holmes, Ruth Bradley, and Smith, Betty Sharp (1977). *Beginning Cherokee.* Norman: University of Oklahoma Press.

48. *Cheyenne (1862)*
Algonquian; Montana, Oklahoma, and Wyoming; $t = 32$, $l = 0$, $n = 32$, $\% = 0$, $ci = -1.00$.

Hayden, Ferdinand Vandeveer (1862). *Contributions to the ethnography and philology of the Indian tribes of the Missouri Valley.* Philadelphia: C. Sherman.

49. *Cheyenne (1915)*
Algonquian; Montana, Oklahoma, and Wyoming; $t = 71$, $l = 0$, $n = 71$, $\% = 0$, $ci = -1.00$.

Petter, Rodolphe (1915). *English-Cheyenne dictionary.* Kettle Falls, Wash.: Mennonite Mission.

50. *Cheyenne (1976–1984)*
Algonquian; Montana, Oklahoma, and Wyoming; $t = 69$, $l = $ E:1, n $= 69$, $\% = 2$, $ci = -0.99$.

Glenmore, Josephine Stands in Timber, and Leman, Wayne (1984). *Cheyenne topical dictionary.* Busby, Mont.: Cheyenne Translation Project.
The Language Research Department of the Northern Cheyenne (1976). *English-Cheyenne student dictionary.* Lame Deer, Mont.: Title VII ESEA Bilingual Education Program.

51. *Chickasaw*
Muskogean; Mississippi; $t = 70$, $l = 8$ (E:5, S:3), $n = 62$, $\% = 11$, $ci = -0.77$.

Humes, Jesse, and Humes, Vinnie May (James) (1973). *A Chickasaw dictionary.* Ada, Ok.: Chickasaw Nation.

Note: Since 1993, another Chickasaw dictionary has become available (Munro and Willmond 1994).

52. *Chinantec (Ojitlán)*
Otomanguean; Oaxaca, Mexico; $t = 38$, $l = $ S:2, $n = 36$, $\% = 5$, ci $= -0.89$.

Smith, Pablo, and Smith, Dorotea (1955). *Vocabulario Chinanteco (Dialecto de Ojitlán, Oaxaca).* México, D.F.: Instituto Lingüístico de Verano.

53. *Chipewyan*
Athapascan-Eyak; Manitoba, Saskatchewan; $t = 61$, $l = 8$ (F:6, E:2), $n = 55$, $\% = 13$, $ci = -0.77$.

Elford, Leon W., and Elford, Marjorie (1981). *English-Chipewyan dictionary.* Prince Albert, Saskatchewan: Northern Canada Evangelical Mission.

54. *Chippewa (Red Lake and Pillager Bands)*
Algonquian; Minnesota; $t = 41$, $l = $ F:1, $n = 40$, $\% = 2$, $ci = -0.95$.

Schuster, Ronald J. (1970). *Chippewa language dictionary: Red Lake and Pillager Bands dialect.* (No other bibliographic information supplied.)

55. *Chiriguano*
Tupí-Guaraní; Santa Cruz, Bolivia; $t = 46$, $l = $ S:13, $n = 36$, $\% = 28$, $ci = -0.50$.

Romano, Santiago, and Cattunar, Hermán (1916). *Diccionario Chiriguano-Español y Español-Chiriguano compilado teniendo à la vista diversos manuscritos de Antiguos Misioneros del*

Apostòlico Colegio Santa María de los Angeles de Tarija y articularmente el diccionario Chiriguano etimològico del R. P. Doroteo Giannecchini. Tarija, Bolivia.

Schmidt, Max (1938). Los Chiriguanos e Izozós. *Revista de la Sociedad Científica del Paraguay* 4:1–115.

56. *Choctaw*
Muskogean; Mississippi; $t = 71$, $l = 12$ (E:10, S:3), $n = 66$, % = 17, $ci = -0.76$.

Byington, Cyrus (1915). *A dictionary of the Choctaw language.* Washington, D.C.: U.S. Government Printing Office.

Watkins, Ben (1892). *Complete Choctaw definer, English with Choctaw definition.* Van Buren, Ark.: J. W. Baldwin.

Wright, Allen (1880). *Chahta leksikon: A Choctaw in English definition.* St. Louis: Presbyterian Publishing Company.

57. *Chol (Tila)*
Mayan; Chiapas, Mexico; $t = 60$, $l = $ S:34, $n = 35$, % = 57, $ci = -0.02$.

Aulie, H. Wilbur, and Aulie, Evelyn W. de (1978). *Diccionario Ch'ol-Español Español-Ch'ol.* México, D.F.: Instituto Lingüístico de Verano.

Josserand, J. Kathryn, and Hopkins, Nicholas A. (1988). *Chol (Mayan) dictionary database.* Final performance report, National Endowment for the Humanities grant RT-20643–86.

Schumann G., Otto (1973). *La lengua Chol, de Tila (Chiapas).* México, D.F.: Centro de Estudios Mayas.

58. *Choróti*
Matacoan; Boqueron, Paraguay and Paraguayan Chaco; $t = 39$, $l = $ S:3, $n = 36$, % = 8, $ci = -0.85$.

Hunt, Richard J. (1915). *El Choratio Yófuaha.* Liverpool: Henry Young.

59. *Cocopa*
Yuman; Baja California and Arizona; $t = 71$, $l = 40$ (S:35, E:4), $n = 42$, % = 56, $ci = -0.03$.

Crawford, James M. (1979). Spanish loan words in Cocopa. *Journal of California and Great Basin Anthropology Papers in Linguistics* 1:117–132.

Crawford, James M. (1989). *Cocopa dictionary.* Berkeley: University of California Press.

60. *Cofan*
Isolate; Putumayo, Colombia; $t = 36$, $l = $ S:22, $n = 14$, % = 61, $ci = +0.22$.

Borman, M. B. (1976). *Vocabulario Cofan.* Quito: Instituto Lingüístico de Verano.

61. *Colorado*
Barbacoan; Pinchincha, Ecuador; $t = 31$, $l = $ S:13, $n = 19$, % = 42, $ci = -0.19$.

Moore, Bruce R. (1966). *Diccionario Castellano-Colorado, Colorado-Castellano.* Quito: Instituto Lingüístico de Verano.

Seler, Eduard (1960). *Gesammelte Abhandlungen zur Amerikanischen Sprach- und Altertumskunde.* Graz: Adademische Druck-U. Verlagsanstalt.

62. *Comanche*
Uto-Aztecan; Oklahoma and Texas; $t = 69$, $l = 12$ (E:8, S:5), n = 65, % = 17, $ci = -0.77$.

Casagrande, Joseph B. (1954–1955). Comanche linguistic acculturation I, II, III. *International Journal of American Linguistics* 20:140–151, 217–237; 21:8–25.

Robinson, Lila Wistrand, and Armagost, James (1990). *Comanche dictionary and grammar.* Dallas: Summer Institute of Linguistics.

63. *Comecrudo (1886)*
Isolate; Tamaulipas, Mexico; $t = 36$, $l = $ S:5, $n = 31$, % = 14, $ci = -0.72$.

Swanton, John R. (1940). *Linguistic materials from the tribes of southern Texas and northeastern Mexico*. Washington, D.C.: U.S. Government Printing Office.

64. *Cora*
Uto-Aztecan; Nayarit, Mexico; $t = 46$, $l = $ S:37, $n = 11$, % = 80, $ci = +0.57$.

Casad, Eugene H. (1988). Post-conquest influence on Cora (Uto-Aztecan). In William Shipley (ed.), *In honor of Mary Haas: From the Haas Festival Conference on Native American Linguistics*, pp. 77–136. Berlin: Mouton de Gruyter.
McMahon, Ambrosio, and McMahon, María Aiton (1959). *Cora y Español*. México, D.F.: Instituto Lingüístico de Verano.

65. *Cree*
Algonquian; Canada; $t = 72$, $l = 10$ (E:8, F:3), $n = 69$; % = 14, $ci = -0.82$.

Lacombe, Albert (1874). *Dictionnaire de la langue des Cris*. Montréal: C. O. Beauchemin and Volois.
Watkins, Edward A. (1938). *A dictionary of the Cree language*. Toronto: General Synod of the Church of England in Canada.

66. *Creek (Muskokee)*
Muskogean; Georgia; $t = 76$, $l = 12$ (S:8, E:5), $n = 65$, % = 16, $ci = -0.70$.

Loughridge, Robert M., and Hodge, David M. (1890). *English and Muskokee dictionary*. St. Louis: Printing House of J. T. Smith.

67. *Crow*
Siouan; Montana; $t = 42$, $l = $ E:1, $n = 42$, % = 2, $ci = -0.98$.

Lowie, Robert H. (1960). *Crow word lists*. Berkeley: University of California Press.

68. *Cuicatec*
Otomanguean; Oaxaca, Mexico; $t = 74$, $l = $ S:46, $n = 30$, % = 62, $ci = +0.22$.

Anderson, E. Richard, and Roque, Hilario Concepción (1983). *Diccionario Cuicateco*. México, D.F.: Instituto Lingüístico de Verano.

69. *Cuna (1890–1913)*
Chibchan; Panama; $t = 38$, $l = 15$ (S:14, E:1), $n = 26$, % = 40, $ci = -0.29$.

Pinart, Alphonse Louis (1890). *Vocabulario Castellano-Cuna*. Paris: Ernest Leroux.
Prince, J. Dyneley (1913). Grammar and glossary of the Tule language of Panama. *American Anthropologist* 13:480–528.

70. *Cuna (1944–1985)*
Chibchan; Panama; $t = 69$; $l = 27$ (S:24, E:6), $n = 50$, % = 39, $ci = -0.33$.

Duke, James A. (1960). *Darien dictionary*. Balboa, Canal Zone, Panama.
Erice, Jesús (1985). *Diccionario de la lengua Kuna*. Panama: Impresora de la Nación.
Holmer, Nils M. (1952). *Ethno-linguistic Cuna dictionary*. Göteborg, Sweden: Elanders Boktryckeri Aktiebolag.
Puig, Manuel María (1944). *Diccionario de la lengua Caribe Cuna*. La Estrella de Panama.

71. *Cupeño*
Uto-Aztecan; California; $t = 62$, $l = $ S:60, $n = 8$, % = 97, $ci = +0.84$.

Hill, Jane H., and Nolasques, Rosinda (1973). *Mulu'wetam: The first people: Cupeño oral history and language*. Banning, Cal.: Malki Museum Press.

72. *Dakota (Santee dialect)*
Siouan; North and South Dakota; $t = 75$, $l = 3$ (F:2, E:1), $n = 74$, % = 4, $ci = -0.95$.

Working Indians Civil Association (1969). *An English-Dakota dictionary.* Ft. Pierre, S.D.: Working Indians Civil Association.

73. *Dakota (Teton dialect, 1866)*
    Siouan; North and South Dakota; $t = 49$, $l = $ F:2, $n = 47$, $\% = 4$, $ci = -0.92$.

    Hyer, Joseph, and Starring, William (1968). *Dictionary of the Sioux language.* New Haven, Conn.: Yale University Press.

74. *Dakota (Teton dialect, 1970–1974)*
    Siouan; North and South Dakota; $t = 68$, $l = 0$, $n = 68$, $\% = 0$, $ci = -1.00$.

    Buechel, Eugene (1970). *A dictionary of the Teton Dakota Sioux language, Lakota-English: English-Lakota.* Pine Ridge, S.D.: Red Cloud Indian School.
    Karol, Joseph S., and Rozman, Stephen L. (1974). *Everyday Lakota: An English-Sioux dictionary for beginners.* St. Francis, S.D.: Rosebud Educational Society.

75. *Delaware (eighteenth century)*
    Algonquian; New Jersey; $t = 52$, $l = 15$ (E:11, Du:3, G:1), $n = 38$, $\% = 29$, $ci = -0.44$.

    Zeisberger, David (1887). *Zeisberger's Indian dictionary, English, German, Iroquois—the Onondaga and Algonquin—the Delaware.* Cambridge: John Wilson.

76. *Delaware (1839)*
    Algonquian; New Jersey; $t = 32$, $l = 4$ (Du:3, E:1), $n = 29$, $\% = 13$, $ci = -0.78$.

    Brinton, Daniel G., and Anthony, Albert Seqaqkind (1888). *A Lenâpé-English dictionary.* The Pennsylvania Students' Series, Vol. 1. Philadelphia: Historical Society of Pennsylvania.

    Note: Since 1993, another Delaware dictionary has become available (O'Meara 1996).

77. *Diegueño*
    Yuman; California; $t = 39$, $l = $ S:31, $n = 18$, $\% = 80$, $ci = +0.33$.

    Couro, Ted, and Hutcheson, Christina (1973). *Dictionary of Mesa Grande Diegueño.* Banning, Cal.: Malki Museum Press.

78. *Eastern Ojibwa*
    Algonquian; Ontario; $t = 63$, $l = 6$ (E:3, F:3), $n = 59$, $\% = 10$, $ci = -0.84$.

    Bloomfield, Leonard (1957). *Eastern Ojibwa.* Ann Arbor: University of Michigan Press.
    Rhodes, Richard A. (1985). *Eastern Ojibwa-Chippewa-Ottawa dictionary.* Berlin: Mouton.

79. *East Greenlandic Eskimo*
    Eskimo-Aleut; Greenland; $t = 44$, $l = 6$ (Da:4, N:2), $n = 38$, $\% = 14$, $ci = -0.73$.

    Gessain, Robert, Dorais, Louis-Jacques, and Enel, Catherine (1982). *Vocabulaire du Groenlandais de l'Est.* Documents du Centre de Recherches Anthropologiques du Musée de l'Homme.
    Robbe, Pierre, and Dorais, Louis-Jacques (1986). *Tunumiit Oraasiat: The East Greenlandic Inuit language.* Québec: Centre d'Etudes Nordiques de l'Université Laval.

80. *Ecuadorean Quechua (1892–1924)*
    Quechumaran; Ecuador; $t = 36$, $l = $ S:8, $n = 30$, $\% = 22$, $ci = -0.61$.

    Grimm, Juan M. (1896). *La lengua Quichua (Dialecto de la República del Ecuador).* Friburgo de Brisgovia.
    Paris, Julio (1892). *Ensayo de gramática de la lengua Quichua tal como se habla actualmente entre los Indios de la República del Ecuador.* Quito: Imprenta del Clero.
    Paris, Julio (1924). *Gramática de la lengua Quichua actualmente en uso entre los Indígenas del Ecuador.* Cuenca, Ecuador: Padres de la Congregación del Santísimo Redentor.

81. *Ecuadorean Quechua (1942–1955)*
    Quechumaran; Ecuador; $t = 40$, $l = $ S:8, $n = 33$, $\% = 20$, $ci = -0.63$.

    Cordero, Luis (1955). *Diccionario Quichua-Español-Quichua.* Quito: Casa de la Cultura Ecuatoriana.
    Murgueytio, Reinaldo (1945). *Yachay-Huasi: Libro de lectura para escuelas campesinas y normales rurales del Ecuador.* Quito: Editorial Gráfica de la Escuela Central Técnica.
    Sheppard, J. J. (1942). *The Quichua language.* Quito: Pan American Society of Tropical Research.

82. *Eskimo (Kangiryuarmiut)*
    Eskimo-Aleut; Canadian Western Arctic; $t = 38$, $l = $ E:4, $n = 34$, $\% = 11$, $ci = -0.79$.

    Lowe, Robert (1983). *Kangiryuarmiut Uqauhingita Numiktittitdjutingit: Basic Kangiryuarmiut Eskimo dictionary.* Inuvik, Northwest Territories: Committee for Original Peoples Entitlement.

83. *Eskimo (Kuskoquim district)*
    Eskimo-Aleut; Alaska; $t = 33$, $l = $ R:19, $n = 15$, $\% = 58$, $ci = +0.12$.

    Schultze, Augustus (1894). *Grammar and vocabulary of the Eskimo language of North-Western Alaska, Kuskoquim District.* Bethlehem, Penn.: Moravian Publication Office.

84. *Eskimo (North Slope Iñupiaq)*
    Eskimo-Aleut; Alaska; $t = 42$, $l = 7$ (R:5, E:4), $n = 37$, $\% = 17$, $ci = -0.72$.

    MacLean, Edna Ahgeak (1980). *Abridged Iñupiaq and English dictionary.* Fairbanks, Alaska: Alaska Native Language Center.
    Webster, Donald H., and Zibell, Wilfried (1970), *Iñupiat Eskimo dictionary.* Fairbanks, Alas.: Summer Institute of Linguistics.

85. *Eskimo (Siglit)*
    Eskimo-Aleut; Canadian Western Arctic; $t = 38$, $l = $ E:5, $n = 33$, $\% = 13$, $ci = -0.74$.

    Lowe, Robert (1984). *Siglit Inuvialuit Uquasiita Kipuktirutait: Basic Siglit Inuvialuit Eskimo dictionary.* Inuvik, Northwest Territories: Committee for Original Peoples Entitlement.

86. *Eskimo (Uummarmiut)*
    Eskimo-Aleut; Canadian Western Arctic; $t = 32$, $l = $ E:4, $n = 28$, $\% = 13$, $ci = -0.75$.

    Lowe, Robert (1984). *Uummarmiut Uqalungiha Mumikhitchirutingit: Basic Uummarmiut Eskimo dictionary.* Inuvik, Northwest Territories: Committee for Original Peoples Entitlement.

87. *Eyak*
    Athapascan-Eyak; Alaska; $t = 52$, $l = 13$ (R:11, E:2), $n = 43$, $\% = 25$, $ci = -0.58$.

    Krauss, Michael E. (1970). *Eyak dictionary.* University of Alaska and Massachusetts Institute of Technology (1963–1970).

88. *Gitksan*
    Tsimshianic; British Columbia; $t = 31$, $l = $ E:4, $n = 27$, $\% = 13$, ci $= -0.74$.

    Hindle, Lonnie, and Rigsby, Bruce (1973). *A short practical dictionary of the Gitksan language.* Northwest Anthropological Research Notes, Vol. 7, No. 1.

89. *Guahibo*
    Guahiban; Apure, Venezuela; $t = 38$, $l = $ S:25, $n = 13$, $\% = 66$, $ci = +.032$.

    Krisologo B., Pedro Juan (1965). *Diccionario Español – Wa-Jibi (Guahibo).* Caracas: Instituto Caribe de Antropología y Sociología.
    Pérez, Manuel Cipriano (1935). Vocabulario del dialecto Guahibo del Vichada. *Anales de la Universidad Central de Venezuela* 23:209–237.

Pérez, Manuel Cipriano (1936). Vocabulario del dialecto Guahibo del Vichada. *Boletín de la Academia de Ciencias Físicas, Matemáticas y Naturales* 3:467–500.

90. *Guajajara*
    Tupí-Guaraní; Maranhão, Brazil; t = 39, l = 8 (P:8, S:1), n = 33, % = 21, ci = -0.64.

Abreu, Fróes (1931). *Na terra das palmeiros*. Rio de Janeiro: Officina Industrial Graphica.
Cruz, Olímpio (1972). *Vocabulário de quatro dialetos dos Indios do Maranhão: Guajajara, Canela, Urubu e Guajá*. Departamento de Cultura do Maranhão.
Roberts, F. J., and Symes, S. P. (1936). Vocabulary of the Guajajara dialect. *Journal de la Société des Américanistes de Paris* 28:209–248.
Snethlage, E. Heinrich (1931). Unter nordostbrasilianischen Indianern. *Zeitschrift für Ethnologie* 62:111–205.

91. *Guajira (1878–1913)*
    Maipuran; La Guajira, Colombia; t = 45, l = S:27, n = 25, % = 60, ci = +0.04.

Celedon, Rafael (1878). *Gramática, catecismo, i vocabulario de la lengua Goajira*. Paris: Maisonneuve I.
Oramas, Luis R. (1913). *Contribución al estudio de la lengua Guajira*. Caracas: Lit. y Tip. del Comercio.
Uterga, Esteban de (1895). *Idioma Goagiro*. Roma: Tipografia de la Sac. Congr.

92. *Guajira (1963–1977)*
    Maipuran; La Guajira, Colombia; t = 57, l = S:37, n = 25, % = 65, ci = +0.21.

Hildebrant, Martha (1963). *Diccionario Guajiro-Español*. Caracas: Comisión Indigenista.
Jusayú, Miguel Angel (1977). *Diccionario de la lengua Guajira*. 2 vols. Caracas: Centro de Lenguas Indígenas.

93. *Guaraní (c. 1639)*
    Tupí-Guaraní; Paraguay; t = 42, l = S:9, n = 36, % = 21, ci = -0.64.

Montoya, Antonio Ruíz (1876). *Gramática y diccionarios de la lengua Tupi ó Guarani*. Vienna: Faesy y Frick.

94. *Guaraní (1903–1928)*
    Tupí-Guaraní; Paraguay; t = 41, l = S:20, n = 25, % = 49, ci = -0.12.

Bottignoli, Justo (1926). *Diccionario Guarani-Castellano y Castellano-Guarani*. Asunción, Paraguay: Turín.
Obelar, Raimundo D. (1914). *Vocabulario Guaraní*. Asunción, Paraguay: Talleres de "Ariel."
Solari, Benjamin T. (1928). *Ensayo de filología: Breve vocabulario Español-Guaraní*. Buenos Aires: Imprenta y Casa Editora "Coni."
Vera, Florencio (1903). *Diccionario gramatical Guaraní-Español*. Asunción, Paraguay: Talleres Mons. Lasagra.

95. *Guaraní (1947–1987)*
    Tupí-Guaraní; Paraguay; t = 70, l = 27 (S:26, P:1), n = 65, % = 39, ci = -0.54.

Dacunda Diaz, M. Ricardo (1987). *Gran diccionario de lengua Guaraní*. Buenos Aires: Ediciones Guairacä.
Guasch, Antonio (1961). *Diccionario Castellano-Guaraní y Guaraní-Castellano*. Sevilla: Gráficas La Gavidia.
Jover Peralta, Anselmo, and Osuna, Tomás (1950). *Diccionario Guaraní-Español, Español-Guaraní*. Buenos Aires: Editorial Tupã.
Mayans, Antonio Ortiz (1949). *Diccionario Guaraní-Castellano, Castellano-Guaraní*. Buenos Aires: Talleres Gráficos "Victoria."
Muniagurria, Saturnino (1947). *El Guaraní*. Buenos Aires: Imprenta y Casa Editora "Coni."

96. *Guaraní (Mbüa dialect)*
Tupí-Guaraní; Paraná, Brazil; $t = 41$, $l = 15$ (P:14, S:1), $n = 28$, % = 37, $ci = -0.32$.

Dooley, Robert A. (1982). *Vocabulário do Guarani*. Brasília, D.F.: Summer Institute of Linguistics.

97. *Guarayo*
Tupí-Guaraní; Santa Cruz, Bolivia and Bolivian Chaco; $t = 33$, $l = $ S:17, $n = 18$, % = 52, $ci = -0.03$.

Hoeller, Alfredo (1932). *Guarayo-Deutsches Wörterbuch*. Guarayos, Bolivia: Verlag der Mission sprokura der P. P. Franziskaner, Hall in Tirol.
Schmidt, Max (1936). Los Guarayú. *Revista de la Sociedad Científica del Paraguay* 3:158–190.

98. *Guaymi*
Chibchan; Panama; $t = 33$, $l = 20$ (S:14, E:8), $n = 15$, % = 61, $ci = +0.15$.

Alphonse, Ephraim S. (1956). *Guaymí grammar and dictionary with some ethnological notes*. Washington, D.C.: U.S. Government Printing Office.

99. *Gwichin (1876)*
Athapascan-Eyak; Yukon, Canada; $t = 56$, $l = $ E:1, $n = 55$, % = 2, $ci = -0.96$.

Petitot, Émile (1876). *Dictionnaire de la langue Dènè-Dindjié, dialects: Montagnais ou Chippewayan, Peaux de Lièvre et Loucheux*. Paris: Ernest Leroux.

100. *Gwichin (1976)*
Athapascan-Eyak; Yukon, Canada; $t = 36$, $l = 6$ (F:5, E:1), $n = 31$, % = 17, $ci = -0.69$.

Ritter, John (1976). *Gwichin (Loucheux) Athapaskan noun dictionary*. Whitehorse, Yukon Territory: Queen's Printer for the Yukon.

101. *Haida (Kaigani dialect)*
Isolate; Alaska; $t = 36$, $l = $ F:3, $n = 33$, % = 8, $ci = -0.83$.

Lawrence, Erma (1977). *Haida dictionary*. Fairbanks: Alaska Native Language Center.

102. *Haisla*
Wakashan; British Columbia; $t = 33$, $l = 3$ (E:2, F:1), $n = 31$, % = 9, $ci = -0.85$.

Lincoln, Neville J., and Rath, John C. (1986). *Phonology, dictionary and listing of roots and lexical derivates of the Haisla language of Kitlope and Kitimaat, B.C.* Ottawa: National Museums of Canada.

103. *Heiltsuk (dialect of Kwakiutl)*
Wakashan; British Columbia; $t = 33$, $l = $ E:9, $n = 27$, % = 27, ci = -0.55.

Rath, John C. (1981). *A practical Heiltsuk-English dictionary with a grammatical introduction*. Ottawa: National Museums of Canada.

104. *Hidatsa*
Siouan; North Dakota; $t = 43$, $l = $ E:1, $n = 42$, % = 2, $ci = -0.95$.

Mathews, Washington (1873). *Grammar and dictionary of the language of the Hidatsa (Minnetarees, Grosventres of the Missouri)*. New York: Cramoisy Press.
Mathews, Washington (1874). *Hidatsa (Minnetaree) English dictionary*. New York: Cramoisy Press.
Mathews, Washington (1877). *Ethnography and philology of the Hidatsa Indians*. Washington, D.C.: U.S. Government Printing Office.

105. *Hopi*
Uto-Aztecan; Arizona; $t = 68$, $l = 19$ (S:17, E:2), $n = 50$, % = 28, $ci = -0.46$.

Albert, Roy, and Shaul, David Leedom (1985). *A concise Hopi and English lexicon*. John Benjamins Publishing Company.
Parsons, Elsie Clews (1936). *Hopi journal of Alexander M. Stephen*. New York: Columbia University Press.
Seaman, P. David (1985). *Hopi dictionary*. Flagstaff: Arizona Board of Regents.

106. *Huambisa*
Jivaroan; Loreto, Peru; $t = 38$, $l = $ S:25, $n = 15$, % = 66, $ci = +0.26$.

Anonymous (1979). *Palabras y frases utiles en algunos idiomas de la Selva Peruana*. Perú: Instituto Lingüístico de Verano.
Jakway, Martha (1987). *Vocabulario Huambisa*. Yarinacocha, Pucallpa, Perú: Instituto Lingüístico de Verano.
Larson, Mildred (1957). *Comparación de los vocabularios Aguaruna y Huambisa*. Cuzco, Perú: Revista Peruana de Cultura.

107. *Huastec*
Mayan; San Luis Potosí, Mexico; $t = 32$, $l = $ S:12, $n = 20$, % = 38, $ci = -0.25$.

Larsen, Ramón (1955). *Vocabulario Huasteco del Estado de San Luis Potosí*. México, D.F.: Instituto Lingüístico de Verano.
McQuown, Norman A. (1984). A sketch of San Luis Potosí Huastec. In Victoria Reifler Bricker (ed.), *Supplement to the Handbook of Middle American Indians*, Vol. 2, pp. 83–142. Austin: University of Texas Press.

108. *Huave (San Mateo)*
Isolate; Oaxaca, Mexico; $t = 47$, $l = $ S:33, $n = 18$, % = 70, ci = +0.32.

Stairs Kreger, Glenn Albert, and Stairs, Emily Florence Scharfe de (1981). *Diccionario Huave de San Mateo del Mar*. México, D.F.: Instituto Lingüístico de Verano.
Warkentin, Milton, and Warkentin, Clara (1952). *Vocabulario Huave*. México, D.F.: Instituto Lingüístico de Verano.

109. *Huichol*
Uto-Aztecan; Nayarit and Jalisco, Mexico; $t = 33$, $l = $ S:17, n = 17, % = 52, $ci = 0.00$.

McIntosh, John B. (1949). *Huichol texts and dictionary*. Collection of Manuscripts on Middle American Cultural Anthropology, no. 27. University of Chicago Library, Chicago.
McIntosh, Juan B., and Grimes, José (1954). *Vocabulario Huichol-Castellano, Castellano-Huichol*. México, D.F.: Instituto Lingüístico de Verano.

110. *Huitoto*
Huitotoan; Amazonas, Colombia; $t = 39$, $l = $ S:7, $n = 36$, % = 18, $ci = -0.74$.

Anonymous (1979). *Palabras y frases utiles en algunos idiomas de la Selva Peruana*. Perú: Instituto Lingüístico de Verano.
Burtch, Shirley (1983). *Diccionario Huitoto Murui*. Yarinacocha, Pucallpa, Perú: Instituto Lingüístico de Verano.
Kinder, Leopoldo Von (1936). *Gramática y vocabulario de la lengua Huitota*. Boletín de Estudios Histórico, Suplemento No. 4. República de Colombia: Departamento de Nariño.
Minor, Eugene E., and Minor, Dorothy Hendrich de (1971). *Vocabulario Huitoto Muinane*. Yarinacocha, Perú: Instituto Lingüístico de Verano.
Minor, Eugene E., and Minor, Dorothy A. (1987). *Vocabulario bilingüe: Huitoto-Español, Español-Huitoto (Dialecto Minica)*. Bogotá: Editorial Townsend.

111. *Illinois (c. 1700)*
Algonquian; Illinois; $t = 48$, $l = 0$, $n = 48$, % = 0, $ci = -1.00$.

Gravier, James (c. 1690). Dictionary of the Illinois language. Manuscript.
Le Boulanger, Joseph Ignatius (1865). *French-Illinois dictionary.* New York: Cramoisy Press.

112. *Ingalik*
Athapascan-Eyak; Alaska; $t = 38$, $l = 18$ (R:17, E:1), $n = 29$, $\% = 47$, $ci = -0.29$.

Kari, James (1978). *Deg Xinag: Ingalik noun dictionary.* Fairbanks: Alaska Native Language Center.

113. *Insular Carib (1665–1666)*
Maipuran; Caribbean islands; $t = 35$, $l = 11$ (S:7, F:4), $n = 26$, $\% = 31$, $ci = -0.43$.

Breton, Raymond (1665). *Dictionnaire Caraibe-François, meslé de quantité de remarques historiques pour l'esclaircissement de la langue.* Auxerre, France: Gilles Bouquet.
Breton, Raymond (1666). *Dictionnaire François-Caraibe.* Auxerre, France: Gilles Bouquet.

114. *Inuit Eskimo*
Eskimo-Aleut; Quebec and Labrador; $t = 64$, $l = 19$ (E:14, G:3, F:1, N:1), $n = 58$, $\% = 30$, $ci = -0.61$.

Dorais, Louis-Jacques (1978). *Lexique analytique du vocabulaire Inuit moderne au Québec-Labrador.* Québec: Les Presses de l'Université Laval.
Schneider, Lucien (1985). *Ulirnaisigutiit: An Inuktitut-English dictionary of northern Quebec.* Québec: Les Presses de l'Université Laval.

115. *Iroquois*
Iroquoian; New York and Quebec; $t = 40$, $l = 5$ (F:2, Du:2, E:1), $n = 35$, $\% = 13$, $ci = -0.75$.

Cuoq, Jean-André (1882). *Lexique de la langue Iroquoise.* Montréal: J. Chapleau et Fils.

116. *Ixcatec*
Otomanguean; Oaxaca, Mexico; $t = 37$, $l = $ S:17, $n = 22$, $\% = 46$, $ci = -0.14$.

Fernández de Miranda, María Teresa (1953). Las formas posesivas en Ixcateco. In *Memoria del Congreso Científico Mexicano, Vol. 12, Ciencias Sociales,* pp. 159–174. México, D.F.: Universidad Autónoma Nacional de México.
Fernández de Miranda, María Teresa (1961). *Diccionario Ixcateco.* México, D.F.: Instituto Nacional de Antropología e Historia.
Gudshinsky, Sarah C. (1958). *Proto-Popotecan: A comparative study of Popolocan and Mixtecan.* Baltimore: Waverly Press.

117. *Ixil*
Mayan; Quiché, Guatemala; $t = 59$, $l = $ S:46, $n = 27$, $\% = 78$, ci = +0.32.

Kaufman, Terrence (1974). *Ixil dictionary.* Technical Report No. 1. Irvine: Laboratory of Anthropology, University of California.

118. *Jacaltec*
Mayan; Huehuetenango, Guatemala; $t = 41$, $l = $ S:29, $n = 13$, $\% = 71$, $ci = +0.39$.

Craig, Colette Grinevald (1977). *The structure of Jacaltec.* Austin: University of Texas Press.
Day, Christopher (1973). *The Jacaltec language.* The Hague: Mouton.
Day, Christopher (1977). Diccionario Jacaltec-Español: The vocabulary of a Mayan language of Guatemala. Manuscript, in the files of the author.

119. *Jíbaro*
Jivaroan; Oriente, Ecuador; $t = 36$, $l = $ S:18, $n = 23$, $\% = 50$, $ci = -0.15$.

Caillet, Luis María (1930–1933). Vocabulario Castellano-Jívaro, según el dialecto que hablan en la actualidad los Indios de Arapicos. *El Oriente Dominicano* 3:179–181, 217–218; 4:29–31, 70, 103–105, 152–153, 186–187; 5:2, 51, 104, 132, 165; 6:15.

Duroni, Salvador (1928). *Diccionario de bolsillo del idioma Jíbaro.* Cuenca, Ecuador: J. M. Astudillo Regalado.

Farabee, William Curtis (1922). *Indian tribes of Eastern Peru.* Cambridge, Mass.: Peabody Museum.

Ghinassi, P. Juan (1938). *Gramática teórico-práctica y vocabulario de la lengua Jíbara.* Quito: Talleres Gráficos de Educación.

Karsten, Rafael (1921). *La lengua de los Indios Jíbaros (Shuara) del Oriente del Ecuador.* Översikt av Finska Vetenskaps-Societetens Förhandlingar Bd. LXIV. 1921–1922. Helsinki: Avd. B. No. 2.

Salesianos, Los Misioneros (1924). Diccionario Jibaro-Castellano y Castellano-Jibaro. *Boletín de la Academia Nacional de Historia* 9:1–67.

120. *Jicarilla Apache*
Athapascan-Eyak; Arizona and New Mexico; $t = 57$, $l = 23$ (S:20, E:5), $n = 45$, % = 40, $ci = -0.39$.

Mersol, Stanley Alfonse (1976). A sociolinguistic-conceptual-cultural-ethnographic Jicarilla Apache-English dictionary: The Dulce Springs dialect. Ph.D.thesis, University of California, Irvine.

121. *Kaapor*
Tupí-Guaraní; Maranhão, Brazil; $t = 39$, $l = $ P:9, $n = 34$, % = 23, $ci = -0.64$.

Cruz, Olímpio 1972. *Vocabulário de quatro dialetos dos Indios do Maranhão: Guajajara, Canela, Urubu e Guajá.* Maranhão, Brazil: Departmento de Cultura do Maranhão.

Kakumasu, James Y., and Kakumasu, Kiyoko (1988). *Dicionário por tópicos Urubu-Kaapor-Português.* Brasília: Summer Institute of Linguistics.

122. *Kaingang (1888–1920)*
Ge; Paraná, Brazil; $t = 36$, $l = $ P:8, $n = 32$, % = 22, $ci = -0.67$.

Ambrosetti, Juan B. (1983). *Los Indios Kaingánques de San Pedro, Misiones República Argentina.* Argentina: Libreros y Editores del Poligono SRL.

Barcatta de Val Floriana, Mansueto (1918). Una critica ao "Vocabulario da Lingua dos Kainjgang" do Visconde de Taunay. *Revista de Museu Paulista* 10:565–628.

Barcatta de Val Floriana, Mansueto (1920). Diccionarios Kainjgang-Portuguez e Portuguez-Kainjgang. *Revista do Museu Paulista* 12:1–392.

Taunay, Alfredo d'Escragnolle, Vizconde de (1888). Vocabulario do dialecto Caingang (Corôados de Guarapuava) Provincia do Paraná. *Revista do Instituto Histórico e Geográfico Brasileiro* 51:285–310.

123. *Kaingang (1986)*
Ge: Paraná, Brazil; $t = 65$, $l = $ P:42, $n = 30$, % = 65, $ci = +0.18$.

Tempski, Edwino Donato (1986). *Caingângues—gente do mato.* Brazil: Curitiba Paraná.

124. *Kalispel*
Salishan; Montana; $t = 67$, $l = 11$ (F:8, E:4), $n = 61$, % = 16, $ci = -0.75$.

Missionaries of the Society of Jesus (1877). *A dictionary of the Kalispel or Flat-head Indian language.* Montana: St. Ignatius Print.

125. *Karok*
Isolate; California; $t = 50$, $l = $ E:12, $n = 41$, % = 24, $ci = -0.58$.

Bright, William (1952). Linguistic innovations in Karok. *International Journal of American Linguistics* 18:53–62.

Bright, William (1957). *The Karok language.* Berkeley: University of California Press.

126. *Kawaiisu*
Uto-Aztecan; California; $t = 37$, $l = 26$ (S:25, E:1), $n = 12$, % = 70, $ci = +0.38$.

Zigmond, Maurice L., Booth, Curtis G., and Munro, Pamela (1991). *Kawaiisu: A grammar and dictionary with texts.* Berkeley: University of California Press.

127. *Kekchi*
Mayan; Alta Verapaz, Guatemala; $t = 64$, $l = $ S:44, $n = 36$, $\% = 69$, $ci = +0.13$.

Anonymous (1930). *Vocabulario Quecchi-Español.* Cobán, Alta Verapaz: Rosales Ponce e Hijos.
Campbell, Lyle (1976). Kekchi linguistic acculturation: A cognitive approach. In Marlys McClaran (ed.), *Mayan Linguistics,* pp. 90–97. Los Angeles: American Indian Studies Center.
Curley Garcia, Francisco (1967). *Vocabulario del dialecto o lengua Gkec-Chí.* Guatemala, C.A.
Haeserijn V., Esteban (1979). *Diccionario K'ekchi' Español.* Guatemala: Editorial "Piedra Santa."
Rosales Ponce, Emilio (1948). *Vocabulario Quecchi-Español.* Cobán, Alta Verapaz, Guatemala: Dirección de la Imprenta "El Norte" en Cobán.
Sedat S., Guillermo (1955). *Nuevo diccionario de las lenguas K'ekchi' y Española.* Chamelco, Alta Verapaz, Guatemala: Instituto Indigenista Nacional.

128. *Keresan (Santa Ana Pueblo)*
Isolate; New Mexico; $t = 38$, $l = $ S:26, $n = 14$, $\% = 68$, $ci = +0.32$.

Davis, Irvine (1964). *The language of Santa Ana Pueblo.* Bulletin 191, Anthropological Papers No. 69. Washington, D.C.: Smithsonian Institution, Bureau of American Ethnology.

129. *Kickapoo*
Algonquian; originally Wisconsin; $t = 42$, $l = 6$ (E:4, F:1, S:1), $n = 36$, $\% = 14$, $ci = -0.64$.

Voorhis, Paul H. (1988). *Kickapoo vocabulary.* Memoir 6, Algonquian and Iroquoian Linguistics. Winnipeg, Canada: Algonquian and Iroquoian Linguistics.

130. *Kiliwa*
Yuman; Baja California; $t = 56$, $l = 0$, $n = 56$, $\% = 0$, $ci = -1.00$.

Mixco, Mauricio J. (1977). The Kiliwa response to Hispanic culture. *Proceedings of the Annual Meeting of the Berkeley Linguistics Society* 3:12–23.
Mixco, Mauricio J. (1985). *Kiliwa dictionary.* Salt Lake City: University of Utah.

131. *Kiowa*
Tanoan; Oklahoma; $t = 42$, $l = $ E:2, $n = 40$, $\% = 5$, $ci = -0.90$.

Harrington, John P. (1928). *Vocabulary of the Kiowa language.* Washington, D.C.: U.S. Government Printing Office.

132. *Klamath (1890)*
Isolate; Oregon; $t = 57$, $l = 21$ (E:19, F:2) $n = 44$, $\% = 37$, ci $= -0.40$.

Gatschet, Albert Samuel (1890). *The Klamath Indians of southwestern Oregon.* Washington, D.C.: U.S. Government Printing Office.

133. *Klamath (1963)*
Isolate; Oregon; $t = 46$, $l = 26$ (E:22, F:4), $n = 21$, $\% = 56$, ci $= +0.11$.

Barker, M. A. R. (1963). *Klamath dictionary.* Berkeley: University of California Press.

134. *Koasati*
Muskogean; Alabama; $t = 74$, $l = 9$ (S:7, F:2), $n = 66$, $\% = 12$, $ci = -0.77$.

Kimball, Geoffrey (1992). Field notes. Department of Anthropology, Tulane University, New Orleans.

Note: Kimball (1994) published a Koasati dictionary after 1993.

135. *Lake Miwok*
Miwok-Costanoan; California; $t = 65$, $l = $ S:53, $n = 17$, % $= 82$, $ci = +0.55$.

Callaghan, Catherine A. (1965). *Lake Miwok dictionary.* Berkeley: University of California Press.

136. *Lengua*
Maskoian; Paraguayan Chaco; $t = 40$, $l = $ S:3, $n = 37$, % $= 8$, ci $= -0.85$.

Coryn, Alfredo (1922). Los Indios Lenguas: Sus costumbres y su idioma. *Anales de la Sociedad Científica Argentina* 93:221–282.
Lowes, R. H. G. (1954). Alphabetical list of Lengua Indian words with English equivalents (Paraguayan Chaco). *Journal de la Société des Américanistes de Paris* 43:86–107.

137. *Mahican (c. 1755)*
Algonquian; New York and Vermont; $t = 31$, $l = 15$ (E:12, Du:3), $n = 17$, % $= 48$, $ci = -0.06$.

Day, Gordon M. (1975). *The Mots Loups of Father Mathevet.* National Museum of Man, Publications in Ethnology, No. 8. Ottawa: National Museums of Canada.

138. *Maidu*
Maiduan; California; $t = 39$, $l = 21$ (E:15, S:6), $n = 20$, % $= 54$, $ci = +0.03$.

Shipley, William F. (1963). *Maidu texts and dictionary.* Berkeley: University of California Press.

139. *Makká*
Matacoan; Paraguayan Chaco; $t = 42$, $l = $ S:3, $n = 40$, % $= 7$, ci $= -0.88$.

Belaieff, Juan (1940). El Maccá. *Revista de la Sociedad Científica del Paraguay* 4:1–110.
Hunt, Richard J. (1915). *El Choroti o Yófuaha.* Liverpool: Henry Young.
Kysela, Vladimiro (1931). Tribu indígena Maccá. *Revista de la Sociedad Científica del Paraguay* 3:43–49.
Schmidt, Max (1937). Los Tapietés. *Revista de la Sociedad Científica del Paraguay* 4:36–76.

140. *Makú*
Kalianan; Amazonas, Brazil; $t = 35$, $l = 12$ (S:10, P:2), $n = 26$, % $= 34$, $ci = -0.40$.

Giacone, Antonio (1955). *Pequena gramática e dicionário Português Ubde-Nehern ou Macú.* Amazonas, Brasil: Escola Salesiana de Artes Gráficas.
Rivet, Paul, Kok, P. P., and Tastevin, Constant (1924–1925). Nouvelle contribution a l'etude de la langue Makú. *International Journal of American Linguistics* 3:133–192.

141. *Maliseet (dialect of Passamaquoddy)*
Algonquian; Maine; $t = 33$, $l = $ E:8, $n = 25$, % $= 24$, $ci = -0.52$.

Chamberlain, Montague (1899). *Maliseet vocabulary.* Cambridge, Mass.: Harvard Cooperative Society.

142. *Mandan*
Siouan; North Dakota; $t = 44$, $l = $ E:1, $n = 44$, % $= 2$, $ci = -0.98$.

Hollow, Robert Charles, Jr. (1965). A Mandan dictionary. Ph.D. thesis, University of California, Berkeley.

143. *Mapuche (1777)*
Araucanian; Chile; $t = 38$, $l = $ S:12, $n = 27$, % $= 32$, $ci = -0.41$.

Havestadt, Bernardi (1777). *Chilidúgú, sive res Chilensis.* Monasterii Westphaliae.

144. *Mapuche (1898–1916)*
Araucanian; Bio-Bio, Chile; $t = 50$, $l = $ S:33, $n = 27$, % $= 66$, $ci = +0.12$.

Augusta, Félix José de (1916). *Diccionario Araucano-Español, Español-Araucano, tomo primero and tomo segundo.* Santiago, Chile: Imprenta Universitaria.

Grasserie, Raoul de la (1898). *Langue Auca (ou langue indigène du Chili).* Paris: J. Maisonneuve.

145. *Mapuche (1944–1990)*
Araucanian; Bio-Bio, Chile; $t = 52$, $l = $ S:32, $n = 30$, % = 62, $ci = $ +0.04.

Calendino, Francisco (1987). *Diccionario Mapuche básico.* Bahía Blanca-Buenos Aires: Centro Universitario Salesiano del Sur Argentino.

Erize, Esteban (1960). *Diccionario comentado Mapuche-Español.* Buenos Aires: Cuadernos del Sur, Instituto de Humanidades, Universidad Nacional del Sur.

Flury, Lazaro (1944). *Guiliches: tradiciones, leyenda, apuntes gramaticales y vocabulario de la zona Pampa-Araucana.* Argentina: La Universidad Córdoba.

Harmelink M., Bryan L.(1990). *Vocabulario y frases utiles en Mapudugun.* Temuco, Chile: Universidad de la Frontera.

Moesbach, Ernesto Wilhelm de (1978). *Diccionario Español-Mapuche.* Argentina: Siringa Libros.

146. *Mataco*
Matacoan; Argentine Chaco; $t = 49$, $l = $ S:10, $n = 41$, % = 20, ci = -0.63.

Hunt, Richard J. (1937). Mataco-English and English-Mataco dictionary. In Walter Kaudern (ed.), *Ethnological studies,* Vol. 5, pp. 1–98. Göteborg, Sweden: Gothenburg Ethnographical Museum.

Hunt, Richard J. (1940). *Mataco grammar.* Tucumán, Argentina: Instituto de Antropología.

Lafone y Quevedo, Samuel A. (1896). Grupo Mataco-Mataguayo del Chaco: Dialecto Vejoz. *Boletín del Instituto Geográfico Argentino* 17:121–176.

Lehmann-Nitsche, Robert (1910–1911). Vocabulario Chorote ó Solote. *Revista del Museo de la Plata* 17:111–130.

Lehmann-Nitsche, Robert (1926). Vocabulario Mataco (Chaco Salteño). *Boletín de la Academia Nacional de Ciencias (Argentina)* 28:251–266.

Remedi, Joaquín (1896). Los Indios Matacos y su lengua . . . con vocabularios ordenados por Samuel A. Lafone y Quevedo. *Boletín del Instituto Geográfico Argentino* 17:331–362.

Remedi, Joaquín (1904). Vocabulario Mataco-Castellano. *Anales de la Sociedad Científica Argentina* 58:119–181.

147. *Mazahua*
Otomanguean; Mexico State, Mexico; $t = 45$, $l = $ S:22, $n = 27$, % = 49, $ci = $ - 0.11.

Anonymous (1958). *Cartilla Mazahua.* México, D.F.: Instituto Lingüístico de Verano.

Muro, Mildred Kiemele (1975). *Vocabulario Mazahua-Español y Español-Mazahua.* México: Biblioteca Enciclopédica del Estado de México.

Stewart, Donald, and Stewart, Shirley Gamble de (1954). *Vocabulario Mazahua.* México, D.F.: Instituto Lingüístico de Verano.

148. *Menominee*
Algonquian; Wisconsin; $t = 70$, $l = 5$ (F:3, E:2), $n = 65$, % = 7, $ci = $ -0.86.

Bloomfield, Leonard (1962). *The Menomini language.* New Haven, Conn.: Yale University Press.

Bloomfield, Leonard (1975). *Menomini lexicon.* Milwaukee, Wisc.: Milwaukee Public Museum Publications in Anthropology and History.

Great Lakes Inter-Tribal Council (1975). *Omæqnomenew-Ktketwanan: English-Menominee, Menominee-English word list.* Milwaukee: University of Wisconsin.

149. *Mescalero Apache*
Athapascan-Eyak; New Mexico; $t = 46$, $l = $ S:14, $n = 35$, % = 30, $ci = $ -0.46.

Breuninger, Evelyn, Hugar, Elbys, and Lathan, Ellen Ann (1982). *Mescalero Apache dictionary.* Mescalero, N.M.: Mescalero Apache Tribe.

150. *Miami*
Algonquian; Indiana; $t = 54$, $l = $ F:1, $n = 53$, % = 3, $ci = $ -0.96.

Voegelin, Charles F. (1938a). *Shawnee stems and the Jacob P. Dunn Miami dictionary, part I.* Indianapolis: Indiana Historical Society.

Voegelin, Charles F. (1938b). *Shawnee stems and the Jacob P. Dunn Miami dictionary, part II.* Indianapolis: Indiana Historical Society.

Voegelin, Charles F. (1939). *Shawnee stems and the Jacob P. Dunn Miami dictionary, part III.* Indianapolis: Indiana Historical Society.

Voegelin, Charles F. (1940a). *Shawnee stems and the Jacob P. Dunn Miami dictionary, part IV.* Indianapolis: Indiana Historical Society.

Voegelin, Charles F. (1940b). *Shawnee stems and the Jacob P. Dunn Miami dictionary, part V.* Indianapolis: Indiana Historical Society.

151. *Micmac (1888)*
Algonquian; Nova Scotia; $t = 69$, $l = 13$ (F:7, E:5, Du:1, G:1), $n = 60$, % = 19, $ci = -0.68$.

Rand, Silas Tertius (1888). *Dictionary of the language of the Micmac Indians who reside in Nova Scotia, New Brunswick, Prince Edward Island, Cape Breton and Newfoundland.* Halifax: Nova Scotia Printing Company.

152. *Micmac (1984)*
Algonquian; Nova Scotia; $t = 58$, $l = 13$ (F:8, E:4, Du:1), $n = 48$, % = 22, $ci = -0.60$.

DeBlois, Albert D., and Metallic, Alphonse (1984). *Micmac lexicon.* Ottawa: National Museums of Canada.

153. *Minto (Lower Tanana)*
Athapascan-Eyak; Alaska; $t = 34$, $l = $ R:16, $n = 21$, % = 47, ci = -0.15.

Krauss, Michael E. (1974). *Minto Nenana Athabaskan noun dictionary.* Fairbanks: Alaska Native Language Center.

154. *Miskito (1848–1894)*
Misumalpan; Nicaragua; $t = 49$, $l = 27$ (E:23, S:4), $n = 28$, % = 55, $ci = -0.02$.

Adam, Lucien (1891). *Langue Mosquito.* Paris: J. Maisonneuve.

Cotheal, Alexander I. (1848). A grammatical sketch of the language spoken by the Indians of the Mosquito Shore. *Transactions of the American Ethnological Society* 2:235–264.

Grunewald, Eduard (1879). Moskito-Deutsches und Deutsch-Moskito Wörterbuch. *Proceedings of the International Congress of Americanists* 3:379–397.

Ziock, Henry (1894). *Dictionary of the English and Miskito languages.* Herrnhut, Saxony: Gustav Winter.

155. *Miskito (1948–1986)*
Misumalpan; Nicaragua; $t = 66$, $l = 45$ (E:40, S:7), $n = 37$, % = 68, $ci = +0.12$.

Anonymous (1986). *Diccionario elemental: Miskito-Español, Español-Miskito.* Managua, Nicaragua: Centro de Investigación y Documentación de la Costa Atlántica.

Heath, George Reineke, and Marx, Werner G. (1961), *Diccionario Miskito-Español, Español-Miskito.* Tegucigalpa, Honduras: Papeleria e Imprenta Calderón.

Marx, Werner G. (1948). *Cartilla Miskito-Español.* Tegucigalpa, Honduras: Papeleria e Imprenta Calderón.

156. *Mississaga*
Algonquian; Ontario; $t = 35$, $l = 6$ (F:4, E: 2), $n = 29$, % = 17, $ci = -0.66$.

Chamberlain, Alexander Francis (1892). *The language of the Mississaga Indians of Skāgog.* Press of MacCalla and Company.

157. *Mixe (Totontepec)*
Mixe-Zoque; Oaxaca, Mexico; $t = 52$, $l = $ S:25, $n = 28$, % = 48, $ci = -0.06$.

Schoenhals, Alvin, and Schoenhals, Louise C. (1965). *Vocabulario Mixe de Totontepec*. México, D.F.: Instituto Lingüístico de Verano.

158. *Mixtec (1593)*
Otomanguean; Oaxaca, Mexico; t = 50, l = S:2, n = 49, % = 4, ci = -0.94.

Alvarado, Francisco de (1962). *Vocabulario en lengua Mixteca*. México, D.F.: Instituto Nacional Indigenista e Instituto Nacional de Antropología e Historia.

159. *Mixtec (Chayuco)*
Otomanguean; Oaxaca, Mexico; t = 37, l = S:11, n = 26, % = 30, ci = -0.41.

Pensinger, Brenda J. (1974). *Diccionario Mixteco: Mixteco del Este de Jamiltepec Pueblo de Chayuco*. México, D.F. Instituto Lingüístico de Verano.

160. *Mixtec (San Juan Colorado)*
Otomanguean; Oaxaca, Mexico; t = 42, l = S:12, n = 31, % = 29, ci = -0.45.

Campbell, Sara Stark, Peterson, Andrea Johnson, and Lorenzo Cruz, Filiberto (1986). *Diccionario Mixteco de San Juan Colorado*. México, D.F.: Instituto Lingüístico de Verano.

161. *Mocho*
Mayan; Chiapas, Mexico; t = 58, l = S:53, n = 11, % =91, ci = +0.73.

Kaufman, Terrence (1967). Preliminary Mochó vocabulary. Working paper No. 5, Laboratory for Language-Behavior Research, University of California, Berkeley.

162. *Mocovi*
Guaycuran; Argentine Chaco; t = 33, l = S:9, n = 25, % = 27, ci = -0.49.

Adam, Lucien (1889). *Grammaire comparée des dialectes de la famille Guaicurú (Abipone, Mocovi, Toba, Mbaya)*. Paris: J. Maisonneuve.
Koch-Grünberg, Theodor (1903). Die Guaikurú-Gruppe. *Mitteilungen der Anthropologischen Gesellschaft in Wien* 33:45–69.
Lafone y Quevedo, Samuel Alexander (1892). *Vocabulario Mocoví-Español*. Buenos Aires: Talleres del Museo de la Plata.

163. *Mohawk*
Iroquoian; New York; t = 59, l = 8 (E:4, Du:2, F:2), n = 52, % = 14, ci = -0.75.

Bonvillain, Nancy, and Francis, Beatrice (1971). *Mohawk-English dictionary*. Albany: University of the State of New York.
Huot, Martha Champion (1948). Some Mohawk words of acculturation. *International Journal of American Linguistics* 14:150–154.
Michelson, Gunther (1973). *A thousand words of Mohawk*. Ottawa: National Museum of Man.

164. *Mojave*
Yuman; Arizona; t = 47, l = 16 (S:14, E:5), n = 34, % = 34, ci = -0.38.

Munro, Pamela, and Brown, Nellie (1976). *A Mojave dictionary*. Parker, Ariz.: Colorado River Tribes Adult Education.

165. *Montagnais (Chipewyan)*
Athapascan-Eyak; Northwest Territory; t = 70, l = F:4, n = 68, % = 6, ci = -0.91.

Le Goff, Laurent (1916). *Dictionnaire Français-Montagnais*. Lyon: Société Saint-Augustin, Desclée, De Brouwer.
Petitot, Émile (1876). *Dictionnaire de la langue Dènè-Dindjié, dialects: Montagnais ou Chippewayan, Peaux de Lièvre et Loucheux*. Paris: Ernest Leroux, Editeur.

166. *Montagnais (dialect of Cree, 1901)*
Algonquian; Quebec; $t = 73$, $l = $ F:6, $n = 69$, $\% = 8$, $ci = -0.86$.

Lemoine, George (1901). *Dictionnaire Français-Montagnais*. Boston: W. B. Cabot and P. Cabot.

167. *Montagnais (dialect of Cree, c. 1980)*
Algonquian; Quebec; $t = 55$, $l = $ F:5, $n = 50$, $\% = 9$, $ci = -0.82$.

Comité Culturel des Montagnais de La Romaine (1978). *Lexique Montagnais-Français*. La Romaine, Québec: Comité Culturel des Montagnais de La Romaine.
McNulty, Gerry E., and Basile, Marie-Jeanne (1981). *Lexique Montagnais-Français du parler de Mingan*. Québec: Université Laval.

168. *Mopan*
Mayan; Belize; $t = 38$, $l = $ S:26, $n = 18$, $\% = 68$, $ci = +0.21$.

Ulrich, Mateo, and Ulrich, Rosemary de (1976). *Diccionario bilingüe Maya Mopán y Español y Maya Mopán*. Guatemala: Instituto Lingüístico de Verano.

169. *Nahuatl (1571)*
Uto-Aztecan; Valley of Mexico; $t = 61$, $l = $ S:22, $n = 45$, $\% = 36$, $ci = -0.38$.

Molina, Alonso de (1571). *Vocabulario en lengua Castellana y Mexicana*. Méjico.

170. *Nahuatl (1611)*
Uto-Aztecan; Valley of Mexico; $t = 34$, $l = $ S:18, $n = 23$, $\% = 53$, $ci = -0.15$.

Arenas, Pedro de (1611). *Vocabulario manual de las lenguas Castellana y Mexicana, en que se contienen las palabras, y respuestas más comunes y ordinarias que se suelen ofrecer en el trato y comunicación entre Españoles e Indios*. México.

171. *Nahuatl (Huazalinguillo dialect)*
Uto-Aztecan; Hidalgo, Mexico; $t = 38$, $l = $ S:16, $n = 23$, $\% = 42$, $ci = -0.18$.

Kimball, Geoffrey (1980). *A dictionary of the Huazalinguillo dialect of Nahuatl with grammatical sketch and readings*. New Orleans: Center for Latin American Studies.

172. *Nahuatl (Sierra de Zacapoaxtla)*
Uto-Aztecan; Puebla, Mexico; $t = 33$, $l = $ S:15, $n = 21$, $\% = 46$, $ci = -0.18$.

Key, Harold, and Key, Mary Ritchie de (1953). *Vocabulario Mejicano de la Sierra de Zacapoaxtla, Puebla*. México, D.F.: Instituto Lingüístico de Verano.

173. *Nahuatl (Tetelcingo)*
Uto-Aztecan; Morelos, Mexico; $t = 50$, $l = $ S:39, $n = 14$, $\% = 78$, $ci = +0.50$.

Brewer, Forrest, and Brewer, Jean G. (1971). *Vocabulario Mexicano de Tetelcingo, Morelos*. México, D.F.: Instituto Lingüístico de Verano.
Key, Harold (1954). *Vocabularies for languages of the Uto-Aztecan family*. Microfilm Collection of Manuscripts on Middle American Cultural Anthropology, No. 38, University of Chicago Library, Chicago.
Pittman, Richard S. (1949). *Aztec (Nahuatl) texts and dictionary*. Collection of Manuscripts on Middle American Cultural Anthropology, No. 27, University of Chicago Library, Chicago.

174. *Nahuatl (Xalita)*
Uto-Aztecan; Guerrero, Mexico; $t = 47$, $l = $ S:35, $n = 12$, $\% = 75$, $ci = +0.49$.

Ramírez de Alejandro, Cleofas, and Dakin, Karen (1979). *Vocabulario Náhuatl de Xalitla, Guerrero*. México, D.F.: Centro de Investigaciones Superiores del INAH.

175. *Natchez*
Isolate; Louisiana; $t = 47$, $l = $ E:1, $n = 46$, $\% = 2$, $ci = -0.96$.

Van Tuyl, Charles D. (1979). *The Natchez: annotated translations from Antoine Simon le Page du Pratz's* Histoire de la Louisiane *and a short English-Natchez dictionary.* Oklahoma City: Oklahoma Historical Society.

176. *Navajo (1910)*
Athapascan-Eyak; New Mexico; $t = 56$, $l = 10$ (S:9, E:1), $n = 48$, $\% = 18$, $ci = -0.68$.

Franciscan Fathers (1910). *An ethnologic dictionary of the Navaho language.* Saint Michaels, Ariz.: Franciscan Fathers.

177. *Navajo (1950–1980)*
Athapascan-Eyak; New Mexico; $t = 72$, $l = 13$ (S:12, E:1), $n = 60$, $\% = 18$, $ci = -0.65$.

Haile, Berard (1950). *A stem vocabulary of the Navaho language: Navaho-English.* St. Michaels, Ariz.: St. Michaels Press.
Haile, Berard (1951). *A stem vocabulary of the Navaho language: English-Navaho.* St. Michaels, Ariz.: St. Michaels Press.
Wall, Leon, and Morgan, William (1958). *Navajo-English dictionary.* Window Rock, Ariz.: Navajo Agency.
Young, Robert W., and Morgan, William (1980). *The Navajo language: A grammar and colloquial dictionary.* Albuquerque: University of New Mexico Press.

Note: A useful appendage to the last source is Young and Morgan (1992).

178. *Nez Perce*
Sahaptin-Nez Perce; Idaho, Oregon, and Washington; $t = 59$, $l = $ E:2, $n = 57$, $\% = 3$, $ci = -0.93$.

Morvillo, Anthony (1895). *A dictionary of the Numípu or Nez Perce language.* Montana: St. Ignatius' Mission Print.

Note: Since 1993, another Nez Perce dictionary has become available (Aoki 1994).

179. *Northern Sierra Miwok*
Miwok-Costanoan; California; $t = 60$, $l = 53$ (S:40, E:17), $n = 12$, $\% = 88$, $ci = +0.68$.

Callaghan, Catherine A. (1987). *Northern Sierra Miwok dictionary.* Berkeley: University of California Press.

180. *Northern Tutchone*
Athapascan-Eyak; Yukon; $t = 32$, $l = 7$ (E:4, F:3), $n = 25$, $\% = 22$, $ci = -0.56$.

Ritter, John (1976). *Mayo Indian language noun dictionary.* Whitehorse, Yukon Territory: Yukon Indian Cultural Education Society.

181. *North Mam*
Mayan; Huehuetenango, Guatemala; $t = 56$, $l = $ S:38, $n = 22$, $\% = 68$, $ci = +0.29$.

Maldonado Andrés, Juan, Ordonez Domingo, Juan, and Ortiz Domingo, Juan (1983). *Diccionario de San Ildefonso Ixtahuacan Huehuetenango.* Hannover, Germany: Verlag für Ethnologie.

182. *Ocaina*
Huitoto; Loreto, Peru; $t = 35$, $l = $ S:5, $n = 32$, $\% = 14$, $ci = -0.77$.

Anonymous (1979). *Palabras y frases utiles en algunos idiomas de la Selva Peruana.* Yarinacocha, Perú: Instituto Lingüístico de Verano.
Leach, Ilo M. (1969). *Vocabulario Ocaina.* Yarinacocha, Perú: Instituto Lingüístico de Verano.
Rivet, Paul, and Wavrin, Robert de (1953). Les Nonuya et les Okáina. *Journal de la Société des Américanistes de Paris* 42:333–389.

183. *Ofo*
Siouan; Mississippi; $t = 38$, $l = 0$, $n = 38$, $\% = 0$, $ci = -1.00$.

Dorsey, James Owen, and Swanton, John R. (1912). *A dictionary of the Biloxi and Ofo languages*. Washington, D.C.: U.S. Government Printing Office.

184. *Ojibwa (Mille Lacs area of Central Minnesota)*
Algonquian; Minnesota; $t = 59$, $l = $ F:3, $n = 56$, $\% = 5$, $ci = -0.90$.

Nichols, John, and Nyholm, Earl (1979). *Ojibwewi-Ikidowinan: An Ojibwe word resources book*. Saint Paul: Minnesota Archaeological Society.

185. *Ojibwa (Odawa dialect)*
Algonquian; Ottawa; $t = 42$, $l = $ F:2, $n = 40$, $\% = 5$, $ci = -0.90$.

Piggott, Glyne L., and Grafstein, Ann (1983). *An Ojibwa lexicon*. Ottawa: National Museums of Canada.

186. *Okanagan (Colville dialect)*
Salishan; British Columbia and Washington; $t = 50$, $l = 17$ (F:11, E:6), $n = 34$, $\% = 34$, $ci = -0.34$.

Mattina, Anthony (1987). *Colville-Okanagan dictionary*. Missoula: University of Montana, Occasional Papers in Linguistics.

187. *Ona*
Chon; Tierra del Fuego, Argentina and Chile; $t = 44$, $l = $ S:6, $n = 42$, $\% = 14$, $ci = -0.82$.

Beauvoir, José María (1901). *Pequeño diccionario del idioma Fueguino-Ona con su correspondiente Castellano*. Buenos Aires: Escuela Tipográfica Salesiana.
Beauvoir, José María (1915). *Los Shelknam, indígenas de la Tierra del Fuego*. Buenos Aires: Libreria del Colegio Pio IX.
Tonelli, D. Antonio (1926). *Grammatica e glossario della lingua degli Ona-Selknám della Terra del Fuoco*. Torino, Italy: Società Editrice Internazionale.

188. *Oneida*
Iroquoian; New York; $t = 38$, $l = 3$ (Du:2, F:1), $n = 35$, $\% = 8$, $ci = -0.84$.

Antone, Angela, et al. (1981). *Tekalihwathé: Thá*. London: Centre for the Research and Teaching of Canadian Native Languages, University of Western Ontario.

189. *Onondaga (seventeenth century)*
Iroquoian; New York; $t = 48$, $l = 3$ (Du:2, F:1), $n = 45$, $\% = 6$, $ci = -0.88$.

Shea, John Gilmary (1860). *French-Onondaga dictionary, from a manuscript of the seventeenth century*. New York: Cramoisy Press.

190. *Onondaga (eighteenth century)*
Iroquoian; New York; $t = 56$, $l = 5$ (Du:2, E:2, F:1), $n = 51$, $\% = 9$, $ci = -0.82$.

Zeisberger, David (1887). *Zeisberger's Indian dictionary, English, German, Iroquois—the Onondaga and Algonquin—the Delaware*. Cambridge: John Wilson.

191. *Osage*
Siouan; Kansas and Oklahoma; $t = 61$, $l = 2$ (F:1, S:1), $n = 59$, $\% = 3$, $ci = -0.93$.

La Flesche, Francis (1932). *A dictionary of the Osage language*. Washington, D.C.: U.S. Government Printing Office.

192. *Otomi (c. 1770)*
Otomanguean; Hidalgo?, Mexico; $t = 47$, $l = $ S:12, $n = 37$, $\% 26$, $ci = -0.53$.

Buelna, Eustaquio (ed.) (1893). *Luces del Otomí o gramática del idioma que hablan los Indios Otomíes en la República Mexicana. Compuesto por un Padre de la Compañía de Jesús.* México: Imprenta del Gobierno Federal.

Neve y Molina, Luis de (1767). *Reglas de ortografía, diccionario y arte del idioma Otomi.* México: Imprenta de la Bibliotheca Mexicana.

193. *Otomi (1826–1841)*
Otomanguean; Hidalgo?, Mexico; $t = 68$, $l =$ S:32, $n = 49$, $\% = 47$, $ci = -0.25$.

Lopez Yepes, Joaquín (1826). *Catecismo y declaración de la Doctrina Cristiana en lengua Otomí, con un vocabulario del mismo idioma.* México: Impreso en la Oficina del Ciudadano Alejandro Valdés.

Piccolomini, Enea Silvio Vincenzo (1841). *Grammatica della lingua Otomí esposta in Italiano.* Roma: Nella Tipografia de Propaganda Fide.

194. *Otomi (Mezquital dialect)*
Otomanguean; Hidalgo, Mexico; $t = 51$, $l =$ S:13, $n = 41$, $\% = 26$, $ci = -0.55$.

Hess, Hernán (1956). *Diccionario Otomí del Mezquital Español Inglés.* México, D.F.: Instituto Lingüístico de Verano.

Wallis, Ethel Emilia (1956). *Diccionario Castellano-Otomí-Otomí-Castellano.* Itsmiquilpan, México: Instituto Lingüístico de Verano.

195. *Otomi (Santiago Mexquititlán)*
Otomanguean; Hidalgo?, Mexico; $t = 73$, $l =$ S:40, $n = 41$, $\% = 55$, $ci = -0.01$.

Hekking, Ewald, and Andrés de Jesús, Severiano (1989). *Diccionario Español-Otomí de Santiago Mexquititlán.* Campanas, Querétaro, México: Universidad Autónoma de Querétaro.

196. *Oyampi*
Tupí-Guaraní; French Guiana; $t = 32$, $l = 16$ (F:9; P:6, Du:2), $n = 18$, $\% = 50$, $ci = -0.06$.

Grenand, Françoise (1989). *Dictionnaire Wayapi-Français.* Paris: Centre National de la Recherche Scientifique.

Olson, Roberta (1978). *Dicionário por tópicos nas línguas Olampí (Wajapi)– Português.* Brasília, D.F.: Summer Institute of Linguistics.

197. *Pacific Gulf Yupik*
Eskimo-Aleut; Alaska; $t = 45$, $l =$ R:33, $n = 12$, $\% = 73$, $ci = +0.47$.

Leer, Jeff (1978). *A conversational dictionary of Kodiak Alutiiq.* Fairbanks: Alaska Native Language Center.

198. *Páez*
Panaquitan; Caucá, Colombia; $t = 43$, $l =$ S:25, $n = 19$, $\% = 58$, $ci = +0.14$.

Slocum, Marianna C., and Gerdel, Florence L. (1983). *Diccionario Páez-Español, Español-Páez.* Lomalinda, Meta, Colombia: Editorial Townsend.

199. *Pame*
Otomanguean; San Luis Potosí, Mexico; $t = 47$, $l =$ S:16, $n = 36$, $\% = 34$, $ci = -0.43$.

Maza, Antonio de la (1947). La nación Pame. *Boletín de la Sociedad Mexicana de Geografía y Estadística* 63:493–575.

Olson, Donald (1963). Spanish loan words in Pame. *International Journal of American Linguistics* 29:219–221.

Soustelle, Jacques (1951). Documents sur les langages Pame et Jonaz du Mexique Central (Hidalgo, Querétaro, San Luis Potosí). *Journal de la Société des Américanistes* 40:1–20.

200. *Panamint Shoshone*
Uto-Aztecan; Nevada; $t = 58$, $l = 41$ (S:32, E:12), $n = 25$, $\% = 71$, $ci = +0.28$.

Dayley, Jon P. (1989). *Tümpisa (Panamint) Shoshone dictionary.* Berkeley: University of California Press.

201. *Passamaquaddy*
Algonquian; Maine; $t = 43$, $l = 14$ (E:11, F:3), $n = 29$, % = 33, $ci = -0.35$.

Leavitt, R. M., and Francis, D. A. (eds.) (1986). *Le Sourd's Passamaquoddy-Maliseet and English dictionary.* Perry, M.: Passamaquoddy-Maliseet Bilingual Program.

202. *Peaux-de-Lièvres (= Hare)*
Athapascan-Eyak; Northwest Territory; $t = 56$, $l = $ F:1, $n = 55$, % = 2, $ci = -0.96$.

Petitot, Émile (1876). *Dictionnaire de la langue Dènè-Dindjié, dialects: Montagnais ou Chippewayan, Peaux de Lièvre et Loucheux.* Paris: Ernest Leroux.

203. *Peruvian Quechua (1560–1619)*
Quechumaran; Peru; $t = 31$, $l = $ S:5, $n = 28$, % = 16, $ci = -0.74$.

Domingo de Santo Tomás (1560). *Lexicon o vocabulario de la lengua general del Peru.*
Holguin, Diego Gonsález (1608). *Vocabulario de la lengua general de todo el Peru llamada lengua Quichua.*
Pardo, Luis A. (1945). Vocabulario segundo del Castellano al Indico por el Padre Diego de Torres Rubio en 1619, aumentado despúes con los vocablos de la lengua Chinchaisuyo, por el Padre Juan de Figueredo. *Revista Universitaria* 34:111–166.

204. *Peruvian Quechua (1864–1908)*
Quechumaran; Peru; $t = 40$, $l = $ S:16, $n = 31$, % = 40, $ci = -0.38$.

Markham, Clements R. ([1864] 1972). *Contributions towards a grammar and dictionary of Quichua.* Osnabrück, Germany: Biblio Verlag.
Sala, Gabriel (1905–1908). Diccionario, gramática y catecismo Castellano, Inga, Amueixa y Campa. *Boletín de la Sociedad Geográfica de Lima* 17:149–227, 311–356, 469–490; 19:102–120, 211–240.

205. *Piaroa*
Salivan; Amazonas, Venezuela; $t = 51$, $l = $ S:20, $n = 32$, % = 39, $ci = -0.24$.

Krisologo B., Pedro Juan (1976). *Manual glotológico del idioma Wo'tiheh.* Caracas: Centro de Lenguas Indígenas.

206. *Pima*
Uto-Aztecan; Arizona; $t = 67$, $l = 51$ (S:50, E:4), $n = 30$, % = 76, $ci = +0.31$.

Saxton, Dean, Saxton, Lucille, and Enos, Susie (1983). *Dictionary Papago/Pima-English, English-Papago/Pima.* Tucson: University of Arizona Press.
Willenbrink, Antonine (1935). *Notes on the Pima Indian language.* Franciscan Fathers of California.

207. *Pipil*
Uto-Aztecan; El Salvador; $t = 53$, $l = $ S:43, $n = 21$, % = 79, ci = +0.40.

Campbell, Lyle (1985). *The Pipil language of El Salvador.* Berlin: Mouton.
Jiménez, Tomás Fidias (1937). *Idioma Pipil ó Nahuat de Cuzcatlán y Tunalán hoy República de El Salvador en la América Central.* San Salvador: Tipografía "La Union."

208. *Piro*
Maipuran; Loreto, Peru; $t = 61$, $l = $ S:38, $n = 34$, % = 62, $ci = +0.07$.

Anonymous (1979). *Palabras y frases utiles en algunos idiomas de la Selva Peruana.* Yarinacocha, Pucallpa, Perú: Instituto Lingüístico de Verano.

Matteson, Esther (1965). *The Piro (Arawakan) language*. Berkeley: University of California Press.
Nies, Joyce (1986). *Diccionario Piro*. Yarinacocha, Pucallpa, Perú: Instituto Lingüístico de Verano.

209. *Plains Cree ("Y" dialect)*
      Algonquian; Alberta; $t = 75$, $l = 4$ (F:3, E:1), $n = 72$, % = 5, $ci = -0.91$.

      Anderson, Anne (1975). *Plains Cree dictionary in the "Y" dialect*. Edmonton, Canada: University of Chicago.

210. *Plains Miwok*
      Miwok-Costanoan; California; $t = 58$, $l = 53$ (S:52, E:3), $n = 7$, % = 91, $ci = +0.79$.

      Callaghan, Catherine A. (1984). *Plains Miwok dictionary*. Berkeley: University of California Press.

211. *Pocomam*
      Mayan; Jilotepec, Guatemala; $t = 32$, $l =$ S:25, $n = 7$, % = 78, $ci = +0.56$.

      Zinn, Raymond, and Zinn, Gail (n.d.). *Dictionary Pocomam Oriental*. Guatemala: Summer Institute of Linguistics.

      Note: Since 1993, another Pocomam dictionary has become available (McArthur and McArthur 1995).

212. *Popoloca (San Vicente Coyoctepec)*
      Otomanguean; Puebla, Mexico; $t = 50$, $l =$ S:33, $n = 18$, % = 66, $ci = +0.30$.

      Barrera, Bartolo, and Dakin, Karen (1978). *Vocabulario Popoloca de San Vicente Coyoctepec, Popoloca-Español, Español-Popoloca*. México, D.F.: Cuadernos de la Casa Chata.

213. *Popoluca (Oluta)*
      Mixe-Zoque; Veracruz, Mexico; $t = 45$, $l =$ S:26, $n = 20$, % = 58, $ci = +0.13$.

      Clark, Lawrence E. (1981). *Diccionario Popoluca de Oluta*. México, D.F.: Instituto Lingüístico de Verano.

214. *Popoluca (Sayula)*
      Mixe-Zoque; Veracruz, Mexico; $t = 40$, $l =$ S:28, $n = 12$, % = 70, $ci = +0.40$.

      Clark, Lorenzo, and Clark, Nancy Davis de (1960). *Vocabulario Popoluca de Sayula*. México, D.F.: Instituto Lingüístico de Verano.
      Clark, Lawrence E. (1977). Linguistic acculturation in Sayula Popoluca. *International Journal of American Linguistics* 43:128–138.

215. *Quechua (Ancash, 1905)*
      Quechumaran; Ancash, Peru; $t = 37$, $l =$ S:27, $n = 12$, % = 73, ci = +0.41.

      Religiosos Franciscanos Misioneros de los Colegios de Propaganda (1905). *Fide del Perú. Vocabulario políglota Incaico*. Lima: Tipografía del Colegio de Propaganda Fide del Perú.

216. *Quechua (Ancash, 1972)*
      Quechumaran; Ancash, Peru; $t = 31$, $l =$ S:18, $n = 15$, % = 58, ci = +0.10.

      Swisshelm, Germán (1972). *Un Diccionario del Quechua de Huaraz*. Huaraz, Perú: Estudios Culturales Benedictinos.

217. *Quechua (Ayacucho, 1905)*
      Quechumaran; Ayacucho, Peru; $t = 37$, $l =$ S:23, $n = 19$, % = 62, $ci = +0.11$.

Religiosos Franciscanos Misioneros de los Colegios de Propaganda (1905). *Fide del Perú.
Vocabulario políglota Incaico.* Lima: Tipografía del Colegio de Propaganda Fide del Perú.

218. *Quechua (Ayacucho, 1969)*
Quechumaran; Ayacucho, Peru; $t = 58$, $l = $ S:47, $n = 15$, % = 81, $ci = +0.55$.

Parker, Gary John (1969). *Ayacucho Quechua grammar and dictionary.* The Hague: Mouton.

219. *Quechua (Cajamarca)*
Quechumaran; Cajamarca, Peru; $t = 43$, $l = $ S:35, $n = 11$, % = 81, $ci = +0.56$.

Quesada S., Felix (1976). *Diccionario Quechua: Cajamarca-Cañaris.* Lima: Instituto de Estudios
Peruanos.

220. *Quechua (Cochabamba)*
Quechumaran; Cochabamba, Bolivia; $t = 36$, $l = $ S:27, $n = 9$, % = 75, $ci = +0.50$.

Herrero, Joaquín, and Sánchez de Lozada, Federico (1974). *Diccionario Quechua-Castellano,
Castellano-Quechua.* Cochabamba, Bolivia: Instituto de Idiomas, Padres de Maryknoll.

221. *Quechua (Cuzco, 1905)*
Quechumaran; Cuzco, Peru; $t = 37$, $l = $ S:21, $n = 19$, % = 57, ci = +0.05.

Religiosos Franciscanos Misioneros de los Colegios de Propaganda (1905). *Fide del Perú.
Vocabulario políglota Incaico.* Lima: Tipografía del Colegio de Propaganda Fide del Perú.

222. *Quechua (Cuzco, 1976)*
Quechumaran; Cuzco, Peru; $t = 42$, $l = $ S:31, $n = 12$, % = 74, ci = +0.45.

Cusihuaman Gutierrez, Antonio (1976). *Diccionario Quechua: Cuzco-Collao.* Lima: Instituto de
Estudios Peruanos.

223. *Quechua (Junin, 1905)*
Quechumaran; Junin, Peru; $t = 37$, $l = $ S:25, $n = 19$, % = 68, ci = +0.16.

Religiosos Franciscanos Misioneros de los Colegios de Propaganda (1905). *Fide del Perú.
Vocabulario políglota Incaico.* Lima: Tipografía del Colegio de Propaganda Fide del Perú.

224. *Quechua (Junin, 1976)*
Quechumaran; Junin, Peru; $t = 44$, $l = $ S:32, $n = 16$, % = 73, ci = +0.36.

Cerron-Palomino, Rodolfo (1976). *Diccionario Quechua: Junin-Huanca.* Lima: Instituto de
Estudios Peruanos.

225. *Quiche*
Mayan; Quiché?, Guatemala; $t = 46$, $l = $ S:17, $n = 35$, % = 37, ci = -0.39.

Henne Pontious, David (1980). *Diccionario Quiche-Español.* Guatemala, C.A.: Instituto
Lingüístico de Verano.
León, Juan de (1954). *Diccionario Quiche-Español.* Guatemala: Editorial Landivar.
Teletor, Celso Narciso (1959). *Diccionario Castellano-Quiché y voces Castellano-Pocomam.*
Guatemala, C.A.

Note: Since 1993, another Quiche dictionary has become available (Ajpacaja Tum et al. 1996).

226. *Quileute*
Chimakuan; Washington State; $t = 41$, $l = 11$ (E:9, F:2), $n = 30$, % = 26, $ci = -0.46$.

Powell, James V., and Woodruff, Fred, Sr. (1976). *Quileute dictionary.* Northwest
Anthropological Research Notes, Vol. 10, No. 1, part 2, Memoir No. Three.

227. *Ranquelche*
Araucanian; La Pampa, Argentina; $t = 53$, $l = $ S:34, $n = 28$, % = 64, $ci = $ +0.11.

Barbará, Federico (1879). *Manual ó vocabulario de la lengua Pampa y del estilo familiar.* Buenos Aires: Mayo de C. Casavalle.
Rosas, Juan Manuel de (1947). *Gramática y diccionario de la lengua Pampa.* Buenos Aires: Editorial Albatros.
Siemiradzki, Josef V. (1898). Beiträge zur ethnographie der südamerikanischen Indianer. *Mitteilungen der Anthropologischen Gesellschaft in Wien* 28 (n.f. vol. 18):127–170.

228. *Seneca*
Iroquoian; New York; $t = 57$, $l = 2$ (Du:1, F:1), $n = 55$, % = 4, $ci = $ -0.93.

Chafe, Wallace L. (1967). *Seneca morphology and dictionary.* Washington, D.C.: Smithsonian Press.

229. *Seri*
Isolate: Sonora, Mexico; $t = 41$, $l = $ S:7, $n = 36$, % = 17, $ci = $ -0.71.

Moser, Edward, and Moser, Mary B. (1961). *Seri-Castellano, Castellano-Seri.* México, D.F.: Instituto Lingüístico de Verano.

230. *Shuswap*
Salishan; British Columbia; $t = 41$, $l = 13$ (E:8, F:6), $n = 30$, % = 32, $ci = $ -0.42.

Kuipers, Aert H. (1974). *The Shuswap language: Grammar, texts, dictionary.* The Hague: Mouton.
Kuipers, Aert H. (1975). *A classified English-Shuswap word-list.* Lisse, Holland: Peter de Ridder Press.

231. *Siberian Yupik Eskimo*
Eskimo-Aleut; Alaska; $t = 37$, $l = 15$ (E:10, R:5), $n = 28$, % = 41, $ci = $ -0.35.

Badten, Linda Womkon, Kaneshiro, Vera Oovi, and Oovi, Marie (1987). In Steven A. Jacobson (ed.), *A dictionary of the St. Lawrence Island/Siberia Yupik Eskimo language.* Fairbanks: Alaska Native Language

232. *Slave*
Athapascan-Eyak; Alberta, British Columbia, and Northwest Territory; $t = 55$, $l = $ F:4, $n = 52$, % = 7, $ci = $ -0.87.

Gouy, Edouard (1930). Dictionnaire Français-Esclave. Manuscript, Dartmouth College Library, Hanover, N.H.

233. *Songish (North Straits Salish)*
Salishan; Washington State; $t = 38$, $l = 10$ (E:7, F:3), $n = 28$, % = 26, $ci = $ -0.47.

Mitchell, Majorie Ruth (1968). A dictionary of Songish, a dialect of Straits Salish. M.A. thesis, University of Victoria, Victoria, British Columbia.

234. *Southern Ojibwa*
Algonquian; Minnesota; $t = 53$, $l = $ F:1; $n = 52$, % = 2, $ci = $ -0.96.

Blessing, Fred K. (1954). A Southern Ojibwa glossary. *The Minnesota Archaeologist* 19:2-57.

235. *Southern Sierra Miwok*
Miwok-Costanoan; California; $t = 63$, $l = 51$ (S:40, E:12), $n = 18$, % = 81, $ci = $ +0.52.

Broadbent, Sylvia (1964). *The Southern Sierra Miwok language.* Berkeley: University of California Press.

236. *Southern Ute*
Uto-Aztecan; Colorado; $t = 61$, $l = 23$ (S:16, E:7), $n = 40$, % = 38, $ci = -0.28$.

Givón, Talmy (1979). *Ute dictionary.* Ignacio, Col.: Ute Press.

237. *Squamish*
Salishan; British Columbia; $t = 31$, $l = 11$ (E:7, F:4), $n = 21$, % = 36, $ci = -0.32$.

Kuipers, Aert H. (1967). *The Squamish language: Grammar, texts, dictionary.* The Hague: Mouton.
Kuipers, Aert H. (1969). *The Squamish language: Grammar, texts, dictionary: part II.* The Hague: Mouton.

238. *Sumo*
Misumalpan; Nicaragua; $t = 62$, $l = 44$ (E:38, S:9), $n = 27$, % = 71, $ci = +0.27$.

Houwald, Götz von (1980), *Diccionario Español-Sumu, Sumu-Español.* Managua, Nicaragua: Ministerio de Educación.

239. *Tanaina*
Athapascan-Eyak; Alaska; $t = 50$, $l = 36$ (R:35, E:1), $n = 30$, % = 72, $ci = +0.12$.

Kari, James (1977). *Dena'ina noun dictionary.* Fairbanks: Alaska Native Language Center.
Tenenbaum, Joan M. (1975). *Nondalton Tanaina noun dictionary.* Fairbanks: Alaska Native Language Center.

240. *Tarahumara (1915–1920)*
Uto-Aztecan; Chihuahua, Mexico; $t = 44$, $l = $ S:25, $n = 22$, % = 57, $ci = +0.07$.

Ferrero, H. José (1920). *Pequeña gramatica y diccionario de la lengua Tarahumara.* México: Imprenta Dirigida por J. Aguilar Vera.
Griggs, Jorge (c. 1915). *Diccionario de la lengua Tarahumara.* Chihuahua, México: Talleres Tipográficos de la Escuela de Artes y Oficios á Cargo de Manuel Gómez.

241. *Tarahumara (1952–1972)*
Uto-Aztecan; Chihuahua, Mexico; $t = 51$, $l = $ S:25, $n = 29$, % = 49, $ci = -0.08$.

Hilton, K. Simon (1959). *Tarahumara y Español.* México, D.F.: Instituto Lingüístico de Verano.
Lionnet, Andrés (1972). *Los elementos de la lengua Tarahumara.* México, D.F.: Universidad Nacional Autónoma de México.
Thord-Gray, I. (1955). *Tarahumara-English, English-Tarahumara dictionary.* Coral Gables, Fl.: University of Miami Press.

242. *Tarascan (1559)*
Isolate; Michoacán, Mexico; $t = 54$, $l = $ S:19, $n = 40$, % = 35, $ci = -0.39$.

Gilberti, Maturino (1901). *Diccionario de la lengua Tarasca ó de Michoucán.* México: Tipografía de la Oficina Impresora del Timbre.

243. *Taurepän*
Carib; Amazonas, Venezuela; $t = 40$, $l = 17$ (S:12, P:8, E:1), n = 27, % = 43, $ci = -0.25$.

Armellada, Cesareo de (1944). *Gramática y diccionario de la lengua Pemon (Arekuna, Taurepan, Kamarakoto) (familia Caribe).* Caracas: C.A. Artes Graficas.
Koch-Grünberg, Theodor (1928). *Vom Roroima zum Orinoco. Ergebnisse einer Reise in Nordbrasilien und Venezuela in den Jahren 1911–1913.* Stuttgart: Verlag Strecker und Schröder.
Rondon, Cándido M. S., and Barbosa de Faria, Joao (1948). *Esbôço gramatical; Vocabulário, lendas e cânticos dos Indios Ariti (Parici).* Rio de Janeiro: Conselho Nacional de Proteçao aos Indios.

244. *Tehuelche*
    Chon; Chubut, Argentina; $t = 34$, $l =$ S:11, $n = 28$, % = 33, ci = -0.50.

Barbará, Federico (1879). *Manual ó Vocabulario de la lengua Pampa y del estilo familiar.* Buenos Aires: Mayo de C. Casavalle.

Lista, Ramón (1896). Los Tehuelches de la Patagonia. *Anales de la Sociedad Científica Argentina* 42:35–43.

Roncagli, G. (1884). Raccolta di vocaboli della lingua Tehuelche: Da Punta Arena a Santa Crus. *Bollettino della Società Geografia Italiana* 9:782–784.

Schmid, Theophilus (1910). *Two linguistic treatises on the Patagonian or Tehuelche language.* Buenos Aires: Coni.

245. *Tequistlatec*
    Isolate; Oaxaca, Mexico; $t = 58$, $l =$ S:42, $n = 26$, % = 72, ci = +0.28.

Turner, Paul, and Turner, Shirley (1971). *Chontal to Spanish-English dictionary Spanish to Chontal.* Tucson: University of Arizona Press.

Waterhouse, Viola, and Parrot, Muriel (1970). Diccionario de la Sierra Chontal. Manuscript in the files of the author.

246. *Tewa*
    Tanoan; New Mexico; $t = 34$, $l =$ S:22, $n = 16$, % = 65, ci = +0.18.

Dozier, Edward P. (1956). Two examples of linguistic acculturation: The Yaqui of Sonora and Arizona and the Tewa of New Mexico. *Language* 32:146–157.

247. *Thompson (Nitklakapamuk)*
    Salishan; British Columbia; $t = 43$, $l = 9$ (E:8, F:1), $n = 34$, % = 21, ci = -0.58.

Good, J. B. (1880). *A vocabulary and outlines of grammar of the Nitlakapamuk or Thompson Tongue, (the Indian language spoken between Yale, Lillooet, Cache Creek and Nicola Lake.) together with a Chinook dictionary, adapted for use in the Province of British Columbia.* Victoria, British Columbia: St. Paul's Mission Press.

Note: Since 1993, another Thompson dictionary has become available (Thompson and Thompson 1996).

248. *Ticuna*
    Isolate; Amazonas, Colombia; $t = 41$, $l = 24$ (P:16, S:9), $n = 20$, % = 59, ci = +0.10.

Alviano, Fidelis de (1944). *Gramática, dicionário, verbos, e frases e vocabulário. Prático da língua dos Indios Ticunas.* Rio de Janeiro: Instituto Histórico e Geográfico Brasileiro.

Anderson, Lambert (1958). Vocabulario breve del idioma Ticuna. *Tradición* 8:53–68.

Anonymous (1979). *Palabras y frases utiles en algunos idiomas de la Selva Peruana.* Perú: Instituto Lingüístico de Verano.

Rondon, Cándido M. S., and Barbosa de Faria, Joao (1948). *Esbôço gramatica; vocabulário; lendas e canticos dos Indios Ariti (Parici).* Rio de Janeiro,: Conselho Nacional de Proteçao aos Indios.

249. *Toba (1884–1925)*
    Guaycuruan; Argentine Chaco; $t = 41$, $l =$ S:12, $n = 35$, % = 29, ci = -0.56.

Bárcena, Alonso (1893). *Arte de la lengua Toba.* La Plata, Argentina: Talleres de Publicaciones del Museo.

Carabassa, Hilario B. (1910). *El Trópico del Capricornio Argentino ó 37 años entre los Indios Tobas.* Buenos Aires: Establecimiento Gráfico de Alberto Monkes Belgrano.

Carranza, Anjel Justiniano (1884). *Expedicion al Chaco Austral.* Buenos Aires: Imprenta Europea.

Ducci, Zacarías (1909). Vocabulario Toba-Castellano. *Boletín del Instituto Geográfico Argentino* 22:68–88; 23:23–53.

Lehmann-Nitsche, Robert (1925). Vocabulario Toba (Río Pilcomayo y Chaco Oriental). *Boletín de la Academia Nacional de Ciencias.* 28:179–196.

250. *Toba (1943–1980)*
Guaycuruan; Argentine Chaco; $t = 51$, $l = $ S:18, $n = 45$, % = 35, $ci = $ -0.53.

Buckwalter, Alberto S. (1980). *Vocabulario Toba.* Chaco, Argentina: Talleres Gráficos Granchavoff.
Flury, Lazaro (1951). *Tradiciones, leyendas y vida de los Indios del Norte.* Buenos Aires: Ciordia and Rodriguez.
Susnik, Branislava J. (1962). Vocabulario ineditos de los idiomas Emok-Tobay Choroti, recogidos por el Dr. Max Schmidt. *Boletín de la Sociedad Científica del Paraguay y del Museo Etnográfico* 6:1–32.
Tebboth, Tomás (1943). Diccionario Toba. *Revista del Instituto de Antropología de la Universidad de Tucumán,* Volumen 3, Número 2.
Vellard, Jehan A. (1969). *Vocabulario Toba.* Buenos Aires: Universidad de Buenos Aires.

251. *Tojolabal*
Mayan; Chiapas, Mexico; $t = 71$, $l = $ S:53, $n = 44$, % = 75, $ci = $ +0.13.

Lenkersdorf, Carlos (1979). *B'omak'umal Tojol Ab'al-Kastiya.* México, D.F.: Editorial Nuestro Tiempo.
Lenkersdorf, Carlos (1981). *B'omak'umal Kastiya-Tojol Ab'al.* México, D.F.: Editorial Nuestro Tiempo.
Mendenhall, Celia Douglass, and Supple, Julia (1948). *Tojolabal dictionary.* Summer Institute of Linguistics.

252. *Tonkawa*
Isolate; Texas; $t = 39$, $l = $ S:5, $n = 35$, % = 13, $ci = $ -0.77.

Hoijer, Harry (1949). *An analytical dictionary of the Tonkawa language.* Berkeley: University of California Press.

253. *Totonac (La Sierra dialect)*
Totonacan; Veracruz, Mexico; $t = 36$, $l = $ S:21, $n = 16$, % = 58, $ci = $ +0.14.

Aschmann, Herman Pedro (1973). *Castellano-Totonaco Totonaco-Castellano dialecto de la Sierra.* México, D.F.: Instituto Lingüístico de Verano.

254. *Totonac (Xicotepec de Juárez)*
Totonacan; Pueblo, Mexico; $t = 52$, $l = $ S:43, $n = 12$, % = 83, ci = +0.60.

Reid, Aileen A., and Bishop, Ruth G. (1974), *Diccionario Totonaco de Xicotepec de Juárez, Puebla.* México, D.F.: Instituto Lingüístico de Verano.

255. *Trique (Chicahuaxtla)*
Otomanguean; Oaxaca, Mexico; $t = 51$, $l = $ S:21, $n = 31$, % = 41, $ci = $ -0.21.

Good, Claude (1978). *Diccionario Triqui de Chicahuaxtla.* México, D.F.: Instituto Lingüístico de Verano.

256. *Trique (Copala)*
Otomanguean; Oaxaca, Mexico; $t = 54$, $l = $ S:33, $n = 26$, % = 61, $ci = $ +0.13.

Hollenbach, Elena E. de (1973). La aculturación lingüística entre los Triques de Copala, Oaxaca. *América Indígena* 33:65–95.

257. *Tucano*
Tucanoan; Amazonas, Brazil; $t = 42$, $l = $ P:16, $n = 29$, % = 38, $ci = $ -0.31.

Gallo M., Carlos I. (1972). *Diccionario Tucano-Castellano*. Mitú, Colombia: Grupo Lingüístico de La Amazonia Colombo-Brasileña.
Giacone, Antonio (n.d.). *Pequena gramática e dicionário da lingua Tucana*. Amazonas, Brasil: Velho Lino de Lino Aguiar.
Tamayo L., César (1988). *Mi primer diccionario Español-Tuyuca, Tuyuca-Español*.

258. *Tunica*
Isolate; Mississippi; $t = 56$, $l = $ F:3, $n = 53$, $\% = 5$, $ci = -0.89$.

Haas, Mary R. (1953). *Tunica dictionary*. Berkeley: University of California Press.

259. *Tupí (1621)*
Tupí-Guaraní; Brazil; $t = 31$, $l = 0$, $n = 31$, $\% = 0$, $ci = -1.00$.

Anonymous (1621). *Vocabulario na lingua Brasilica*. Manuscrito Português-Tupí do seculo XVII, coordenado e prefaciado por Plinio Ayrosa. Volume XX da Coleçao Departamento de Cultura, São Paulo—1938.

260. *Tupí (1795)*
Tupí-Guaraní; Brazil; $t = 33$, $l = $ P:3, $n = 30$, $\% = 9$, $ci = -0.82$.

Ayrosa, Plinio M. da Silva (1934). Diccionario Portuguez e Brasiliano. *Revista do Museu Paulista* 18:17–319.

261. *Tupí (1854–1894)*
Tupí-Guaraní; Brazil; $t = 42$, $l = $ P:12, $n = 32$, $\% = 29$, $ci = -0.48$.

Barbosa Rodrigues, Joao (1894). *Vocabulario indigena*. Rio de Janeiro: Typ. de. G. Leuzinger and Filhos.
Chaffanjon, Jean (1889). *L'Orénoque et le Caura*. Paris: Librairie Hachette.
Gonçalves Dias, Antonio (1854). Vocabularío da Lingua Geral usada hoje en dia no Alto-Amazonas. *Revista do Instituto Histórico e Geográfico do Brazil* 17:553–576.
Martius, Karl Friedrich Phillip von (1863). *Glossaria Linguarum Brasiliensium*. Erlangen, Germany: Druck von Junge and Sohn.

262. *Tupí (1950–1979)*
Tupí-Guaraní; Brazil; $t = 49$, $l = $ P:10, $n = 42$, $\% = 20$, $ci = -0.65$.

Barbosa, A. Lemos (1967). *Pequeno vocabulário Tupi-Português*. Rio de Janeiro: Livraria São José.
Boudin, Max H. (1978). *Dicionário de Tupi moderno (dialeto Tembé-Ténêtéhar do Alto do Rio Gurupi)*. São Paulo: Conselho Estadual de Artes e Ciências Humanas.
Masucci, Oberdan (1979). *Dicionário Tupi Português e vice-versa*. Rio de Janeiro: Brasilivros-Editorae Distribuidora.
Mauro, Humberto (1950). Vocabulário dos têrmos Tupis de "O Selvagem" de Couto de Magalhaes. *Revista do Instituto Histórico e Geográfico Brasileiro* 208:197–242.

263. *Tupí (Nheengatu dialect)*
Tupí-Guaraní; Amazonas, Brazil; $t = 46$, $l = $ P:16, $n = 36$, $\% = 35$, $ci = -0.44$.

Stradelli, Ermano (1929). Vocabulários da Língua Geral Portuguez-Nheêngatú e Nheêngatú-Portuguez. *Revista do Instituto Histórico e Geográfico Brasileiro* Tomo 104, 158:9–768.
Tastevin, Constant (1910). *La langue Tapïhïya dite Tupï ou Neëñgatu (Belle Langue)*. Vienne: Libraire de L'université.
Tavera-Acosta, Bartolomé (1907). *En el sur (dialectos indígenas de Venezuela)*. Bolívar: Imprenta y Encuadernación de Benito Jimeno Castro.

264. *Tzeltal (1888)*
Mayan; Chiapas, Mexico; $t = 45$, $l = $ S:10, $n = 35$, $\% = 22$, $ci = -0.56$.

Pineda, Vicente (1888). *Gramática de la lengua Tzel-tal y diccionario de la misma.* Chiapas, México: Tip. del Gobierno.

265. *Tzeltal (Bachajón)*
     Mayan; Chiapas, Mexico; $t = 51$, $l = $ S:34, $n = 18$, % $= 67$, $ci = +0.31$.

     Slocum, Marianna C., and Gerdel, Florencia L. (1971). *Vocabulario Tzeltal de Bachajón.* México, D.F.: Instituto Lingüístico de Verano.

266. *Tzeltal (Oxchuc)*
     Mayan; Chiapas, Mexico; $t = 36$, $l = $ S:17, $n = 21$, % $= 47$, $ci = -0.11$.

     Robles U., Carlos (1966). *La dialectología Tzeltal y el diccionario compacto.* México, D.F.: Instituto Nacional de Antropología e Historia.
     Sarles, Harvey B. (1961). *Monosyllable dictionary of the Tzeltal language.* Chicago: University of Chicago, Department of Anthropology, Chiapas Project.
     Slocum, Marianna C. (1953). *Vocabulario Tzeltal-Español.* México, D.F.: Instituto Lingüístico de Verano.

267. *Tzeltal (Tenejapa)*
     Mayan; Chiapas, Mexico; $t = 50$, $l = $ S:29, $n = 26$, % $= 58$, $ci = +0.06$.

     Berlin, Brent, and Kaufman, Terrence (1962). Diccionario del Tzeltal de Tenejapa, Chiapas. Manuscript, Stanford University Libraries, Stanford, Cal.

268. *Tzotzil (San Andrés)*
     Mayan; Chiapas, Mexico; $t = 51$, $l = $ S:31, $n = 25$, % $= 61$, $ci = +0.12$.

     Delgaty, Alfa Hurley, and Ruíz Sánchez, Agustín (1978). *Diccionario Tzotzil de San Andrés.* México, D.F.: Instituto Lingüístico de Verano.

269. *Tzotzil (San Bartolome)*
     Mayan; Chiapas, Mexico; $t = 43$, $l = $ S:32, $n = 12$, % $= 74$, $ci = +0.47$.

     Sarles, Harvey B. (n.d.). A dictionary of a Tzotzil language as spoken in San Bartolome de los Llanos (Venustiano Carranza), Chiapas, Mexico. Manuscript, University of Pittsburgh Library, Pittsburgh.

270. *Tzotzil (Zinacantán, late sixteenth century)*
     Mayan; Chiapas, Mexico; $t = 51$, $l = $ S:20, $n = 36$, % $= 39$, $ci = -0.31$.

     Laughlin, Robert M. (1988). *The great Tzotzil dictionary of Santo Domingo Zinacantán.* Washington, D.C.: Smithsonian Institution Press.

271. *Tzotzil (Zinacantán, 1950–1975)*
     Mayan; Chiapas, Mexico; $t = 64$, $l = $ S:49, $n = 23$, % $= 77$, $ci = +0.41$.

     Laughlin, Robert M. (1975). *The great Tzotzil dictionary of San Lorenzo Zinacantán.* Washington, D.C.: Smithsonian Institution Press.
     Weathers, Kenneth (1950). *Diccionario Español-Tzotzil y Tzotzil-Español.* México, D.F.: Instituto Lingüístico de Verano.

272. *Uarao*
     Uarao; British Guiana and Venezuela; $t = 53$, $l = 22$ (S:19, Du:3, E:3), $n = 39$, % $= 42$, $ci = -0.32$.

     Barral, Basilio de (1979). *Diccionario Warao-Castellano, Castellano-Warao.* Caracas: Talleres de "El Polígota."
     Edwards, Walter F. (1980). *A short dictionary of the Warau language of Guyana.* Guyana: Amerindian Languages Project, University of Guyana.
     Williams, James (1928–1929). The Waray Indians of Guiana and vocabulary of their language. *Journal de la Société des Américanistes de Paris* 20:193–252; 21:201–261.

273. *Ute (1849–1880)*
     Uto-Aztecan; Colorado?; $t = 40$, $l = $ S:7, $n = 34$, $\% = 18$, $ci = -0.68$

     Selman, Morman V. (n.d.). *Dictionary of the Ute Indian language*. Provo, Utah: M. H. Graham
     Printing Co.

274. *Vejoz*
     Matacoan; Argentine Chaco; $t = 39$, $l = $ S:6, $n = 35$, $\% = 15$, $ci = -0.74$.

     Hunt, Richard J. (1913). *El Vejoz*. Buenos Aires: Universidad Nacional de la Plata.
     Lafone y Quevedo, Samuel Alexander (1896). Los Indios Matacos y su lengua por el P. J. Remedi,
     con vocabularios ordenados. *Boletín del Instituto Geográfico Argentino* 17:319–363.
     Lehmann-Nitsche, Robert (1910–1911). Vocabulario Chorote ó Solote. *Revista del Museo de la
     Plata* 17:111–130.
     Milanesio, Domingo (1918). *Etimología Araucana*. Buenos Aires: Imprenta "San Martín."
     Schmidt, Max (1937). Los Guisnais. *Revista de la Sociedad Científica del Paraguay* 4:1–35.

275. *Wappo*
     Yukian; California; $t = 67$, $l = $ S:58, $n = 10$, $\% = 87$, $ci = +0.73$.

     Sawyer, Jesse O. (1964a). The implications of Spanish /r/ and /rr/ in Wappo history. *Romance
     Philology* 18:165–177.
     Sawyer, Jesse O. (1964b). Wappo words from Spanish. *Publications in Linguistics, University of
     California* 34:163–169.
     Sawyer, Jesse O. (1965). *English-Wappo vocabulary*. Berkeley: University of California Press.

276. *Washo*
     Isolate; California; $t = 40$, $l = 26$ (E:22, S:5), $n = 22$, $\% = 65$, $ci = +0.10$.

     Bright, William (1960). Animals of acculturation in the California Indian languages. *University
     of California Publications in Linguistics* 4:215–246.
     Jacobsen, Jr., William Horton (1964). A grammar of the Washo language. Ph.D. thesis, University
     of California, Berkeley.

277. *Western Apache*
     Athapascan-Eyak; Arizona; $t = 64$, $l = 13$ (S:11, E:2), $n = 56$, $\% = 20$, $ci = -0.67$.

     Perry, Edgar, Quintero, Canyon Z., Sr., Davenport, Catherine D., and Perry, Corrine B. (1972).
     Western Apache dictionary. Fort Apache, Ariz.: White Mountain Apache Culture Center.

278. *West Greenlandic Eskimo*
     Eskimo-Aleut; Greenland; $t = 59$, $l = 11$ (Da:9, N:2), $n = 50$, $\% = 19$, $ci = -0.66$.

     Robbe, Pierre, and Dorais, Louis-Jacque (1986). *Tunumiit Oraasiat: The East Greenlandic Inuit
     language*. Québec: Centre d'Etudes Nordiques de l'Université Laval.
     Schultz-Lorentzen, Christian W. (1927). *Dictionary of the West Greenland Eskimo language*.
     Kobenhavn: Meddeleser om Grønland.

279. *Wintu*
     Wintun; California; $t = 42$, $l = 16$ (E:12, S:6), $n = 27$, $\% = 38$, $ci = -0.26$.

     Pitkin, Harvey (1985). *Wintu dictionary*. Berkeley: University of California Press.

280. *Yakima (Sahaptin dialect)*
     Sahaptin-Nez Perce; Washington State; $t = 38$, $l = 5$ (F:3, E:2), $n = 33$, $\% = 13$, $ci = -0.74$.

     Pandosy, M. C. (1862). *Grammar and dictionary of the Yakama language*. New York: Cramoisy
     Press.

281. *Yaqui*
      Uto-Aztecan; Sonora, Mexico; $t = 40$, $l = $ S:33, $n = 8$, % = 83, $ci = $ +0.63.

      Johnson, Jean B. (1962). *El idioma Yaqui.* México, D.F.: Instituto Nacional de Antropología e Historia.
      Spicer, Edward H. (1943). Linguistic aspects of Yaqui acculturation. *American Anthropologist* 45:410–426.

      Note: This language case may be the same dialect as Cahita (case 28).

282. *Yavapai (Tolkapaya dialect)*
      Yuman; Arizona; $t = 62$, $l = 15$ (S:14, E:1), $n = 48$, % = 24, ci = -0.53.

      Munro, Pamela (1992). Field notes. Department of Linguistics, University of California, Los Angeles.

283. *Yavapai (Tonto dialect)*
      Yuman; Arizona; $t = 35$, $l = 0$, $n = 35$, % = 0, $ci = $ -1.00.

      Gatschet, Albert S. (1887). Der Yuma-Sprachstamm. *Zeitschrift für Ethnologie* 9:365–418.

284. *Yucatec (1850–1883)*
      Mayan; Yucatán, Mexico; $t = 45$, $l = $ S:4, $n = 43$, % = 9, $ci = $ -0.87.

      Berendt, C. Hermann (1870). *Diccionario Español-Maya del Convento de San Francisco en Mérida.* Mérida.
      Brasseur de Bourbourg, Charles Etienne (1870). *Manuscrit Troano. Estudes sur le système graphique et la langue des Mayas tome second.* Paris: Imprimerie Impériale.
      Charencey, Charles Felix Hyacinthe de (1883). Vocabulaire Français-Maya. *Actes de la Société Philologique* 13:1–87.
      Michelon, Oscar (1976). *Diccionario de San Francisco.* Verlagsanstalt Graz, Austria: Akademische Druck-u.

285. *Yuki*
      Yukian; California; $t = 42$, $l = 14$ (S:8, E:6), $n = 30$, % = 33, $ci = $ -0.38.

      Sawyer, Jesse O., and Schlicher, Alice (1984). *Yuki vocabulary.* Berkeley: University of California Press.

286. *Zapotec (1578)*
      Otomanguean; Oaxaca, Mexico; $t = 57$, $l = $ S:12, $n = 52$, % = 21, $ci = $ -0.70.

      Córdova, Juan de (1942). *Vocabulario Castellano-Zapoteco.* México, D.F.: Instituto Nacional de Antropología e Historia.

      Note: A useful supplement to this source is Whitecotton and Whitecotton (1993).

287. *Zapotec (sixteenth century)*
      Otomanguean; Oaxaca, Mexico; $t = 42$, $l = $ S:5, $n = 39$, % = 12, $ci = $ -0.81.

      México, La Junta Colombina de (1893). *Vocabulario Castellano-Zapoteco.* México: Oficina Tipográfica de la Secretaría de Fomento.

288. *Zapotec (Juárez)*
      Otomanguean; Oaxaca, Mexico; $t = 49$, $l = $ S:30, $n = 21$, % = 61, $ci = $ +0.18.

      Nellis, Neil, and Nellis, Jane Goodner de (1983). *Diccionario Zapoteco de Juárez.* México, D.F.: Instituto Lingüístico de Verano.

289. *Zapotec (Mitla)*
      Otomanguean; Oaxaca, Mexico; $t = 62$, $l = $ S:48, $n = 16$, % = 77, $ci = $ +0.52.

Fernández de Miranda, María Teresa (1964). Los prestamos Españoles en el Zapoteco de Mitla. *Anales del Instituto de Antropología e Historia* 17:259–274.

Stubblefield, Morris, and Stubblefield, Carol Miller de (1991). *Diccionario Zapoteco de Mitla, Oaxaca.* México, D.F.: Instituto Lingüístico de Verano.

290. *Zoque (1672)*
Mixe-Zoque; Chiapas, Mexico; $t = 32$, $l = $ S:4, $n = 30$, $\% = 16$, $ci = -0.81$.

Grasserie, Raoul de la (1898). *Langue Zoque et langue Mixe.* Paris: J. Maisonneuve.

291. *Zoque (Copainalá)*
Mixe-Zoque; Chiapas, Mexico; $t = 32$, $l = $ S:14, $n = 18$, $\% = 44$, $ci = -0.13$.

Harrison, Roy, Harrison, Margaret, and García H., Cástulo (1981). *Diccionario Zoque de Copainalá.* México, D.F.: Instituto Lingüístico de Verano.

292. *Zuni*
Isolate; New Mexico; $t = 52$, $l = 14$ (S:10, E:4), $n = 42$, $\% = 27$, $ci = -0.54$.

Curtis, Edward S. (1926). *The North American Indian.* Vol. 17. Norwood, Mass.: Plimpton Press.

Hart, E. R. (1973). *A glossary of common Zuni terms.* Zuni, N.M.: The Pueblo of Zuni.

Keech, Roy A. (1937). A Zuni Indian vocabulary. *National Archaeological News* 1(4):2–3, (5):2–3, (6):2–3, (7):12–13, (8):11–12.

Newman, Stanley (1958). *Zuni dictionary.* Bloomington, Ind.: Research Center in Anthropology, Folklore, and Linguistics.

REFERENCES

(Note: For lexical sources for the 292 language cases, see appendix B.)

Adair, James (1775). *The history of the American Indians*. London.

Aikhenvald, Alexandra Y. (1996). Areal diffusion in Northwest Amazonia: The case of Tariana. *Anthropological Linguistics* 38:73–116.

Ajpacaja Tum, Pedro Florentino, Chox Tum, Manuel Isidro, Tepaz Raxuleu, Francisco Lucas, and Guarchaj Ajtzalam, Diego Adrian (1996). *Diccionario K'iche'*. La Antigua, Guatemala: Proyecto Lingüístico Francisco Marroquín.

Albert, Roy, and Shaul, David Leedom (1985). *A concise Hopi and English lexicon*. John Benjamins.

Alexander, J. T. (1971). *A dictionary of the Cherokee Indian language*. Raleigh: North Carolina State Library.

Andersen, Elaine S. (1978). Lexical universals of body-part terminology. In Joseph H. Greenberg et al. (eds.), *Language universals, Volume 3, Word structure*, pp. 335–368. Stanford, Cal.: Stanford University Press.

Anderson, Eugene N. (1997). Fun with Colonial Maya dictionaries, or how I enjoyed my Christmas vacation. Paper presented at the 20th Annual Conference of the Society of Ethnobiology, Athens, Ga.

Aoki, Haruo (1994). *Nez Perce dictionary*. Berkeley: University of California Press.

Appel, René, and Muysken, Pieter (1987). *Language contact and bilingualism*. London: Edward Arnold.

Atran, Scott (1990). *Cognitive foundations of natural history: Towards an anthropology of science*. Cambridge: Cambridge University Press.

Aubin, George F. (1975). *A Proto-Algonquian dictionary*. Ottawa: National Museums of Canada.

Bakker, Peter (1989a). "The language of the coast tribes is half Basque": A Basque-American Indian Pidgin, 1540–1640. *Anthropological Linguistics* 31:117–147.

Bakker, Peter (1989b). Two Basque loanwords in Micmac. *International Journal of American Linguistics* 55:258–261.

Bakker, Peter (1992). "A language of our own": The genesis of Michif—the mixed Cree-French language of the Canadian Métis. Thesis, University of Amsterdam, Amsterdam.

Bakker, Peter (1993). European-Amerindian language contact in North America: Pidgins, creoles, and mixed languages. *Native American Studies* 7:17–22.

Bakker, Peter (1995). Nederlandse leenwoorden in Noordamerikaanse Indianentalen. *Yumtzilob* 7:5–16.

Bakker, Peter (1997). *A language of our own: The genesis of Michif, the mixed Cree-French language of the Canadian Métis.* New York: Oxford University Press.

Bakker, Peter, and Grant, Anthony P. (1994). Interethnic communication in Canada, Alaska and adjacent areas. Manuscript.

Baldwin, Stuart J. (1994). Blackfoot neologisms. *International Journal of American Linguistics* 60:69–72.

Bartelt, Guillermo (1992). Chileno: A maritime pidgin among California Indians. *California Linguistic Notes* 23:25–28.

Bartholomew, Doris (1955). Palabras prestadas del Español en el dialecto Otomi hablado en San Felipe y Santiago, Jiquipilco, México. *Revista Mexicana de Estudios Antropológicos* 14:169–171.

Barto, Craig J. (1979). Spanish loanwords in Walapai. M.A. thesis, University of Kansas, Lawrence.

Bartram, William ([1879] 1909). Observations on the Creek and Cherokee Indians. With prefatory and supplementary notes by E. G. Squier. Report. Complete. *Transactions of the American Ethnological Society* 3:1–81.

Basso, Keith H. (1967). Semantic aspects of linguistic acculturation. *American Anthropologist* 69:471–477.

Bates, Dawn, Hess, Thom, and Hilbert, Vi (1994). *Lushootseed dictionary.* Seattle: University of Washington Press.

Berkhofer, Robert F., Jr. (1978). *The white man's Indian: Images of the American Indian from Columbus to the present.* New York: Knopf.

Berlin, Brent (1972). Speculations on the growth of ethnobotanical nomenclature. *Language in Society* 1:51–86.

Berlin, Brent (1990). The chicken and the egg-head revisited: Further evidence for the intellectualist bases of ethnobiological classification. In Darrell A. Posey et al. (eds.), *Ethnobiology: Implications and applications, Vol. 1, Proceedings of the First International Congress of Ethnobiology, Belém, 1988*, pp. 19–33. Bélem, Brazil: Museu Paraense Emílio Goeldi.

Berlin, Brent (1992). *Ethnobiological classification: Principles of categorization of plants and animals in traditional societies.* Princeton, N.J.: Princeton University Press.

Berlin, Brent, Breedlove, Dennis E., and Raven, Peter H. (1973). General principles of classification and nomenclature in folk biology. *American Anthropologist* 70:290–299.

Berlin, Brent, and Kay, Paul (1969). *Basic color terms: Their universality and evolution.* Berkeley: University of California Press.

Beverley, Robert (1705). *The history and present state of Virginia, in four parts . . . By a native and inhabitant of the place.* London.

Bierwisch, Manfred (1967). Some semantic universals of German adjectives. *Foundations of language* 3:1–36.

Blanchet, Francis Norbet (1878). *Dictionary of the Chinook Jargon.* Victoria, British Columbia: M. W. Watt.

Blom, Frans, and La Farge, Oliver (1927). *Tribes and temples.* Middle American Research Institute, Publication 1. New Orleans: Tulane University.

Bloomfield, Leonard (1933). *Language.* New York: Holt, Rinehart, and Winston.

Bloomfield, Leonard (1946). Algonquian. In Harry Hoijer et al. (eds.), *Linguistic structures of Native America*, pp. 85–129. New York: Viking Fund Publications in Anthropology.

Boas, Franz (1930). Spanish elements in modern Nahuatl. In John D. Fitz-Gerald, and Pauline Taylor (eds.), *Todd Memorial Volumes, Philological Studies*, Vol. 1, pp. 85–89. Freeport, N.Y.: Books for Libraries Press.

Bonvillain, Nancy (1978). Linguistic change in Akwesasne Mohawk: French and English influences. *International Journal of American Linguistics* 44:31–39.

Bourne, Edward Gaylord (1904). *Narratives of the career of Hernando De Soto.* 2 vols. New York: Trail Makers.

Boynton, Sylvia S. (1982). Mikasuki grammar in outline. Ph.D. thesis, University of Florida, Gainesville.

Bright, William (1952). Linguistic innovations in Karok. *International Journal of American Linguistics* 18: 53–62. (Reprinted in Bright 1976:98–115.)

Bright, William (1960a). Animals of acculturation in the California Indian languages. *University of California Publications in Linguistics* 4:215–246. (Reprinted in Bright 1976:121–162.)

Bright, William (1960b). A note on the southwestern words for cat. *International Journal of American Linguistics* 26:167–168.

Bright, William (1967). Inventory of descriptive materials. In Norman A. McQuown (ed.), *Handbook of Middle American Indians, Volume 5, Linguistics,* pp. 9–62. Austin: University of Texas Press.

Bright, William (1968). *A Luiseño dictionary.* Berkeley: University of California Publications in Linguistics.

Bright, William (1973). North American Indian language contact. In Thomas A. Sebeok (ed.), *Current trends in linguistics,* Vol. 10, pp. 713–726. The Hague: Mouton. (Reprinted in Bright 1976:210–217.)

Bright, William (1976). *Variation and change in language.* Stanford, Cal.: Stanford University Press.

Bright, William (1979a). Hispanisms in Cahuilla. *Journal of California and Great Basin Anthropology Papers in Linguistics* 1:101–116.

Bright, William (1979b). Notes on Hispanisms. *International Journal of American Linguistics* 45:267–271.

Bright, William (1993). The Aztec triangle: Three-way language contact in New Spain. In Laura A. Buszard-Welcher, Lionel Wee, and William Weigel (eds.), General session and parasession on the place of morphology in a grammar. *Proceedings of the Eighteenth Annual Meeting of the Berkeley Linguistics Society,* pp. 22–36. Berkeley, Cal.: Berkeley Linguistics Society.

Bright, William (1997). Notes on Hispanisms: California. Forthcoming in *Festschrift for Sidney Lamb.*

Bright, William, and Bright, Elizabeth (1959). Spanish words in Patwin. *Romance Philology* 13:161–164. (Reprinted in Bright 1976:116–120.)

Bright, William, and Sherzer, Joel (1976). Areal features in North American Indian languages. In William Bright, *Variation and change in language,* pp. 228–268. Stanford, CA: Stanford University Press.

Bright, William, and Thiel, Robert A. (1965). Hispanisms in a modern Aztec dialect. *Romance Philology* 18:444–452.

Briggs, Lucy T. (1981). Aymarization: An example of language change. In M. J. Hardman (ed.), *The Aymara language in its social and cultural context,* pp. 127–145. Gainesville: University Presses of Florida.

Brinton, Daniel G. (1873). On the language of the Natchez. *Proceedings of the American Philosophical Society* 13:483–499.

Brown, Cecil H. (1976). General principles of human anatomical partonomy and speculations on the growth of partonomic nomenclature. *American Ethnologist* 3:400–424.

Brown, Cecil H. (1977a). Folk botanical life-forms: Their universality and growth. *American Anthropologist* 79:317–342.

Brown, Cecil H. (1977b). Lexical universals and the human language faculty. In M. Saville-Troike (ed.), *Georgetown University round table on languages and linguistics 1977,* pp. 75–91. Washington D.C.: Georgetown University Press.

Brown, Cecil H. (1979). Folk zoological life-forms: Their universality and growth. *American Anthropologist* 81:791–817.

Brown, Cecil H. (1983). Where do cardinal direction terms come from? *Anthropological Linguistics* 25:121–161.

Brown, Cecil H. (1984). *Language and living things: Uniformities in folk classification and naming.* New Brunswick, N.J: Rutgers University Press.

Brown, Cecil H. (1985a). Mode of subsistence and folk biological taxonomy. *Current Anthropology* 26:43–64.

Brown, Cecil H. (1985b). Polysemy, overt marking, and function words. *Language Sciences* 7:283–332.

Brown, Cecil H. (1987a). The linguistic history of Mayan *year* (*haʔab'). *Anthropological Linguistics* 29:362–388.

Brown, Cecil H. (1987b). Polysémie, l'attribution d'une marque et le concept "semaine." *Recherches Amérindiennes au Québec* 27(4):37–50.

Brown, Cecil H. (1989a). Lexical universals and semantic primitives. *Quaderni di Semantica* 10:279–295.

Brown, Cecil H. (1989b). Naming the days of the week: A cross-language study of lexical acculturation. *Current Anthropology* 30:536–550.

Brown, Cecil H. (1989c). Universal constraints on polysemy and overt marking. *Quaderni di Semantica* 10:33–50.

Brown, Cecil H. (1990). A survey of category types in natural language. In S. L. Tsohatzidis (ed.), *Meanings and prototypes: Studies in linguistic categorization*, pp. 17–47. London: Routledge.

Brown, Cecil H. (1991). Hieroglyphic literacy in ancient Mayaland: Inferences from linguistic data. *Current Anthropology* 32:489–496.

Brown, Cecil H. (1992). British names for American birds. *Journal of Linguistic Anthropology* 2:30–50.

Brown, Cecil H. (1994). Lexical acculturation in Native American languages. *Current Anthropology* 35:95–117.

Brown, Cecil H. (1995). Lexical acculturation and ethnobiology: Utilitarianism versus intellectualism. *Journal of Linguistic Anthropology* 5:51–64.

Brown, Cecil H. (1996a). Lexical acculturation, areal diffusion, lingua francas, and bilingualism. *Language in Society* 25:261–282.

Brown, Cecil H. (1996b). A widespread marking reversal in languages of the southeastern United States. *Anthropological Linguistics* 38:439–460.

Brown, Cecil H. (1998). Spanish loanwords in languages of the southeastern United States. *International Journal of American Linguistics* 64:148–167.

Brown, Cecil H., Kolar, John, Torrey, Barbara J., Truong-Quang, Tipawan, and Volkman, Phillip (1976). Some general principles of biological and non-biological folk classification. *American Ethnologist* 3:73–85.

Brown, Cecil H., and Witkowski, Stanley R. (1980). Language universals. In David Levinson and Martin J. Malone (authors and eds.), *Toward explaining human culture: A critical review of the findings of worldwide cross-cultural research*, pp. 359–384. New Haven, Conn.: HRAF Press.

Brown, Cecil H., and Witkowski, Stanley R. (1981). Figurative language in a universalist perspective. *American Ethnologist* 8:596–615.

Brown, Cecil H., and Witkowski, Stanley R. (1983). Polysemy, lexical change and cultural importance. *Man* 18:72–89.

Brunel, Gilles (1987). L'enfant de l'oeil: La contribution de Brown à l'ethnoscience. *Recherches Amérindiennes au Québec* 17:51–57.

Burris, Harold W., Jr. (1978). Geometric figure terms: Their universality and growth. *The Journal of Anthropology* 1:18–41.

Byington, Cyrus (1915). *A dictionary of the Choctaw language.* John R. Swanton and Henry S. Halbert (eds.), Bureau of American Ethnography Bulletin 46. Washington, D.C.: U.S. Government Printing Office.

Callaghan, Catherine A. (1994). Untitled comment. *Current Anthropology* 35:108.

Callaghan, Catherine A., and Gamble, Geoffrey (1996). Borrowing. In Ives Goddard (ed.), *Handbook of North American Indians, Volume 17, Languages,* pp. 111–116. Washington, D.C.: Smithsonian Institution.

Calnek, Edward E. (1962). Highland Chiapas before the Spanish conquest. Ph.D. thesis, The University of Chicago, Chicago.

Campbell, Lyle (1976). Kekchi linguistic acculturation: A cognitive approach. In Marlys McClaran (ed.), *Mayan linguistics,* Vol. 1, pp. 90–97. Los Angeles: American Indian Studies Center.

Campbell, Lyle (1977). *Quichean linguistic prehistory.* Berkeley: University of California Press.

Campbell, Lyle, and Kaufman, Terrence (1976). A linguistic look at the Olmec. *American Antiquity* 41:80–89.

Campbell, Lyle, and Kaufman, Terrence (1985). Mayan linguistics: Where are we now? *Annual Review of Anthropology* 14:187–198.

Campbell, Lyle, Kaufman, Terrence, and Smith-Stark, Thomas C. (1986). Meso-America as a linguistic area. *Language* 62:530–570.

Canart, Paul (1979). *Studies in comparative semantics.* New York: St. Martin's Press.

Carter, George F. (1971). Pre-Columbian chickens in America. In Carroll L. Riley, J. Charles Kelley, Campbell W. Pennington, and Robert L. Rands (eds.), *Man across the sea: Problems of Pre-Columbian contacts,* pp. 178–218. Austin: University of Texas Press.

Casad, Eugene H. (1988). Post-conquest influences on Cora (Uto-Aztecan). In William Shipley (ed.), *In Honor of Mary Haas: From the Haas Festival Conference on Native American Linguistics,* pp. 77–136. Berlin: Mouton de Gruyter.

Casagrande, Joseph B. (1954a). Comanche linguistic acculturation I. *International Journal of American Linguistics* 20.140–151.

Casagrande, Joseph B. (1954b). Comanche linguistic acculturation II. *International Journal of American Linguistics* 20.217–237.

Casagrande, Joseph B. (1955). Comanche linguistic acculturation III. *International Journal of American Linguistics* 21.8–25.

Casson, Ronald W. (1994). Untitled comment. *Current Anthropology* 35:108–109.

Catesby, Mark (1731–1743). *The natural history of Carolina, Florida, and Bahama Islands.* 2 vols. London.

Chamberlain, Alexander F. (1894). New words in the Kootenay language. *American Anthropologist* 7:186–192.

Chomsky, Noam (1959). Review of Skinner (1957). *Language* 35:26–58.

Chomsky, Noam (1975). *Reflections on language.* New York: Pantheon.

Clark, Lawrence E. (1977). Linguistic acculturation in Sayula Popoluca. *International Journal of American Linguistics* 43:128–138.

Clark, William P. (1885). *The Indian Sign Language, with brief explanatory notes of the gestures taught deaf-mutes in our institutions for their instruction, and a description of some of the peculiar laws, customs, myths, superstitions, ways of living, code of peace and war signals of our Aborigines.* L. R. Hamersly.

Coones, S. F. (1891). *Dictionary of the Chinook Jargon as spoken on Puget Sound and the Northwest.* Seattle: Lowman and Hanford Stationery and Printing.

Córdova, Juan de (1942). *Vocabulario Castellano-Zapoteco.* México, D.F.: Instituto Nacional de Antropología e Historia.

Cotton, Eleanor Greet, and Sharp, John M. (1988). *Spanish in the Americas.* Washington D.C.: Georgetown University Press.

Crawford, James M. (1975). Southeastern Indian languages. In James M. Crawford (ed.), *Studies in Southeastern Indian languages*, pp. 1–120. Athens, Ga: University of Georgia Press.

Crawford, James M. (1978). *The Mobilian trade language*. Knoxville: University of Tennessee Press.

Crawford, James M. (1979). Spanish loan words in Cocopa. *Journal of California and Great Basin Anthropology Papers in Linguistics* 1:117–132.

Crosby, Alfred W. (1972). *The Columbian exchange: Biological and cultural consequences of 1492*. Westport, Conn.: Greenwood Press.

Crosby, Alfred W. (1991). Metamorphosis of the Americas. In Herman J. Viola and Carolyn Margolis (eds.), *Seeds of Change: A quincentennial commemoration*, pp. 70–89. Washington, D.C.: Smithsonian Institution Press.

Crowley, Cornelius J. (1962). Some remarks on the etymology of the southwestern words for cat. *International Journal of American Linguistics* 28:149–151.

Crowley, Terry (1992). *An introduction to historical linguistics*. Auckland: Oxford University Press.

Crystal, David (1980). *A first dictionary of linguistics and phonetics*. Boulder, Col.: Westview Press.

Davidson, Alan (1992). Europeans' wary encounter with tomatoes, potatoes, and other New World foods. In Nelson Foster and Linda S. Cordell (eds.), *Chilies to chocolate: Food the Americas gave the world*, pp. 1–14. Tucson: University of Arizona Press.

Dávila Garibi, José Ignacio (1967). Préstamos lingüísticos e influencias recíprocas Nahua-Castellanas y Castellano-Nahuas. *Estudios de Cultural Náhuatl* 7:255–265.

Day, Gordon M. (1994). *Volume 1: Abenaki-English, Western Abenaki dictionary*. Hull, Quebec: Canadian Museum of Civilization.

Day, Gordon M. (1995). *Volume 2: English-Abenaki, Western Abenaki dictionary*. Hull, Quebec: Canadian Museum of Civilization.

Derrick-Mescua, Mary T. (1980). A phonology and morphology of Mikasuki. Ph.D. thesis, University of Florida, Gainesville.

Diamond, Jared (1993, February). Speaking with a single tongue. *Discover*, pp. 78–85.

Diebold, A. Richard, Jr. (1961). Incipient bilingualism. *Language* 37:97–111.

Diebold, A. Richard, Jr. (1962). A laboratory of language contact. *Anthropological Linguistics* 4:41–51.

Doak, Ivy G. (1983). *The 1908 word lists of James Teit*. Occasional Papers in Linguistics 1983 No. 3.University of Montana, Missoula.

Dockstader, Frederick J. (1955). Spanish loanwords in Hopi: A preliminary checklist. *International Journal of American Linguistics* 21:157–159.

Dorsey, James Owen, and Swanton, John R. (1912). *A dictionary of the Biloxi and Ofo languages*. Smithsonian Institution Bureau of American Ethnology Bulletin 47. Washington, D.C.: U.S. Government Printing Office.

Douaud, Patrick C. (1985). *Ethnolinguistic profile of the Canadian Métis*. Canadian Ethnology Service Paper 99.

Dozier, Edward P. (1956). Two examples of linguistic acculturation: The Yaqui of Sonora and Arizona and the Tewa of New Mexico. *Language* 32:146–157.

Dozier, Edward P. (1967). Linguistic acculturation studies in the Southwest. In Dell H. Hymes (ed.), *Studies in southwestern ethnolinguistics: Meaning and history in languages of the American Southwest*, pp. 389–402. The Hague: Mouton.

Drechsel, Emanuel J. (1979). Mobilian Jargon: Linguistic, sociocultural, and historical aspects of an American Indian lingua franca. Ph.D. thesis, University of Wisconsin, Madison.

Drechsel, Emanuel J. (1981). A preliminary sociolinguistic comparison of four indigenous pidgin languages of North America (with notes towards a sociolinguistic typology in American Indian linguistics). *Anthropological Linguistics* 23:93–112.

Drechsel, Emanuel J. (1983). The question of the *lingua franca* Creek. In Frances Ingemann (ed.), *1982 Mid-America Linguistic Conference Papers*, pp. 388–400. Lawrence: Department of Linguistics, University of Kansas.

Drechsel, Emanuel J. (1984). Structure and function in Mobilian Jargon: Indications for the pre-European existence of an American Indian pidgin. *Journal of Historical Linguistics and Philology* 1:141–185.

Drechsel, Emanuel J. (1996). An integrated vocabulary of Mobilian Jargon, a Native American pidgin of the Mississippi Valley. *Anthropological Linguistics* 38:248–354.

Du Pratz, Antoine S. le Page (1758). *Histoire de la Louisiane.* 3 vols. Paris.

Edmonson, Barbara (1984). Linguistic ability in sixteenth-century Mexico. *International Journal of American Linguistics* 50:343–345.

Emeneau, Murray B. (1962). Bilingualism and structural borrowing. *Proceedings of the American Philosophical Society* 106:430–442.

Emeneau, Murray B. (1980). *Language and linguistic area.* Stanford, Cal.: Stanford University Press.

Feeling, Durbin (1975). *Cherokee-English dictionary.* Cherokee Nation of Oklahoma.

Fernández de Miranda, María Teresa (1964). Los prestamos Españoles en el Zapoteco de Mitla. *Anales del Instituto Nacional de Antropología e Historia* 17:259–274.

Fleisher, Mark Stewart (1976*).* Clallam: A study in Coast Salish ethnolinguistics. Ph.D. thesis, Washington State University, Pullman.

Foster, Nelson, and Cordell, Linda S. (1992). Appendix: Food plants of American origin. In Nelson Foster and Linda S. Cordell (eds.), *Chilies to chocolate: Food the Americas gave the world*, pp. 163–168. Tucson: University of Arizona Press.

Francis, W. Nelson, and Kučera, Henry (1982). *Frequency analysis of English usage: Lexicon and grammar.* Boston: Houghton Mifflin.

Fritz, Gayle J. (1994). Are the first American farmers getting younger? *Current Anthropology* 35:305–309.

Fritz, Gayle J. (1995). New dates and data on early agriculture: The legacy of complex hunter-gatherers. *Annals of the Missouri Botanical Garden* 82:3–15.

Froke, Michael Gregory (1975). Lexical acculturation among the Dakota. M.A. thesis, California State University, Long Beach.

Gallatin, Albert 1836. *A synopsis of the Indian tribes within the United States east of the Rocky Mountains, and in the British and Russian possessions in North America.* Transactions and Collections of the American Antiquarian Society, Vol.2, pp. 1–422. Cambridge: Printed for the Society at the University Press.

Galloway, Brent D. (1990). *A phonology, morphology, and classified word list for the Samish dialect of Straits Salish.* Hull, Quebec: Canadian Museum of Civilization.

Gamble, Geoffrey (1989). Spanish loans in Wikchamni. In Mary Ritchie Key and Henry M. Hoenigswald (eds.), *General and Amerindian ethnolinguistics in remembrance of Stanley Newman*, pp. 123–128. Berlin: Mouton de Gruyter.

Garcilaso de la Vega (El Inca) (1723). *La Florida del Inca. Historia del Adelantado, Hernando de Soto, Gouernador, y Capitan General del Reino de la Florida y de Otros Heroicos Caballeros, Españoles, e Indios.* Madrid.

Garvin, Paul L. (1948). Kutenai lexical innovations. *Word* 4:120–127.

Gatschet, Albert S. (1883). The Shetimasha Indians of St. Mary's Parish, Southern Louisiana. *Transactions of the Anthropological Society of Washington* 2:148–158.

Gatschet, Albert S. (1888). *Tchikilli's Kasi'hta legend in the Creek and Hitchiti languages.* The Transactions of the Academy of Science of St. Louis, Vol. 5. St. Louis, Mo.: R. P. Studley.

Gatschet, Albert S. (1892). Der Yuma-Sprachstamm. *Zeitschrift für Ethnologie* 24:1–18.

Gatschet, Albert S., and Swanton, John R. (1932). *A dictionary of the Atakapa language.* Smithsonian Institution Bureau of American Ethnology Bulletin 108. Washington, D.C.: U.S. Government Printing Office.

Georgiev, Vladimir I. (1977). L'union linguistique balkanique: L'état actuel des recherches. *Linguistique Balkanique* 20:5–15.

Gerhard, Peter (1979). *The southeast frontier of New Spain.* Princeton, N.J.: Princeton University Press.

Gibbs, George (1863). *A dictionary of the Chinook Jargon or trade language of Oregon.* Washington, D.C.: Smithsonian Institution.

Gill, John Kaye (1884). *Dictionary of the Chinook Jargon.* Portland, Ore.: J. K. Gill.

Gillin, John (1947). Modern Latin American culture. *Social Forces* 25:243–248.

Goddard, Ives (1974). Dutch loanwords in Delaware. In Herbert C. Kraft (ed.), *A Delaware Indian symposium,* pp. 153–160. Harrisburg: Pennsylvania Historical and Museum Commission.

Goddard, Ives (1979). Comparative Algonquian. In Lyle Campbell and Marianne Mithun (ed.), *The languages of Native America: Historical and comparative assessment,* pp. 70–132. Austin: University of Texas Press.

González Casanova, P. (1934). *Los hispanismos en el idioma azteca.* México, D.F.: Publicaciones del Museo Nacional.

Good, John B. (1880). *A vocabulary and outlines of grammar of the Nitlakapamuk or Thompson tongue (the Indian language spoken between Yale, Lillooet, Cache Creek and Nicola Lake). Together with a Chinook dictionary, adapted for use in the Province of British Columbia.* Victoria: St. Paul's Mission Press.

Granberry, Julian (1993). A grammar and dictionary of the Timucua language. Tuscaloosa: University of Alabama Press.

Greenberg, Joseph H. (1966). *Language universals with special reference to feature hierarchies.* The Hague: Mouton.

Greenberg, Joseph H. (1969). Language universals: A research frontier. *Science* 166:473–478.

Greenberg, Joseph H. (1975). Research on language universals. *Annual Review of Anthropology* 4:75–94.

Greenberg, Joseph H. (ed.) (1978). *Universals of human language: Volume 3, Word structure.* Stanford, Cal.: Stanford University Press.

Greenberg, Joseph H. (1987). *Language in the Americas.* Stanford, Cal.: Stanford University Press.

Greenfeld, Philip J. (1971). Playing card names in Western Apache. *International Journal of American Linguistics* 37:195–196.

Grimes, Joseph E. (1960). Spanish-Nahuatl-Huichol monetary terms. *International Journal of American Linguistics* 26:162–165.

Grubb, David McC. (1977). *A practical writing system and short dictionary of Kwakw'ala (Kwakiutl).* Ottawa: National Museum of Man.

Gumperz, John J. (1962). Types of linguistic communities. *Anthropological Linguistics* 4(1):28–40.

Haas, Mary R. (1947). Some French loan-words in Tunica. *Romance Philology* 1:145–148.

Haas, Mary R. (1953). *Tunica Dictionary.* University of California Publications in Linguistics, Vol. 6, No. 2, pp. 175–332. Berkeley: University of California Press.

Haas, Mary R. (1968). The last words of Biloxi. *International Journal of American Linguistics* 34:77–84.

Haas, Mary R. (n.d.; c. 1936–1940). Creek vocabulary. Manuscript.

Hall, Robert A., Jr. (1947). A note on Taos k'owena *horse. International Journal of American Linguistics* 13:117–118.

Hammerich, Louis L. (1954). The Russian stratum in Alaskan Eskimo. *Slavic Word* 10:401–428.

Hancock, Ian F. (1971). A survey of the pidgins and creoles of the world. In Dell Hymes (ed.), *Pidginization and creolization of languages,* pp. 509–523. London: Cambridge University Press.

Hardy, Donald E. (1988). The semantics of Creek morphosyntax. Ph.D. thesis, Rice University, Houston.

Hartt, Ch. Fred. (1872). Notes on the Lingoa Geral or Modern Tupí of the Amazonas. *Transactions of the American Philological Association* 3:58–76.

Haugen, Einar (1950). The analysis of linguistic borrowing. *Language* 26:210–231.

Haugen, Einar (1956). *Bilingualism in the Americas: A bibliography and research guide.* Tuscaloosa: University of Alabama Press.

Hays, Terence E. (1982). Utilitarian/adaptationist explanations of folk biological classification: Some cautionary notes. *Journal of Ethnobiology* 2:89–94.

Hays, Terence E. (1994). Sound symbolism, onomatopoeia, and New Guinea frog names. *Journal of Linguistic Anthropology* 4:153–174.

Heath, Shirley B. (1972). *Telling tongues: Language policy in Mexico, colony to nation.* New York: Teachers College Press.

Heinrich, Albert (1971). Some borrowings from German into Eskimo. *Anthropological Linguistics* 13:96–99.

Henderson, Eugenia J. A. (1965). The topography of certain phonetic and morphological characteristics of South East Asian languages. *Lingua* 15:400–434.

Herzog, George (1941). Culture change and language: Shifts in the Pima vocabulary. In Leslie Spier, A. Irving Hallowell, and Stanley S. Newman (eds.), *Language, culture, and personality: Essays in memory of Edward Sapir,* pp. 66–74. Menasha, Wisc.: Sapir Memorial Publication Fund.

Hewson, John (1993). *A computer-generated dictionary of Proto-Algonquian.* Hull, Quebec: Canadian Museum of Civilization.

Hickerson, Nancy P. (1985). Some Kiowa terms for currency and financial transactions. *International Journal of American Linguistics* 51:446–449.

Hill, Jane H. (1994). Untitled comment. *Current Anthropology* 35:109–110.

Hill, Jane H., and Hill, Kenneth C. (1986). *Speaking Mexicano: Dynamics of syncretic language in Central Mexico.* Tucson: University of Arizona Press.

Hill, Kenneth C. (1990). The phonological incorporation of Spanish into Mexicano (Nahuatl). In Jacek Fisiak (ed.), *Historical dialectology,* pp. 273–282. Berlin: Mouton de Gruyter.

Hockett, Charles F. (1948). Implications of Bloomfield's Algonquian studies. *Language* 24:117–131.

Hoenigswald, Henry M. (1960). *Language change and linguistic reconstruction.* Chicago: University of Chicago Press.

Hoijer, Harry (1939). Chiricahua loan-words from Spanish. *Language* 15:110–115.

Hollenbach, Elena E. de (1973). La aculturación lingüística entre Los Triques de Copala, Oaxaca. *América Indígena* 33:65–95.

Holmes, Ruth Bradley, and Smith, Betty Sharp (1976). *Beginning Cherokee.* Norman: University of Oklahoma Press.

Humes, Rev. Jesse, and Humes, Vinnie May (James) (1973). *A Chickasaw dictionary.* Ada, Ok.: The Chickasaw Nation.

Hunn, Eugene (1977). *Tzeltal folk zoology: The classification of discontinuities in nature.* New York: Academic Press.

Hunn, Eugene (1982). The utilitarian factor in folk biological classification. *American Anthropologist* 84:830–847.

Hunn, Eugene (1994). Place-names, population density, and the magic number 500. *Current Anthropology* 35:81–85.

Hunn, Eugene (1996). Columbia Plateau Indian place names: What can they teach us? *Journal of Linguistic Anthropology* 6:3–26.

Huot, Martha Champion (1948). Some Mohawk words of acculturation. *International Journal of American Linguistics* 14:150–154.

Jakobson, Roman (1941). *Kindersprache, Aphasie, und allgemeine Lautgesetze.* Uppsala: Almqvist and Wiksell.

Johnson, Jean Bassett (1943). A clear case of linguistic acculturation. *American Anthropologist* 54:427–434.

Joseph, Brian D. (1983). *The synchrony and diachrony of the Balkan infinitive: A study in areal, general, and historical linguistics.* Cambridge: Cambridge University Press.

Juilland, Alphonse, and Chang-Rodriguez, E. (1964). *Frequency dictionary of Spanish words.* The Hague: Mouton.

Justeson, John S., Norman, William M., Campbell, Lyle, and Kaufman, Terrence (1985). *The foreign impact on Lowland Mayan language and script.* New Orleans: Middle American Research Institute.

Karttunen, Frances (1985). *Nahuatl and Maya in contact with Spanish.* Austin: Department of Linguistics and The Center of Cognitive Science, University of Texas.

Karttunen, Frances, and Lockhart, James (1976). *Nahuatl in the middle years: Language contact phenomena in texts of the colonial period.* Berkeley: University of California Press.

Kaufman, Terrence (1964). Materiales lingüísticos para el estudio de las relaciones internas y externas de la familia de idiomas Mayanos. In Evon Z. Vogt and L. A. Ruz (eds.), *Desarrollo cultural de los Mayas*, pp. 81–136. Mexico City: Universidad Nacional Autónoma de México.

Kaufman, Terrence (1967). *Preliminary Mochó vocabulary.* Berkeley: Laboratory for Language-Behavior Research, University of California.

Kaufman, Terrence (1976). Archaeological and linguistic correlations in Mayaland and associated areas of Meso-America. *World Archaeology* 8:101–118.

Kaufman, Terrence (1994a). The native languages of Latin America. In Christopher Moseley and R. E. Asher (eds.), *Atlas of the world's languages*, pp. 31–33. London: Routledge.

Kaufman, Terrence (1994b). The native Languages of Meso-America. In Christopher Moseley and R. E. Asher (eds.), *Atlas of the world's languages*, pp. 34–45. London: Routledge.

Kaufman, Terrence (1994c). The native languages of South America. In Christopher Moseley and R. E. Asher (eds.), *Atlas of the world's languages*, pp. 46–89. London: Routledge.

Kaufman, Terrence and Norman, William M. (1984). An outline of Proto-Cholan phonology, morphology and vocabulary. In John S. Justeson and Lyle Campbell (eds.), *Phoneticism in Mayan hieroglyphic writing*, pp. 77–166. Albany: Institute for Mesoamerican Studies, State University of New York.

Kennard, Edward A. (1963). Linguistic acculturation in Hopi. *International Journal of American Linguistics* 29:36–41.

Kiddle, Lawrence B. (1952a). The Spanish language as a medium of cultural diffusion in the age of discovery. *American Speech* 27:241–256.

Kiddle, Lawrence B. (1952b). Spanish loan words in American Indian languages. *Hispania* 35:179–184.

Kiddle, Lawrence B. (1964). American Indian reflexes of two Spanish words for cat. *International Journal of American Linguistics* 30:299–304.

Kiddle, Lawrence B. (1978). American Indian borrowings of Spanish *caballo*. In Vladimir Honsa and M. J. Hardman-de-Bautista (eds.), *Papers on linguistics and child language*, pp. 151–167. The Hague: Mouton.

Kimball, Geoffrey (1988). An Apalachee vocabulary. *International Journal of American Linguistics* 54:387–398.

Kimball, Geoffrey (1994). *Koasati dictionary.* Lincoln: University of Nebraska Press.

King, Duane H. and King, Laura H. (1976). Old words for new ideas: Linguistic acculturation in modern Cherokee. *Tennessee Anthropologist* 1:58–62.

Kinkade, M. Dale (1991). *Upper Chehalis dictionary.* Missoula: University of Montana.

Klagstad, Harold L., Jr. (1963). Towards a morpho-syntactic treatment of the Balkan linguistic group. In *American contributions to the 5th International Congress of Slavists, I: Linguistic contributions*, pp. 179–189. The Hague: Mouton.

Kronenfeld, David B. (1974). Sibling typology: Beyond Nerlove and Romney. *American Ethnologist* 1:489–506.

Kronenfeld, David B. (1996). *Plastic glasses and church fathers: Semantic extension from the ethnoscience tradition*. Oxford: Oxford University Press.

Kroskrity, Paul V. (1978). Inferences from Spanish loanwords in Arizona Tewa. *Anthropological Linguistics* 20:340–350.

Kroskrity, Paul V. (1982). Language contact and linguistic diffusion: The Arizona Tewa speech community. In Florence Barkin, Elizabeth A. Brandt, and Jacob Ornstein-Galicia (eds.), *Bilingualism and language contact: Spanish, English, and Native American languages*, pp. 51–72. New York: Teachers College Press.

Kroskrity, Paul V. (1993). *Language, history, and identity: Ethnolinguistic studies of the Arizona Tewa*. Tucson: University of Arizona Press.

Kroskrity, Paul V., and Reinhardt, Gregory A. (1985). On Spanish loans in Western Mono. *International Journal of American Linguistics* 51:231–237.

Landar, Herbert J. (1959). The diffusion of some southwestern words for cat. *International Journal of American Linguistics* 25:273–274.

Landar, Herbert J. (1961). The southwestern words for cat. *International Journal of American Linguistics* 27:370–371.

Langevin, H. L. (1872). *British Columbia*. Ottawa: I. B. Taylor.

Laughlin, Robert M. (1969). The Tzotzil. In Evon Z. Vogt (ed.), *Handbook of Middle American Indians, Volume 7, Ethnology*, pp. 152–194. Austin: University of Texas Press.

Law, Howard W. (1961). Linguistic acculturation in Isthmus Nahuat. In *A. William Cameron Townsend en el vigesimoquinto aniversario del Instituto Lingüístico de Verano*, pp. 555–561. Mexico, D.F.

Lawson, John (1860). *History of Carolina, containing the exact description and natural history of that country*. Raleigh, N.C.

Lee, Dorothy D. (1943). The linguistic aspect of Wintu acculturation. *American Anthropologist* 45:435–440.

Lehiste, Ilse (1988). *Lectures on language contact*. Cambridge, Mass.: MIT Press.

Lehman, Frederic K. (1994). Untitled comment. *Current Anthropology* 35:110–111.

Lenz, Rudolf (1893). Beiträge zur Kenntnis des Amerikanospanischen. *Zeit. für rom. Philol.* 17:188–214.

Lévi-Strauss, Claude (1966). *The savage mind*. London: Weidenfeld and Nicolson.

Lockhart, James (1992). *The Nahuas after the conquest*. Stanford, Cal.: Stanford University Press.

Loewen, Jacob A. (1960). Spanish loanwords in Waunana. *International Journal of American Linguistics* 26:330–344.

Loughridge, Robert M., and Hodge, David (1890). *English and Muskokee dictionary*. St. Louis, Mo.: Printing House of J. T. Smith.

Loukotka, Čestmír (1968). *Classification of South American Indian languages*. Los Angeles: Latin American Center, University of California.

MacCauley, Clay (1887). *The Seminole Indians of Florida*. Fifth Annual Report of the Bureau of American Ethnology, 1883–1884, pp. 469–531. Washington, D.C.: U.S. Government Printing Office.

Malinowski, Bronislaw (1974). *Magic, science, and religion*. London: Souvenir Press.

Mannheim, Bruce (1991). *The language of the Inka since the European invasion*. Austin: University of Texas Press.

Margry, Pierre (1883). *Découvertes et éstablissements des Français dans l'Ouest et dans le Sud de l'Amérique septentrionale (1614–1754)*. Mémoires et documents originaux recueillis et publiés par Pierre Margry, 6 vols. (1875–1886). Paris.

Martin, Gary J. (1992). Borrowed names and exotic plants: The impact of Spanish contact on folk botanical classification in Mexico. Manuscript.

Martin, Jack B. (1987). Mikasuki vocabulary. Manuscript, University of California, Los Angeles.

Martin, Jack B. (1994). Modeling language contact in the prehistory of the southeastern United States. In Patricia B. Kwachka (ed.), *Perspectives on the Southeast: Linguistics, archaeology, and ethnohistory*, pp. 14–24. Athens: University of Georgia Press.

Martinet, André (1952). Diffusion of language. *Romance Philology* 6:5–13.

Masica, Colin P. (1976). *Defining a linguistic area: South Asia.* Chicago: University of Chicago Press.

McArthur, Carolina de, and McArthur, Ricardo (1995). *Diccionario Pocomam y Español.* Instituto Lingüístico de Verano de Centroamérica.

McLendon, Sally (1969). Spanish words in Eastern Pomo. *Romance Philology* 23:39–53.

Miller, Wick R. (1959). Spanish loanwords in Acoma: I. *International Journal of American Linguistics* 25:147–153.

Miller, Wick R. (1960). Spanish loanwords in Acoma: II. *International Journal of American Linguistics* 26:41–49.

Miller, Wick R. (1978). Multilingualism in its social context in aboriginal North America. *Proceedings of the Annual Meeting of the Berkeley Linguistics Society* 4:610–616.

Mixco, Mauricio J. (1977). The Kiliwa response to Hispanic culture. *Proceedings of the Annual Meeting of the Berkeley Linguistics Society* 3:12–23.

Montler, Timothy (1991). *Saanich, North Straits Salish: Classified word list.* Hull, Quebec: Canadian Museum of Civilization.

Moravcsik, Edith A. (1978). Language contact. In Joseph H. Greenberg (ed.), *Universals of human language, Volume 1: Method and theory*, pp. 93–122. Stanford, Cal.: Stanford University Press.

Morice, Adrien-Gabriel (1932). *The Carrier language,* Vols. 1 and 2. St. Gabriel, Osterreich: Internationale de Monographies Linguistiques, Anthropos..

Morínigo, Marcos A. (1931). *Hispanismos en el Guaraní.* Buenos Aires: Universidad de Buenos Aires.

Morris, Brian (1984). The pragmatics of folk classification. *Journal of Ethnobiology* 4:45–60.

Moseley, Christopher, and Asher, R. E. (eds.) (1994), *Atlas of the world's languages.* London: Routledge.

Mougeon, Raymond, and Beniak, Edouard (1989). The extralinguistic correlates of core lexical borrowing. In Keith M. Denning et al. (eds.), *Variation in language: NWAV-XV at Stanford*, pp. 337–347. Stanford, Cal.: Department of Linguistics, Stanford University.

Mullen, Christine (1976). Canadian French loanwords in Spokane as indicators of culture change. M.A. thesis, University of Victoria, British Columbia.

Munro, Pamela (1984). On the Western Muskogean source for Mobilian. *International Journal of American Linguistics* 50:438–450.

Munro, Pamela (1992a). Field notes. Department of Linguistics, University of California, Los Angeles.

Munro, Pamela (1992b). Muskogean cognate sets. Manuscript.

Munro, Pamela, and Willmond, Catherine (1994). *Chickasaw: An analytical dictionary.* Norman: University of Oklahoma Press.

Muntzel, Martha C. (1985). Spanish loanwords in Ocuiltec. *International Journal of American Linguistics* 51:515–518.

Muysken, Pieter (1981). Halfway between Quechua and Spanish: The case for relexification. In A. Highfield and A. Valdman (eds.), *Historiacity and variation in creole studies*, pp. 52–78. Ann Arbor, Mich.: Karoma.

Muysken, Pieter (1984). Linguistic dimensions of language contact. *Revue Quebecoise de Linguistique* 14:49–76.

Nater, Hank F. (1990). *A concise Nuxalk-English dictionary.* Hull, Quebec: Canadian Museum of Civilization.

Nathan, Michele (1977). Grammatical description of the Florida Seminole dialect of Creek. Ph.D. thesis, Tulane University, New Orleans.

Nerlove, Sarah B., and Romney, A. Kimball (1967). Sibling terminology and cross-sex behavior. *American Anthropologist* 69:179–187.

Nicklas, T. Dale (1974). The elements of Choctaw. Ph.D. thesis, University of Michigan, Ann Arbor.

Nordell, Norman (1984). Spanish loan words via Aztec. *Summer Institute of Linguistics Mexico Workpapers* 5:9–23.

Nordenskiöld, Erland (1922). *Deductions suggested by the geographical distribution of some post-Columbian words used by the Indians of South America.* Göteborg, Sweden: Elanders Boktryuckeri Aktiebolag.

Olson, Donald (1963). Spanish loan words in Pame. *International Journal of American Linguistics* 29:219–221.

O'Meara, John (1996). *Delaware-English/English-Delaware dictionary.* Toronto: University of Toronto Press.

Ornstein, Jacob (1976). Sociolinguistic constraints on lexical borrowing in Tarahumara: Explorations in "langue and parole" and "existential bilingualism"—An approximation. *Anthropological Linguistics* 18(2):70–93.

Oswalt, Robert L. (1958). Russian loanwords in southwestern Pomo. *International Journal of American Linguistics* 24:245–247.

Oswalt, Robert L. (1994). History through the words brought to California by the Fort Ross Colony. In Leanne Hinton (ed.), *Flutes of fire: Essays on California Indian languages*, pp. 101–105. Berkeley, Cal.: Heyday Books.

Parker, Steve (1996). Toward a universal form for "yes": Or, rhinoglottophilia and the affirmation grunt. *Journal of Linguistic Anthropology* 6:85–95.

Parsons, Elsie Clews (1941). *Notes on the Caddo.* Memoirs of the American Anthropological Association Number 57. Menasha, Wisc.: American Anthropological Association.

Peñalosa, Fernando (1990). Los prestamos en las narraciones en las lenguas Q'anjob'alanas. *Winak: Boletín Intercultural* 5:176–195.

Pentland, David H. (1982). French loanwords in Cree. *Kansas Working Papers in Linguistics* 7:105–117.

Perry, Edgar, Quintero, Canyon Z., Sr., Davenport, Catherine D., and Perry, Corrine B. (1972). *Western Apache dictionary.* Fort Apache, Ariz.: White Mountain Apache Culture Center.

Pilling, James C. (1887a). *Bibliography of the Eskimo language.* Bulletin 1. Washington, D.C.: Bureau of American Ethnology.

Pilling, James C. (1887b). *Bibliography of the Siouan languages.* Bulletin 5. Washington, D.C.: Bureau of American Ethnology.

Pilling, James C. (1888). *Bibliography of the Iroquoian languages.* Bulletin 6. Washington, D.C.: Bureau of American Ethnology.

Pilling, James C. (1889). *Bibliography of the Muskhogean languages.* Bulletin 9. Washington, D.C.: Bureau of American Ethnology.

Pilling, James C. (1891). *Bibliography of the Algonquian languages.* Bulletin 13. Washington, D.C.: Bureau of American Ethnology.

Pilling, James C. (1892). *Bibliography of the Athapascan languages.* Bulletin 14. Washington, D.C.: Bureau of American Ethnology.

Pilling, James C. (1893a). *Bibliography of the Salishan languages.* Bulletin 16. Washington, D.C.: Bureau of American Ethnology.

Pilling, James C. (1893b). *Bibliography of the Chinookan languages.* Bulletin 15. Washington, D.C.: Bureau of American Ethnology.

Pilling, James C. (1894). *Bibliography of the Wakashan languages.* Bulletin 19. Washington, D.C.: Bureau of American Ethnology.

Pinnow, Heinz-Jürgen (1969). Entlehnungen von Tiernamen in Tsimshian und Na-Déné sowie Grundsätzliches zur Entlehnungsfrage bei Indianersprachen. *Zeitschrift für Ethnologie* 94:82–102.

Pope, John (1792). *A tour through the southern and western territories of the United States of North-America.* Richmond, Va.: John Dixon.

Poplack, Shana, Sankoff, David, and Miller, Christopher (1988). The social correlates and linguistic processes of lexical borrowing and assimilation. *Linguistics* 26:47–104.

Prince, J. Dyneley (1912). An ancient New Jersey Indian jargon. *American Anthropologist* 14:508–524.

Proulx, Paul (1994). Untitled comment. *Current Anthropology* 35:112.

Prunet, Jean-François (1990). The origin and interpretation of French loans in Carrier. *International Journal of American Linguistics* 56:484–502.

Randall, Robert A. (1987). The nature of highly inclusive folk-botanical categories. *American Anthropologist* 89:143–146.

Rankin, Robert L. (1988). Quapaw: Genetic and areal affiliations. In William Shipley (ed.), *In honor of Mary Haas: From the Haas Festival Conference on Native American linguistics,* pp. 629–650. Berlin: Mouton de Gruyter.

Rees-Miller, Janie (1996). Morphological adaptation of English loanwords in Algonquian. *International Journal of American Linguistics* 62:196–202.

Remesal, Antonio (1932). *Historia general de las Indias Occidentales, y particular de la gobernación de Chiapa y Guatemala,* Tomo I. Guatemala: Biblioteca "Goathemala" de la Sociedad de Geografía e Historia.

de Reuse, Willem J. (1994). English loanwords in the native languages of the Chukotka peninsula. *Anthropological Linguistics* 36:56–68.

de Reuse, Willem J. (1995). The functions of Spanish loanwords in 19th century sources on the Western Apache language. Manuscript.

Rhodes, Richard A. (1982). Algonquian trade languages. In William Cowan (ed.), *Papers of the Thirteenth Algonquian Conference,* pp. 1–10. Ottawa: Carleton University.

Rhodes, Richard A. (1985). *Eastern Ojibwa-Chippewa-Ottawa dictionary.* Berlin: Mouton.

Robinson, Lila Wistrand, and Armagost, James (1990). *Comanche dictionary and grammar.* Dallas: Summer Institute of Linguistics.

Romano, Santiago, and Cattunar, Herman (1916). *Diccionario Chiriguano-Español y Español-Chiriguano compilado teniendo à la vista diversos manuscritos de antiguos misioneros del Apostólico Colegio Santa María de los Angeles de Tarija y particularmente el diccionario Chiriguano etimológico del R. P. Dorotéo Giannecchini.* Tarija, Bolivia.

Romans, Bernard (1775). *A concise natural history of east and west Florida.* New York.

Rowe, John H. (1950). Sound patterns in three Inca dialects. *International Journal of American Linguistics* 16:137–148.

Rudes, Blair A. (1987). *Tuscarora roots, stems, and particles: Towards a dictionary of Tuscarora.* Winnipeg: Algonquian and Iroquoian Linguistics.

Salzmann, Zdeněk (1951). Contrastive field experience with language and values of the Arapaho. *International Journal of American Linguistics* 17:98–101.

Salzmann, Zdeněk (1954). The problem of lexical acculturation. *International Journal of American Linguistics* 20.137–139.

Sanchez, Jesus (1885). Glosario de voces castellanas derivadas del idioma Nahuatl ó Mexicana. *Anales del Museo Nacional de México* 3(7a):57–67.

Sankoff, David, Poplack, Shana, and Vanniarajan, S. (1990). The case of the nonce loan in Tamil. *Language Variation and Change* 2:71–101.

Sapir, Edward H. (1921). *Language.* New York: Harcourt, Brace.

Sapir, Edward H. (1931). *Southern Paiute dictionary,* Vol. 65, No. 3. Proceedings of the American Academy of Arts and Sciences.

Sawyer, Jesse O., Jr. (1964a). The implications of Spanish /r/ and /rr/ in Wappo history. *Romance Philology* 18:165–177.

Sawyer, Jesse O., Jr. (1964b). Wappo words from Spanish. *Publications in Linguistics, University of California* 34:163–169.

Seaman, P. David (1985). *Hopi dictionary.* Flagstaff: Northern Arizona University.

Schlichter, Alice (1980). English and Spanish loanwords in Wintu. In Kathryn Klar et al. (eds.), *American Indian and Indoeuropean studies: Papers in honor of Madison S. Beeler,* pp. 221–227. The Hague: Mouton.

Schoolcraft, Henry R. (1855). *Information respecting the history, condition and prospects of the Indian tribes of the United States: Collected and prepared under the direction of the Bureau of Indian Affairs, per act of Congress of March 3D, 1847. Part 5.* Philadelphia: Lippincott, Grambo and Company.

Schwartz, Douglas W. (1983). Havasupai. In Alfonso Ortiz (ed.), *Handbook of North American Indians, Volume 10, Southwest,* pp. 13–24. Washington, D.C.: Smithsonian Institution.

Scotton, Carol Mayers, and Okeju, John (1973). Neighbors and lexical borrowing. *Language* 46:871–889.

Sharpe, Pamela J. (1981). Spanish borrowing into Aymara clothing vocabulary. In M. J. Hardman (ed.), *The Aymara language in its social and cultural context,* pp. 147–174. Gainesville: University Presses of Florida.

Shaterian, Alan William (1983). Phonology and dictionary of Yavapai. Ph.D. thesis, University of California, Berkeley.

Shaul, David L. (1981). Semantic change in Shoshone-Comanche, 1800–1900. *Anthropological Linguistics* 23:344–355.

Shea, John Gilmary (1861). *Early voyages up and down the Mississippi.* Albany, N.Y.

Shea, Kathleen D. (1984). A Catawba lexicon. M.A. thesis, University of Kansas, Lawrence.

Sherzer, Joel (1973). Areal linguistics in North America. In Thomas A. Sebeok et al. (eds.), *Current trends in linguistics, Vol. 10: Linguistics in North America,* pp. 749–795. The Hague: Mouton.

Sherzer, Joel (1976). *An areal-typological study of American Indian languages north of Mexico.* Amsterdam: North-Holland.

Shimkin, Demitri B. (1980). Comanche-Shoshone words of acculturation. *Journal of the Steward Anthropological Society* 11:195–247.

Shipley, William F. (1962). Spanish elements in the indigenous languages of central California. *Romance Philology* 16:1–21.

Shipley, William F. (1963). *Maidu texts and dictionary.* Berkeley: University of California Press.

Silva-Corvalán, Carmen (1994). *Language contact and change: Spanish in Los Angeles.* Oxford: Clarendon.

Silverstein, Michael (1972). Chinook Jargon: Language contact and the problem of multi-level generative systems, I. *Language* 48:378–406.

Silverstein, Michael (1996). Dynamics of linguistic contact. In Ives Goddard (ed.), *Handbook of North American Indians, Volume 17, Languages,* pp. 117–136. Washington, D.C.: Smithsonian Institution.

Singh, R. (1981). Aspects of language borrowing: English loans in Hindi. In P.H. Nelde (ed.), *Sprachkontakt und Sprachkonflikt,* pp. 113–116. Wiesbaden: Steiner.

Skinner, B. F. (1957). *Verbal behavior.* New York: Appleton-Century-Crofts.

Spencer, Robert F. (1947). Spanish loanwords in Keresan. *Southwestern Journal of Anthropology* 3:130–147.

Spicer, Edward H. (1943). Linguistic aspects of Yaqui acculturation. *American Anthropologist* 45:410–425.

Spicer, Edward H. (1962). *Cycles of conquest.* Tucson: University of Arizona Press.

Spier, Leslie (1946). *Comparative vocabularies and parallel texts in two Yuman languages of Arizona.* Albuquerque, New Mexico: University of New Mexico Press.

Stefánsson, Vilhjálmur (1909). The Eskimo trade jargon of Herschel Island. *American Anthropologist* 11:217–232.

Steward, Julian (ed.) (1946). *Handbook of South American Indians.* Washington, D.C.: Smithsonian Institution.

Strachey, William (1849). *The historie of travaile into Virginia Britannia, expressing the cosmographie and commodities of the country, together with the manners and customs of the people.* London: Hakluyt Society Publication.

Sturtevant, William C. (1962). Spanish-Indian relations in southeastern North America. *Ethnohistory* 9:41–94.

Sturtevant, William C. (1971). Creek into Seminole. In Eleanor Burke Leacock and Nancy Oestreich Lurie, *North American Indians in historical perspective,* pp. 92–128. New York: Random House.

Suárez, Jorge A. (1983). *The Mesoamerican Indian languages.* Cambridge: Cambridge University Press.

Swan, James G. (1857). *The Northwest Coast, or, three year's residence in Washington Territory.* New York: Harper and Brothers.

Swanton, John R. (1919). *A structural and lexical comparison of the Tunica, Chitimacha, and Atakapa languages.* Smithsonian Institution Bureau of American Ethnology Bulletin 68. Washington, D.C.: U.S. Government Printing Office.

Swanton, John R. (1946). *The Indians of the southeastern United States.* Smithsonian Institution Bureau of American Ethnology Bulletin 137. Washington, D.C.: U.S. Government Printing Office.

Swiggers, Pierre (1985). Munsee borrowings from Dutch: Some phonological remarks. *International Journal of American Linguistics* 51:594–597.

Swiggers, Pierre (1988). Dutch loanwords in Munsee: The contrastive phonology of borrowing. *Papers and Studies in Contrastive Linguistics* 23:61–68.

Sylestine, Cora, Hardy, Heather K., and Montler, Timothy (1993). *Dictionary of the Alabama language.* Austin: University of Texas Press.

Tagliavini, Carlo (1949). Di alcune denominazioni della "pupilla." *Annali dell' Instituto Universitario di Napoli* 3:341–378.

Tait, Mary (1994). North America. In Christopher Moseley and R. E. Asher (eds.), *Atlas of the world's languages,* pp. 3–30. London: Routledge.

Tate, Charles Montgomery (1889). *Chinook as spoken by the Indians of Washington Territory, British Columbia and Alaska.* Victoria, British Columbia: M. W. Watt.

Taylor, Allan R. (1962). Spanish *manteca* in Alaskan Eskimo. *Romance Philology* 16:30–32.

Taylor, Allan R. (1981). Indian lingua francas. In Charles A. Ferguson, and Shirley Brice Heath (eds.), *Language in the USA,* pp. 175–195. Cambridge: Cambridge University Press.

Taylor, Allan R. (1990). A European loanword of early date in eastern North America. *Anthropological Linguistics* 32:187–210.

Taylor, Douglas (1946). Loan words in Dominica Island Carib. *International Journal of American Linguistics* 12:213–216.

Taylor, Douglas (1948). Loanwords in Central American Carib. *Word* 4:187–195.

Thiel, Robert August (1963). Hispanisms in a modern Aztec dialect. M.A. thesis, University of California, Los Angeles.

Thomas, Edward Harper (1935). *Chinook: A history and dictionary of the Northwest Coast trade jargon.* Portland, Ore.: Metropolitan Press.

Thomason, Sarah Grey (1980). On interpreting "The Indian Interpreter." *Language in Society* 9:167–193.

Thomason, Sarah Grey (1983). Chinook Jargon in areal and historical context. *Language* 59:820–870.

Thomason, Sarah Grey, and Kaufman, Terrence (1988). *Language contact, creolization, and genetic linguistics.* Berkeley: University of California Press.

Thompson, Laurence C., and Thompson, M. Terry (1996). *Thompson River Salish dictionary.* Missoula: University of Montana.

Tovar, Antonio (1961). *Catalogo de las lenguas de America del Sur.* Buenos Aires: Editorial Sudamericana.

Tovar, Antonio (1962). Los prestamos en Mataco: Contacto de Español y lenguas indígenas. *Acta Salmanticensia* 16:461–468.

Trager, George L. (1944). Spanish and English loanwords in Taos. *International Journal of American Linguistics* 10:144–158.

Trigger, Bruce G. (ed.) (1978). *Handbook of North American Indians, Volume 15, Northeast,.* Washington, D.C.: Smithsonian Institution.

Trubetzkoy, Nikolai S. (1939). *Grundzüge der Phonologie.* Prague: Travaux du Cercle Linguistique de Prague, 7.

van Baarle, Peter (1995). Leenwoorden in het Arawak en de contacten tussen Arawakken en Europeanen van 1500 tot 1800. *Yumtzilob* 7:25–53.

Vander Beke, George E. (1929). *French word book.* New York:Macmillan.

van Hout, Roeland, and Muysken, Pieter (1994). Modeling lexical borrowability. *Language Variation and Change* 6:39–62.

Van Tuyl, Charles D. (1979). *The Natchez: Annotated translations from Antoine Simon le Page du Pratz's* Histoire de la Louisiane *and a short English-Natchez dictionary.* Oklahoma Historical Society Series in Anthropology Number 4. Oklahoma City: Oklahoma Historical Society.

Villa Rojas, Alfonso (1969). The Tzeltal. In Evon Z. Vogt (ed.), *Handbook of Middle American Indians, Volume 7, Ethnology,* pp. 195–225. Austin: University of Texas Press.

Viola, Herman J. (1991). Seeds of change. In Herman J. Viola and Carolyn Margolis (eds.), *Seeds of change: A quincentennial commemoration,* pp. 12–15. Washington, D.C.: Smithsonian Institution Press.

Voegelin, Charles F. (1938a). *Shawnee stems and the Jacob P. Dunn Miami dictionary,* Part I. Indianapolis: Indiana Historical Society.

Voegelin, Charles F. (1938b). *Shawnee stems and the Jacob P. Dunn Miami dictionary,* Part II. Indianapolis: Indiana Historical Society.

Voegelin, Charles F. (1939). *Shawnee stems and the Jacob P. Dunn Miami dictionary,* Part III. Indianapolis: Indiana Historical Society.

Voegelin, Charles F. (1940a). *Shawnee stems and the Jacob P. Dunn Miami dictionary,* Part IV. Indianapolis: Indiana Historical Society.

Voegelin, Charles F. (1940b). *Shawnee stems and the Jacob P. Dunn Miami dictionary,* Part V. Indianapolis: Indiana Historical Society.

Voegelin, Charles F., and Hymes, Dell H. (1953). A sample of North American Indian dictionaries with reference to acculturation. *Proceedings of the American Philosophical Society* 97:634–644.

Vogt, Evon Z. (1969). Chiapas highlands. In Evon Z. Vogt (ed.), *Handbook of Middle American Indians, Volume 7, Ethnology,* pp. 133–151. Austin: University of Texas Press.

Wagner, Günter (1931). *Yuchi tales.* Publications of the American Ethnological Society. New York: G. E. Stechert and Co.

Wagner, Günter (1933–1938). Yuchi. In Franz Boas (ed.), *Handbook of American Indian languages,* pp. 300–384. Hamburg: J. J. Augustin.

Watkins, Ben (1892). *Complete Choctaw definer, English with Choctaw definition.* Van Buren, Ark.: J. W. Baldwin.

Weinreich, Uriel (1953). *Languages in contact.* New York: Linguistic Circle of New York.

Whistler, Kenneth W. (1980). An interim Barbareño Chumash dictionary. Manuscript.

Whitecotton, Joseph W., and Whitecotton, Judith Bradley (1993). *Vocabulario Zapoteco-Castellano.* Nashville, Tenn.: Vanderbilt University Publications in Anthropology.

Whitney, William Dwight (1881). On mixture in language. *Transactions of the American Philosophical Association* 12:1–26.

Wierzbicka, Anna (1996). *Semantics: Primes and universals.* Oxford: Oxford University Press.

Williams, Joseph M. (1976). Synaesthetic adjectives: A possible law of semantic change. *Language* 52:461–478.

Williams, Mark (1992). *Hitchiti: An early Georgia language.* LAMAR Institute Publication 21. Watkinsville, Ga.: LAMAR Institute.

Williams, Samuel Cole (1927). *Lieutenant Henry Timberlake's memoirs, 1756–1765; with annotations, introduction, and index.* Johnson City, Tenn..

Williams, Samuel Cole (1930). *Adair's history of the American Indians.* New York: Promontory Press.

Witkowski, Stanley R. (1972). Guttman scaling of semantic distinctions. In P. Reining (ed.), *Kinship studies in the Morgan centennial year,* pp. 167–188. Washington D.C.: Anthropological Society of Washington.

Witkowski, Stanley R., and Brown, Cecil H. (1978). Lexical universals. *Annual Review of Anthropology* 7:427–451.

Witkowski, Stanley R., and Brown, Cecil H. (1981). Lexical encoding sequences and language change: color terminology systems. *American Anthropologist* 83:13–27.

Witkowski, Stanley R., and Brown, Cecil H. (1983). Marking-reversals and cultural importance. *Language* 1983:569–582.

Witkowski, Stanley R., and Brown, Cecil H. (1985). Climate, clothing, and body-part nomenclature. *Ethnology* 24:197–214.

Witkowski, Stanley R., and Brown, Cecil H. (1991). Proto-Mayan time depth. Manuscript.

Witkowski, Stanley R., Brown, Cecil H., and Chase, Paul K. (1981). Where do tree terms come from? *Man* 16:1–14.

Wonderly, William L. (1946). Phonemic acculturation in Zoque. *International Journal of American Linguistics* 12:92–95.

Worth, Dean Stoddard (1963). Russian and Alaskan Eskimo. *International Journal of Slavic Linguistics and Poetics* 7:72–79.

Wright, Allen (1880). *Chahta leksikon.* St. Louis: Presbyterian Publishing Company.

Yasugi, Yoshiho (1995). *Native Middle American languages: An areal-typological perspective.* Osaka, Japan: National Museum of Ethnology.

Young, Robert W., and Morgan, William, Sr. (1980). *The Navajo language: A grammar and colloquial dictionary.* Albuquerque: University of New Mexico Press.

Young, Robert W., and Morgan, William, Sr. (1992). *Analytical lexicon of Navajo.* Albuquerque: University of New Mexico Press.

Zipf, George K. (1935). *The psycho-biology of language.* Boston: Houghton Mifflin.

Zipf, George K. (1949). *Human behavior and the principle of least effort.* Cambridge, Mass.: Addison Wesley.

Index of Languages, Items of Acculturation, Personal and Geographical Names

Subject Index

absolute universals 43
accelerator mass spectrometry 166
acculturated items 5, 7, 8, 14, 17-20, 25, 26, 29, 32, 35, 37, 41, 43, 44, 49, 55, 59, 62-64, 66, 68, 91, 95, 98, 102, 103, 105, 109, 110, 112, 113, 115-117, 119, 120, 122, 144, 145, 158, 160-163, 165
acoustics 38
adjective 14
agricultural chronology of Mesoamerica 166
alcoholic drink 68
altar 68
American birds 51
American pidgins 110, 161
Amerindian settlement 62
analogs 16, 51-54, 62, 68, 69, 160
analyzable native term 20, 21, 32, 34, 39, 115
Andean linguists 71
Anglo-American culture 81
Anglo-American Protestants 82
Anglo-Americans 9, 51, 70, 82
animal calls 37
animal subtypes 48, 51, 52, 56, 65, 66, 160
animals 3, 7-9, 23, 38, 46, 53, 56, 58, 64-66, 69, 70, 94-96, 113, 141, 162-165
anomalies 67, 68
anthropological theorizing 162
arable land 65

areal diffusion 108, 111, 114, 118, 127, 141, 142, 144, 145, 157, 161
areal patterns 83
artifacts 4, 5, 13-15, 20, 23, 32-34, 36, 37, 41, 44, 49, 54, 56, 58-69, 158-160, 163-165
assimilation 20
attitudinal factors 9
automobile parts 7
auxiliary language 117, 120, 142, 144, 149
Aztec empire 110

base element 28, 31, 49
bibliographies 16
bicultural 81
bidialectalism 119
bilabial stops 25
bilingual 11, 12, 14, 16-18, 63, 81, 82, 94, 95, 116, 119, 120, 158
bilingual dictionaries 12, 14, 16, 17
bilingualism 9, 10, 62, 70, 71, 81, 82, 86, 89-93, 95, 104, 105, 108, 116-120, 127, 158, 160, 161
bilingualism in the Americas 10
biological distinctiveness 164
borrowability 55-59, 61-63, 66-69, 159
borrowing 9, 20, 24, 38, 43, 55, 57, 62, 70, 71, 81-86, 90-93, 105, 112, 114-117, 119, 120, 128, 134, 142, 144, 151, 156-158, 161, 165, 166
botanical 13, 49, 52, 141
bread-like concoction 36
brevity of form 30

253